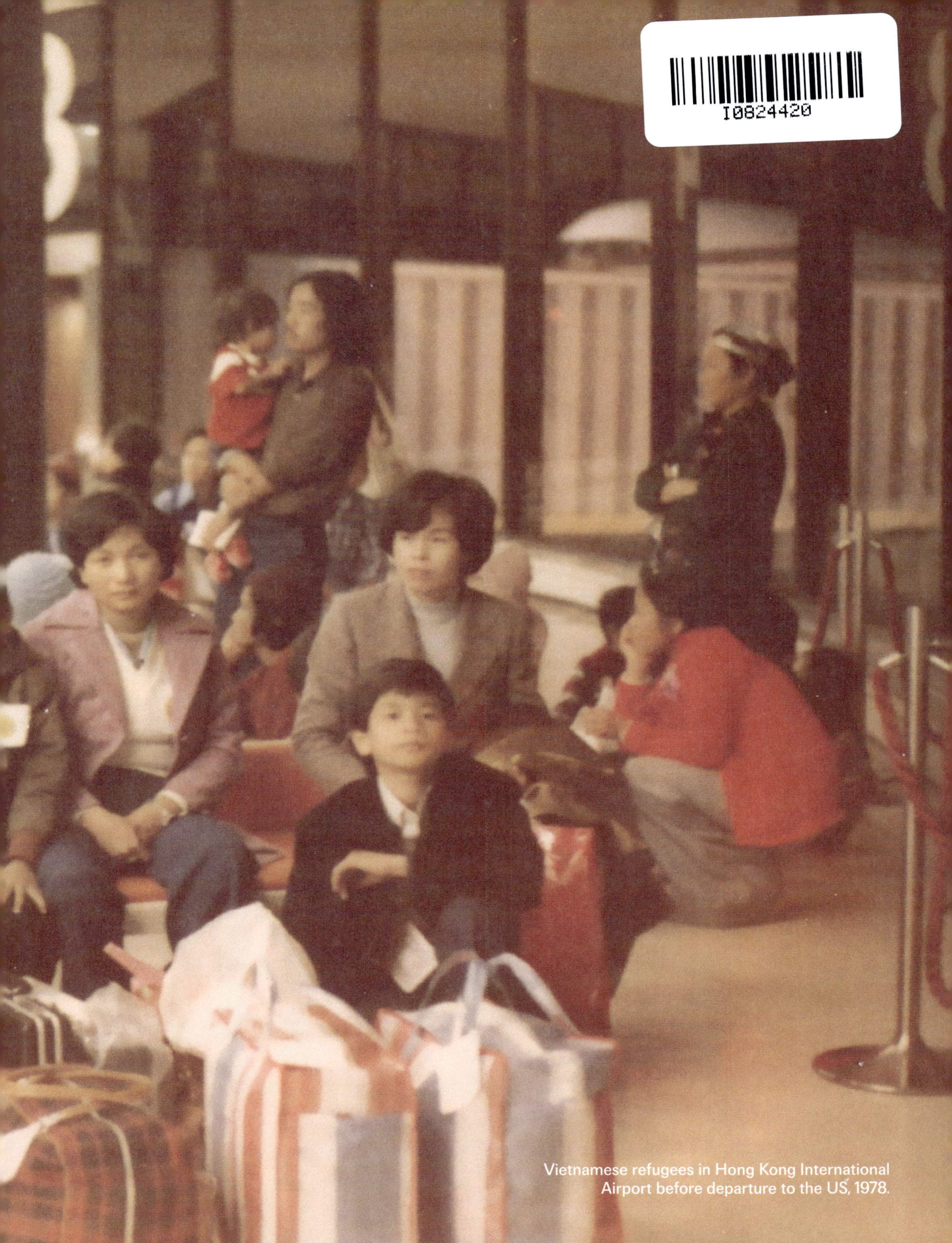

Vietnamese refugees in Hong Kong International Airport before departure to the US, 1978.

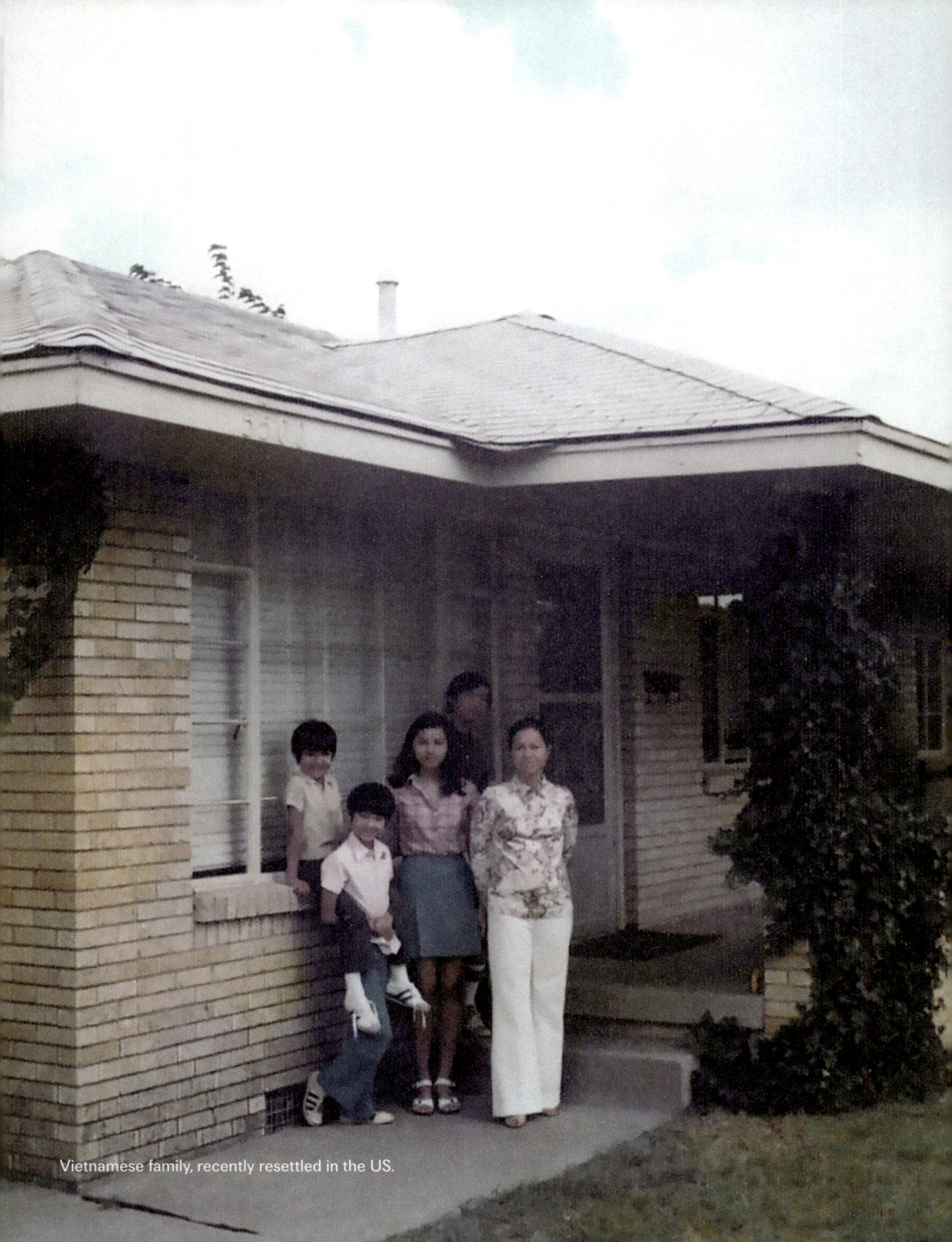

Vietnamese family, recently resettled in the US.

NEWWAVE

Rebellion and Reinvention in the Vietnamese Diaspora

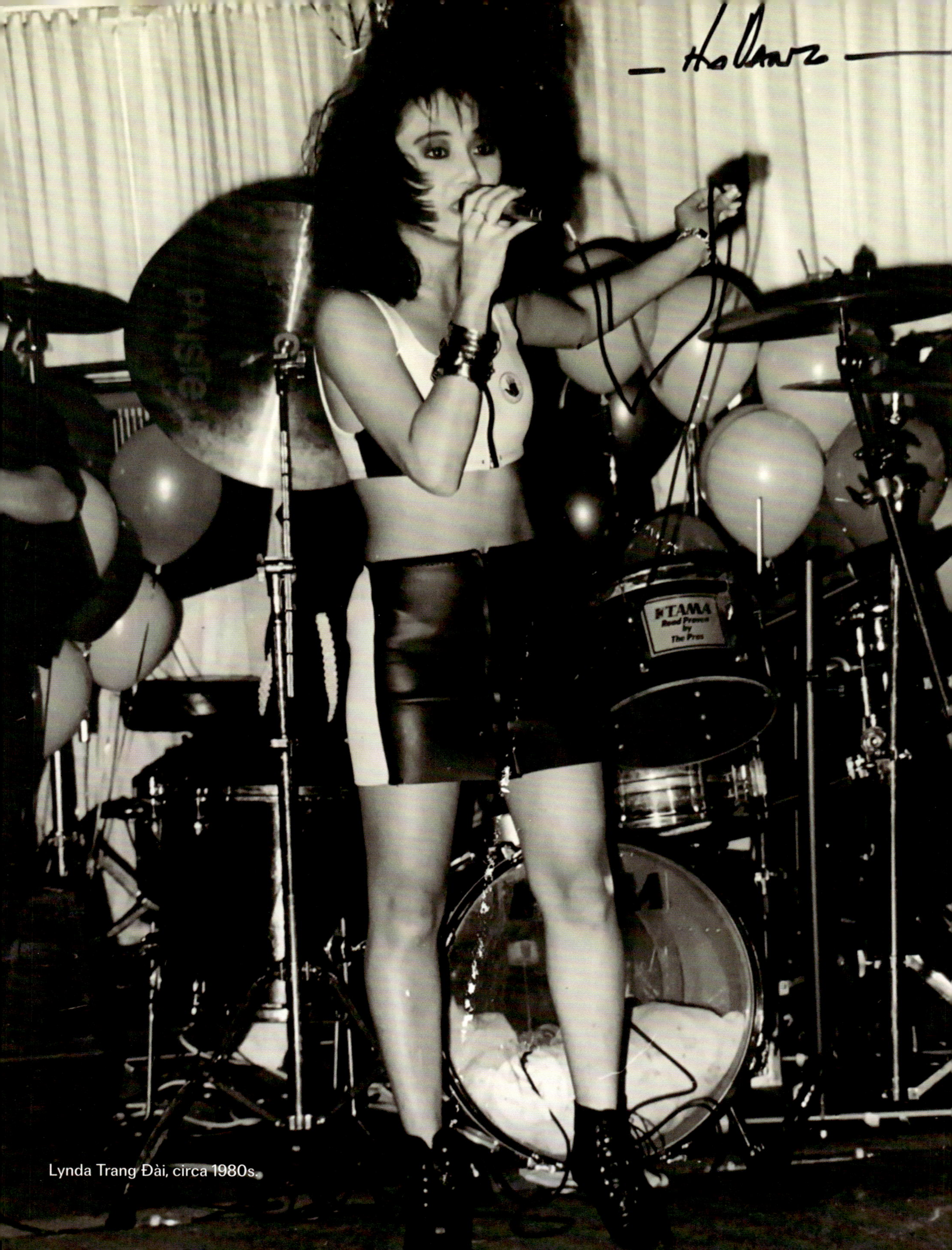

Lynda Trang Đài, circa 1980s.

NEWWAVE

Elizabeth Ai

Rebellion and Reinvention in the Vietnamese Diaspora

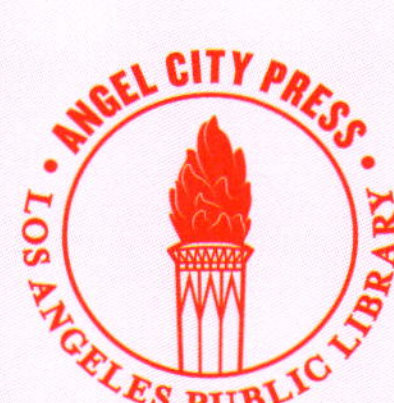

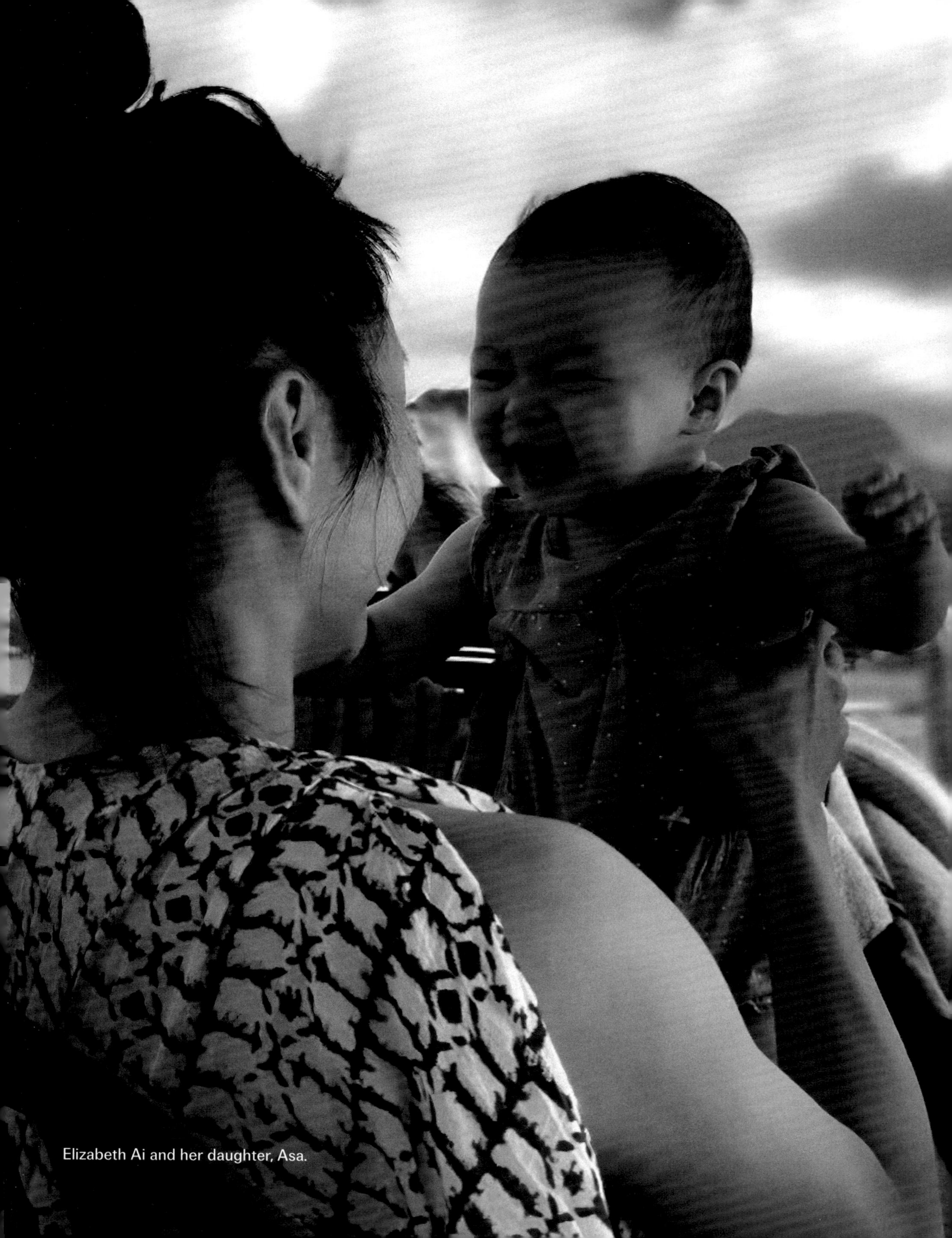

Elizabeth Ai and her daughter, Asa.

For Asa: thank you for being the spark that ignited this journey.

And for the Vietnamese women who endure an invisible war far greater than the one they escaped. May your journeys bring you back to yourselves.

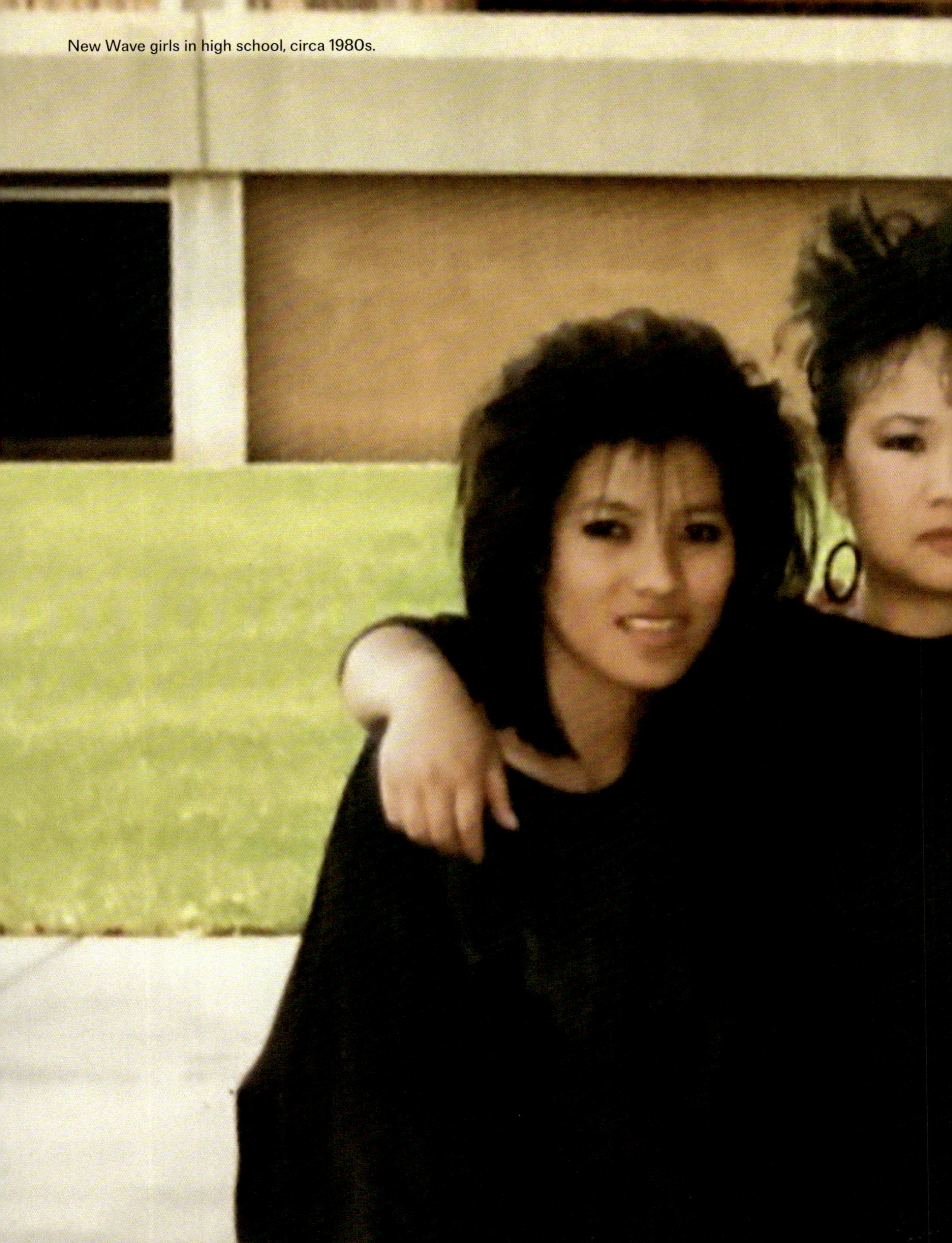

New Wave girls in high school, circa 1980s.

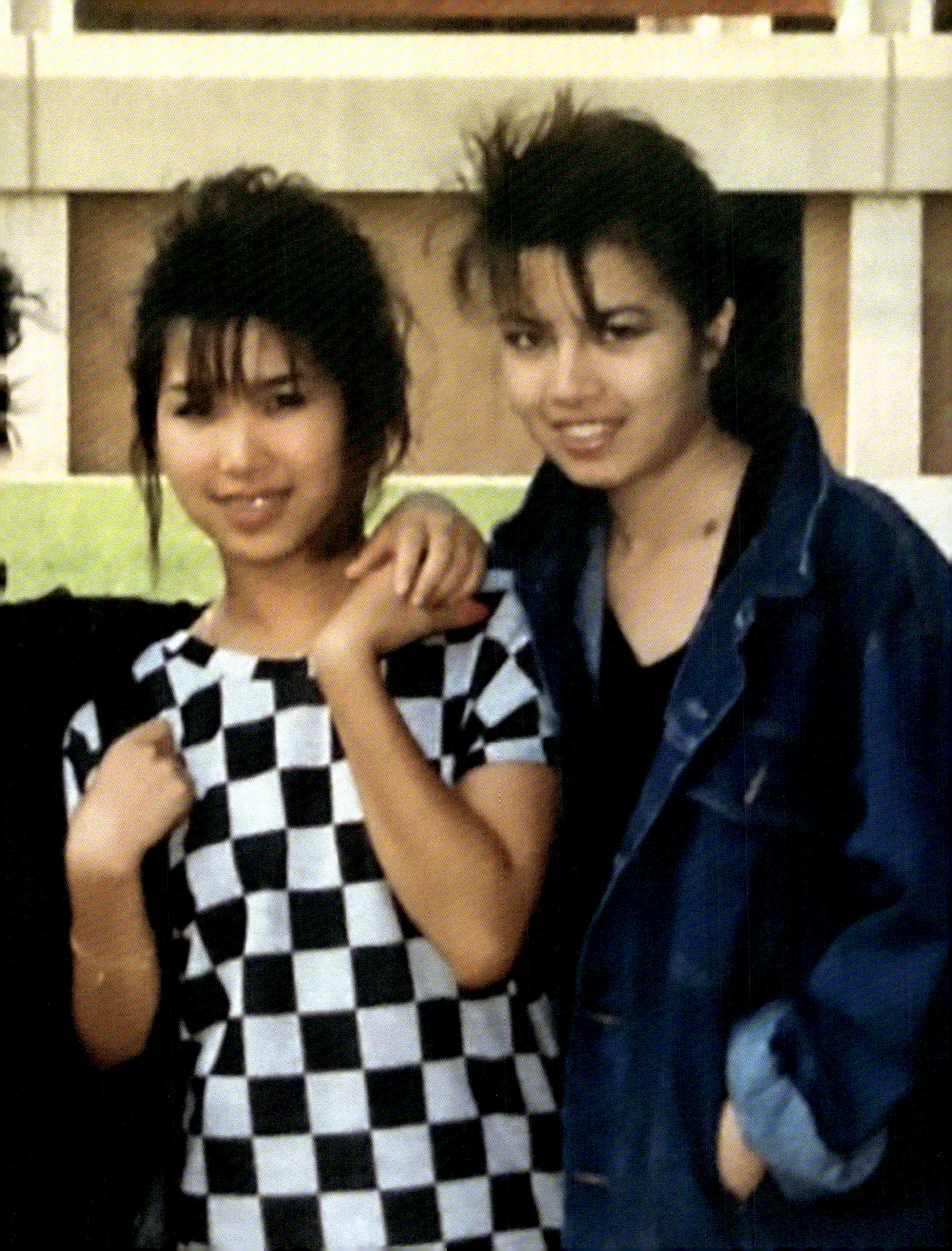

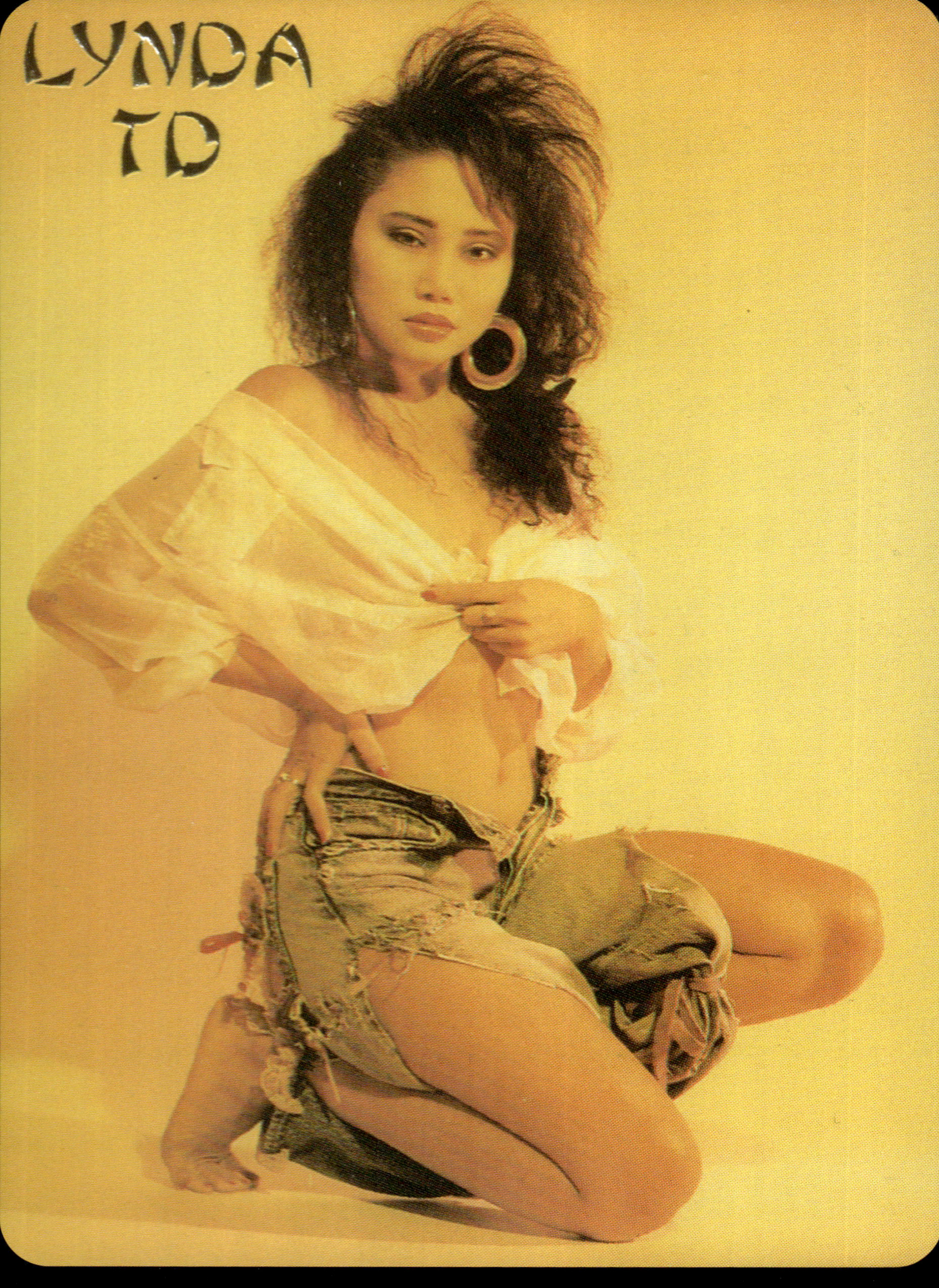

Lynda Trang Đài from the *Crazy Love* album, 1989.

CONTENTS

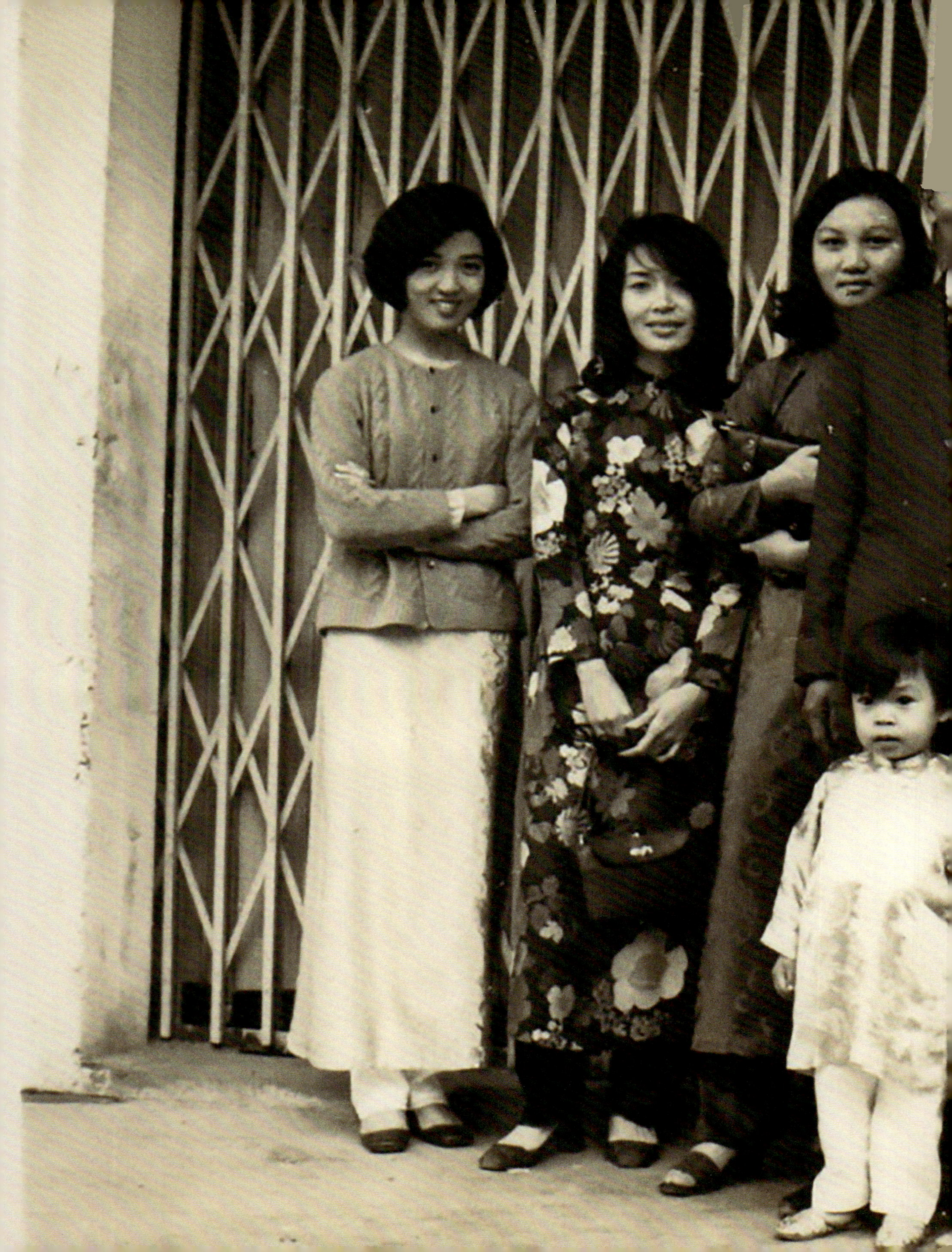

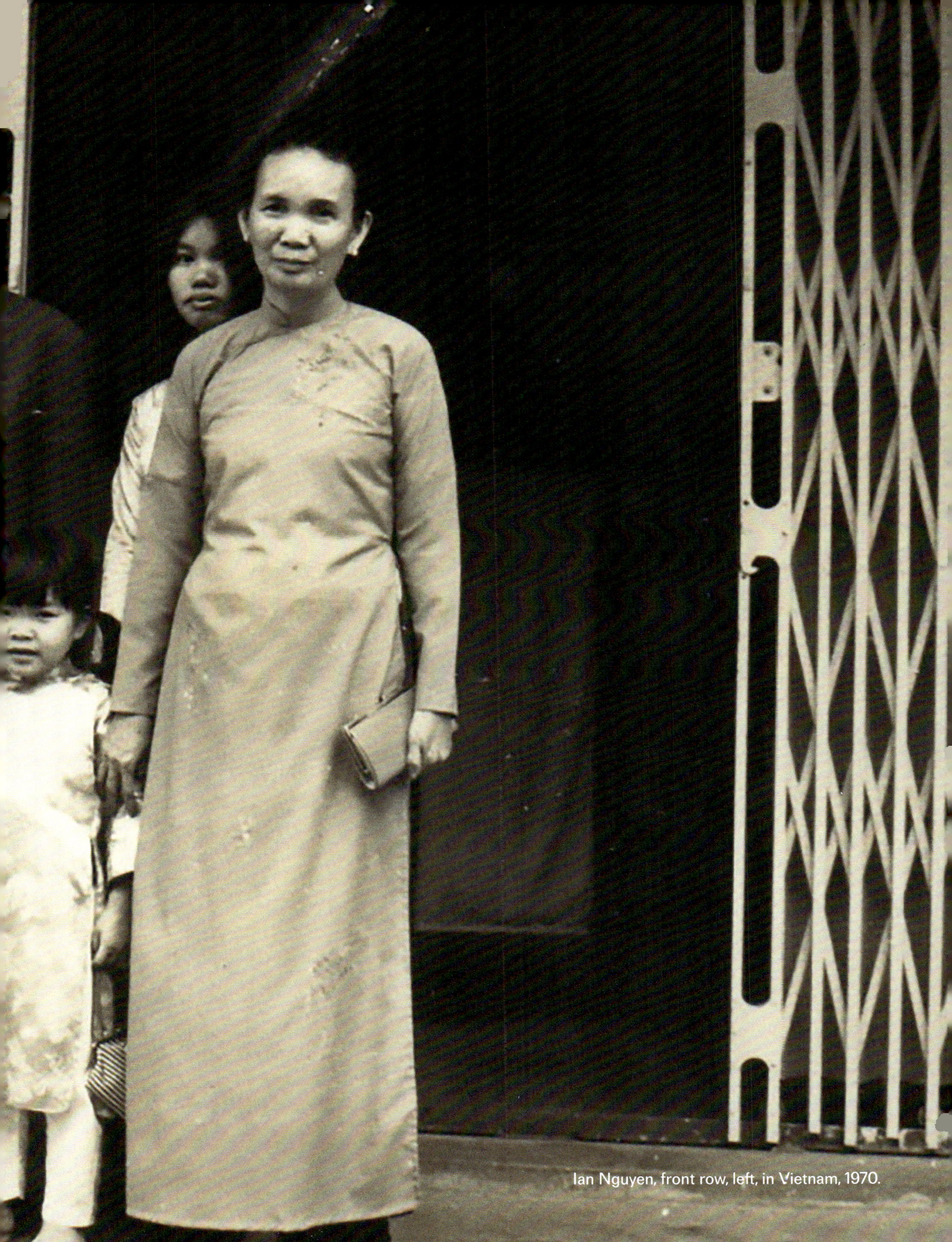

Ian Nguyen, front row, left, in Vietnam, 1970.

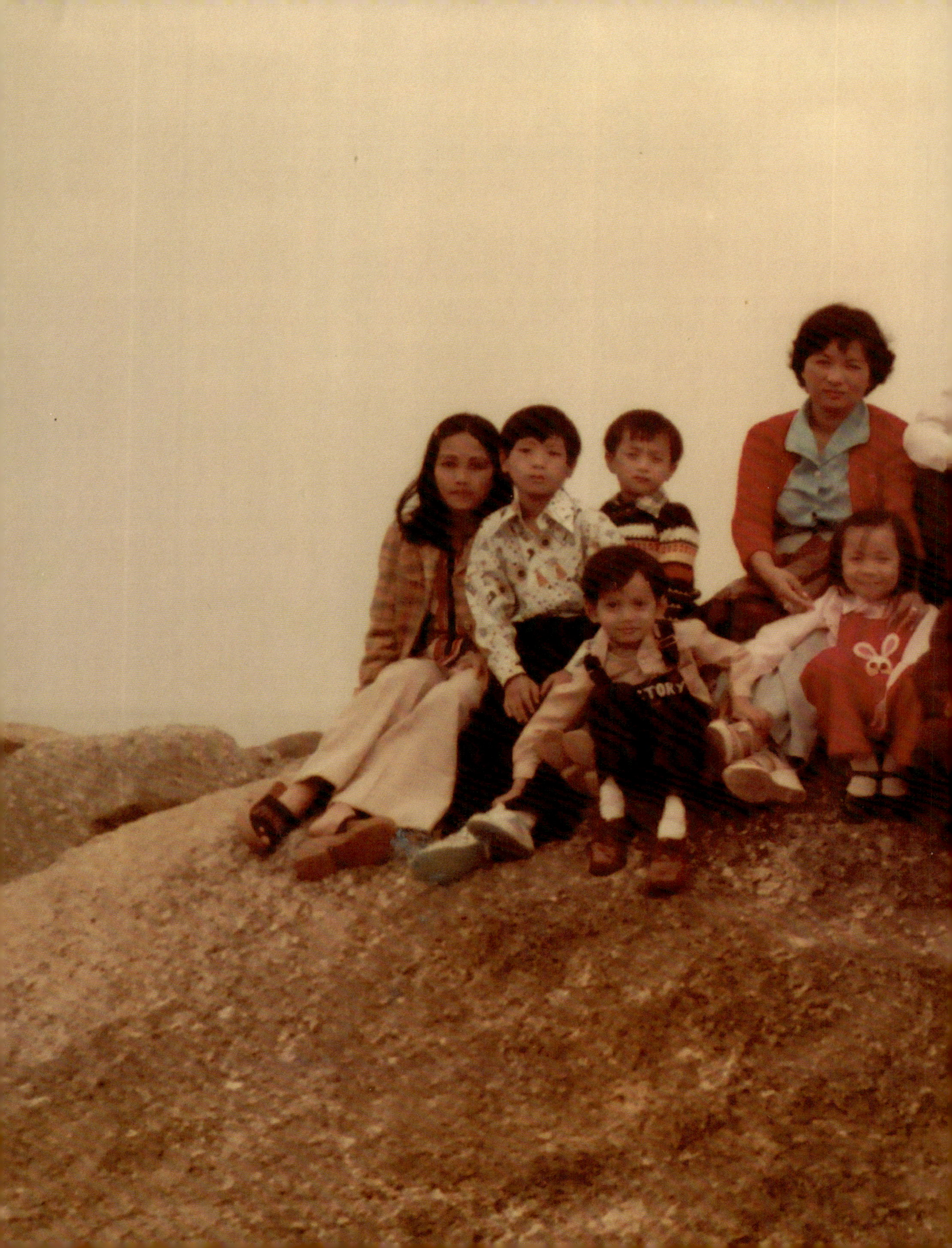

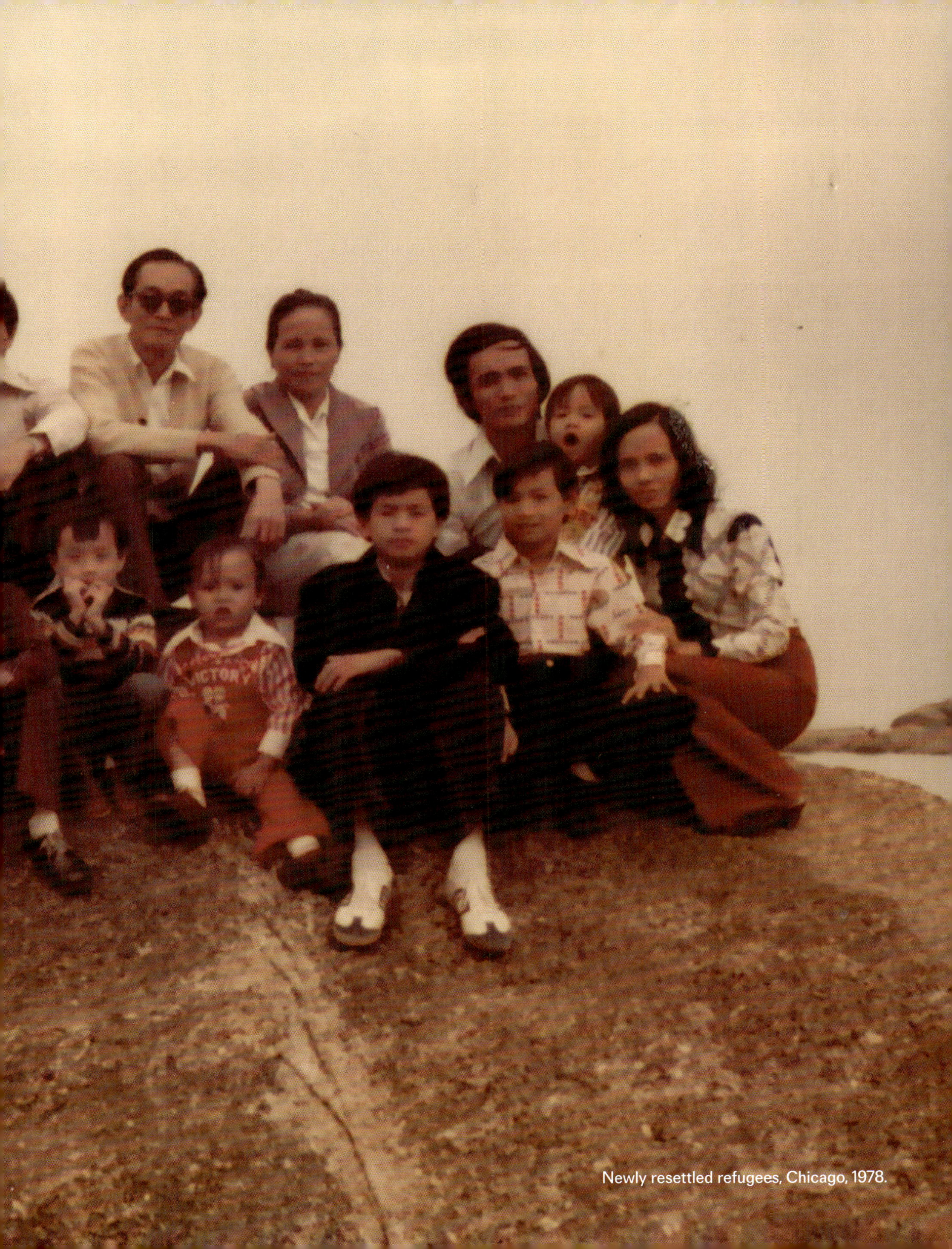

Newly resettled refugees, Chicago, 1978.

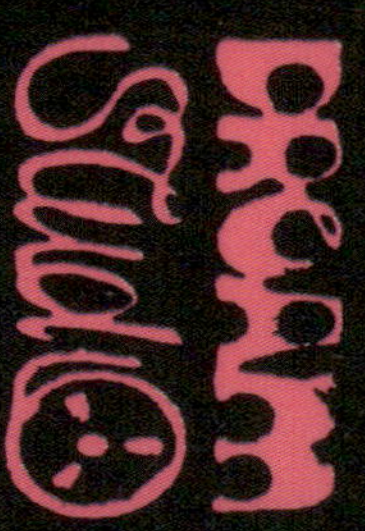

DUY QUANG * CAROL KIM * NHƯ MAI
CÔNG THÀNH * THÁI THẢO

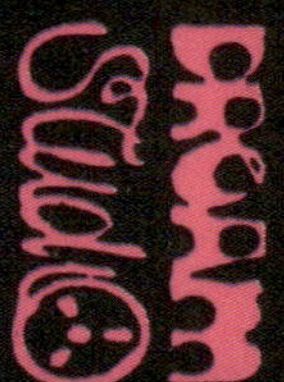

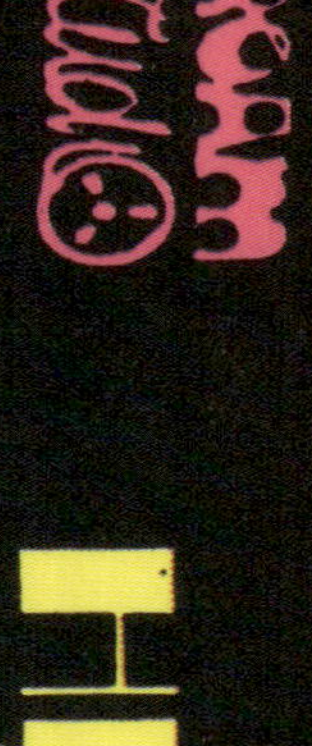

Liên Khúc
HẸN EM 4 MÙA

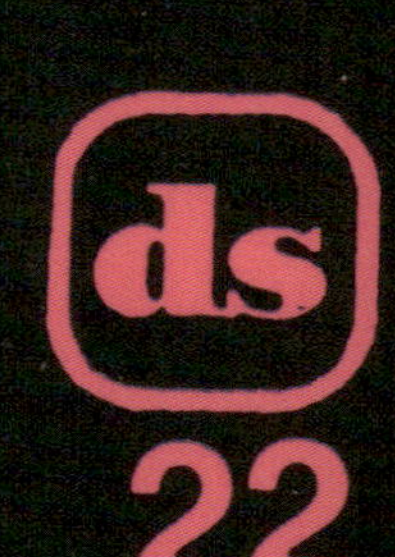

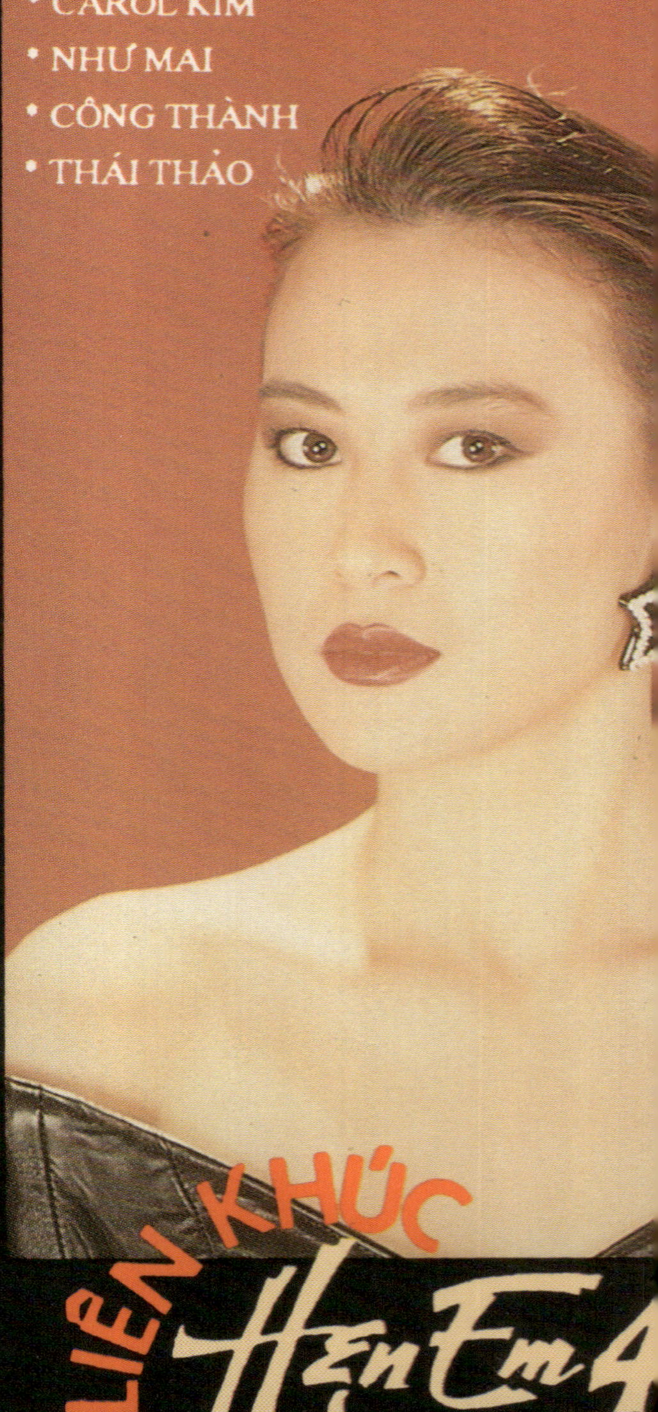

REAM Studio
22

DREAM STUDIO
HÂN HẠNH GIỚI THIỆU

DS001
Dạ Vũ The Dreamers
MỘNG DU
•
DS002
Tiếng Hát Duy Quang
SAO MÀ QUÊN ĐƯỢC
•
DS003
Tiếng Hát Thái Thảo
TÌNH EM
•
DS004
BẾN MƠ 1
DS005
Bên Nhau Ngày Vui
DS006
Duy Quang 2
NỬA ĐOẠN TÌNH BUỒN
•
DS007
Tình Khúc Mai Xuân Hoàng Hạc
NHỮNG NỤ HÔN ĐỜI
•
DS008
Bến Mơ 2
•
DS009
Dạ Vũ The Magic
ĐÊM HUYỀN DIỆU 1
•
DS010
Dạ Vũ The Dreamers 2
OH MÊ LY!

DS011
Tiếng Hát Duy Quang 3
THÀ NHƯ GIỌT MƯA
•
DS012
Tiếng Hát Ngọc Lan - Duy Quang
TÌNH PHAI
•
DS013
Duy Quang Nhạc Tuyển Chọn
•
DS014
Tiếng Hát Kiều Nga - Duy Quang
NGA
•
DS015
Tiếng Hát Ngọc Lan - Duy Quang
Kiều Nga
LỜI THÌ THẦM
•
DS016
Bến Mơ 3
TẠ TỪ
•
DS017
Dạ Vũ Magic
ĐÊM HUYỀN DIỆU 2
•
DS018
Tiếng Hát Duy Quang 4
NỤ HÔN TÌNH SẦU

DS022:
Liên Khúc Hẹn Em 4 Mùa

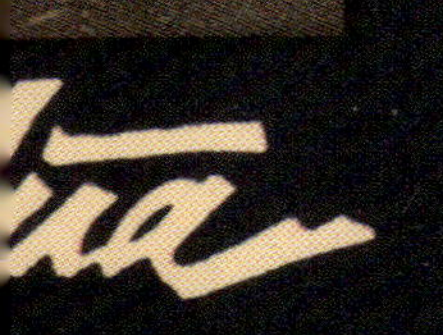

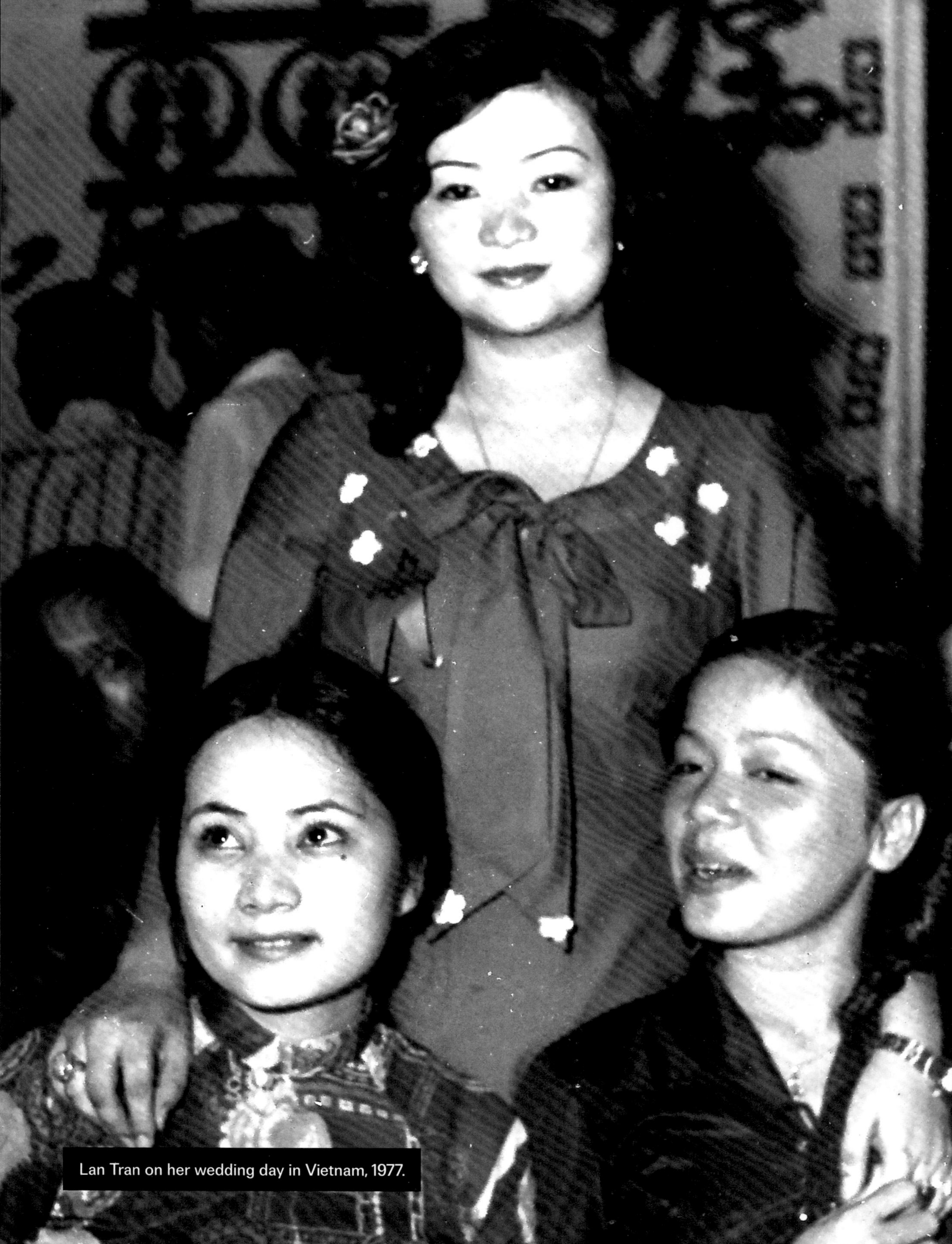

Lan Tran on her wedding day in Vietnam, 1977.

Con người có cố có ông,
như cây có cội,
như sông có nguồn.

Everyone has ancestors,
like every tree has roots,
and every river a source.

– Vietnamese proverb

INTRODUCTION

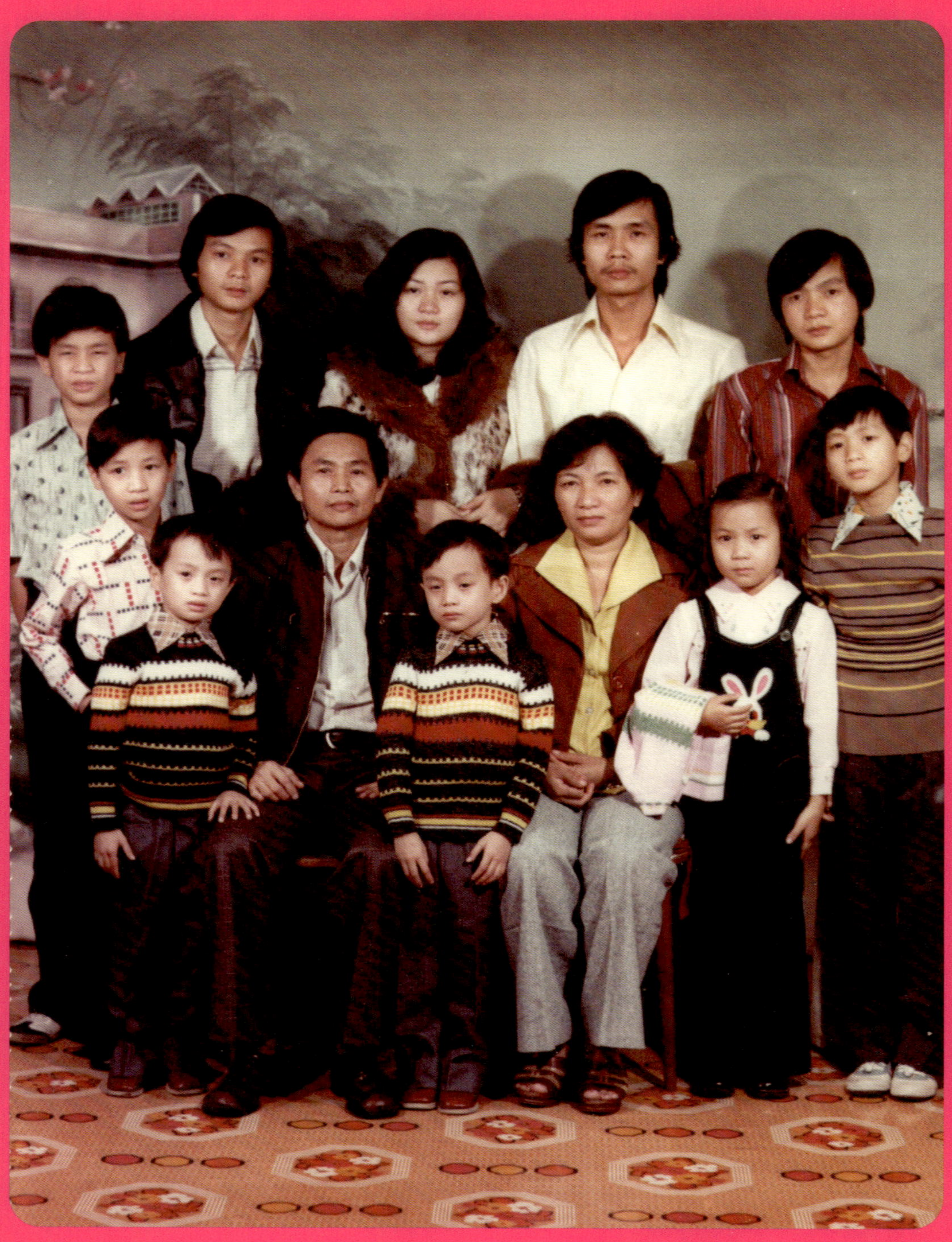

Elizabeth Ai

As a member of the Vietnamese diaspora, I grew up in a loud, chaotic home that buzzed with activity, especially on weekends when relatives from across town would visit to share fruits, sit for tea, or join us for *cúng*—an act of worship—before a large feast. *Cúng* was an expression of gratitude for our ancestors and faith in our Buddhist deities, and it also included wishes for everything from health and happiness to material desires. In our multilingual household, we primarily spoke Vietnamese, with my grandparents using Chinese for conversations they didn't want the children to understand; English mingled with our daily vernacular thanks to my teenage uncles and aunts.

Despite being raised in a Buddhist home where the past and present were believed to coexist, we were explicitly forbidden from discussing our family's past—the successive flights from China and Vietnam, and the profound losses we suffered during these tumultuous and traumatic moments. This inability to ask anything left me grappling with so many unanswered questions: Why did we speak Vietnamese if we were ethnically Chinese? Why was the past off-limits? Why were my divorced parents, who were both alive and well, out of my life?

But I never got those answers, and like many children of the 1980s, I spent countless hours in front of the television, getting fed another version of the past. Growing up as a second-generation Vietnamese American during this period, my perception of our Vietnamese community was predominantly shaped by a violent American media narrative focused on the war, which started in tragedy and ended with the fall of Saigon in 1975. This story, largely shaped through the lens of white male directors and their white male protagonists, failed to capture the complex cultural shifts and the rich diversity that characterized the Vietnamese experience during and after the war. The portrayals were traumatizing and one-dimensional, framing Vietnamese people as either victims or villains—depictions that lacked depth and nuance.

This kind of oversimplification overshadowed the intricate cultural shifts experienced by more than forty-five million Vietnamese people, many of whom faced the formidable challenges of fleeing, resettling, or reunifying. For families like mine, the urgent needs of survival—adapting to new environments, learning a new language, and figuring out how to put food on the table—often superseded the luxury of reflection. Moments for introspection, when they arose, were suppressed to prevent reopening painful wounds. Many adults chose to maintain a

Elizabeth Ai's family in Hong Kong after escaping Vietnam, 1978.

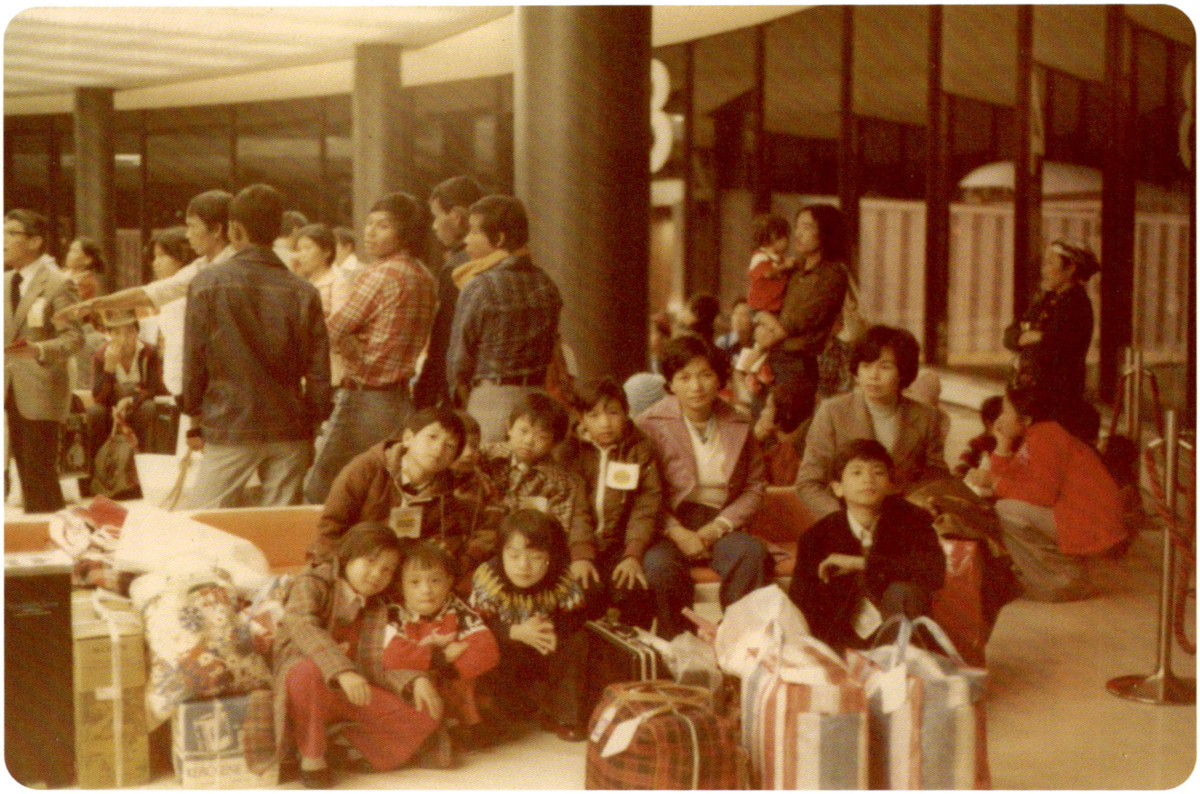

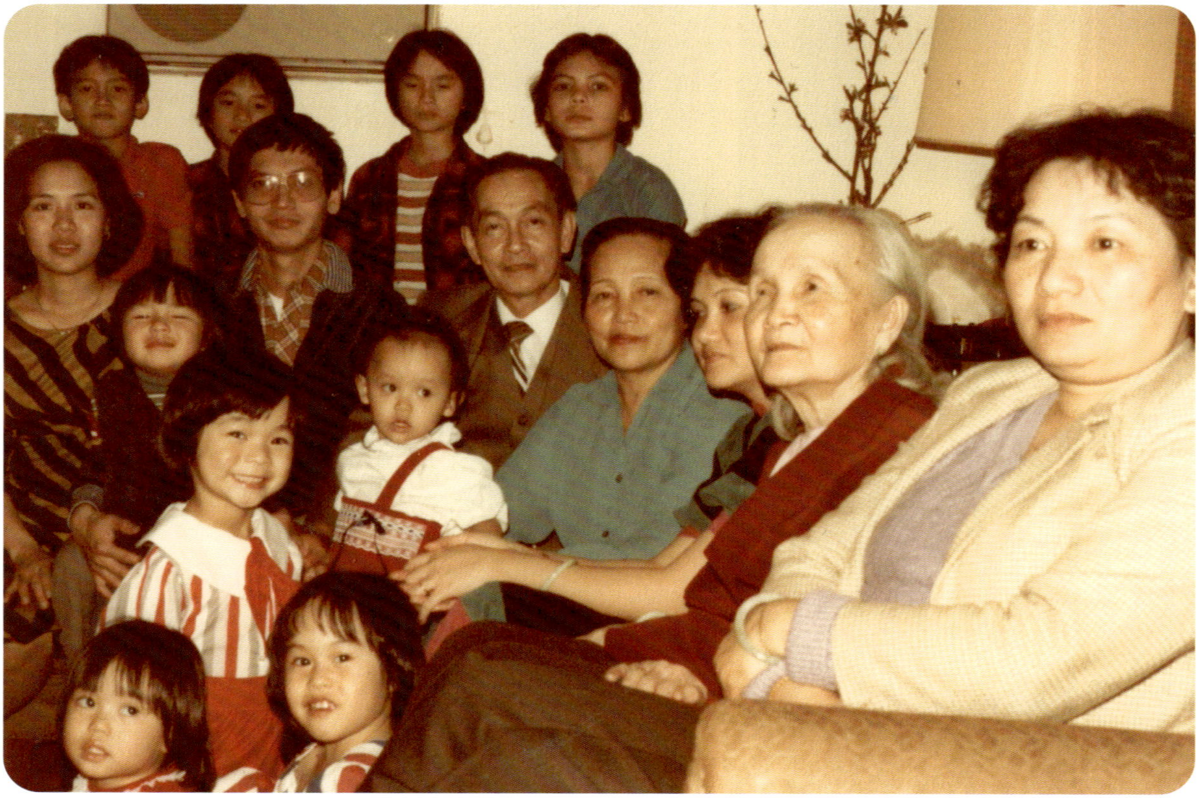

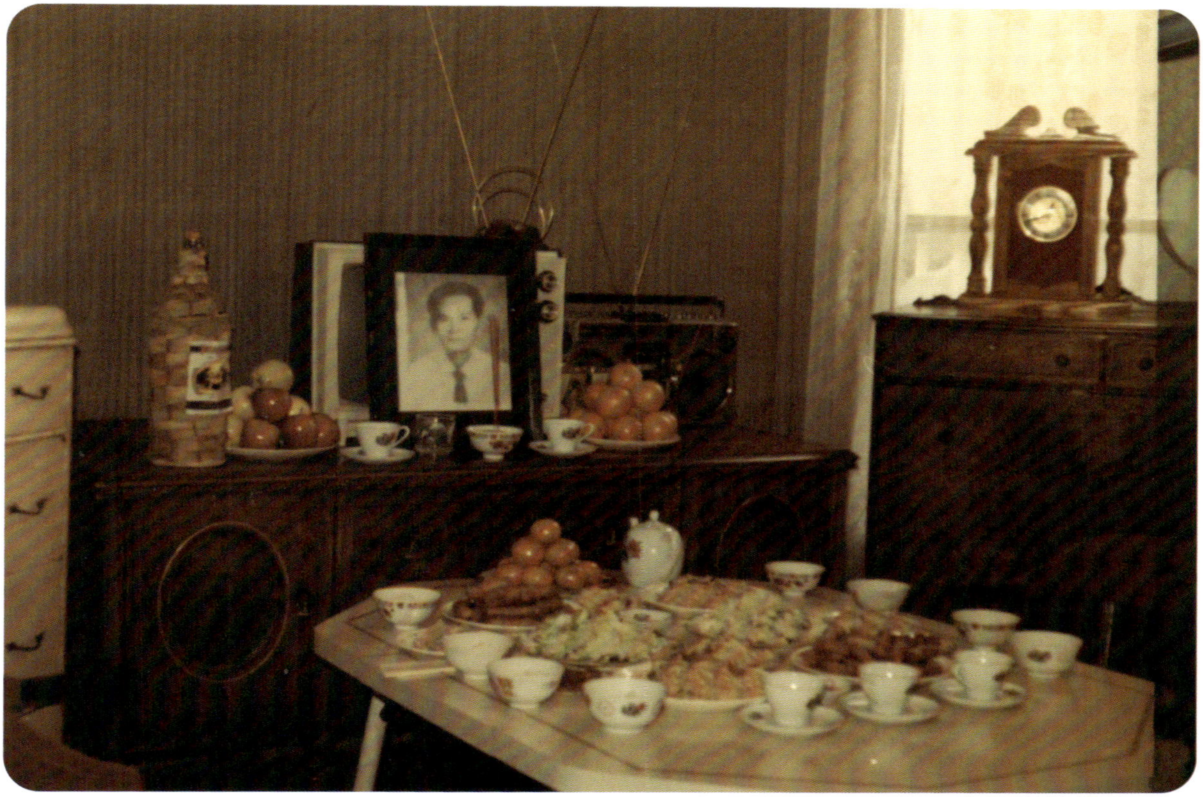

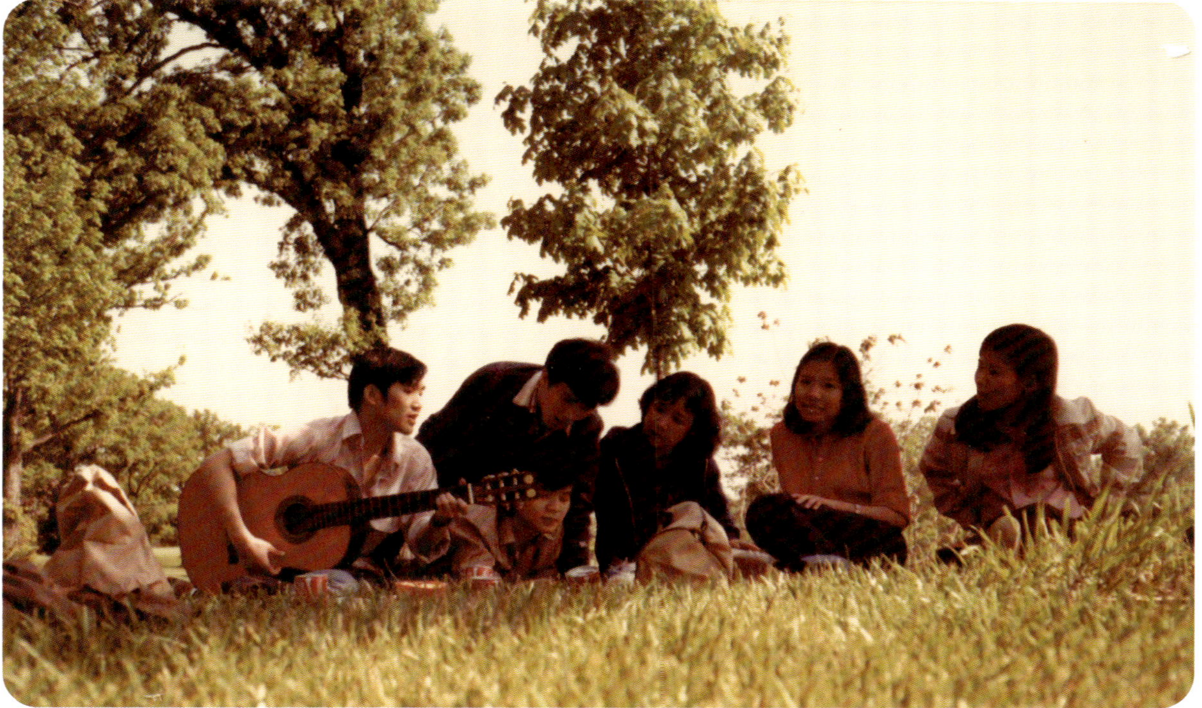

Ai family photos, late 1970s to early 1980s.

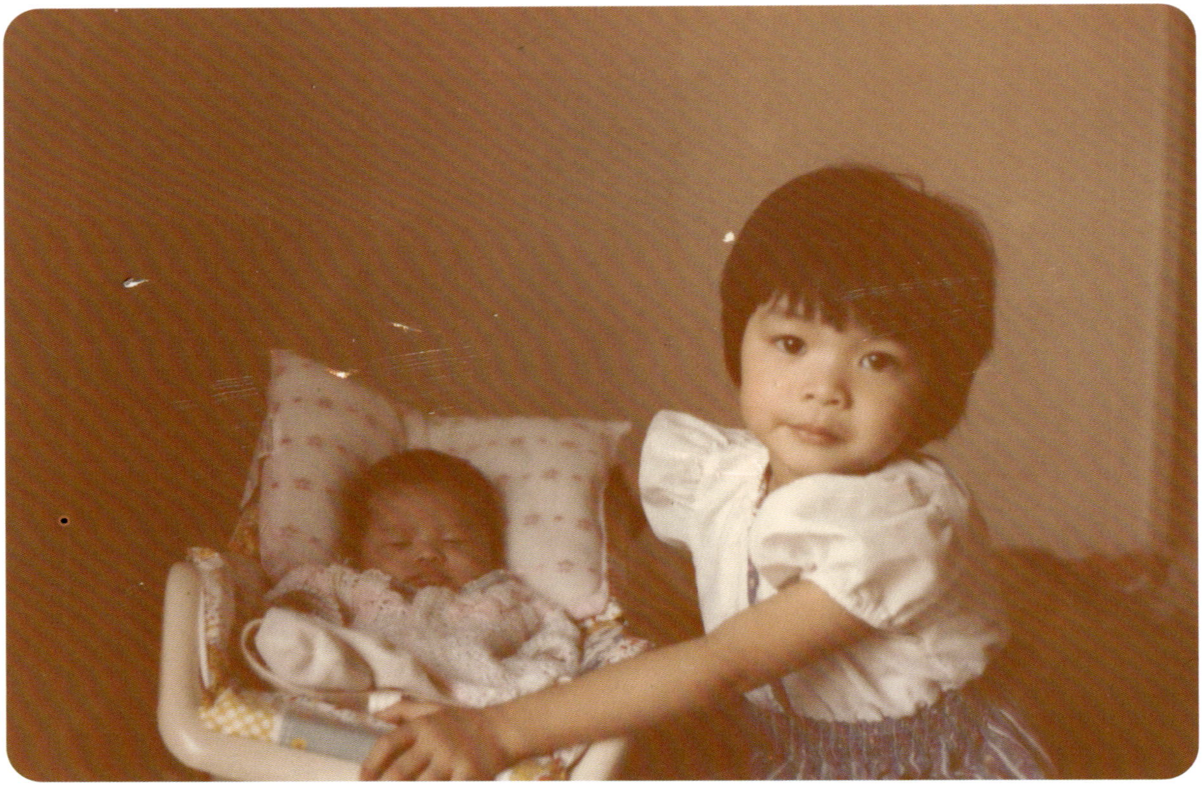

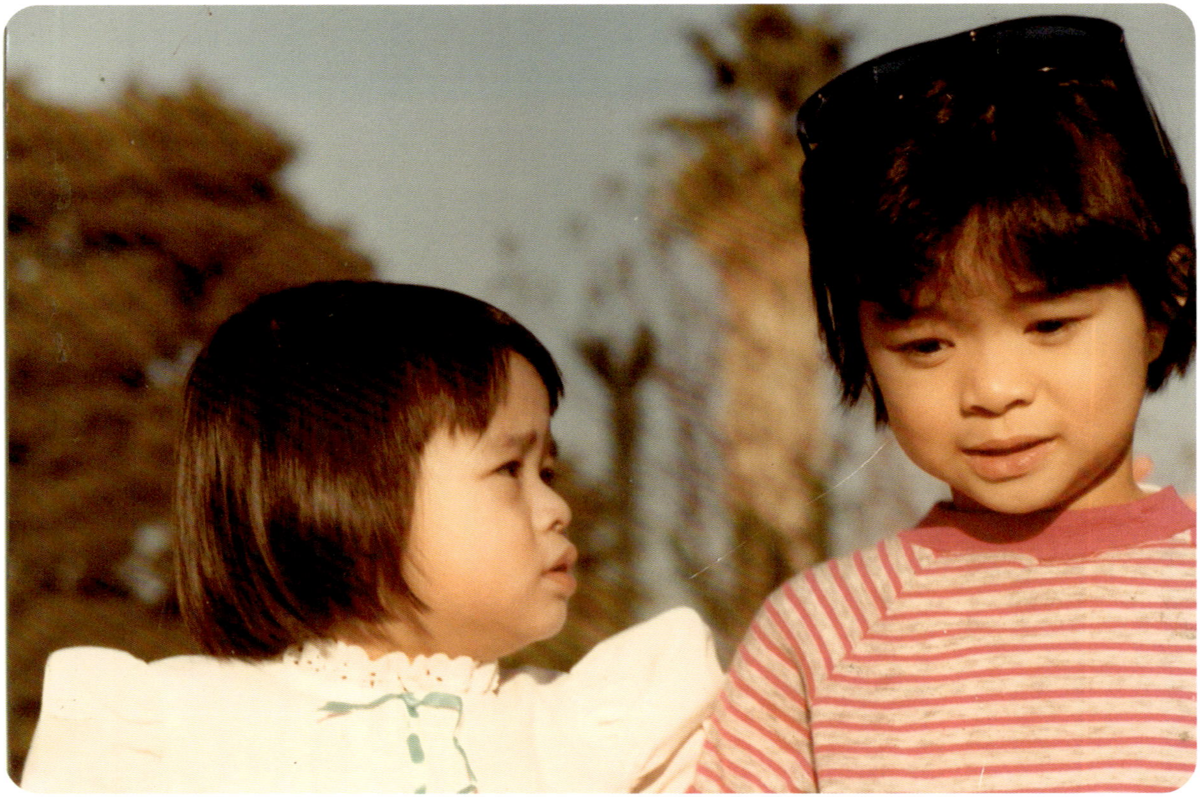

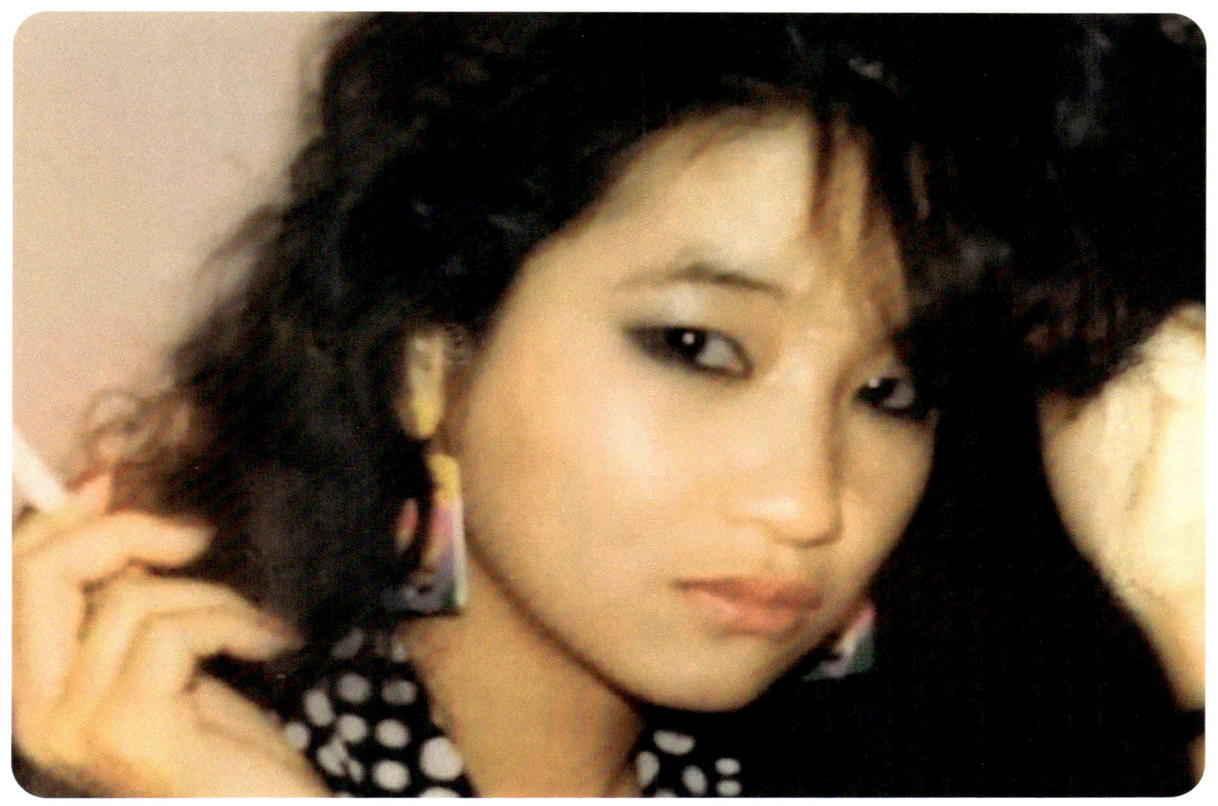

façade of strength for their children, opting for silence instead of sharing their traumatic experiences.

Like many others, my family was drawn to Southern California and found a new beginning in the United States; many refugees settled in Orange County due to its proximity to Camp Pendleton. The warm climate, similar to Vietnam, along with the support from numerous local churches that sponsored refugee families, made this region a hub for the Vietnamese diaspora. By the mid 1980s, Orange County emerged as the heart of the Vietnamese community in America and the location of the first officially sanctioned Little Saigon, straddling the cities of Westminster, Garden Grove, and Santa Ana.

ENTER NEW WAVE MUSIC

Opposite, above: Elizabeth Ai with baby sister Carol Ai, 1983. Opposite, below: Elizabeth (at right) and Carol Ai, 1986. Above: Young New Waver.

The 1980s marked a period of significant cultural transformation, with New Wave music emerging as a vital outlet for Vietnamese youth navigating their dual heritage. During this time, MTV burst onto the scene as a radical force, revolutionizing societal norms with its bold and provocative content that streamed directly into living rooms across America. MTV's

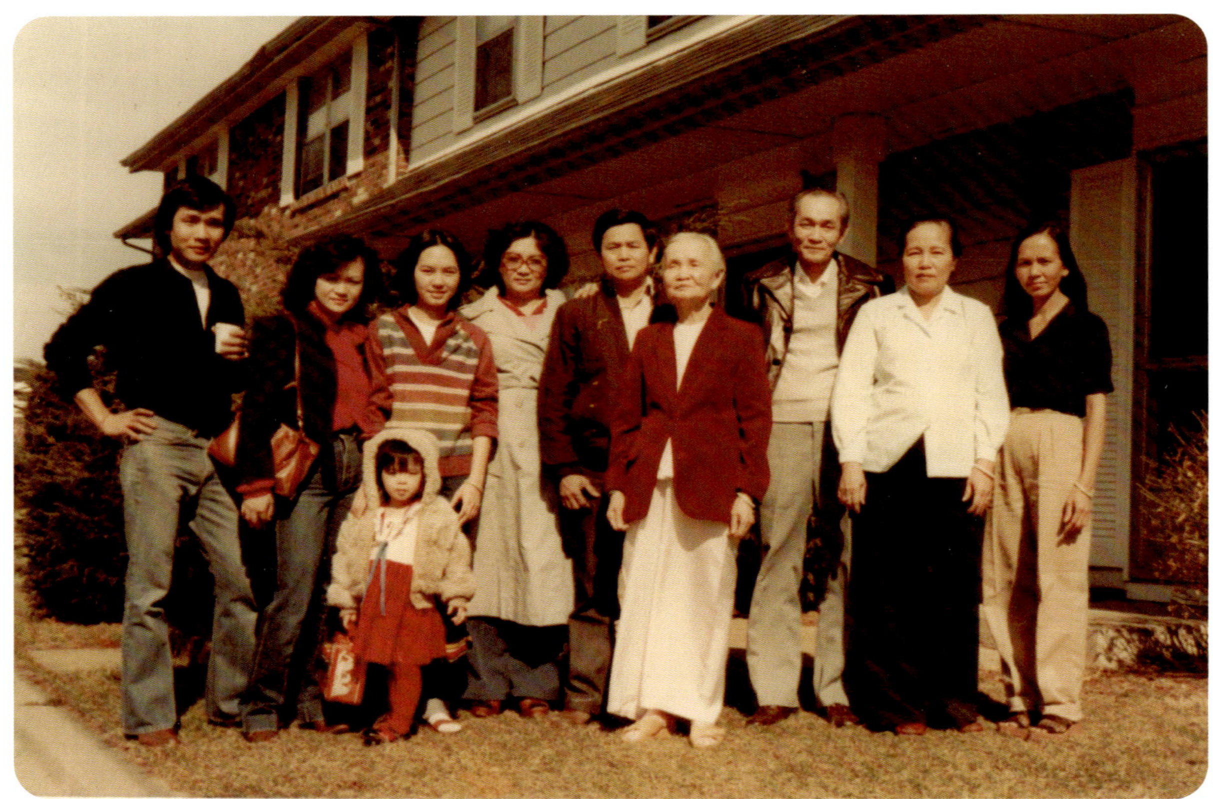

profound impact represented a new era of freedom and rebellion against the established order, resonating deeply with young Vietnamese Americans.

These youths, in the process of forming their own hybrid identities, were particularly drawn to a subgenre of New Wave, one with synthesized sounds that got miscategorized in record shop bins under the UK New Wave labels, where you could also find bands like Depeche Mode, The Cure, New Order, OMD, and the like. This particular subgenre of New Wave was later called Eurodisco, and was predominantly produced by German and Italian artists. This style, characterized by its blend of European synth-pop and American disco beats, was not typically played on American radio, making it a symbol of resistance against both mainstream American culture and traditional Vietnamese expectations. It became more than just a sound; it was a powerful statement of identity and a catalyst for a creative counterculture for Vietnamese youth.

For the "1.5 Generation"—refugees between five and twelve years old, who were born in Vietnam and largely raised in America—as they came of age, the Vietnamese New Wave movement and music embodied their unique cultural position,

Above: Ai family, resettled in the US. Opposite: Elizabeth (standing) and Carol Ai, 1984.

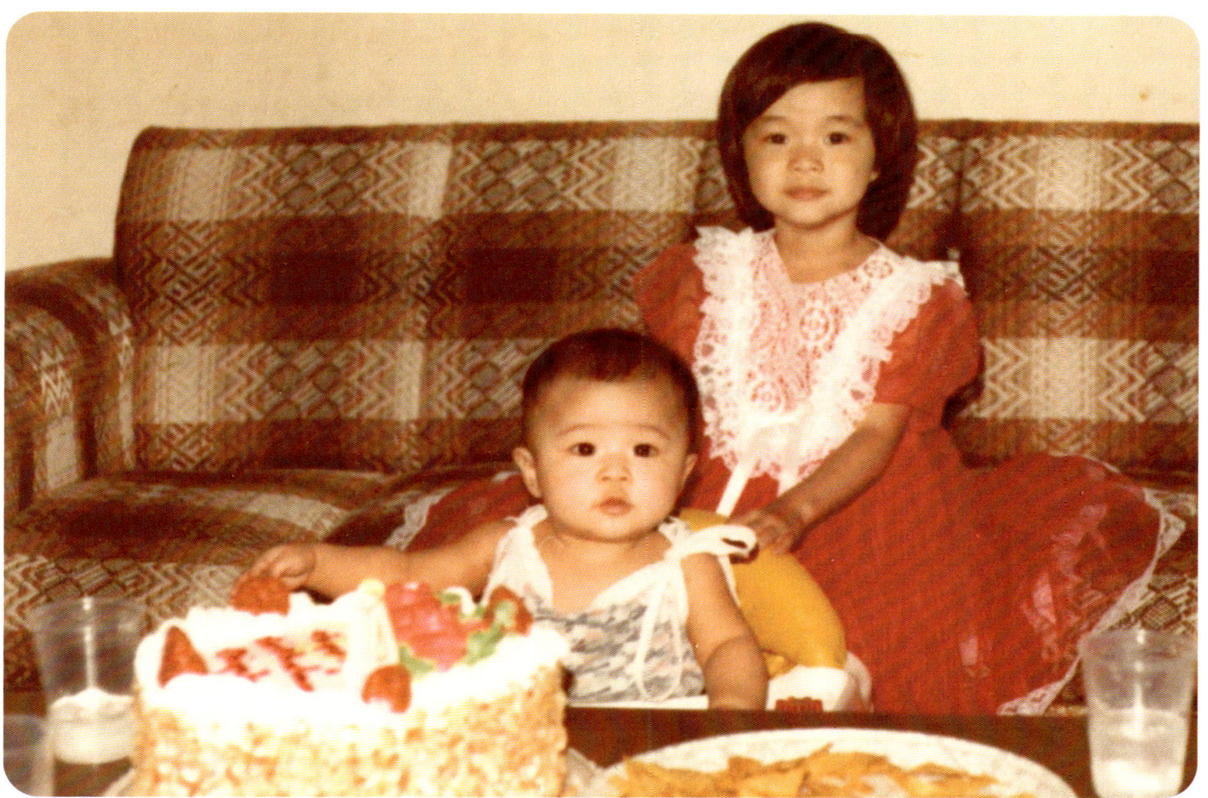

straddling the line between their ancestral heritage and the new world they inhabited. The rarity and distinctiveness of this imported music underscored their departure from both American and Vietnamese norms, serving as the perfect medium for expression and connection within a burgeoning subculture. This movement was more than just music; it encompassed a style, a sound, an atmosphere. It shaped friendships and defined entire worlds. It was a crucial element in their narrative of adaptation, playing a key role in the development of a hybridized identity.

It wasn't until I became a mother myself that I began to fully appreciate the magnitude of what the first generations endured. The loss was profound, extending beyond the physical scars of war to the emotional pain of losing their homeland for a challenging new way of life. In hindsight, I realized that the restrictions on conversations about our past during my childhood disconnected me from a rich cultural heritage I deserved to know. Many of the questions I had as a child were still left unanswered. And because New Wave music was in the background of some of my earliest and fondest memories, I began to dive into those moments to start looking for answers.

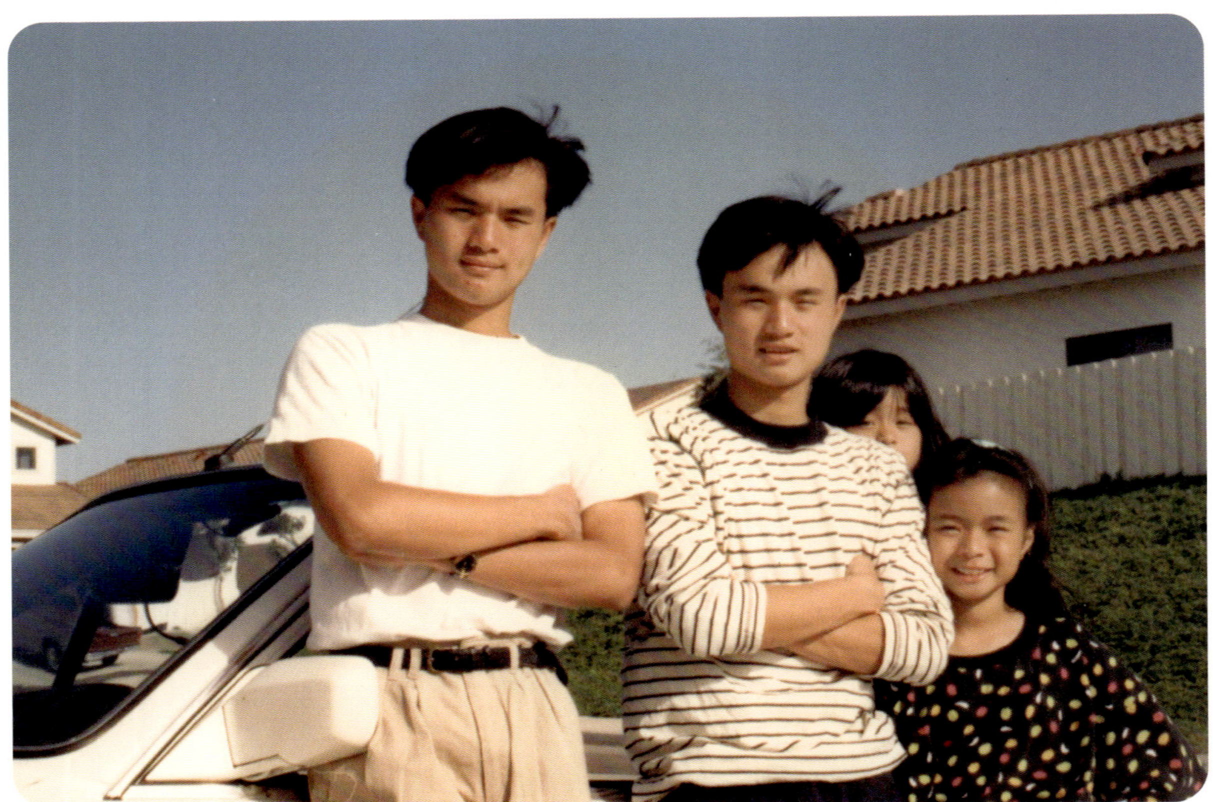

Above: New Wave teens and family, 1988. Opposite: Myra Wu, mid-1980s.

I explored how this music captured our community's distinctive narrative of adaptation and identity. I was fascinated by how the Vietnamese diaspora began to establish its own cultural outlets, building a platform to this music of the youth and giving rise to what some in the community called "Vietnamese Hollywood." Through variety shows and music productions put on by the likes of *Paris by Night*, Asia Entertainment, May Productions, Giáng Ngọc Productions, Lang Van, and dozens of other companies, a vigorous Vietnamese entertainment industry flourished, creating its own stars and its own version of MTV. These productions not only provided entertainment, but also offered a sense of identity and pride, offering an alternative to the American media's depiction of the Vietnamese experience.

As I delved deeper into this era, it became clear that the music was not merely a backdrop but a central element in our story of adaptation and identity. It provided a sense of belonging and offered a way to cope with the displacement and identity struggles that defined our community's experience in America.

Driven by a desire to learn more about this history and tell a more complete story, I embarked on creating my documentary,

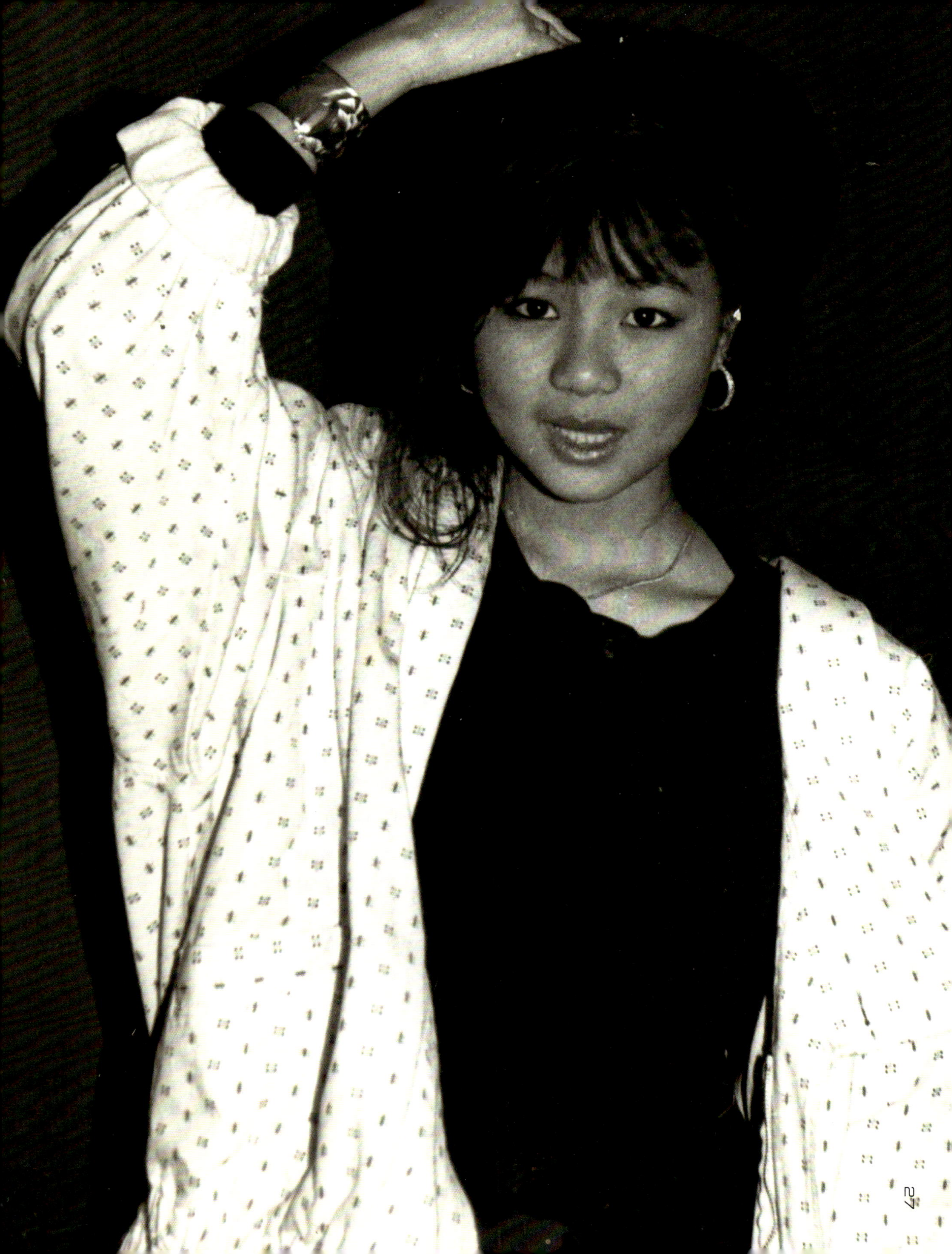

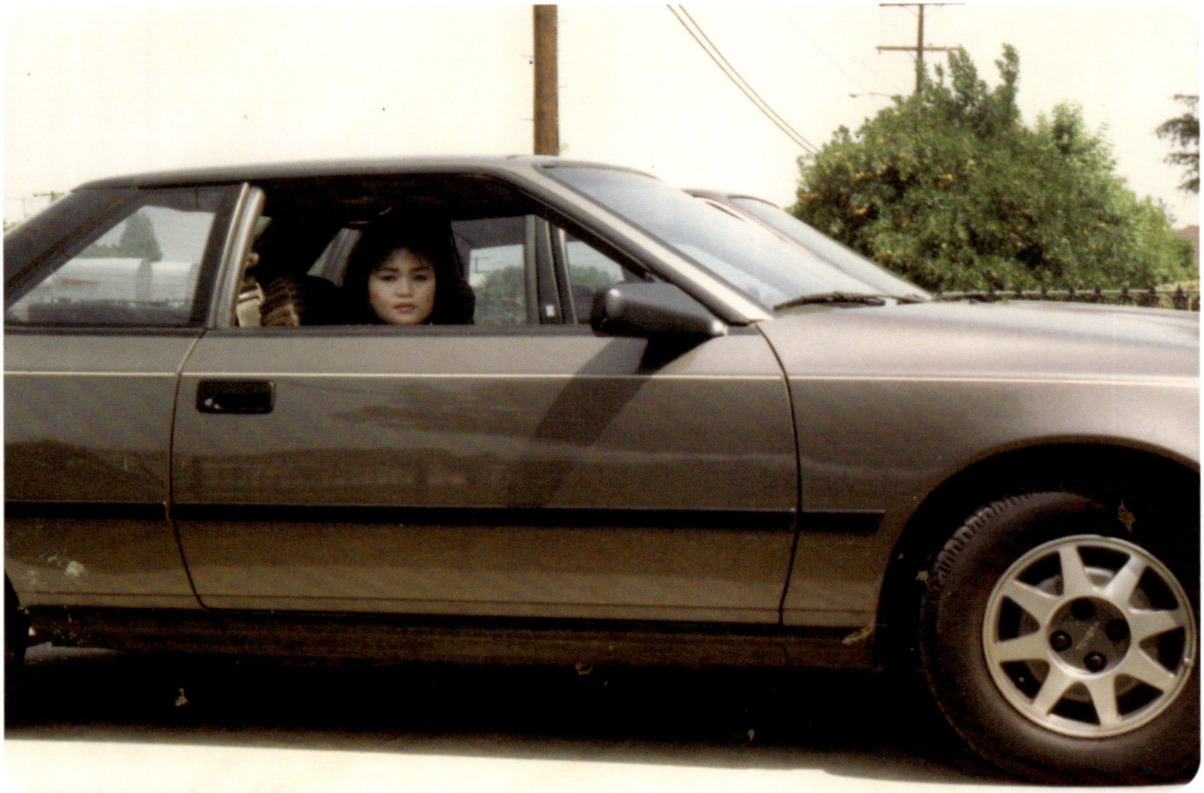

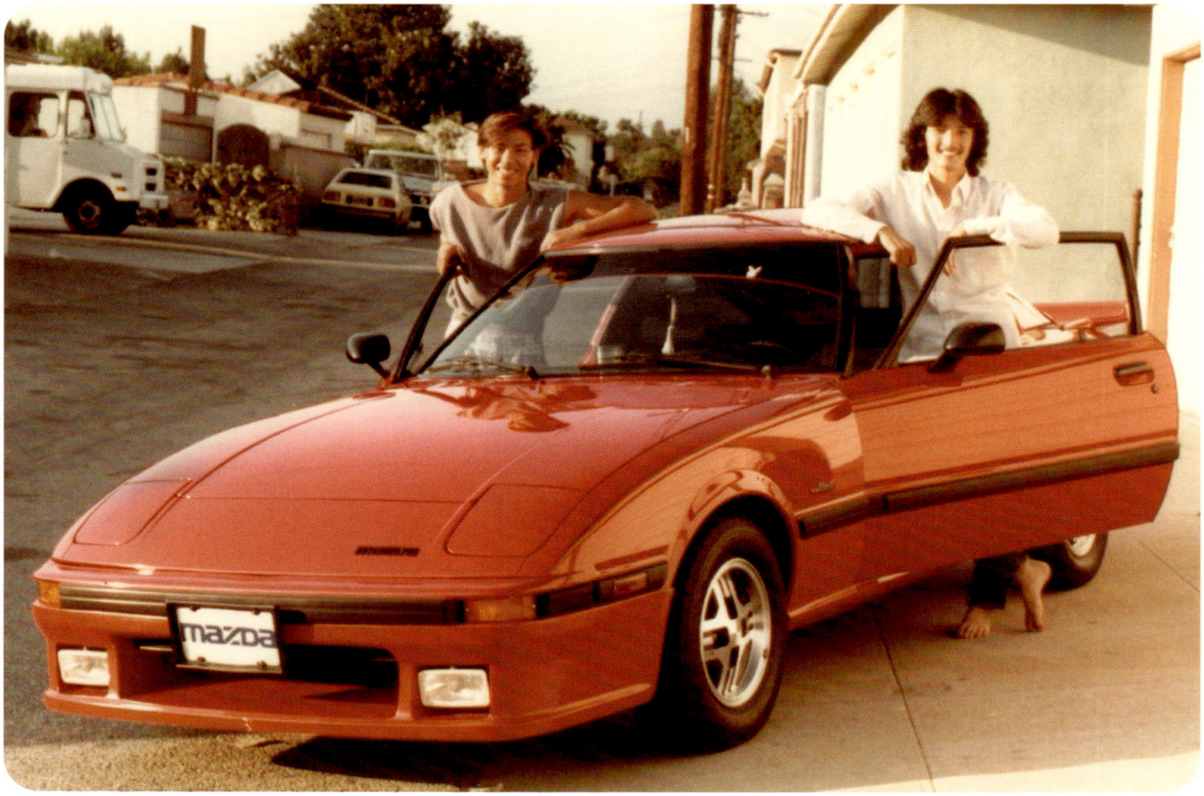

Community archive photos, circa 1980s.

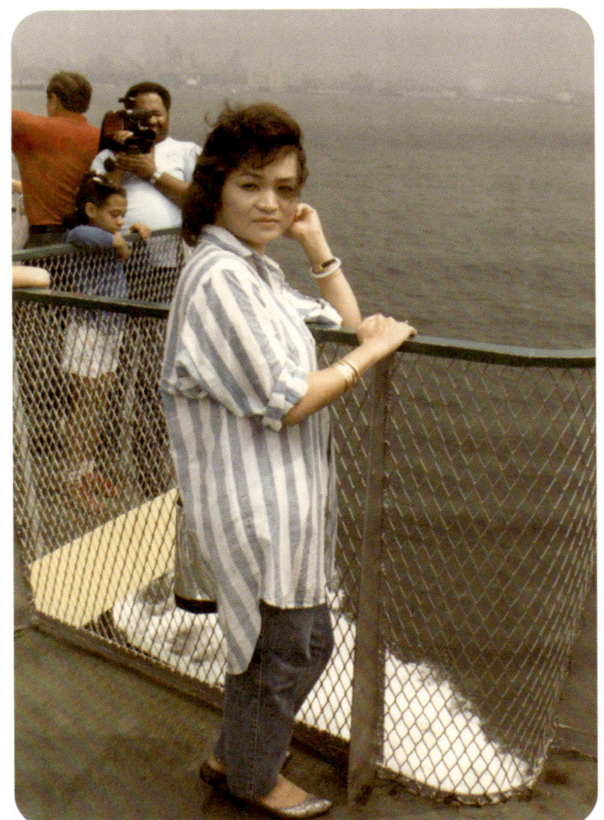

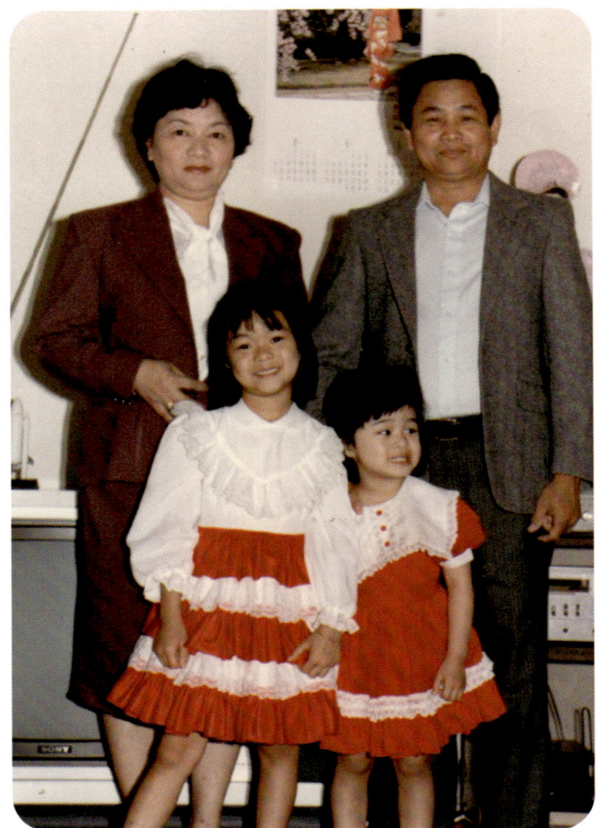

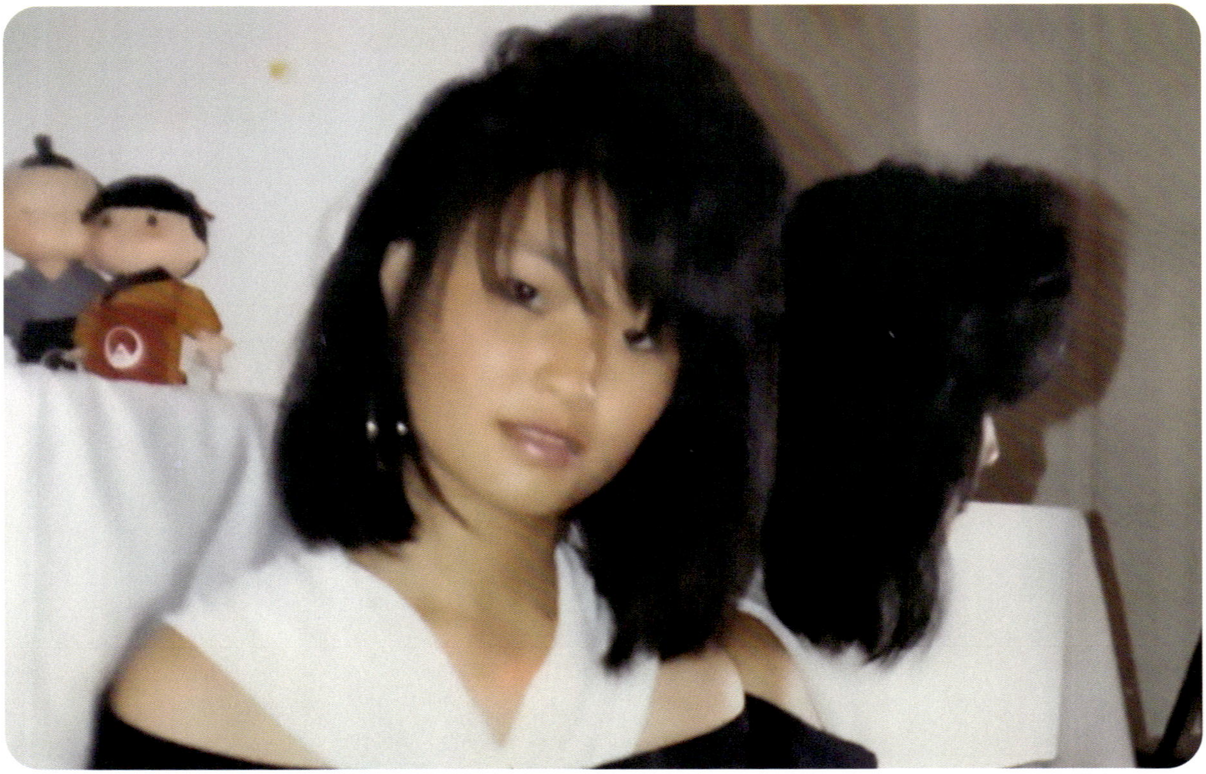

Community archive photos.

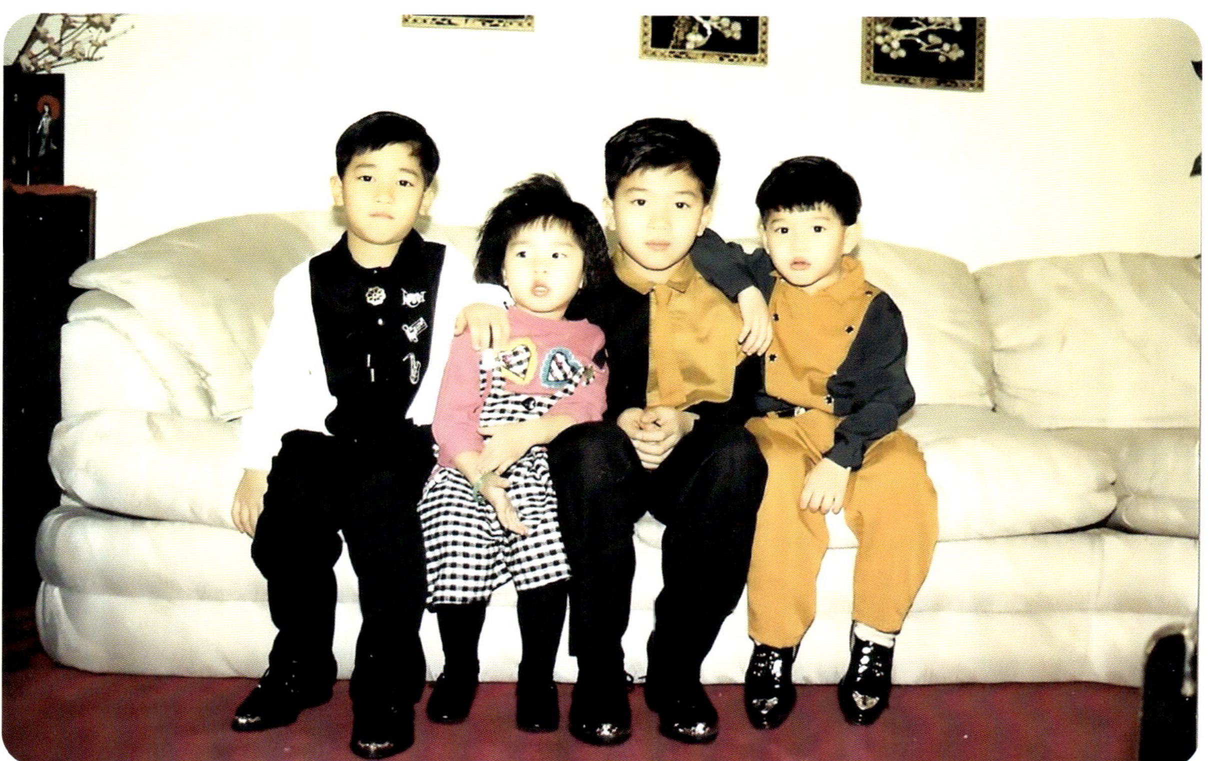

New Wave, in 2018. This project was more than just a film; it was a personal exploration into the pivotal era following the Vietnam War, an attempt to understand and represent the diverse experiences of Vietnamese Americans post-resettlement. In the various ebbs and flows of the research phases, my team and I were able to amass a treasure trove of material on the diaspora that didn't make it into the film. My memories of my childhood were sparse but potent. They conjure a time when my family was poor, didn't know any better, and just could escape through these sounds, this music, the fashion that went along with it. Consequential and trivial at the same time. But as I dove into my family's limited archive, I realized that there weren't very many photos of my uncles and aunts, so I began to cast my questions into the community. Where else could I learn why this world existed? It couldn't have been just us? One question would beget more questions, and before long, I launched an Instagram page just to find more photos and stories like mine. I was on a hunt for archives and connections.

The discovery of these rich stories and insights sparked the creation of this book, designed to provide a comprehensive account and share these invaluable perspectives. Both through the documentary and now this book that you hold, I aim to move

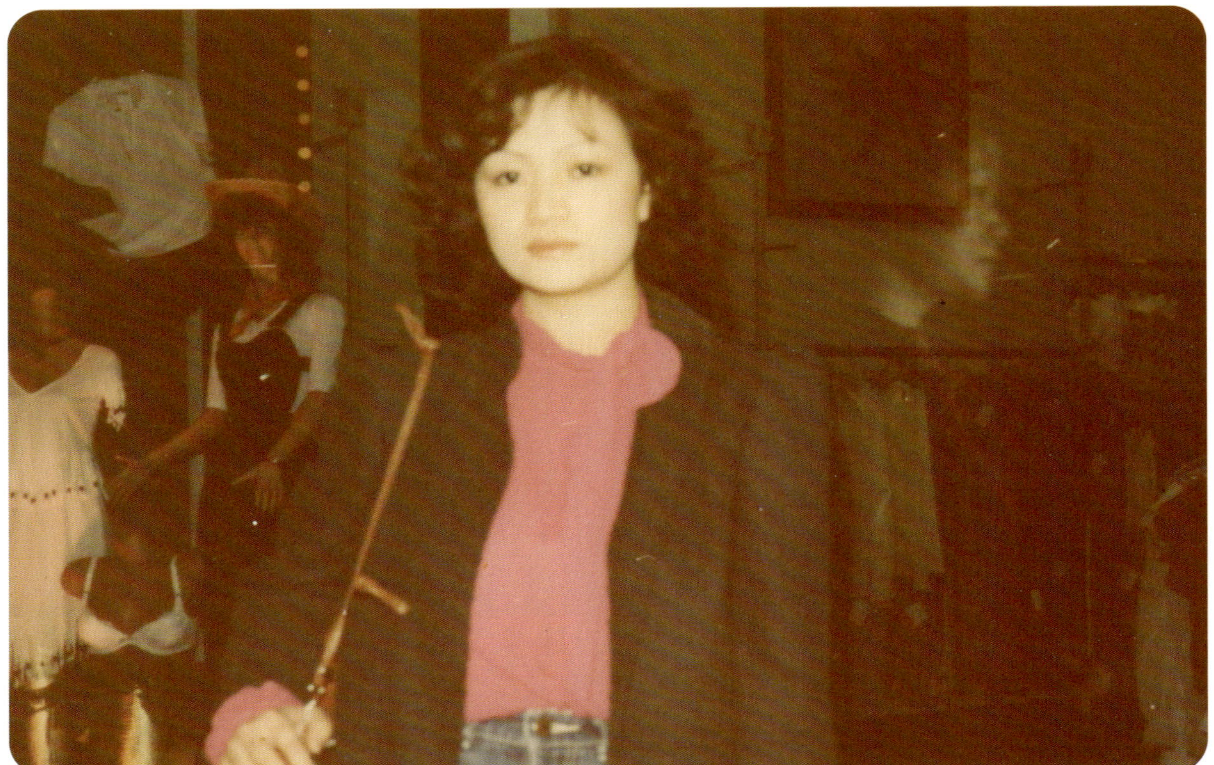

beyond simplified historical narratives and counter the erasure of our experiences by preserving and disseminating the complex story of our community.

This project was not a solitary effort, but the result of collaboration with dozens of dedicated advisors, teammates, and contributions from authors I deeply admire. I am immensely grateful for everyone I encountered during my research who shared their personal stories, opened their hearts, and provided archival evidence of their lives marked by both pain and joy. This book is an act of preservation and reclamation, a means to save our stories from fading into oblivion in the small way that I could offer, memorializing a history that might otherwise disappear.

Above: Lan Tran, circa 1980s. Opposite, above: Lan Tran with daughters, Elizabeth (left) and Carol Ai. Opposite, below: Lan Tran and Elizabeth Ai, California, 1988.

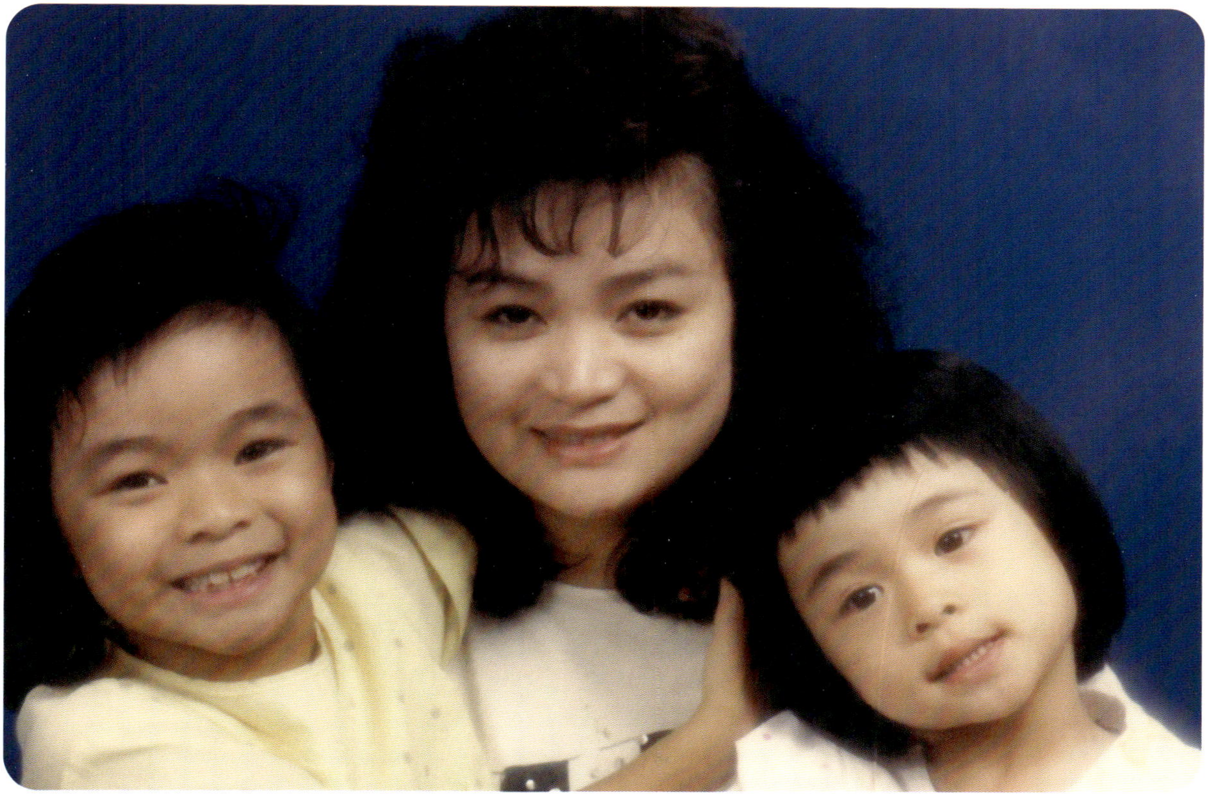

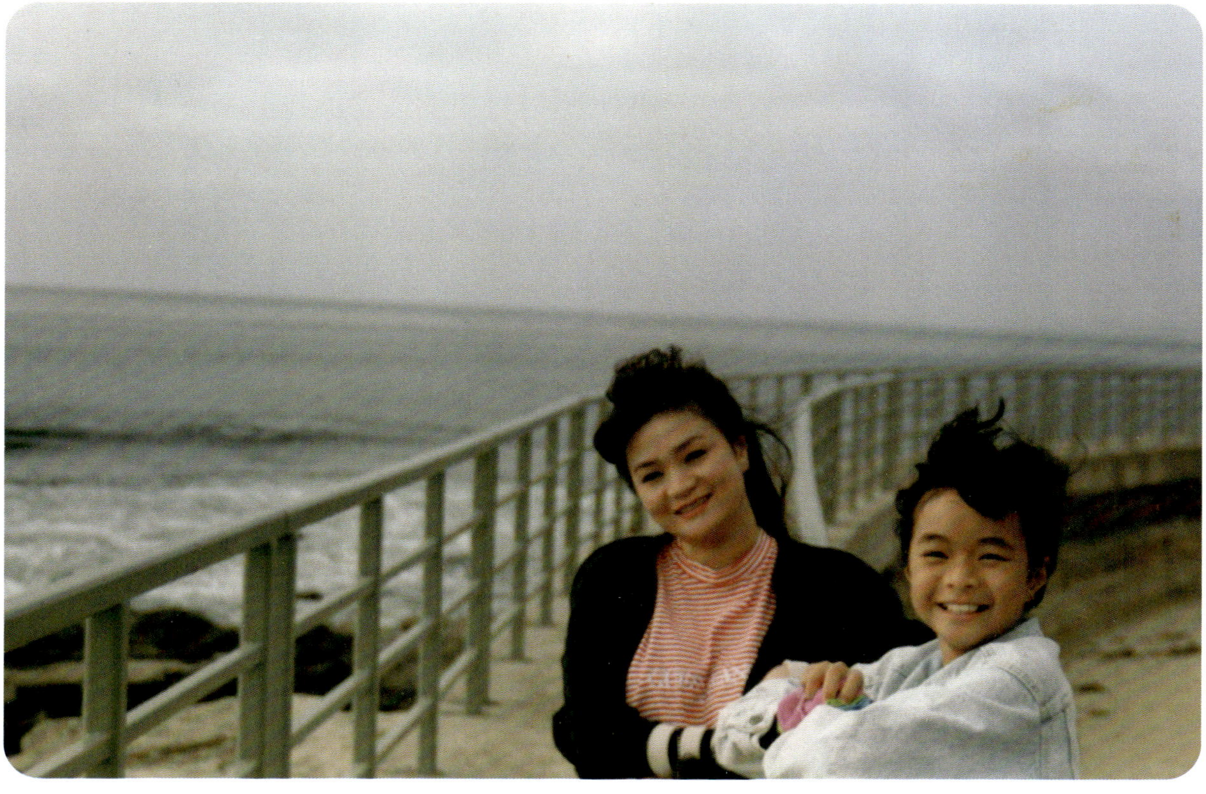

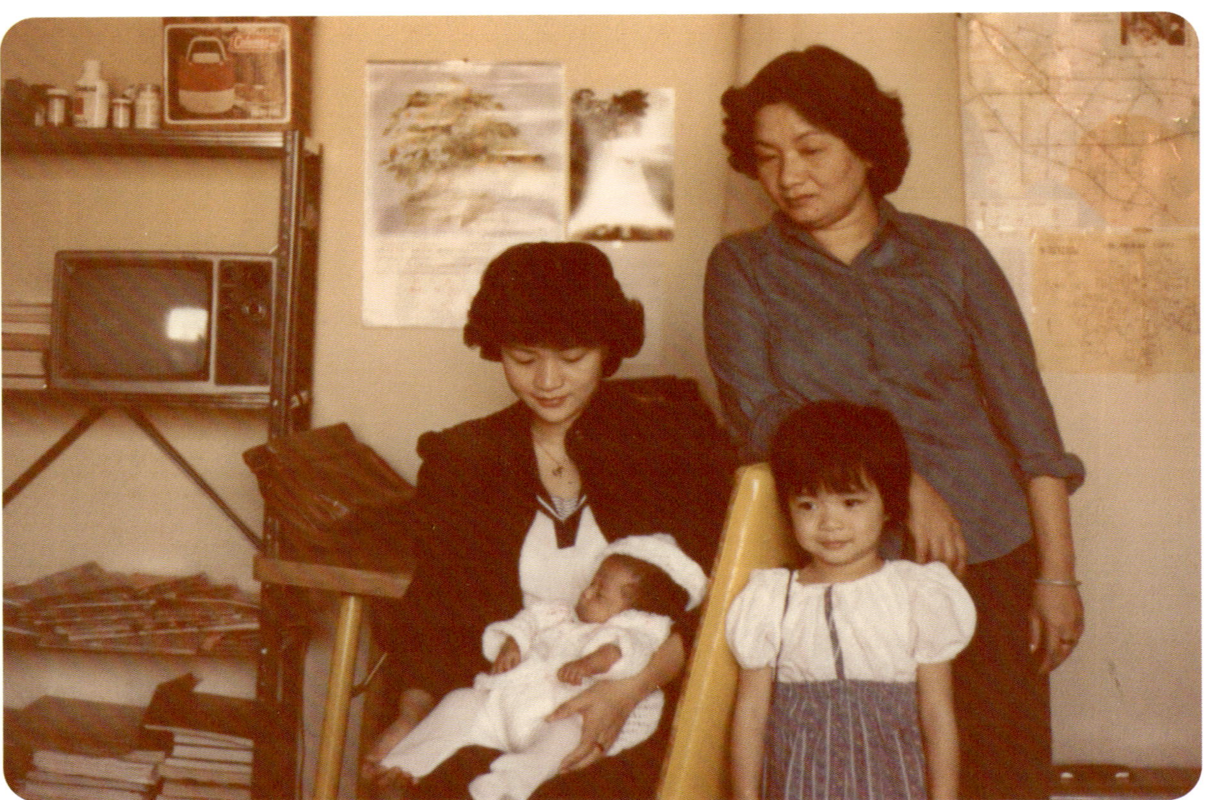

Above: Ai family photo, 1983. Opposite: Elizabeth Ai, 2022.

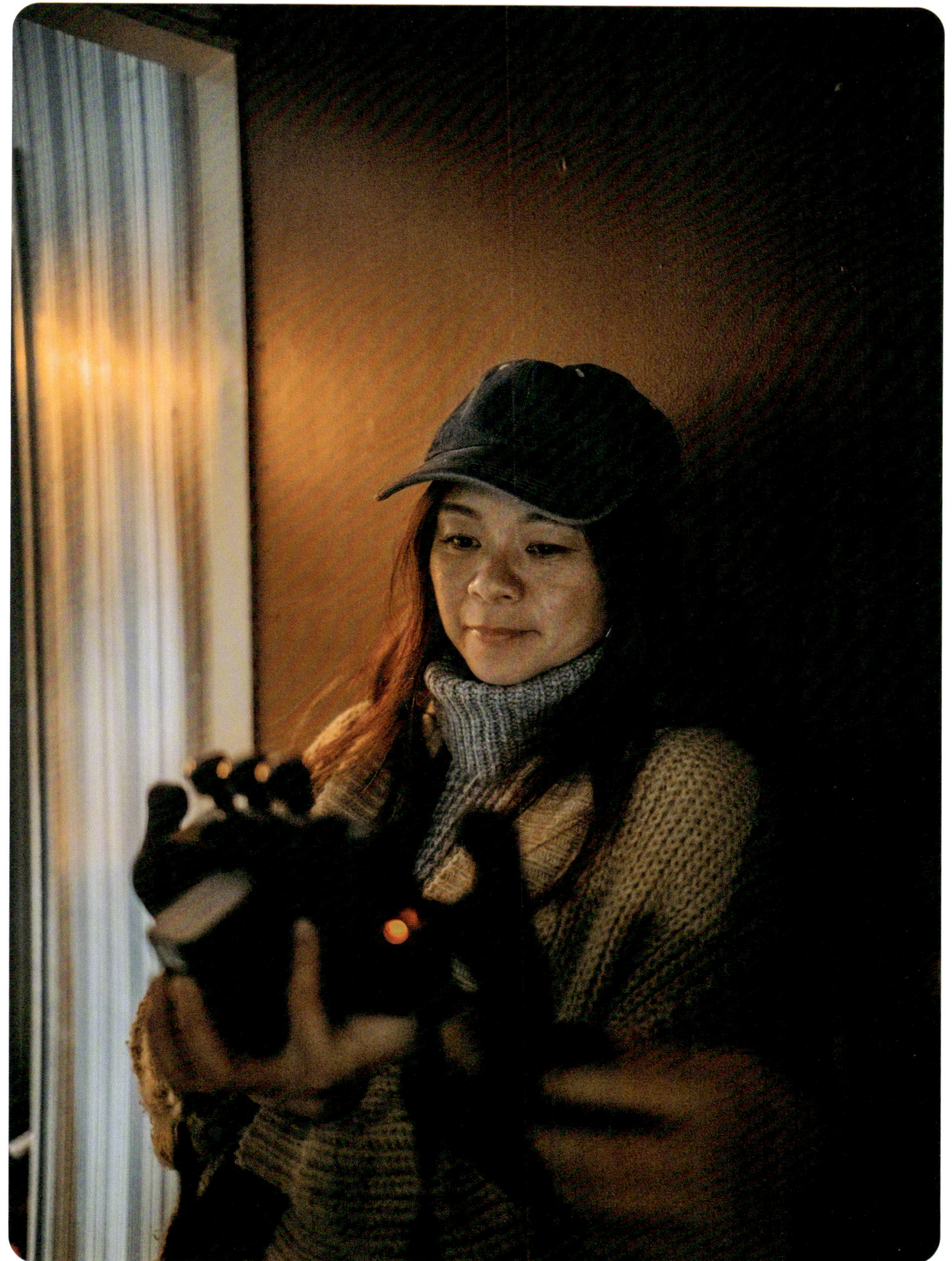

ĐƯỜNG ME THÁNG HẠ

Gởi Diệu Chi

Em đưa tay gầy hứng vài lá rụng
Anh nắm tay em hương ấm chuyền cành
Em chợt mỉm cười đôi mắt long lanh
Chính lúc đó, anh bắt đầu nói hết
Nói nỗi xa em, nói buồn cách biệt
Nói mong manh là những cuộc trùng phùng
Nói bập bềnh là những kiếp ly hương
Nói đứt ruột là những điều quyết định

Chân bước đều chân, tay trong tay ấm
Chiều biệt ly không có sóng trùng khơi
Êm ả đường me, âu yếm ngàn lời
Vạt áo lụa dấu cả trời ấp ủ
Em mãi dặn dò, dặn nhiều chưa đủ
Dặn yêu em dù cách trở trùng dương
Dặn đợi em dù tóc sẽ điểm sương
Dặn rượu tha phương, đừng say quán lạ
Dặn sức khỏe đừng đốt bằng thuốc lá
Ve trên cây ghen em dặn
Xa nhau đừng quên vội đường me xanh tháng hạ

Nguyễn Mộng Giác
trại tị nạn Galang 4/1982

TAMARIND ROAD IN SUMMER

To Diệu Chi

You raise a slim hand to catch the fallen leaves
I hold your hand, revived by your warmth
You suddenly smile with your sparkling eyes
At that moment, I start to say all I must say
That we will be apart, and how sad I feel
That our chances of reunion are slim
That exiled lives are unpredictable
That decisions are gut-wrenching

Together we walk, hand in hand
The day we say goodbye, there are no breaking waves
The tamarind road is paved with our sweet words
Enfolding the sky in your silk *áo dài*
You tell me a litany of demands; it's hardly enough
Telling me to love you despite an ocean apart
Telling me to wait for you even when our hair turns gray
Telling me not to get drunk in strange places
Telling me not to destroy my health with cigarettes
The cicadas on the trees are jealous of your love for me
Don't forget the tamarind road in summer when we are apart

Nguyễn Mộng Giác
Galang Refugee Camp 4/1982

CHAPTER 1

WAR IS OVER?

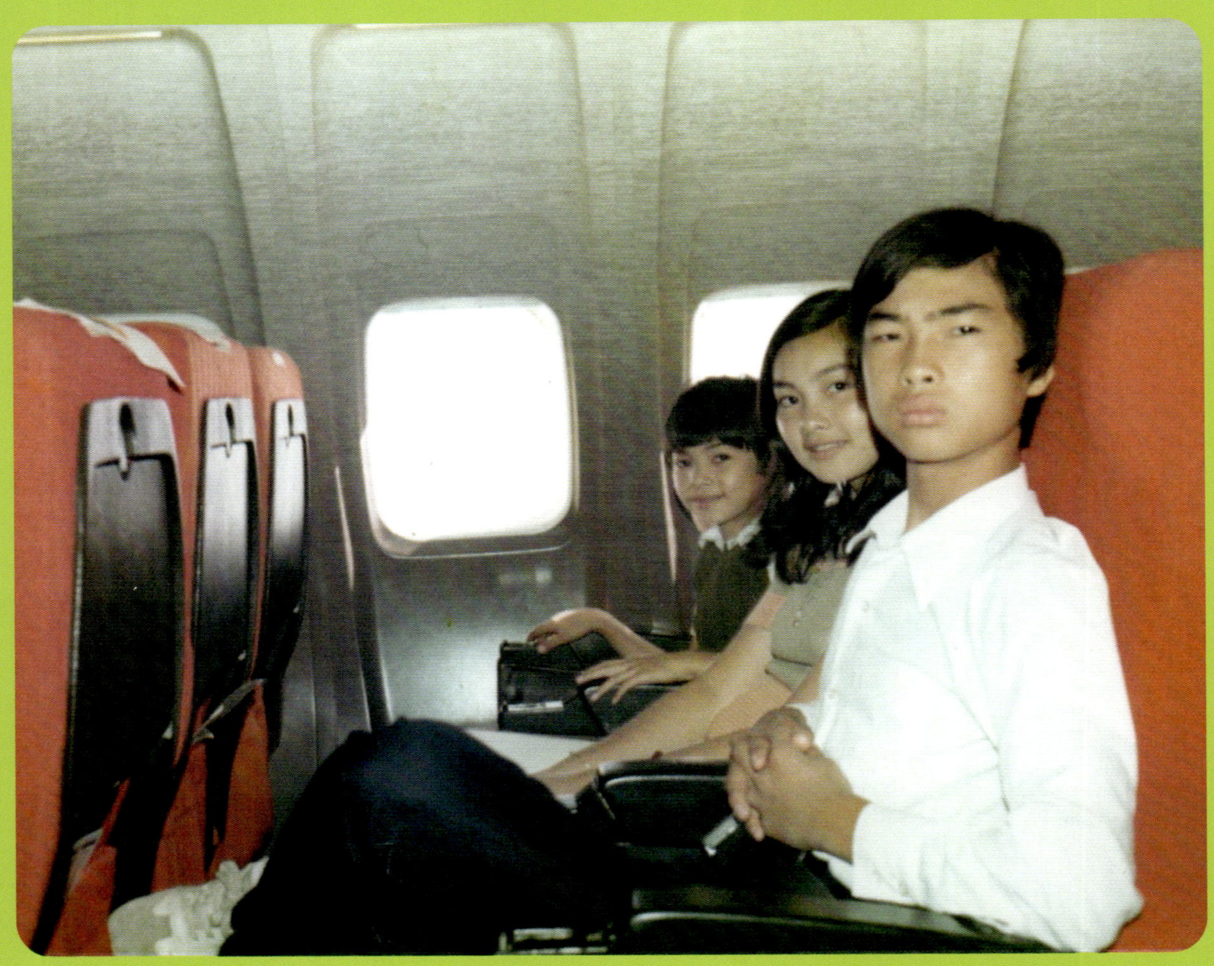

1975

As the gates of Camp Pendleton loomed in the distance, families huddled together, overwhelmed by a palpable tension. The end of the Vietnam War in 1975 had triggered a forced exodus of more than 130,000 Vietnamese refugees to places like this sprawling military base and beyond. It was a migration born not of choice but of necessity, and for many refugees it marked a grim shift from surviving a war-torn homeland to facing the daunting trials of resettlement.

Just one week after the war's end, President Gerald Ford addressed Congress:

> *But out of the 120,000 refugees who are either here or on their way, 60% of those are children. They ought to be given an opportunity.*

Behind his words lay the unspoken truth of American involvement in Vietnam—a war that had now followed them in its consequences.

Camp Pendleton housed more than 50,000 of those refugees. The arid California landscape that rushed past car windows offered a stark contrast to their past lives in the tropics, yet the physical distance they covered did little to sever the emotional ties to the land they had left behind. The transformation from the austere confines of a military base to the suburbs of Orange County was a bitter reminder of their harsh reality. The scent of citrus groves mingling with the ocean breeze was a façade masking the challenges ahead.

Each day, the reality of the refugees' situation grew heavier—a relocation that was more than just physical, but also a deep emotional rupture from all they had known. They were expected to keep quiet, work tirelessly, and show gratitude in a land they had not chosen, under circumstances they had never wanted.

With "Operation New Life" underway at the threshold of US military bases like Camp Pendleton, Fort Chaffee, in Arkansas, Eglin Air Force Base in Florida, and Fort Indiantown Gap in Pennsylvania, Vietnamese refugees continued to struggle for survival under different terms. This "new life" was fraught with barriers, demanding not just adaptability but also suppression of the past in order to navigate an environment that was as unwelcoming as it was indifferent.

Archival image provided by Karyn Bao An Vo.

Though the Vietnam War had ended, the refugees' struggle was far from over. Now, burdened with a grief that had to be quietly endured, they maintained a veneer of gratitude towards

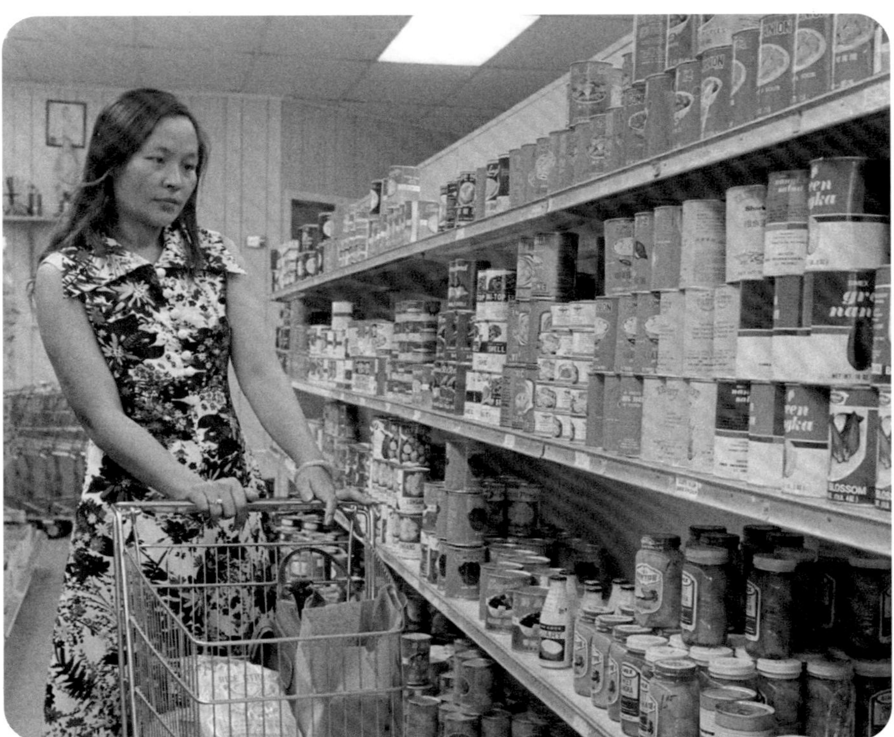

their host country, necessary to navigate the harsh realities ahead, as they were determined to find stability.

As they began their new lives, these families were continually reminded of their displacement by the sparse landscapes and suburban quiet. The streets of Westminster and Garden Grove contrasted starkly with the teeming boulevards of Saigon. Here, orderly roads lined with plain buildings lacked the vibrant chaos and colorful architecture of their tropical homeland. Far from the dense, lively neighborhoods of their past, the absence of familiar sights and sounds intensified their feelings of displacement.

Yet people found ways to connect—through shared workplaces, encounters in local supermarkets, and gatherings at Buddhist temples and Catholic churches. These venues became crucial for maintaining cultural ties and were a foundation for building new ones. As families adapted to local culture and established new routines, the bonds within the community strengthened, offering vital emotional and practical support. There was no choice and no turning back; Orange County had to transform from a mere refuge into a home where the seeds of new life would be sown.

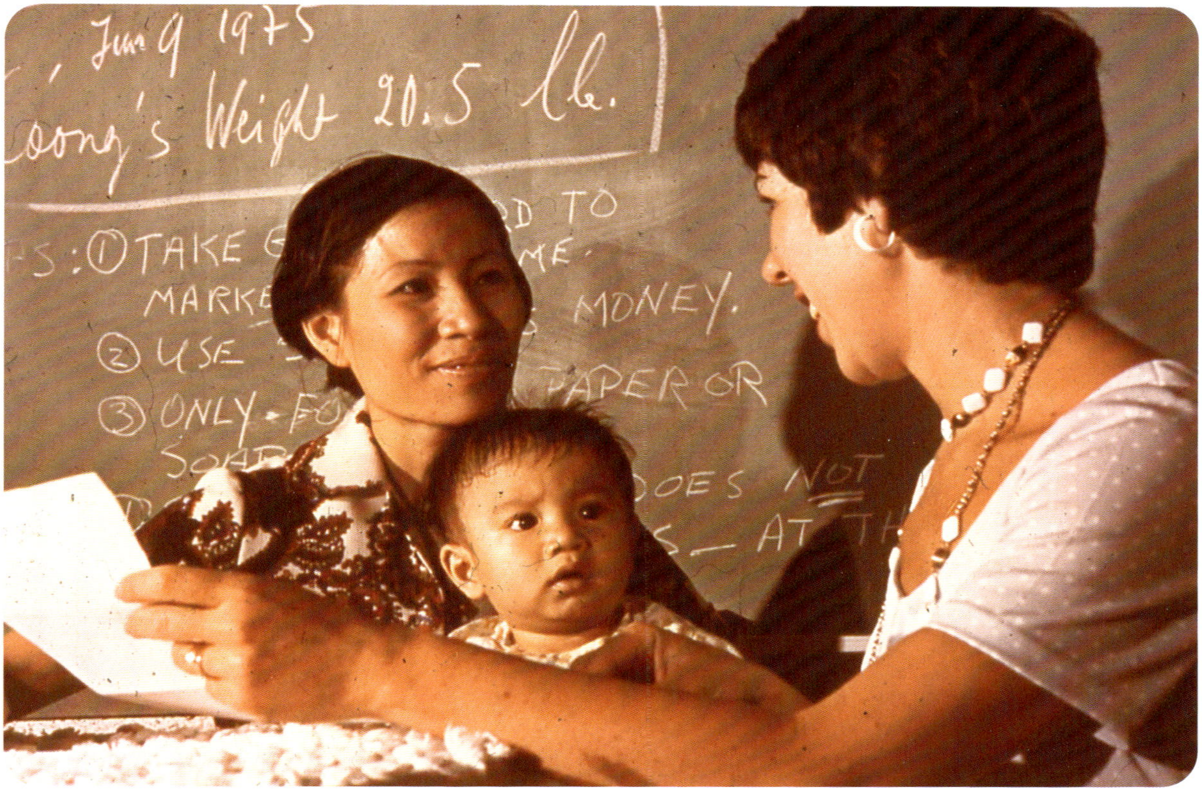

Opposite: Woman shops in a Vietnamese store, Arlington Virginia, 1977. Above: Catherine Nguyen Dinh reviews social services resources with a church's sponsoring member in Alexandria, Virginia, 1975. Right: Future New Wave star Thái Tài at Camp Pendleton, 1975.

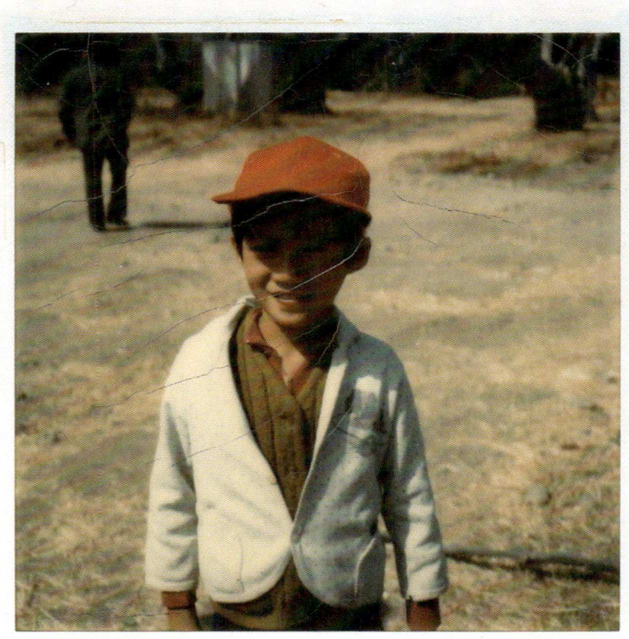

DEPARTMENT OF THE AIR FORCE
HEADQUARTERS 15th AIR BASE WING (PACAF)
APO SAN FRANCISCO 96553

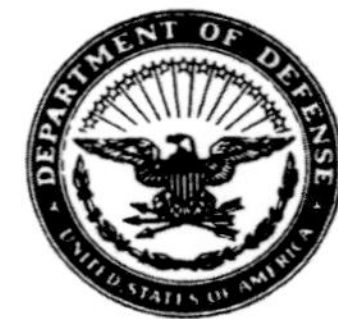

26 SEP 1975

Mr. Le Quang Dieu Toan
c/o M. Jamieson
2835A Kolowalu Street
Honolulu, Hawaii 96822

Dear Mr. Toan

As the Indochinese refugee activities here at Hickam Air Force Base have now been successfully completed, I wish to take this opportunity to express my sincerest appreciation for the prominent part you played in that success as an interpreter.

For most of the orphans and refugees, the trip from their homeland into uncertainty was a traumatic experience, and your presence was most reassuring to them. You were able to comfort many people, children and adults alike, with words of their native tongue. Time and again I saw the surprise and relief on their faces when they discovered there was someone who could explain what was happening to them. Your untiring efforts as a volunteer were truly commendable, and the success attained would not have been possible without the dedicated efforts of people like yourself.

Such unselfish devotion to fellow human beings in need does not go unnoticed, and I would again like to reiterate my sincere appreciation for your valuable assistance.

Sincerely

H. H. Q. CHING, Lt Col, USAF
Deputy Commander for Personnel

Opposite, above: Archival image provided by Karyn Bao An Vo. Opposite, below: Photograph taken in an Indonesian refugee camp, late 1970s. Above: Letter sent to Family Love band member Le Quang Dieu Toan, who interpreted for the Air Force at a refugee camp.

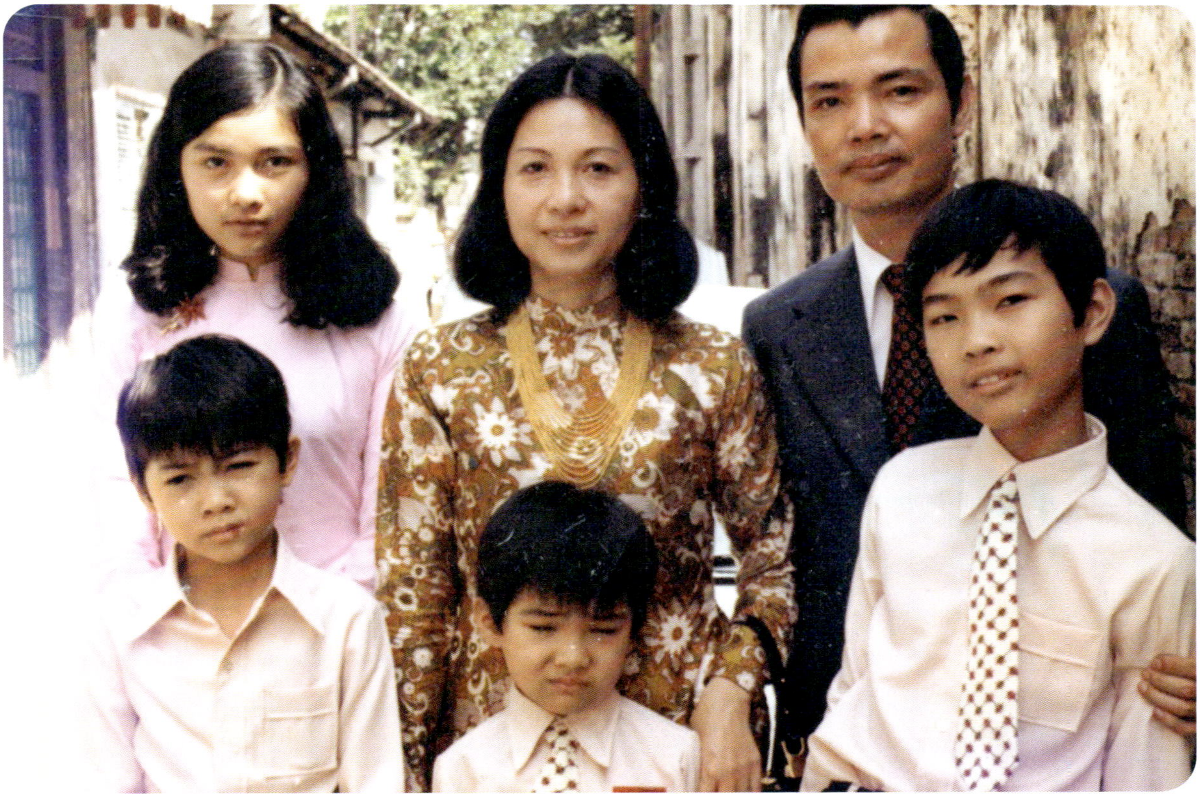

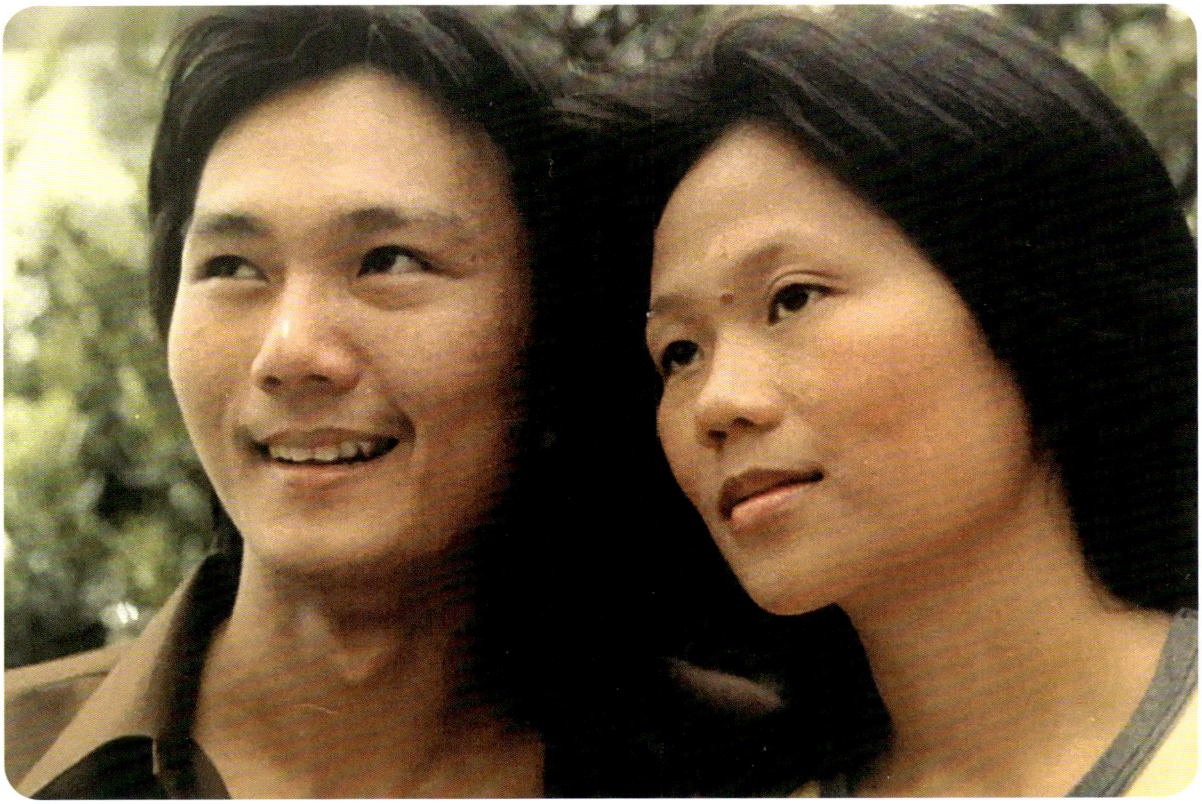

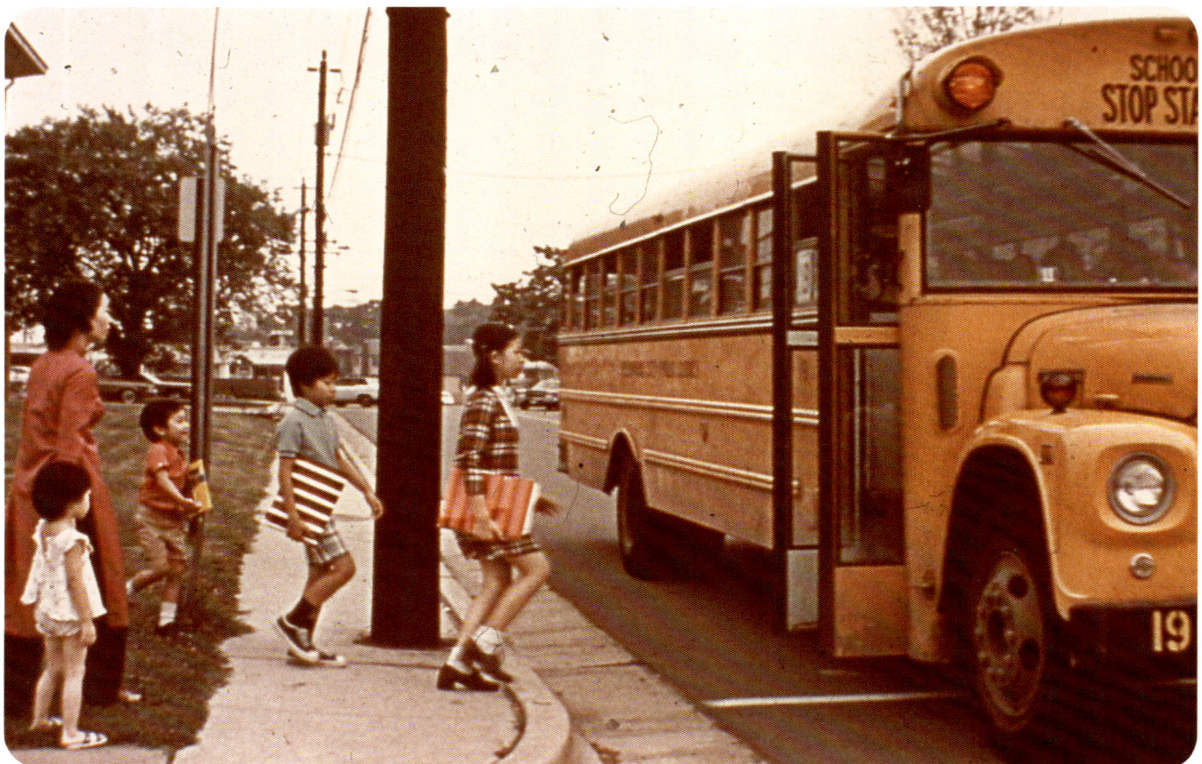

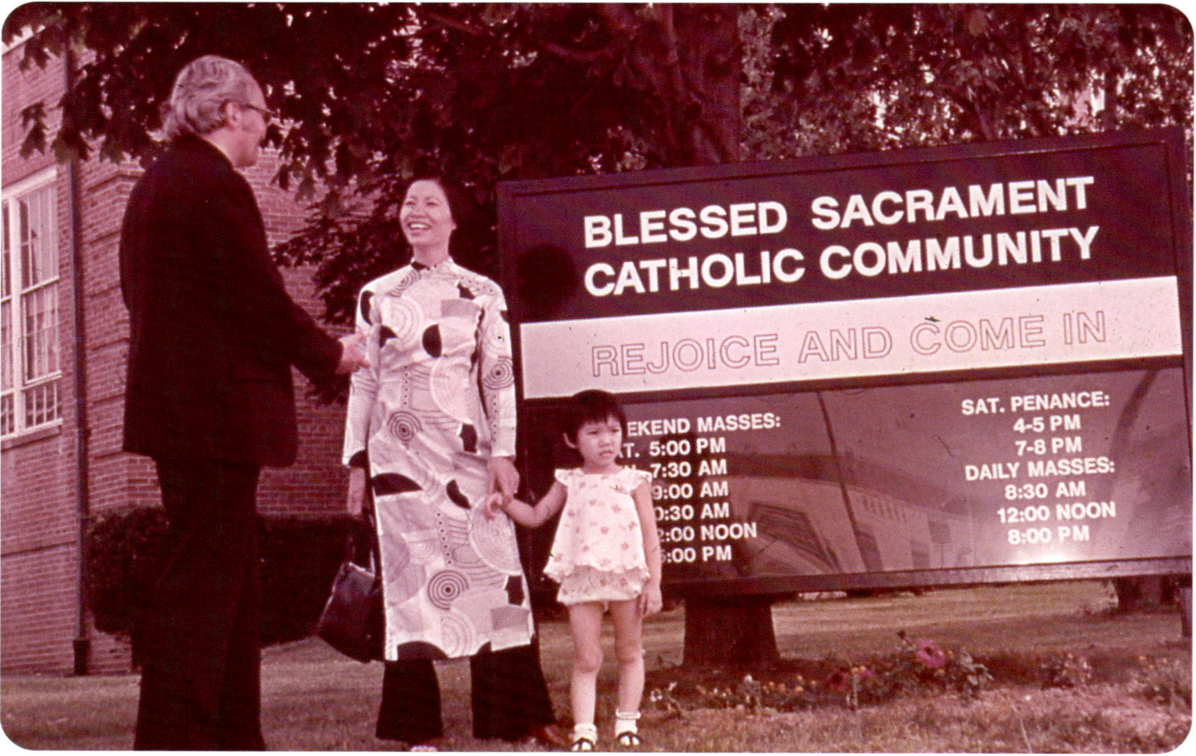

Family photos from Thúy Đinh, Northern Virginia, summer 1975.

WOOD CAT SUMMER, 1975

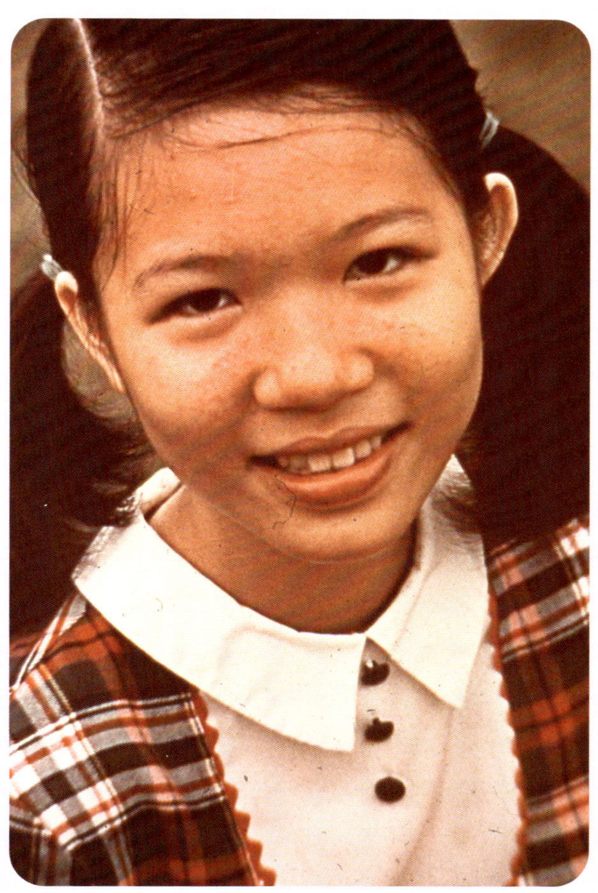

Thúy Đinh

As the first Vietnamese refugees settling in Northern Virginia, my family's arrival was well-documented. A snapshot of my mother holding my baby brother—their first American photograph—was taken by Douglas Chevalier for the *Washington Post* Metro Section upon our landing at Dulles Airport on May 27, 1975.

Sponsored by Blessed Sacrament Catholic Parish of Alexandria, Virginia, our family of ten—from a six-month-old infant to a sixty-one-year-old patriarch—was offered shelter in the parish school before more permanent housing could be found. In June 1975, a photographer from the National Conference of Catholic Charities (NCCC) came to the parish school to document our story, to be included as part of the NCCC's advocacy efforts regarding the refugee crisis.

His photo slides encapsulate us in violet time. My elders have the gaunt faces and sharpened jaws of timeless refugees, but still manage to convey a subtle elegance. The photographer tells us to act natural, but my grandfather says we must look our best. We wear church-donated clothes. My grandmother and mother wear their silk *áo dài* from Vietnam. In one image, while helping my mother select tomatoes at the local co-op, my grandmother casually dangles her Italian leather purse with its dainty silver clasp.

I look juvenile in pigtails, plaid dress, and white bobby socks—a Christmas outfit in June. The pre-owned buckle oxfords bruise my toes. At thirteen,

I already wear size seven-and-a-half in women's shoes. I want to be beautiful, the way Sylvia Vartan sings *la plus belle pour aller danser*, but know beauty needs its own time and place. Like a tangerine from an old Chinese fable, I've been untimely plucked from my native soil, poised to turn sour in my transplanted state.

While the resin-like images enfold us in embryonic time, in reality we were not fixed in time or space, but untethered, light as air. My grandfather had chosen a Catholic parish to sponsor us, correctly intuiting that Blessed Sacrament would be staffed with savvy volunteers to assist our large family: dapper, bolo-tie-wearing Mr. H. would take the adults to the bank to open a checking account; down-to-earth Mrs. W. would register us kids for schools and take us to doctor's appointments; and tall, perky Mrs. M. would help our family apply for food stamps and other social services.

For the most part, our pride guided our social interactions. To avoid seeming needy, we showed our benefactors our nimble curiosity, quick humor, and fluid adaptability.

In reality we were *điếc không sợ súng*—explorers without maps, deaf insurgents oblivious of loud explosions. This sense of freefalling turned our assimilation process into a daily improv session. We navigated by our wits and a natural affinity for theatrics. One night, my grandfather ventured from the parish school to

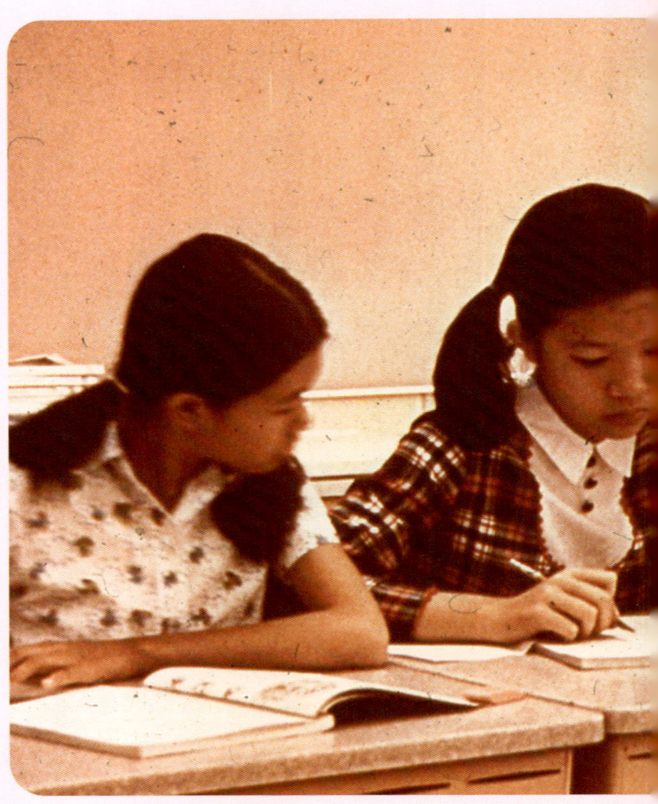

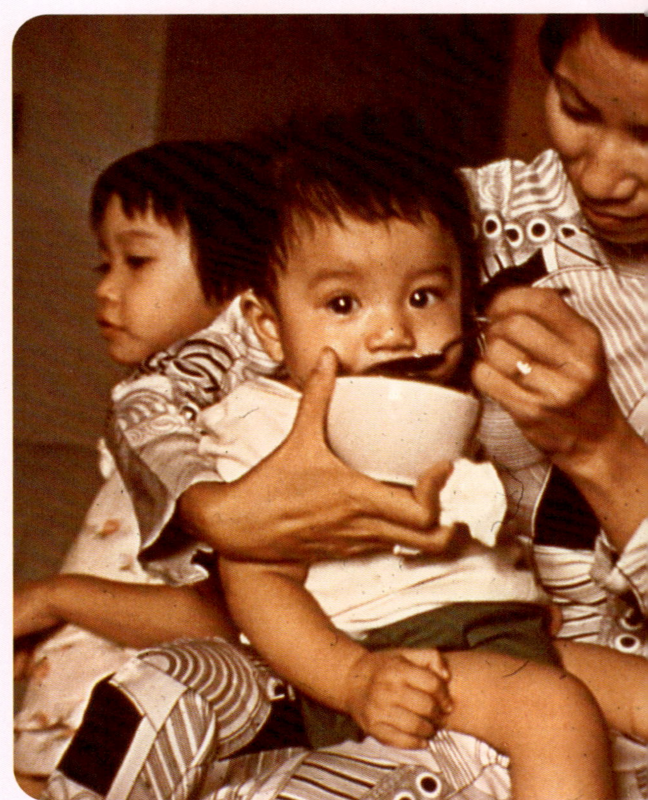

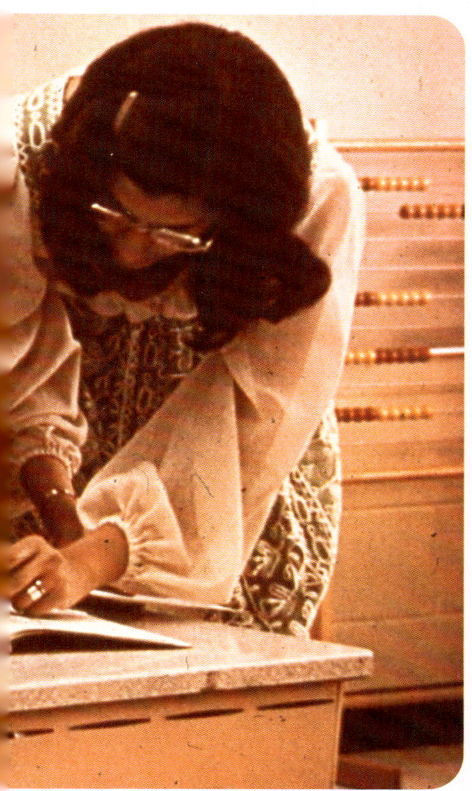

Peoples Drugstore just a couple of blocks down Kenwood Avenue, and told everyone he had traversed miles across the city! But no matter how big the world seemed to us then, we were still reluctant to take up space. All the drama and adventure occurred mostly in our heads.

In mid-1975 there existed only two Vietnamese grocery stores, Saigon Market and Vietnam Center, located on Wilson Boulevard in Arlington—a twelve-minute drive from Blessed Sacrament, which somehow seemed very far to us. Not wishing to overburden church members, my elders would limit our Asian grocery excursions to once a month, so we had to be very frugal with our daily consumption of *nước mắm*!

If overt rebellion became the norm for subsequent generations, then grace under pressure was our ideal—a latent form of resistance, perhaps? At the end of August, before moving into our rental home, my family prepared a Sunday dinner to thank all parish members. We spent our modest savings to shop for ingredients, then stayed up all night to prepare a communal feast of *chả giò*, *yu choy* soup in clarified pork broth, and whole steamed cod seasoned with honey-soy, shiitake, scallions, and fresh ginger. Our dinner was a resounding success. Deflecting praise, my grandfather told our guests we ate like that every day.

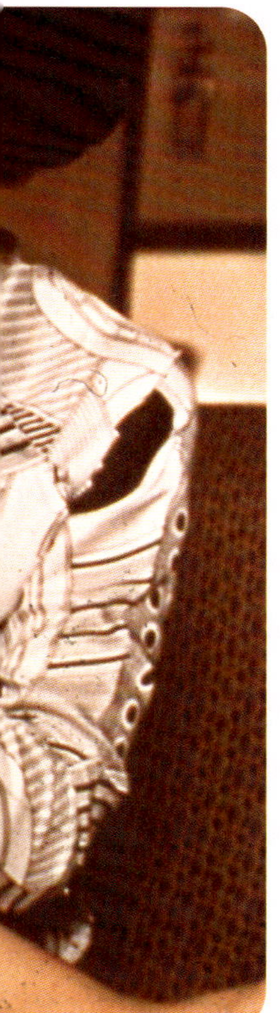

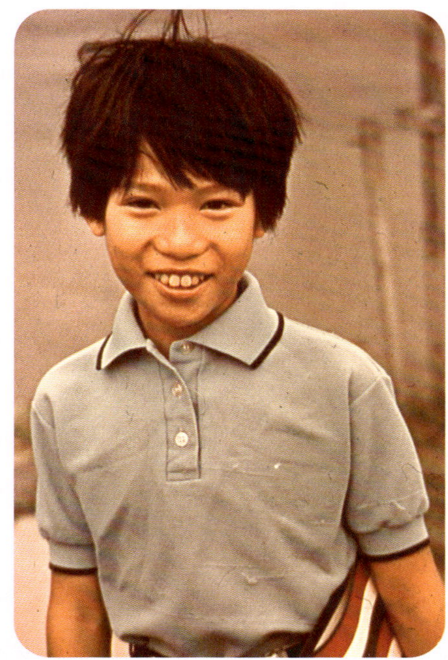

Thúy Đinh's family photos.

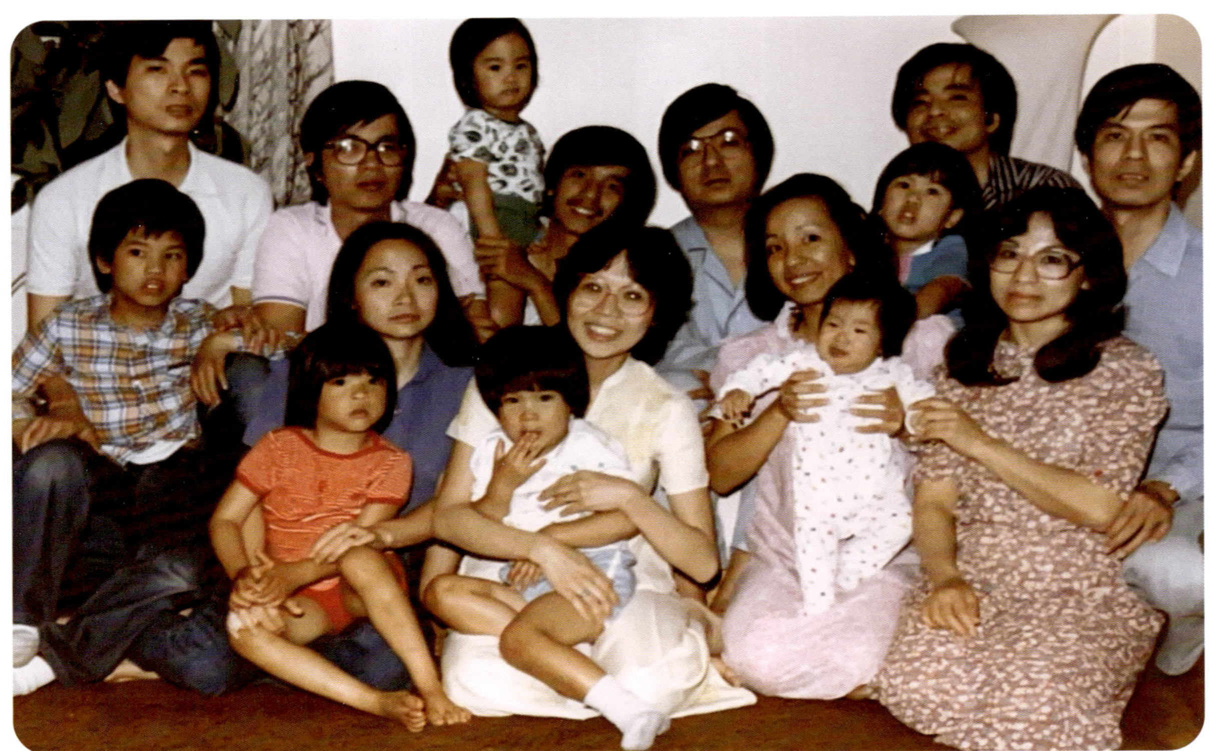

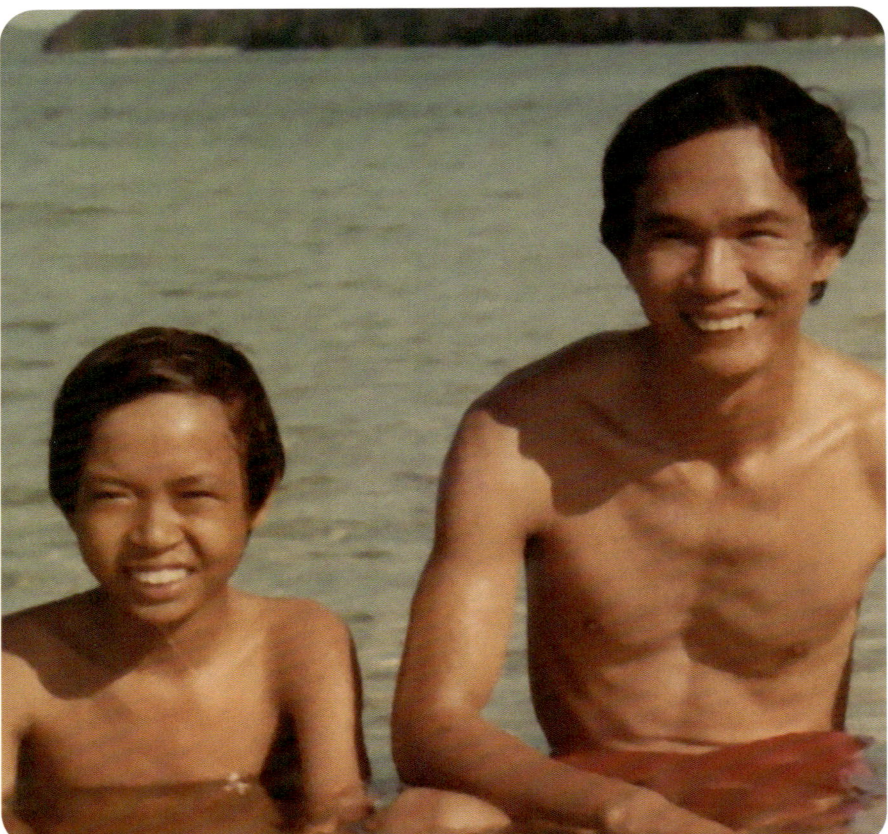

Above: Family photo provided by Thuy-Anh J. Nguyen. Left: Ian Nguyen and his father, Nguyễn Mộng Giác, Galang refugee camp, Indonesia, 1982.

For the children of the "1.5 Generation"—children born in Vietnam and largely raised in America—growing up in Orange County during the 1970s and '80s meant navigating a complex hybridized identity. At home, their parents, fearful of cultural erosion, diligently maintained Vietnamese traditions. Conversations continued in their native tongue and weekends were often spent immersed in community and cultural events. These practices were part of a broader effort to anchor their heritage in the minds of their children.

Outside their homes, however, they encountered a different reality. Their Vietnamese identities were made even more complex in an America still grappling with the aftermath of a contentious and ultimately unsuccessful war. The media's portrayal of the Vietnam War as a symbol of American decline only intensified the stigma these young people endured, solidifying a sense of otherness that pervaded their everyday experiences. The contrast between the inclusive environment at home and the exclusion they often felt in school led to a profound sense of disorientation and even dissociation.

This cultural and emotional dichotomy was taxing on these youth. In their community, there was a strong push from the elders to preserve Vietnamese traditions and values, while the broader societal expectation was to assimilate into Western norms, often at odds with their upbringing. Balancing these competing pressures influenced not only their self-perception but also their social interactions and academic engagement.

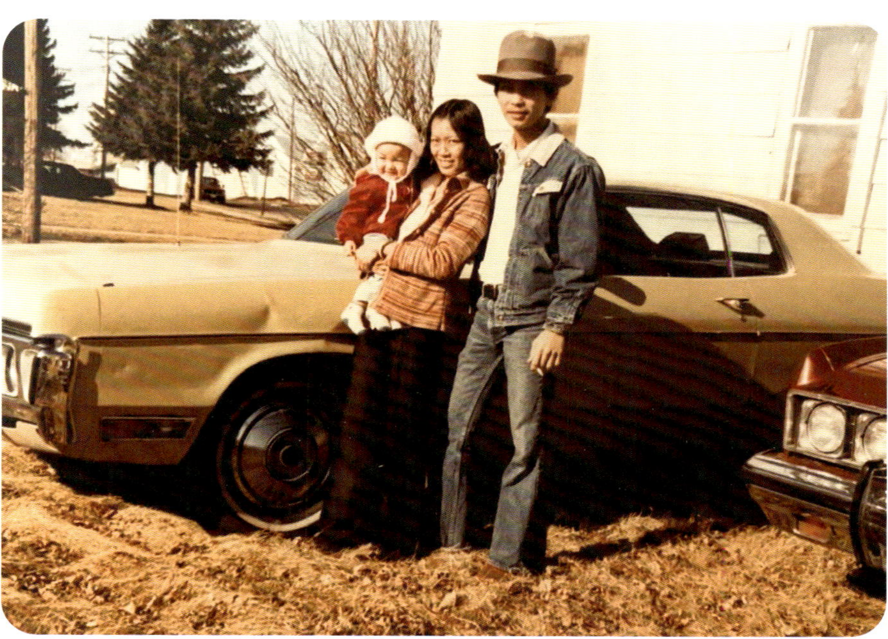

Refugee family in Fort Dodge, Iowa, 1980.

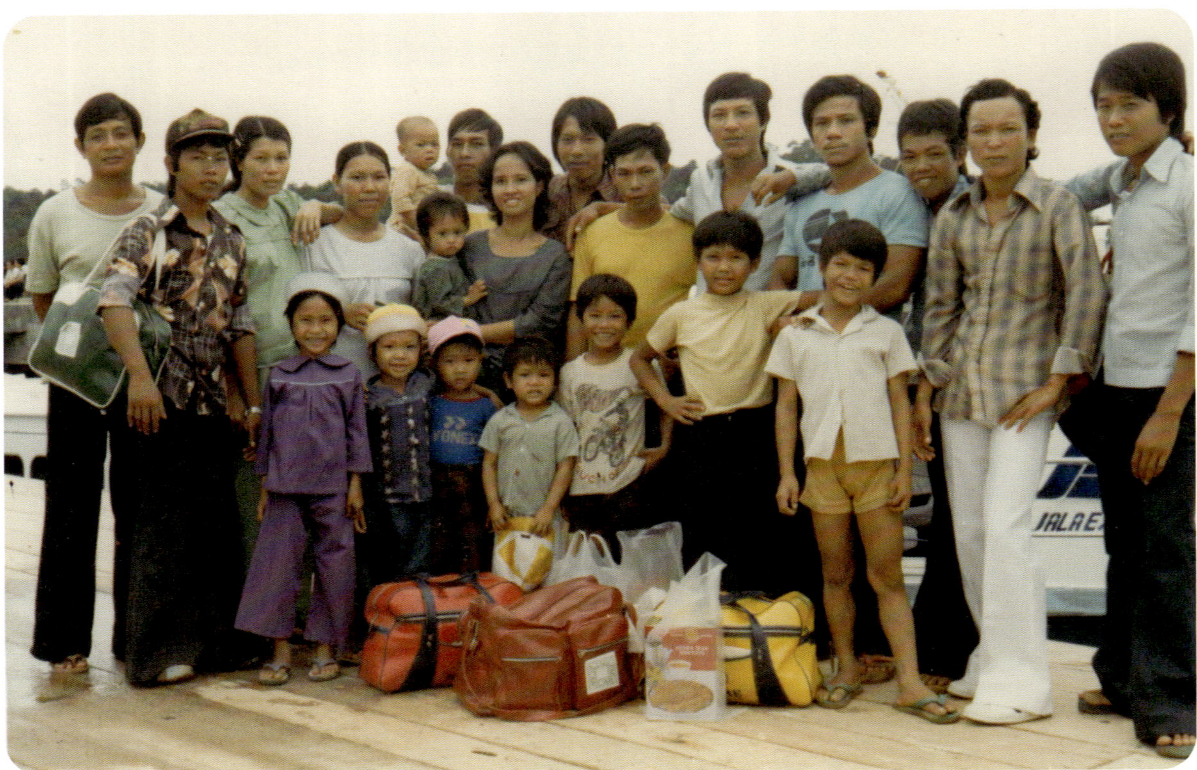

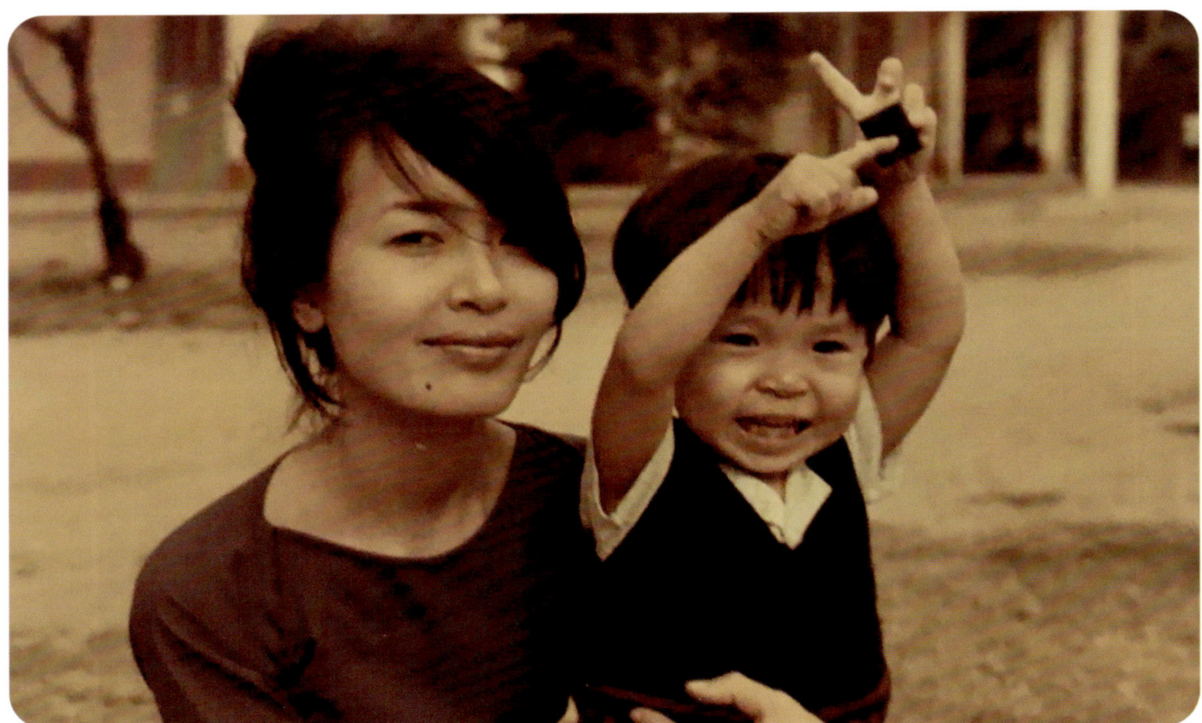

Above: Family photo from Tina Snow Le. Below: Ian Nguyen with his mother, Nguyễn Diệu Chi. Opposite: Vietnamese boat refugees.

OUR PEOPLE

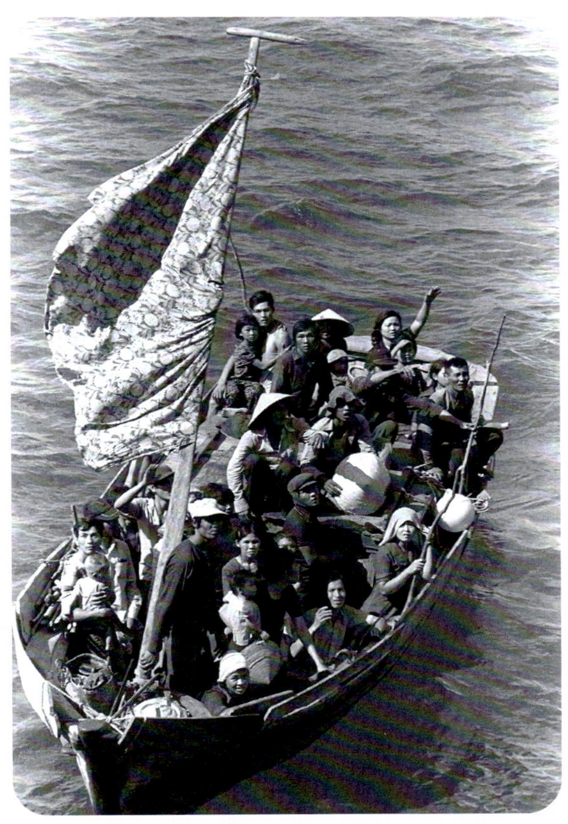

Thúy Võ Đặng

Like others who left Vietnam by boat in the 1980s, my family came to the United States via refugee camps in Malaysia and the Philippines. After resettlement by a Lutheran church in upstate New York in the early '80s, my parents quickly determined that we would only make it in America if we had the social network of other Vietnamese people around us. By then, the "first wave" of 1975 refugees had resettled in areas adjacent to and beyond the four US resettlement camps in California, Florida, Pennsylvania, and Arkansas. Camp Pendleton, located in the boundary space between San Diego and Orange counties, was the first camp to open up for refugee resettlement. From Camp Pendleton, refugees were matched with sponsoring families and churches. A politically conservative region, Orange County drew many people from the 1975 cohort due to scores of faith-based organizations that served refugee resettlement in those early years. With the goal of living near "our people," my large family crossed the US by bus, bound for the state of abundant sunshine and liberal welfare policies.

The chapter of our Orange County, California story found our family of eleven in a two-bedroom apartment in a complex inhabited by many other newly-arrived refugees just like us. Most of us could only string together a few English words at the time. The community around me had experienced war and displacement. We were also encountering the threat of erasure from national narratives in Vietnam and the US. The North claimed to liberate the South and reunify the country, so those who chose to flee the new regime were considered traitors, and their perspectives were erased from nationalist retellings of the past. In the US, Vietnamese people were cast as enemies of democracy (the communists) or weak allies-turned-victims (the South, and, by extension, the refugees). Our stories were distorted to suit a different national reckoning with the American defeat in Vietnam. Mainly, we were seen as embodiments of America's moral victory over communism–refugees who reinforced the narrative of democracy and freedom by "voting with their feet." Many of our elders coped with the loss of home and all that was familiar by working too much, drinking too much, taking their anger out on their kids, and often placing tremendous guilt and pressure on us to honor their sacrifices. Refugee kids did not have it easy at home.

This context is not meant to blame first-generation Vietnamese Americans for what transpired after the war. Shaped by the historical fault lines of a divided country and the hurts that haven't healed, we were all just doing the best we could do. There was a certain scrappiness about all the adults around me who figured out how to sidestep the limits of the scant public assistance they received by pooling together resources, forming *hụi* (informal rotating credit associations) to help

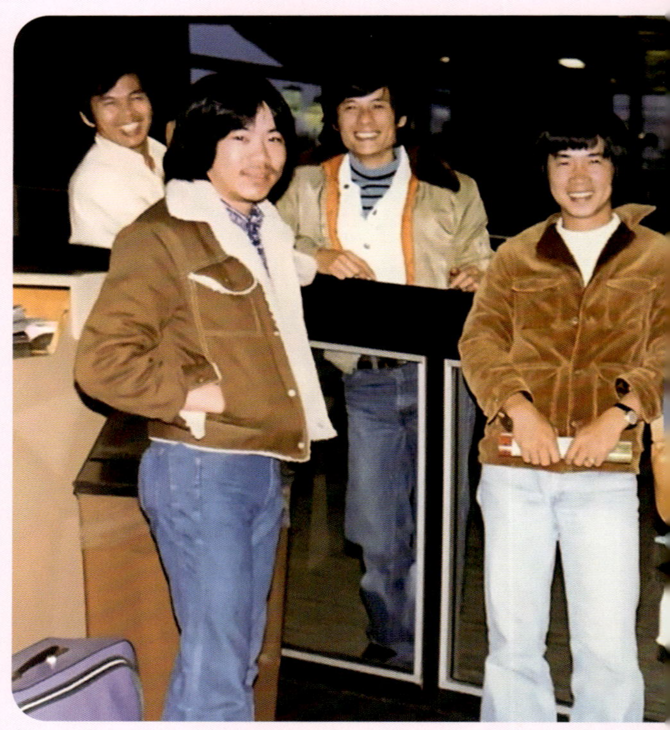

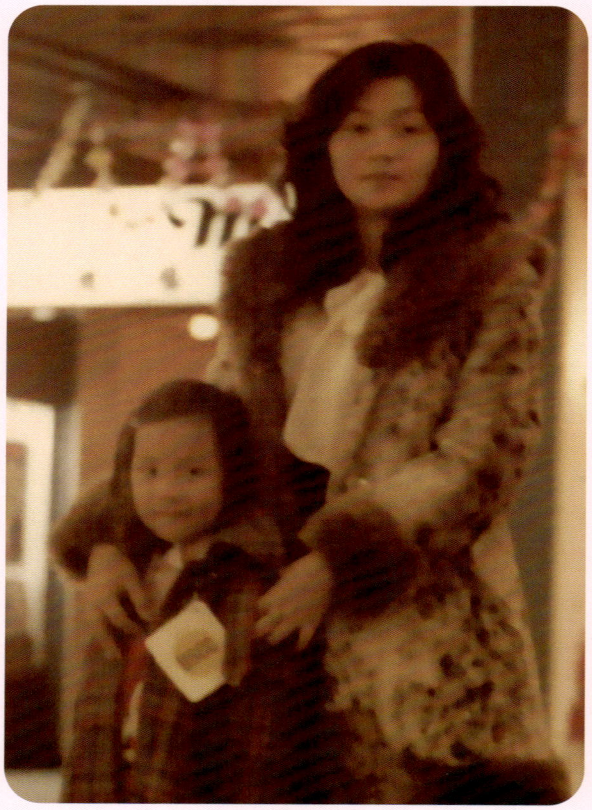

Community archive photos, circa 1970s.

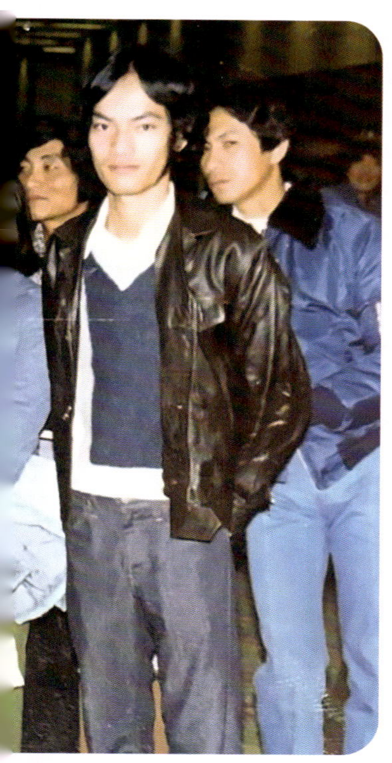

each other buy cars, homes, and start businesses. It was through this first-generation scrappiness that Little Saigon in OC was built up in the span of a decade and now serves as the unofficial capital of the Vietnamese diaspora. Little Saigon became a hub for Vietnamese language news media and entertainment, restaurants, groceries, services and more. It is a space for ongoing negotiations of Vietnamese American identity, culture, and belonging.

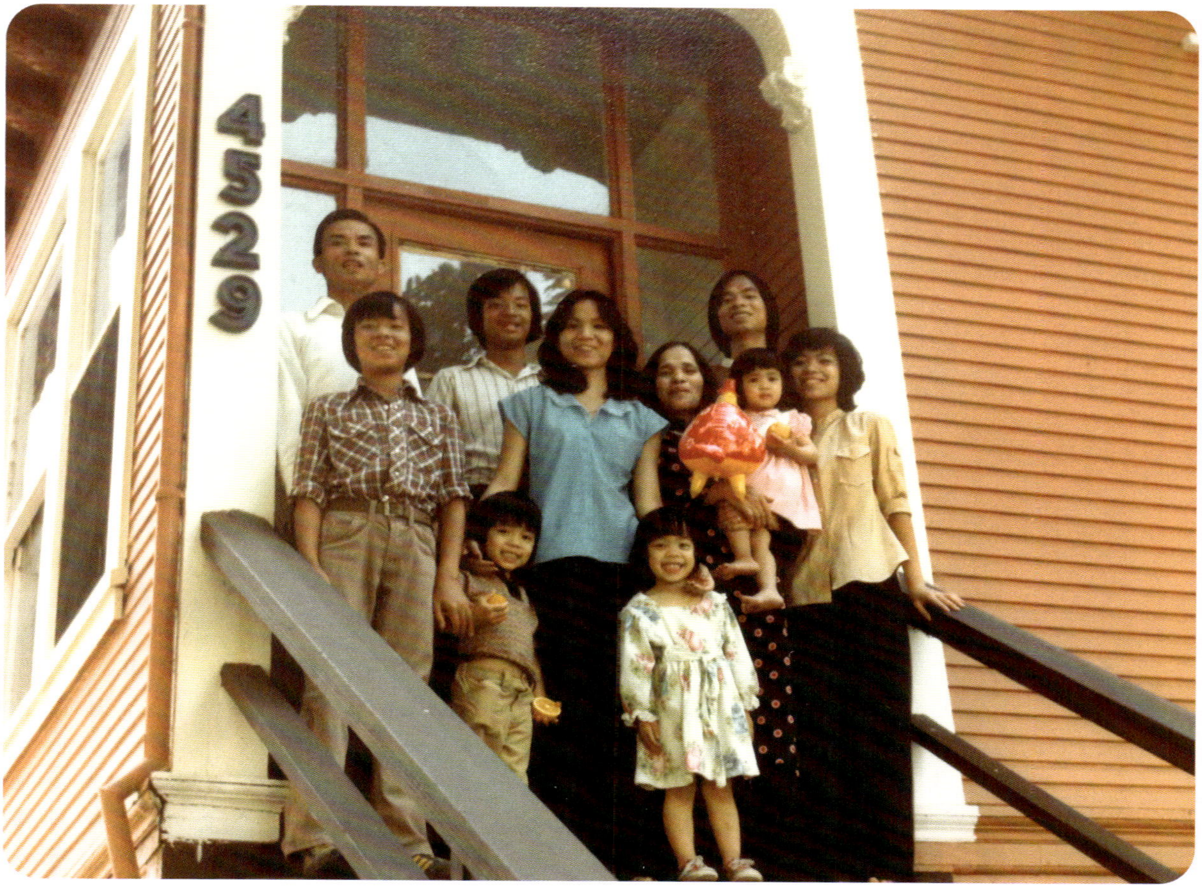

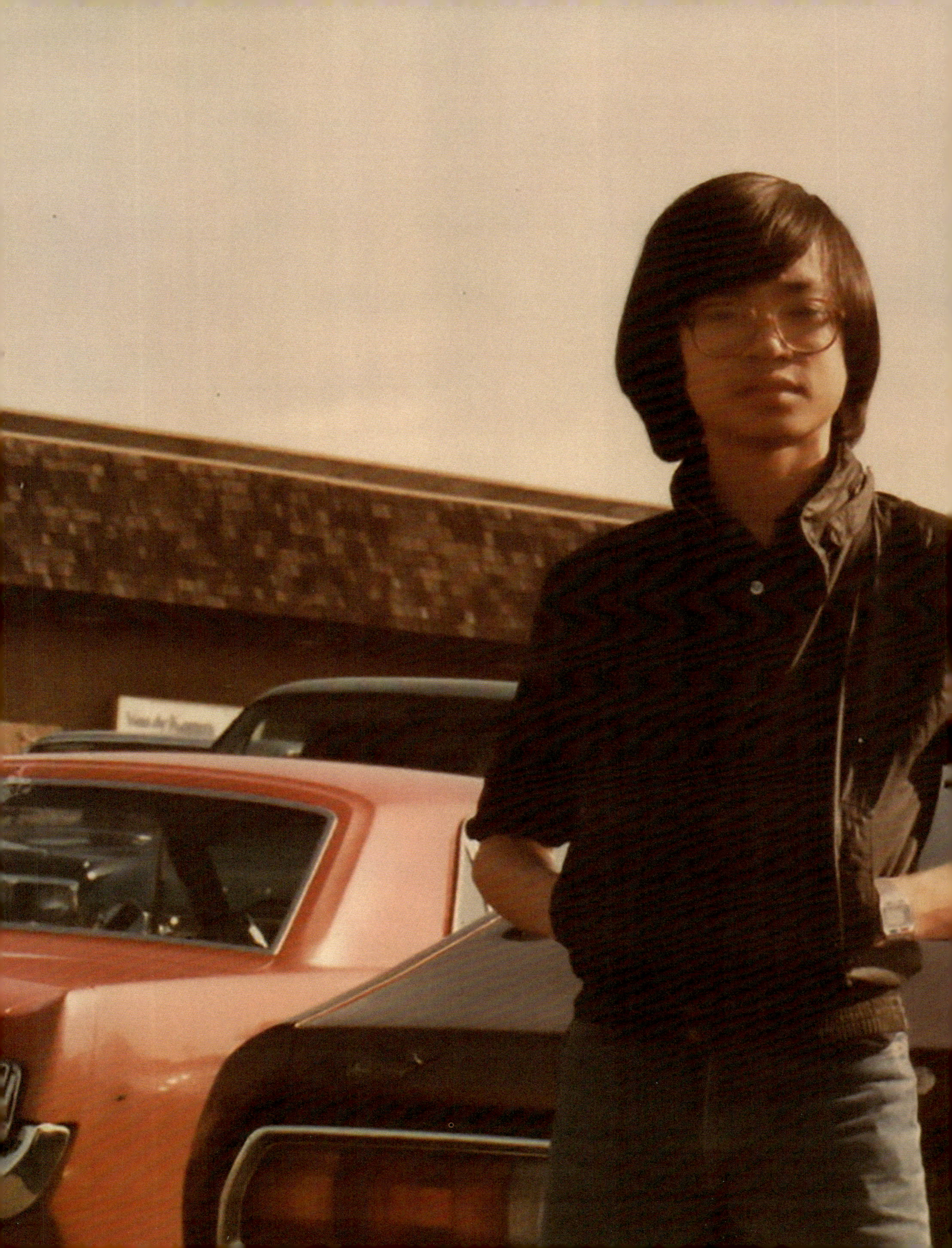

Ian Nguyen, aka DJ BPM, circa 1982.

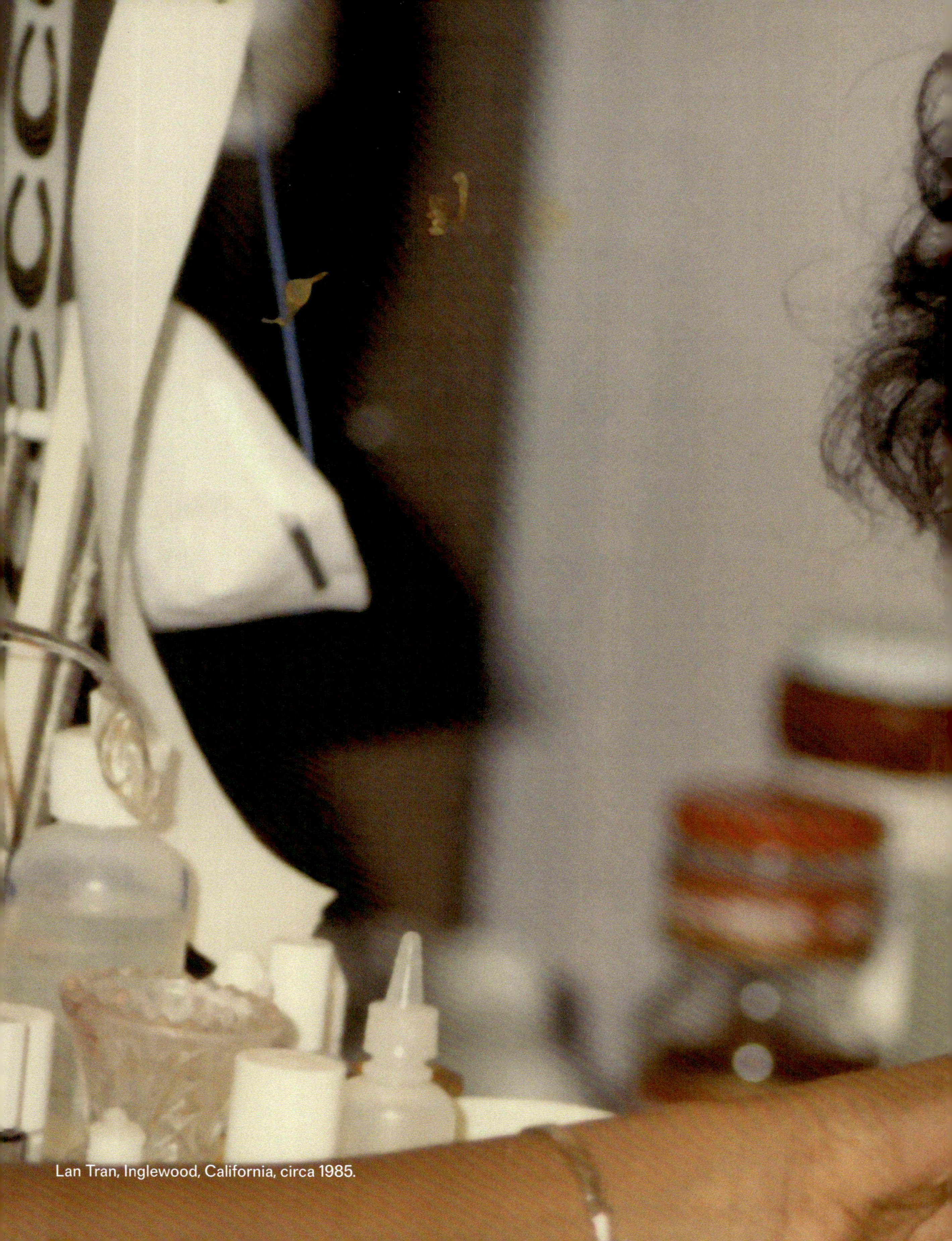

Lan Tran, Inglewood, California, circa 1985.

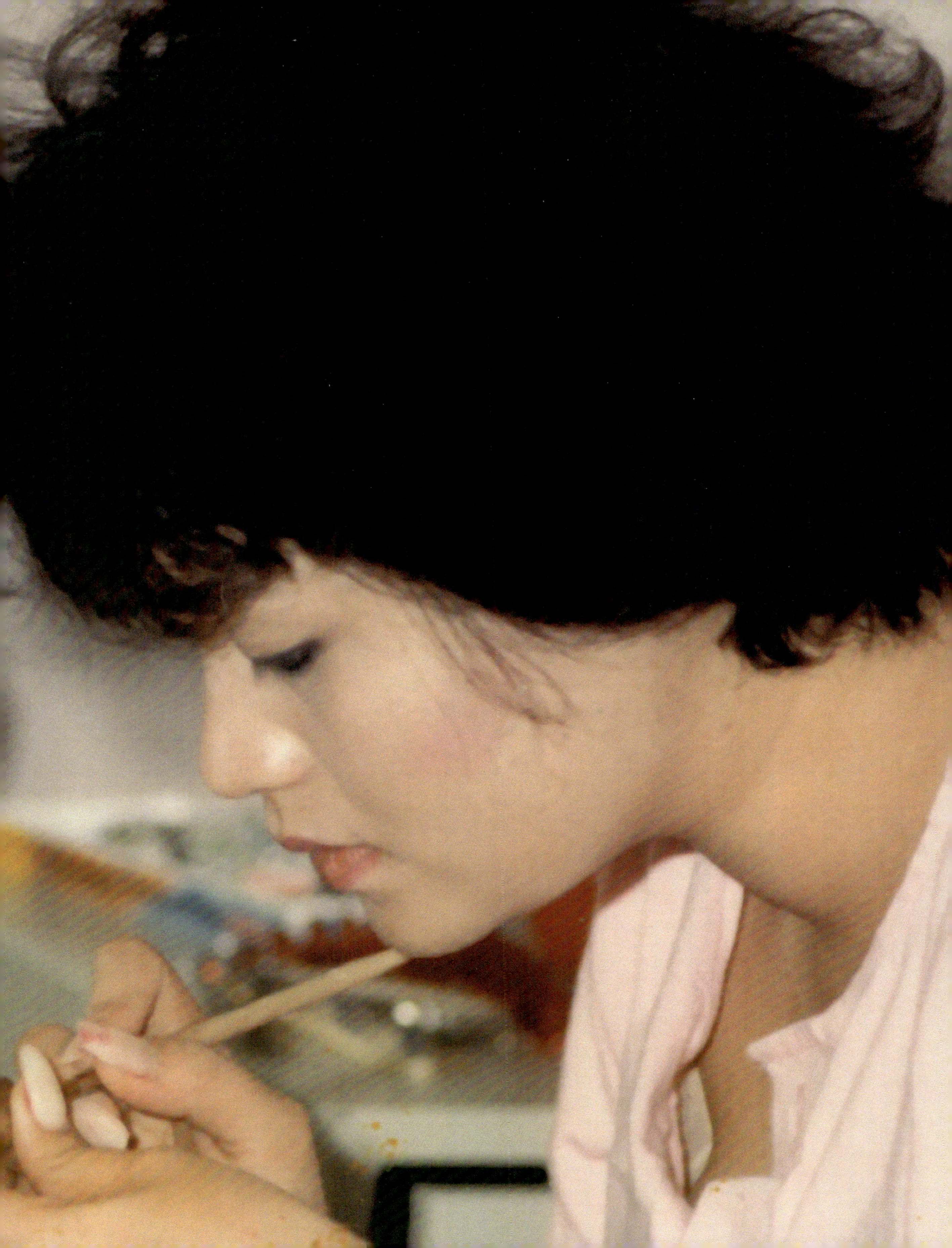

CHAPTER 2

LOST AND FOUND

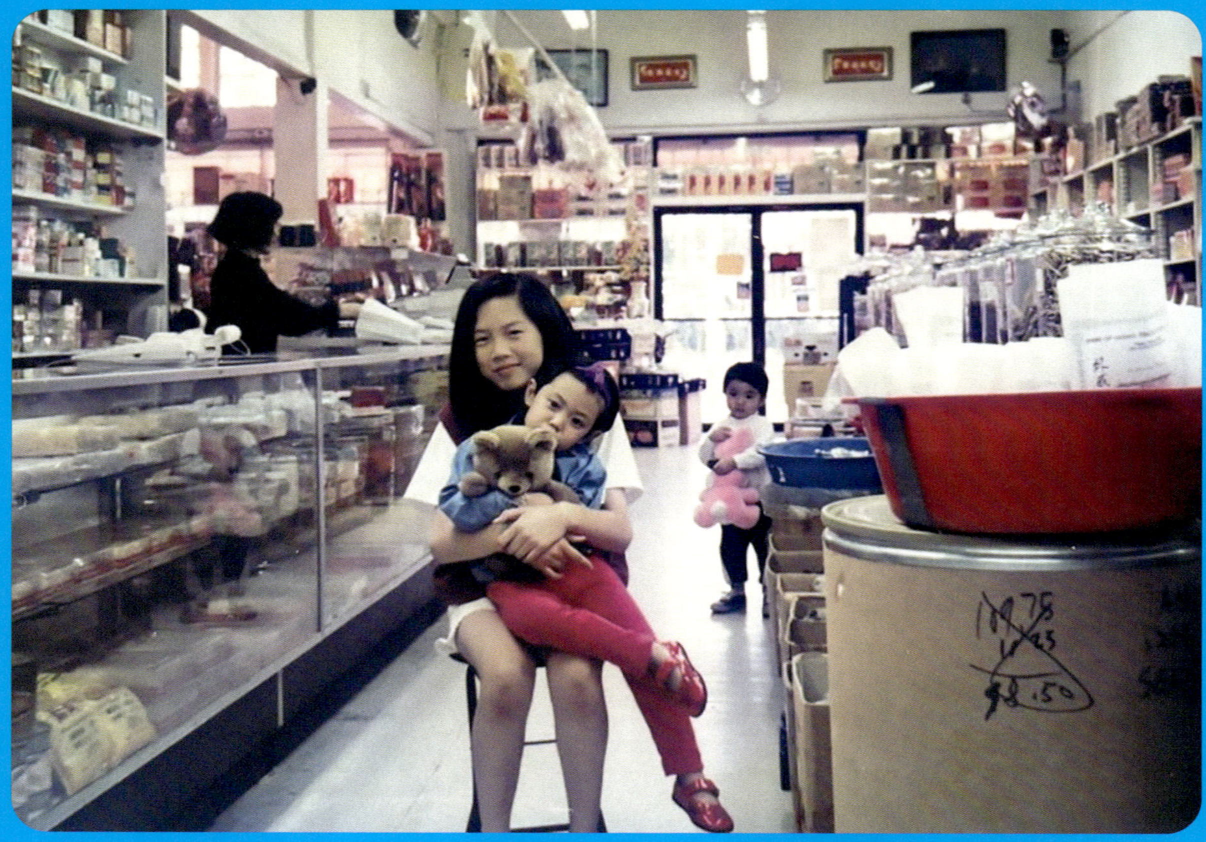

1980s

The late 1970s and early 1980s marked a significant period for the Vietnamese community in Southern California. Following the initial wave of refugees after the Vietnam War, this period saw the arrival of the "boat people" who had fled Vietnam by sea under perilous conditions. These newcomers, seeking refuge and opportunity, differed significantly from the earlier arrivals who came immediately before or after the fall of Saigon in 1975; while the first wave consisted largely of South Vietnam's privileged and military ranks, the new arrivals came predominantly from the lower socioeconomic strata, reflecting a broader spectrum of Vietnamese society.

These immigrants were welcomed by an established network of sponsor families in their new homeland. These sponsors, often relatives who had already established themselves in America, offered guidance through the complexities of American life and provided a little more stability amidst the chaos of resettlement.

Social gatherings quickly became the cornerstone of community life, crucial in fostering a sense of belonging for these displaced families. From shared dinners with relatives to elaborate celebrations of Vietnamese cultural festivals, these events were vital for emotional support and cultural preservation. In the warmth of shared meals and the singing of homeland anthems, bonds were forged, friendships blossomed, and a dynamic community took root.

And as the Vietnamese community grew, so too did its visibility. Refugees began to establish businesses, from

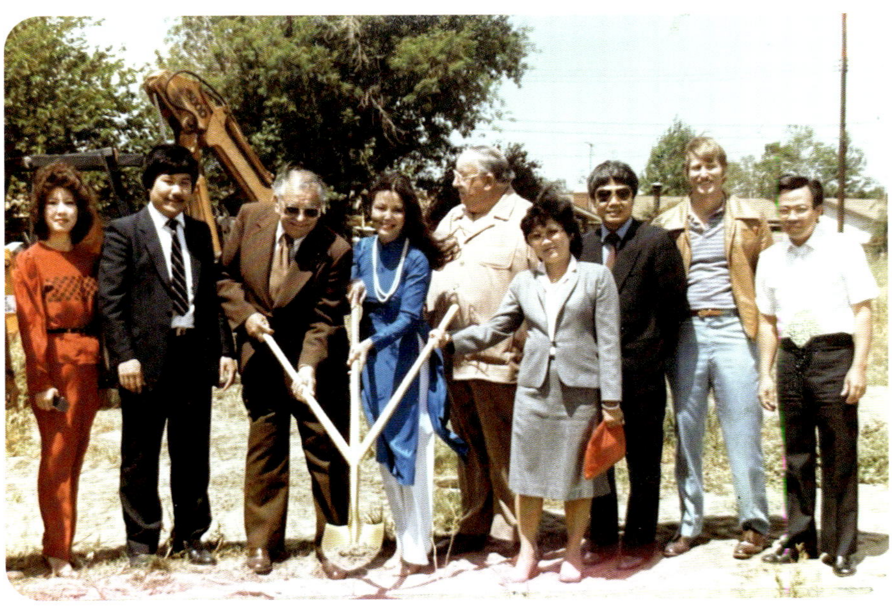

Opposite: Woman and child in Vietnamese grocery store, circa 1980s. Right: Photograph of New Waver Paul Tran's parents (at left), actress, Kiều Chinh (in blue), and other community members at groundbreaking, circa 1982.

N LONG BEACH INDEPENDENT, PRESS-TELEGRAM/SATURDAY, JULY 28, 1979

eather C4

local news

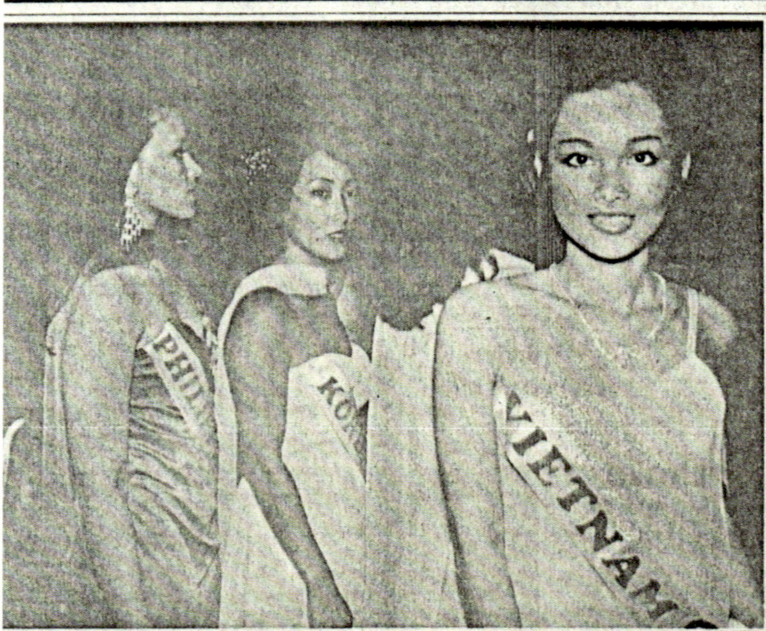

—Staff Photo by LEO HETZEL

NTESTANTS from Vietnam, Korea and the Philippines wait their turn to participate in gown competition Friday night.

Controversy at Orient pageant

By Toni Cordero
Staff Writer

Controversy again swirled around the Miss Orient U.S.A. pageant Friday as selection of the new queen approached.

A contestant charged in an interview with a television station that pageant entrants had invested a lot of money to participate and were not getting their money's worth.

"I myself am not being ripped off because I have not given the pageant any of my money," said Pami Ozaki, as she dressed for the bathing suit contest. "Some of the girls had to come up with $500 in sponsorships to come to the pageant."

She said many of the women were angry because they are not being fed well and some had been charged $25 for a hairdo that amounted to "someone pulling their hair up and putting it in a rubber band." She said they continued to participate in the pageant because they are "silly."

"A lot of the girls here are silly," she said. "They want to go into modeling and acting and they think this is their big break. Many can't even speak English very well. They're led to believe they're here to represent their countries."

She said she had decided to speak out because she was not concerned about the outcome of the pageant and because she doesn't "believe in using people."

However, Remedios Cabacungan, executive director of the pageant, said the girls had been given full meals except for Thursday night because they did not want to eat before the preliminary contest and the hotel had stopped serving food by the time the event had ended.

She also said that the sponsorship money the women put up was used for hotel accommodations and other pageant expenses. She said most had paid about $450.

Another contestant who asked not to be identified also said the women had not been fed full meals. She said the pageant was "not in the least" professional.

Controversy about the pageant, founded three years ago by Mrs. Cabacungan, began earlier this week when Leilani O'Melia, last year's winner, charged that she had not received any of the prizes she had been promised when she was crowned. Miss O'Melia had threatened to shut down the pageant.

But hours before the finals on the Quenn Mary Friday, Miss O'Melia received a notarized contract from pageant officials, including Mrs. Cabacungan, guaranteeing she would get a 17-day trip to the Orient, $1,500 in scholarships and $1,000 for expense money on the trip.

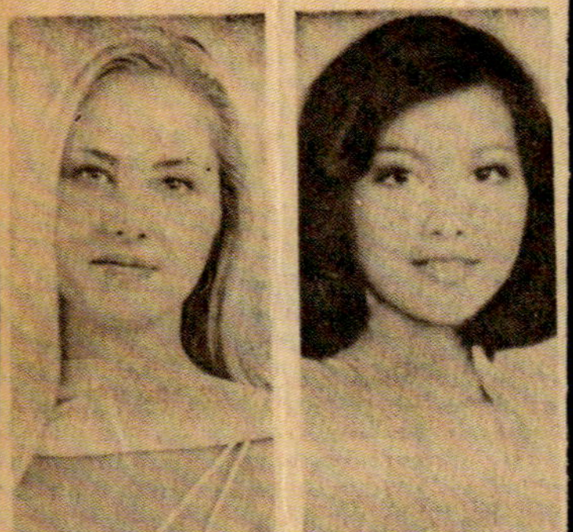

CROWNED Saturday night as Miss Oklahoma City World was Kathy Joplin, left, a 21-year-old pharmacy student. On the right is Que Phuong, a 17-year-old Vietnamese refugee, first runner-up and voted Miss Photogenic in the contest held at the Ramada Inn Central. Miss Joplin will compete in the state contest in June where she hopes to take another step toward the Miss World title.

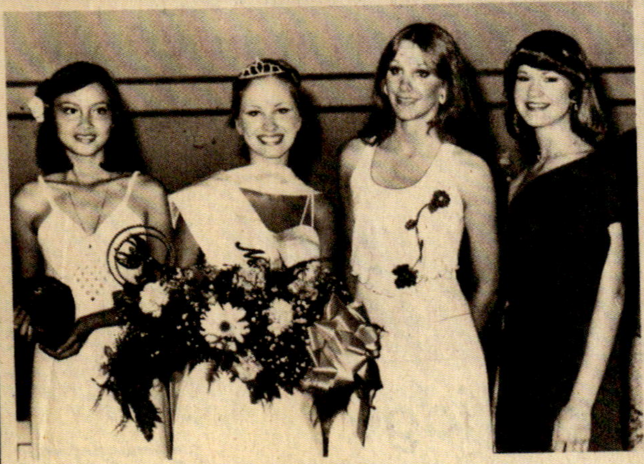

'World' Beauties

Top winners in Saturday night's Miss Oklahoma City World competition include these beauties, from left, TonNuQue Phuong, first runner-up; Kathy Joplin, who won the crown; Anita Garrett, second runner-up, and Karla Price, third runner-up. (Staff Photo by Claude Long)

MISS OKLAHOMA CITY 1977
Que Phuong as 1st runner up.

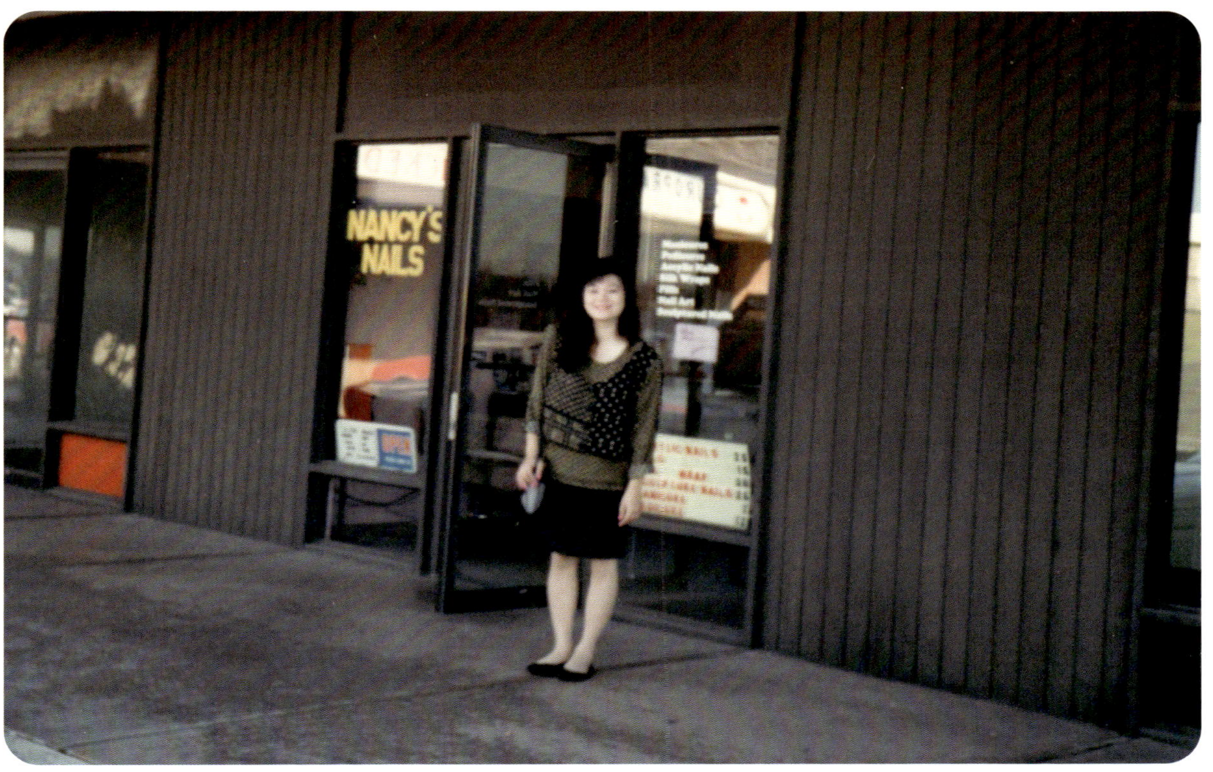

Vietnamese Americans worked to become part of their new communities. Opposite: Que Phuong participated in beauty pageants in the late 1970s and early 1980s. Above: Lan Tran opened a number of nail salons across California.

restaurants to shops selling imported goods. These enterprises did more than cater to the community's needs; they became hubs of cultural exchange within the fabric of everyday life in Orange County.

However, this growth was not met without resistance. By May 1981, tension surfaced as more than a hundred non-Vietnamese Westminster residents signed a petition to "deny granting any license to any Indochinese refugee attempting to set up any business in this Viet town area." This petition was a symptom of broader discontent; many longer-standing residents felt uneasy about the rapid economic changes and the perceived strain on social services caused by the influx of boat refugees.

The unease among the established residents grew as the Vietnamese community continued to expand. Accusations of overcrowding, competition for jobs, and cultural displacement fueled a climate of hostility and mistrust. As the rift between the communities deepened, the seeds of rebellion among the Vietnamese youth began to sprout. Feeling marginalized in their adopted homeland and pressured by the legacy of their parents' sacrifices, these young individuals found themselves at a crossroads leading to a burgeoning counterculture that would soon challenge both their heritage and the societal norms of Orange County.

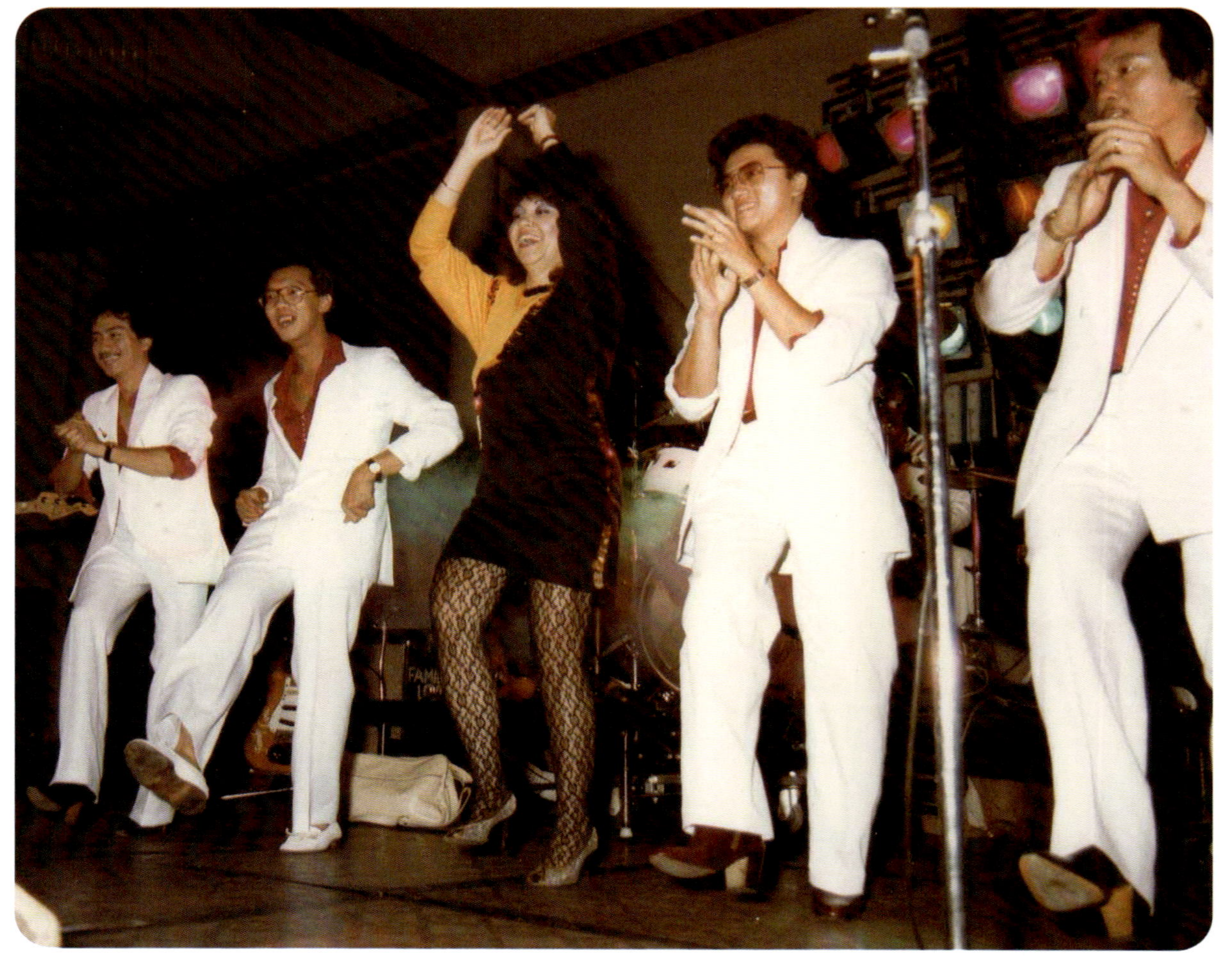

Above and opposite: Family Love Band, 1980s.

Family Love was formed by Lê Trí in 1968 by combining two famous groups of that era: the Flowers and the Rabbits. Christiane Lê and Tami Lê sang, with Lê Trí on keyboard, Minh Hải on guitar, Tường Nga on bass, and Tường Vân on drums. Like many other groups at the time, Family Love performed on American military bases and various nightclubs in Saigon. Lê Toàn joined the group in 1972, and the group started to appear at the "Hippy-A-Gogo" shows in Saigon on the weekends. In a short time, Family Love captured thousands of young fans.

Arriving in America in 1975, Family Love reformed and was invited to perform in the military bases and many night clubs in Honolulu, and quickly gained a lot of non-Vietnamese fans. In 1977, the group signed a one-year contract to tour the Midwest, and was the only Vietnamese band doing floor shows and comedy for an American audience. In 1981, the group relocated to San Jose, California, appearing at a number of Vietnamese night clubs in the Bay Area, and eventually touring across the US. Family Love broke up in 1997, but the band remains popular in Vietnamese communities all over the world.

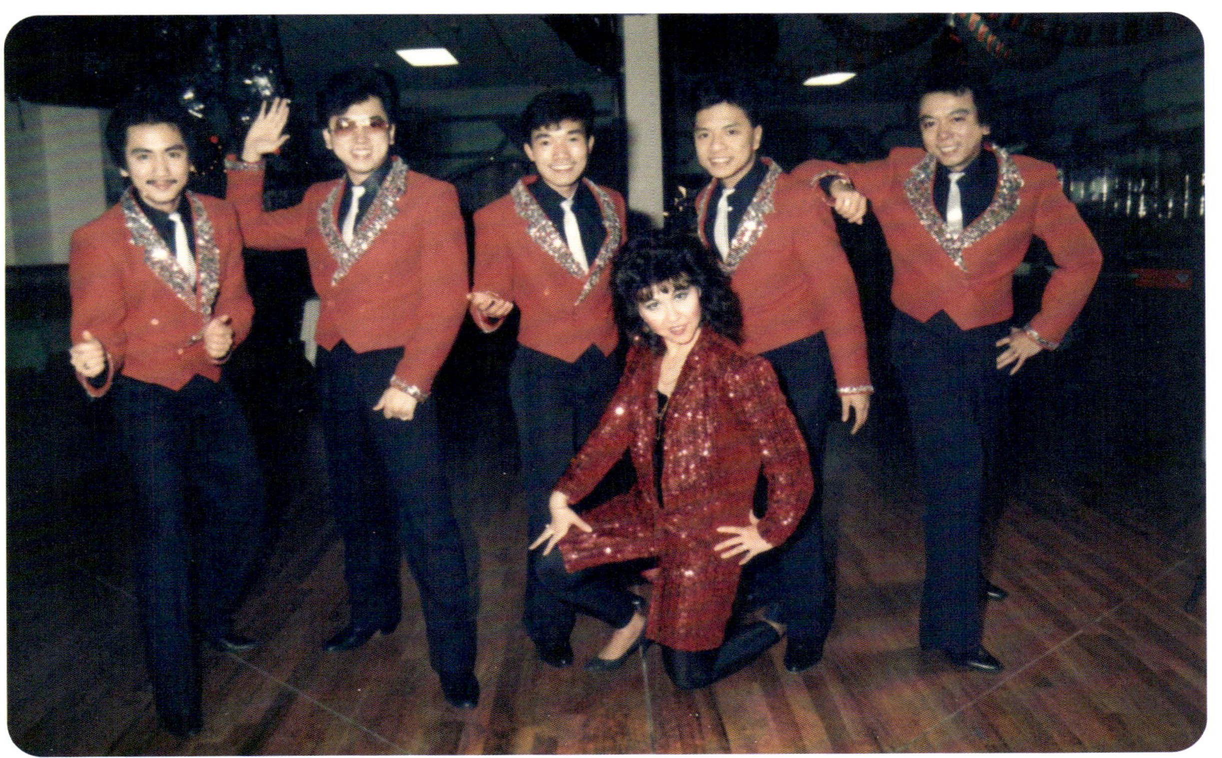

THE MUSIC SCENE OF THE VIETNAMESE DIASPORA

The pulse of the rising Vietnamese community resonated through the streets of Southern California and beyond, as a vibrant diasporic music scene flourished. Church concerts morphed into communal celebrations that drew large crowds, all eager to immerse themselves in the sounds of home. The music, ranging from traditional folk melodies to covers of contemporary American, French, and even Spanish pop hits, served as a bridge connecting generations. It not only preserved the rich cultural heritage of Vietnam but also embraced new influences.

At the heart of this music scene was *Paris By Night*, a variety show that captivated audiences with its dazzling performances and star-studded lineup of displaced Vietnamese artists who were eager to shine on stage once again. For many, particularly in parts of Middle America and elsewhere, where Vietnamese communities were sparse, *Paris By Night* was a crucial cultural link. It was more than just entertainment; it became a portal through which the older generation could dream of their homeland. The traditional melodies from South Vietnam

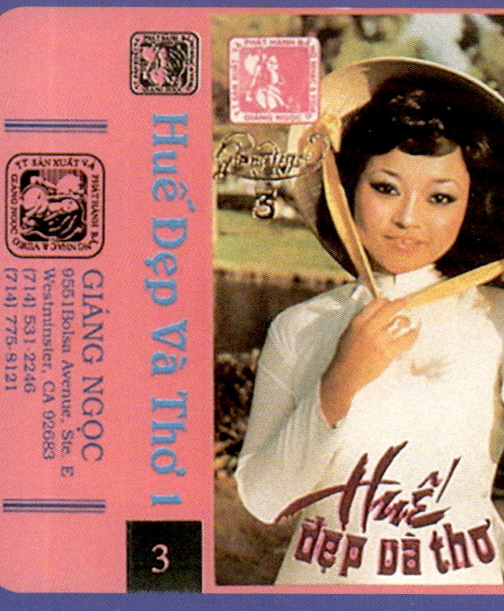

Huế Đẹp Và Thơ 1

3

GIÁNG NGỌC
9551 Bolsa Avenue, Ste. E
Westminster, CA 92683
(714) 531-2246
(714) 775-8121

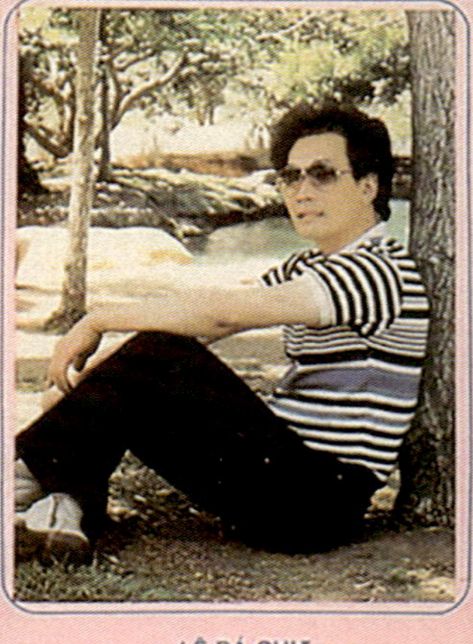

LÊ BÁ CHƯ
Giám Đốc
Trung Tâm Băng Nhạc & Video
GIÁNG NGỌC

XUÂN HỌP MẶT Giáng Ngọc

GIÁNG NGỌC
9551 Bolsa Avenue, Ste. E
Westminster, CA 92683
(714) 531-2246
(714) 491-1672

46

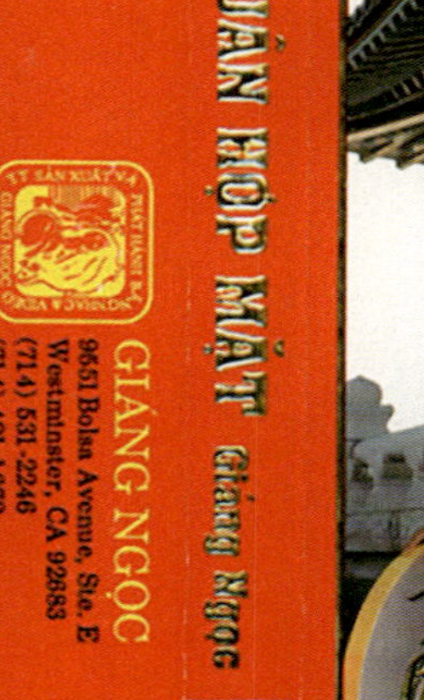

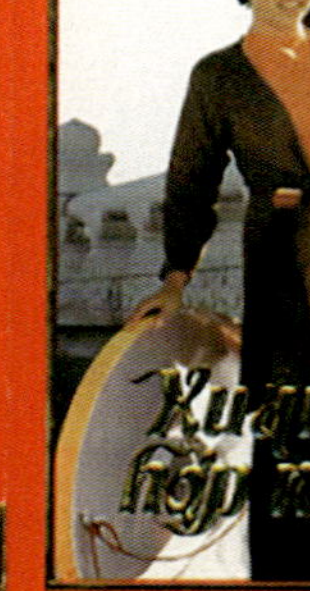

Chiều Vàng
Nhạc tiền chiến

GIÁNG NGỌC
9551 Bolsa Ave, Ste. E
Westminster, CA 92683
(714) 531-2246

43

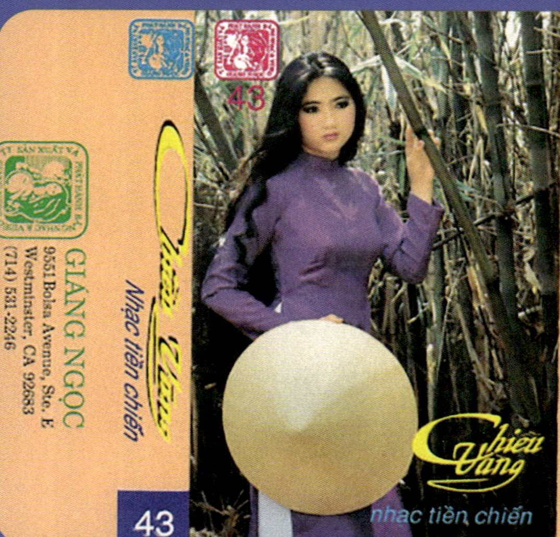

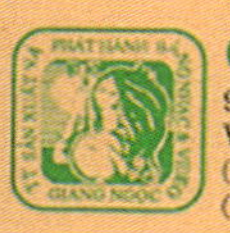

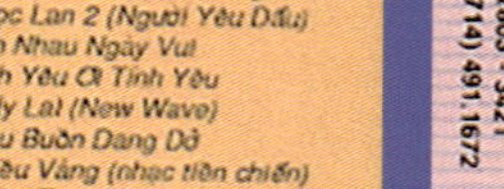

nhạc tiền chiến

GIÁNG NGỌC
9551 Bolsa Avenue, Ste. E
Westminster, CA 92683
(714) 531-2246
(714) 491-1672

- Giáng Ngọc 26: *Mộng Ước*
- Giáng Ngọc 27: *Hồn Trinh Nữ*
- Giáng Ngọc 28: *New Wave Trung Nghĩa 2*
- Giáng Ngọc 29: *Dạ Khúc Cho Tình Nhân*
- Giáng Ngọc 30: *Tình Khúc Lính 2*
- Giáng Ngọc 31: *Giáng Ngọc Tứ Quí*
- Giáng Ngọc 32: *Heartflash Tonight*
- Giáng Ngọc 33: *Sao Rơi Trên Biển*
- Giáng Ngọc 34: *Chiều Lá Đổ*
- Giáng Ngọc 35: *Hoa Biển*
- Giáng Ngọc 36: *Magic For Love*
- Giáng Ngọc 37: *Nguyệt Ánh & Việt Dzũng*
- Giáng Ngọc 38: *Ngọc Lan 2 (Người Yêu Dấu)*
- Giáng Ngọc 39: *Bên Nhau Ngày Vui*
- Giáng Ngọc 40: *Tình Yêu Ơi Tình Yêu*
- Giáng Ngọc 41: *Lady Lai (New Wave)*
- Giáng Ngọc 42: *Điệu Buồn Dang Dở*
- Giáng Ngọc 43: *Chiều Vàng (nhạc tiền chiến)*
- Giáng Ngọc 44: *Chiều Trên Đồi Thông*

LỜI TÌNH BUỒN • Giáng Ngọc

TÌNH KHÚC HOÀNG THANH TÂM

Thư Từ Giao Dịch:
LÊ BÁ CHƯ
TRUNG TÂM GIÁNG NGỌC
9551 Bolsa Ave. Suite E | P.O. Box 3421 Anaheim
Westminster, CA 92683 | CA 92803 - 3421
Tel: (714) 531-2246 | Tel: (714) 491-1672

15

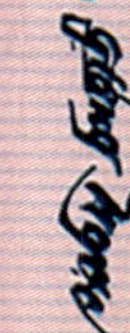

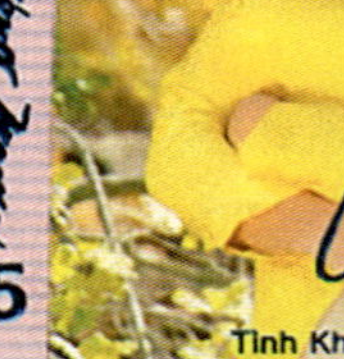

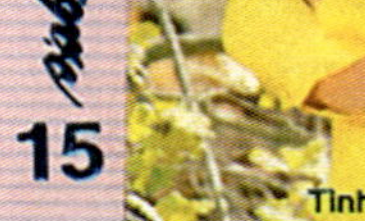

Tình Khú

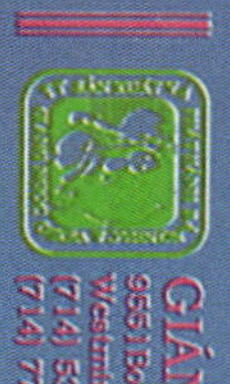

Huế Đẹp Và Thơ 2

8

GIÁNG NGỌC
9551 Bolsa Avenue, Ste. E
Westminster, CA 92683
(714) 531-2246
(714) 775-8121

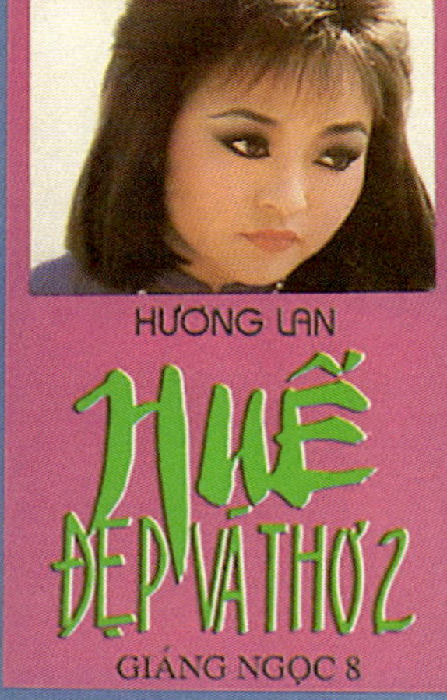

HƯƠNG LAN

HUẾ ĐẸP VÀ THƠ 2

GIÁNG NGỌC 8

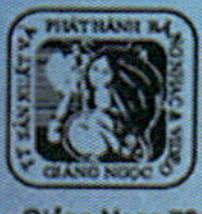

GIÁNG NGỌC
9551Bolsa Avenue, Ste. E
Westminster, CA 92683
(714) 531-2246
(714) 775-8121

- Giáng Ngọc 73: *Biệt Ly*
- Giáng Ngọc 74: *Tìm Quên*
- Giáng Ngọc 75: *Buồn Trong Kỷ Niệm*
- Giáng Ngọc 76: *Come Rock With Me*
- Giáng Ngọc 77: *Huế Mù Sương*
- Giáng Ngọc 78: *Ngủ Đi Em*
- Giáng Ngọc 79: *Ai Cho Tôi Tình Yêu*
- Giáng Ngọc 80: *Nghẹn Ngào*
- Giáng Ngọc 81: *Thiên Đường Tình Ái*
- Giáng Ngọc 82: *Thương Nhớ Một Người*
- Giáng Ngọc 83: *Nhớ Nhau Hoài*
- Giáng Ngọc 84: *Giấc Mơ Qua*
- Giáng Ngọc 85: *Thiệp Hồng Anh Viết Tên Em*
- Giáng Ngọc 86: *Nửa Đêm Ngoài Phố*
- Giáng Ngọc 87: *Xin Gọi Nhau Là Cố Nhân*
- Giáng Ngọc 88: *Quán Nửa Khuya*
- Giáng Ngọc 89: *Tình Nhớ*
- Giáng Ngọc 90: *Lời Về Đất Mẹ*
- Giáng Ngọc 91: *Nửa Đêm Ngoài Phố*
- Giáng Ngọc 92: *Vỹ Dạ Đò Trăng*
- Giáng Ngọc 93: *Nếu Em Về Bên Anh*
- Giáng Ngọc 94: *Ru Ta Ngậm Ngùi*
- Giáng Ngọc 95: *Dạ Vũ Mừng Xuân*
- Giáng Ngọc 96: *Crazy For You*

Sông Nước Tình Quê * Giáng Ngọc 4

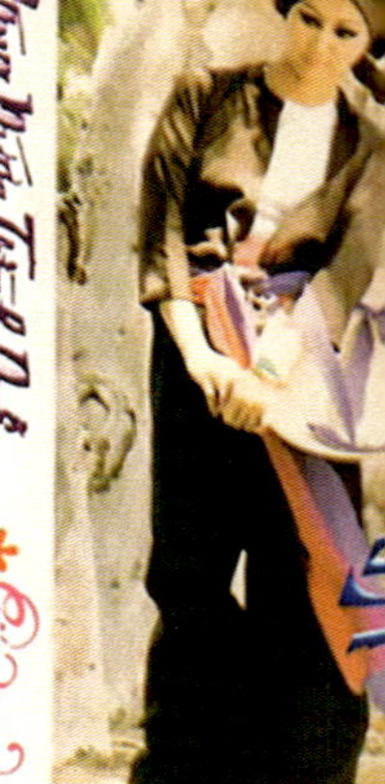

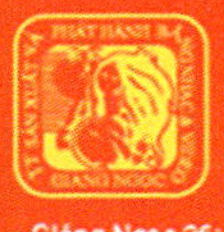

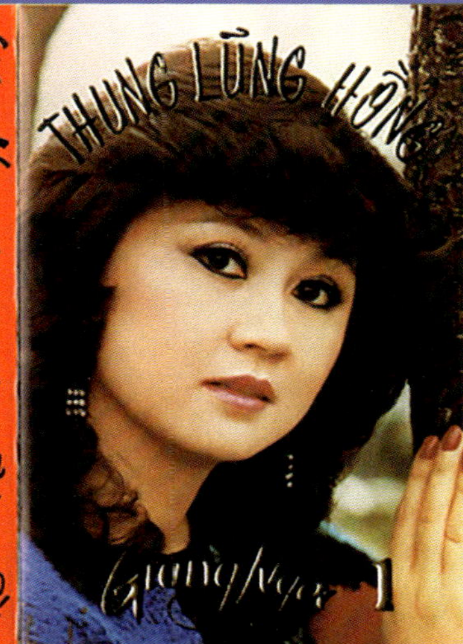

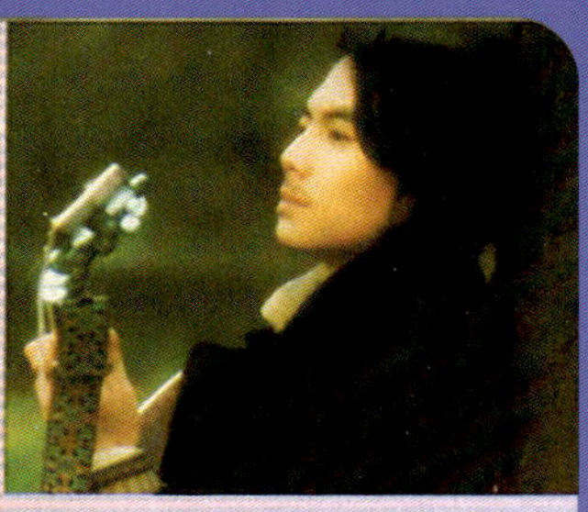

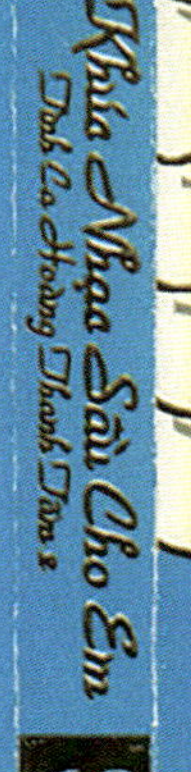
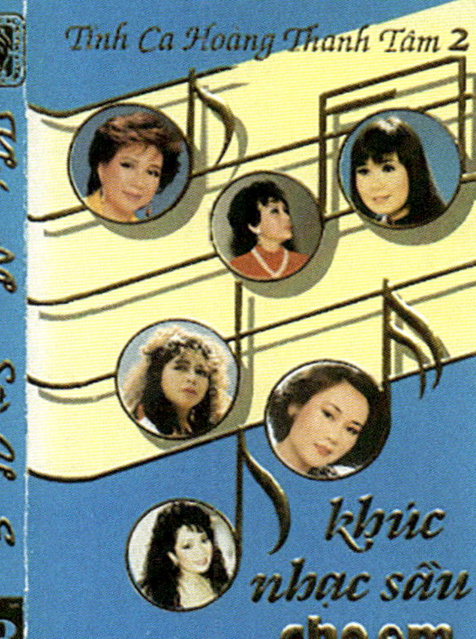

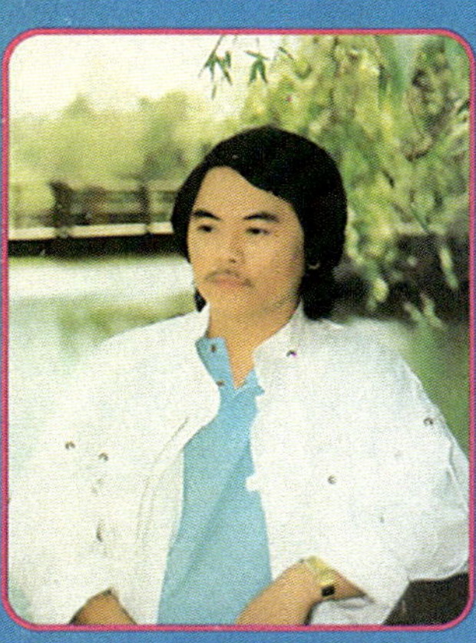

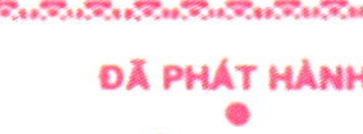

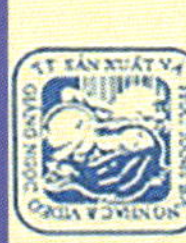
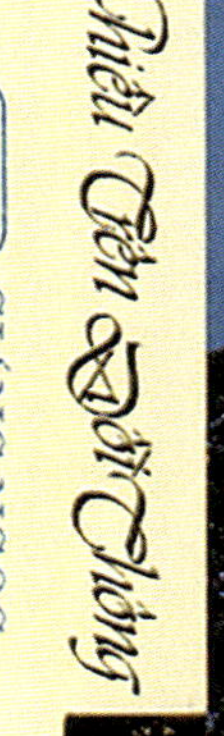

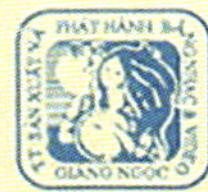

Giáng Ngọc Productions cassette tape covers, which reflect a more traditional Vietnamese aesthetic.

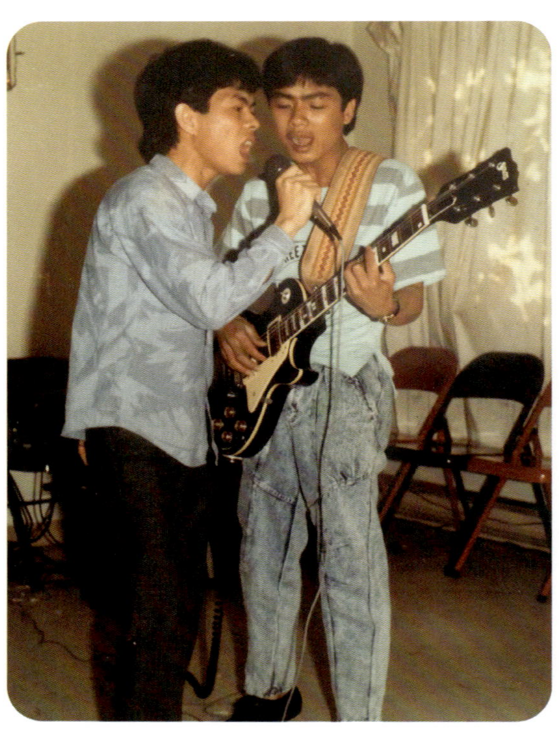

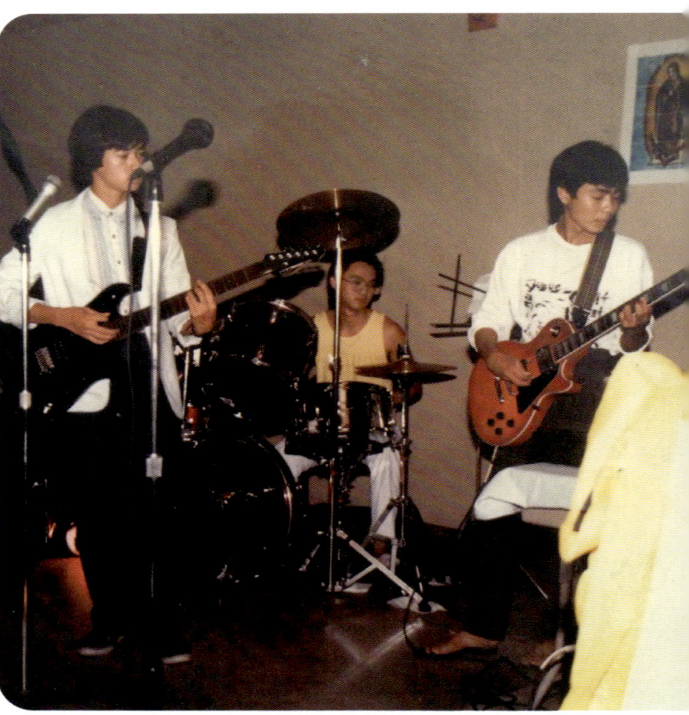

Above: Young Vietnamese Americans began building their own communities, hanging out and starting bands.

performed in the show evoked deep memories and visceral emotions.

The influence of Vietnamese music spread far beyond concert halls. VHS tapes of the shows began to sell out in Vietnamese convenience stores and music shops, bringing this cherished entertainment into living rooms around the world. Through these recordings, *Paris By Night* transformed from a simple variety show into a global phenomenon, fostering a sense of pride and belonging in a world that often felt foreign, and reconnecting Vietnamese in exile with their cultural legacy.

BUILDING LITTLE SAIGON IN ORANGE COUNTY

Once a predominantly white, middle-class suburban area dotted with ample farmland, Westminster, California experienced a decline by the 1970s. The city's fortunes began to transform with the arrival of Vietnamese immigrants. Starting in 1978, the nucleus of Little Saigon formed around Bolsa Avenue. Here, Vietnamese American newcomers revitalized the area by opening businesses in old storefronts previously owned by white residents, injecting new life into the declining retail spaces. Recognizing the growing economic potential, investors soon constructed large shopping

Right: Vietnamese American New Wave teens in the 1980s. Below: Lê Bá Chư (standing) producer of Giáng Ngọc Productions, a popular New Wave label.

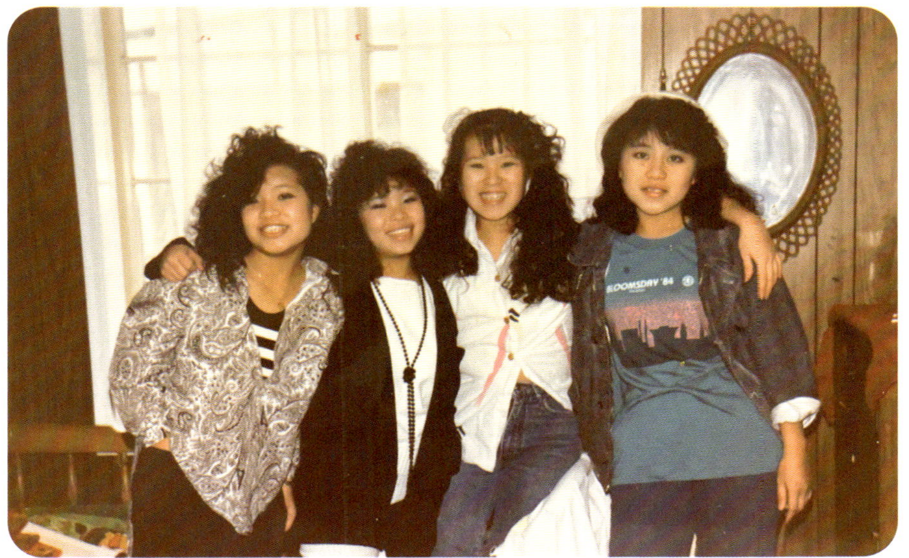

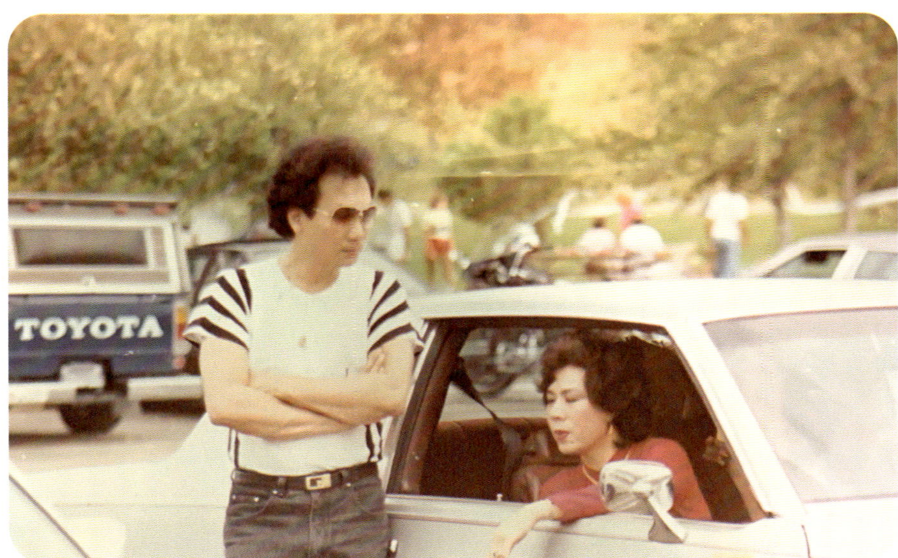

centers that mixed various businesses, establishing the area as a key cultural and commercial hub.

One of the most pivotal developments was the Asian Garden Mall, also known as Phước Lộc Thọ—a name inspired by the Buddhist statues at its entrance. Opened in 1987, it quickly became the cornerstone of Little Saigon in Westminster. As the first and largest Vietnamese American shopping mall, it drew visitors not just from across Orange County but globally, serving as a hub for cultural and political events and symbolizing the community's economic success and cultural preservation.

Amid the burgeoning Vietnamese music scene and cultural expression epitomized by shows like *Paris By Night*, the

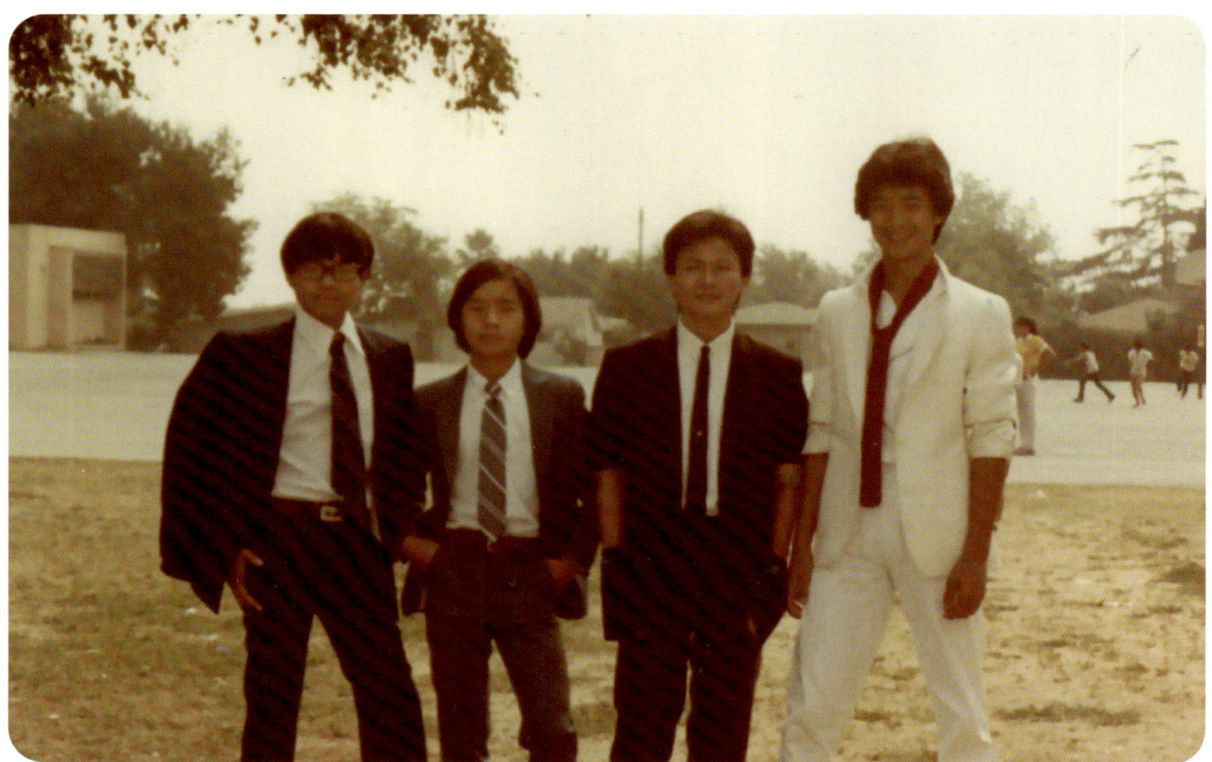

Vietnamese young men pose for a group photo, circa 1980.

entrepreneurial spirit of the Vietnamese community gave rise to the flourishing of Little Saigon. Bolsa Avenue was officially designated Little Saigon by the city council in the late 1980s. These plazas became symbols of strength for a community determined to thrive against all odds.

From Garden Grove to Westminster, and across the country, the concept of Little Saigon spread swiftly, symbolizing hope and opportunity for the Vietnamese diaspora. It offered newcomers a place to preserve their traditions and build a future, enhancing their economic standing and firmly establishing their cultural footprint in Southern California and beyond.

ESCAPE AND REBELLION: THE VIETNAMESE YOUTH COUNTERCULTURE

As the children of the 1.5 generation in the Vietnamese community matured into teenagers, they started to build their own communities. Driven by a need to escape the traumas of their parents' past and the pressures to uphold traditional values, these young individuals turned away from established cultural norms. Rejecting the classic tunes of *Paris By Night* and other

Opposite: New Wave party, San Gabriel Valley, California 1980s.

traditional forms, they carved out new spaces for self-expression, places where they could explore a sense of freedom far removed from the weight of their cultural heritage.

From late-night gatherings in motel rooms to rowdy garage parties, the underground music scene became a gateway to rebellion and liberation. These venues served as sanctuaries where Vietnamese teens could forge their own identities, free from judgment and united by the universal language of music.

Yet, amid the chaos and the noise, deep-seated joy emerged—a relief from the dual pressures of home and school. These gatherings were far more than just a break from societal norms; they were spirited celebrations of life itself, affirming the youths' solidarity in their discontent and their collective desire to craft a unique path. This movement was not just a phase of youthful defiance, but the beginning of the critical part of their journey to self-definition, marking a bold assertion of their individual and collective identities.

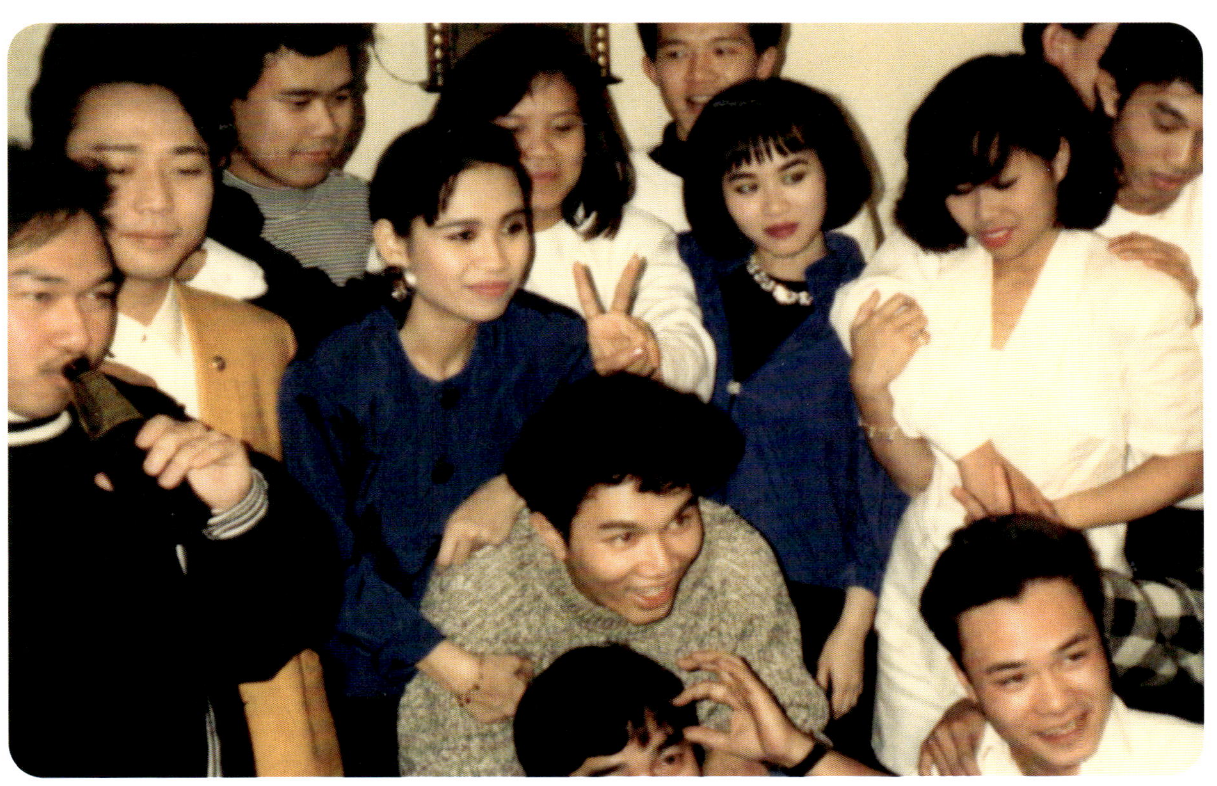

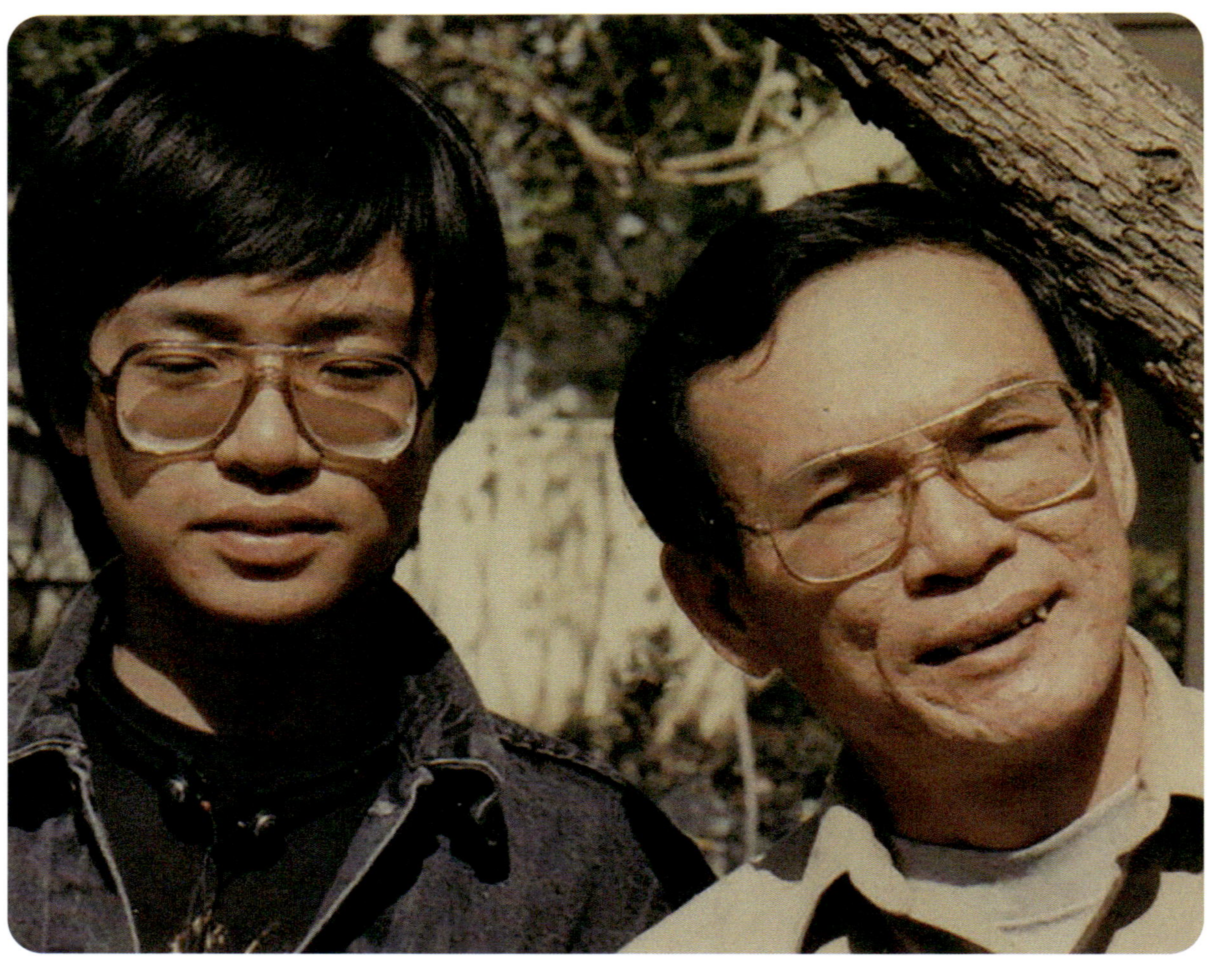

Above: Ian Nguyen, aka DJ BPM, with his father, Nguyễn Mộng Giác. Opposite: Nguyễn Mộng Giác poses with his published books.

New Wave music surged into my life when I was a teenager who had recently arrived in the U.S. in 1985. I believe that was around the "prime time" of New Wave. Although I didn't consider myself a New Waver, I did enjoy dancing at various school and house parties. (Modern Talking was my favorite!) My interests, however, leaned towards a different spectrum—I was deeply engrossed in Vietnamese literature. My father, who was the editor-in-chief for Người Việt Daily News at the time, often brought home books by Vietnamese authors in the diaspora. Nguyễn Mộng Giác was among them. I devoured his epic four-volume historical novel, Sông Côn Mùa Lũ (loosely translated as Côn

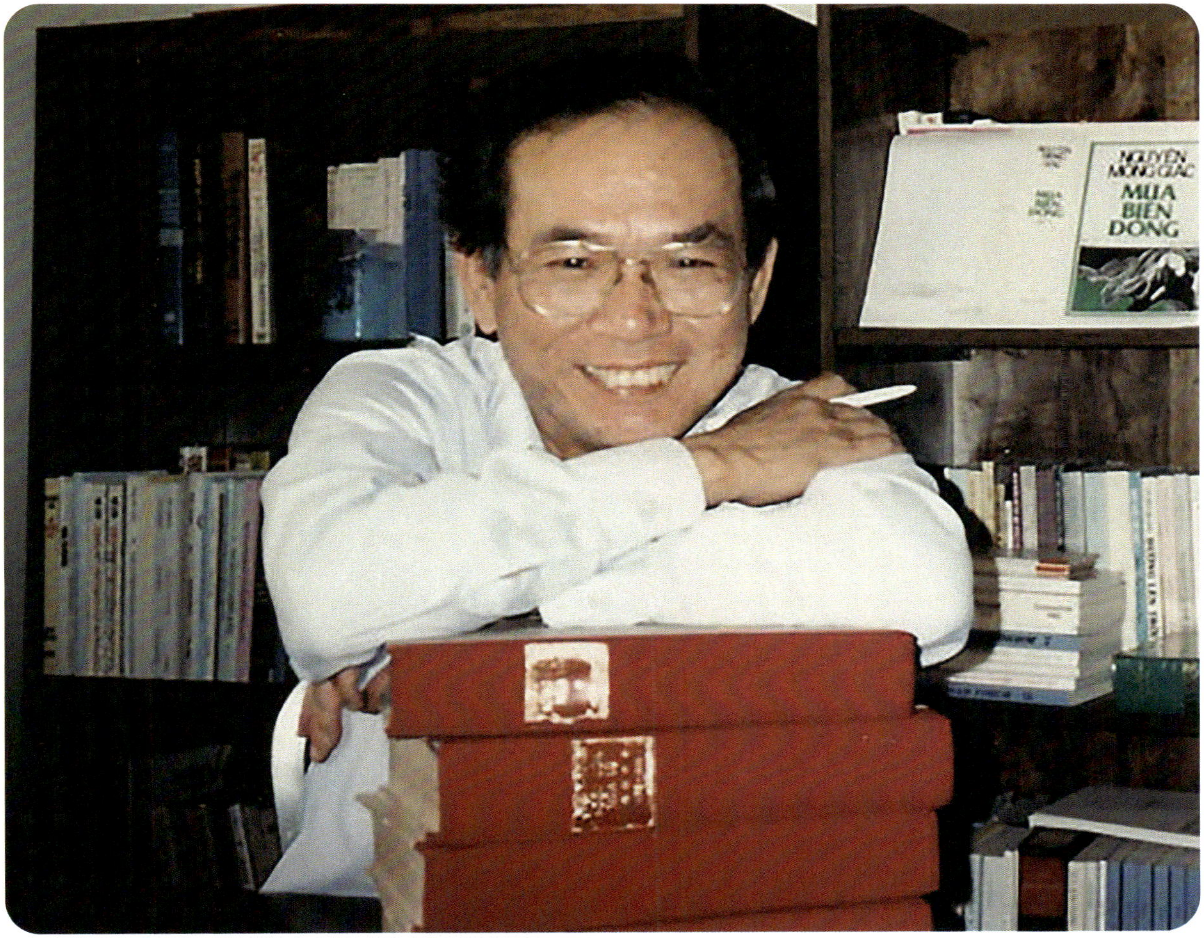

River in Flood Season), which vividly depicted King Quang Trung and the tumultuous history of the eighteenth century through vibrant characters. Nguyễn's other monumental work, Mùa Biển Động (loosely translated as Season of Turbulent Seas), spanned five volumes and provided a contemporary focus on the lives affected by the war in South Vietnam and its aftermath. Some friends and I even dreamed of establishing a library of Vietnamese books. One of our regular activities was inviting Vietnamese authors to discuss their works with us. Nguyễn Mộng Giác was one such guest. I remember we kept him well past midnight, engrossed in discussions about Mùa Biển Động and Sông Côn Mùa Lũ.

— Ysa Le, Executive Director of the Vietnamese American Arts and Letters Association (VAALA)

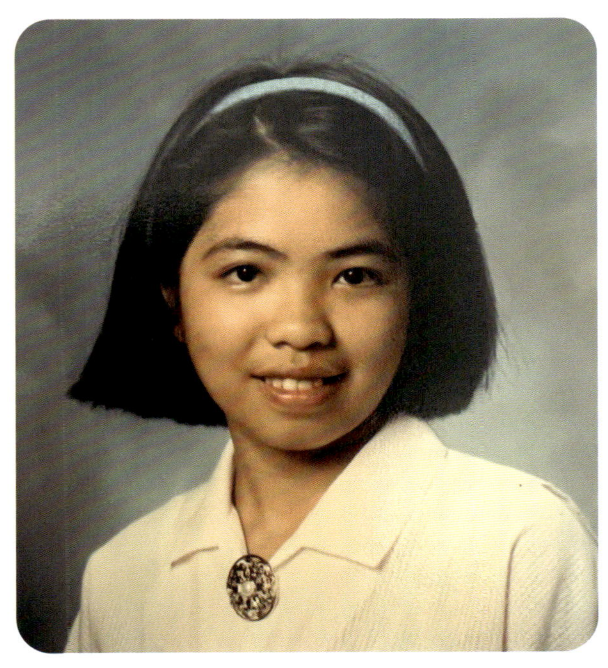

CHAPTER 3

NEW WAVE: IT SOUNDED LIKE THE FUTURE

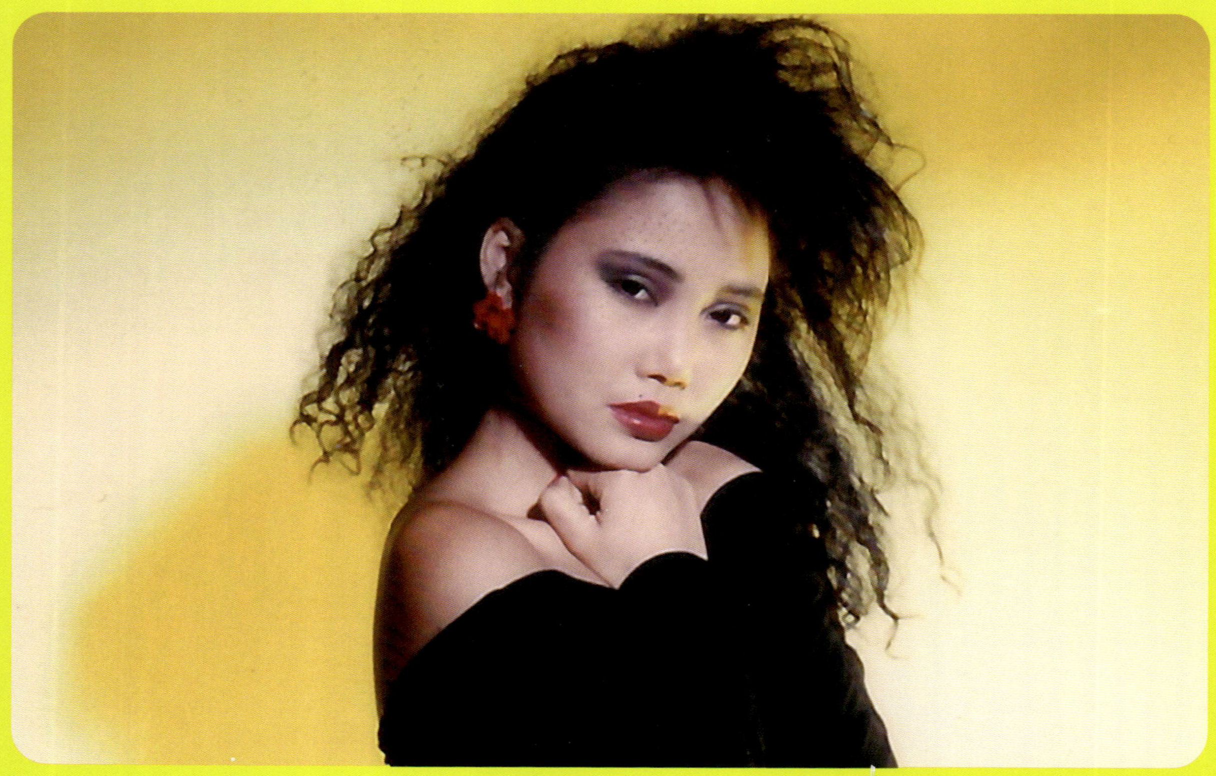

1985

As the 1980s dawned, Vietnamese American youth cultivated a counterculture that was a distinct departure from their parents' traditions. The emergence of MTV as a cultural powerhouse revolutionized not only music, but also fashion, influencing styles across the globe. However, rather than fully adopting the mainstream American pop culture, these young people were drawn to a European aesthetic that offered an alternative to both American norms and the conservative traditions of their Vietnamese heritage.

This European influence manifested in a penchant for New Wave and punk styles, sometimes called "Modern Romantic," which favored gothic and avant-garde looks. Ripped jeans, jackets adorned with safety pins, spiked hair, and bold makeup became symbols of this rebellion. Far from just a fashion statement, these choices were part of a broader rejection of the conventional expectations placed upon them by both their cultural roots and their adopted country.

The underground music scenes provided safe spaces for teenagers to freely express themselves. Here, amidst the synthesized beats and mile-high hair, they formed bonds that transcended cultural and generational divides. Vietnamese American youth found a sense of belonging and freedom. These gatherings were not merely escapes but celebrations of life, offering a counter-narrative to the prescriptive identities they were expected to assume.

As these young individuals forged their unique path, they not only shaped their own identities but also influenced

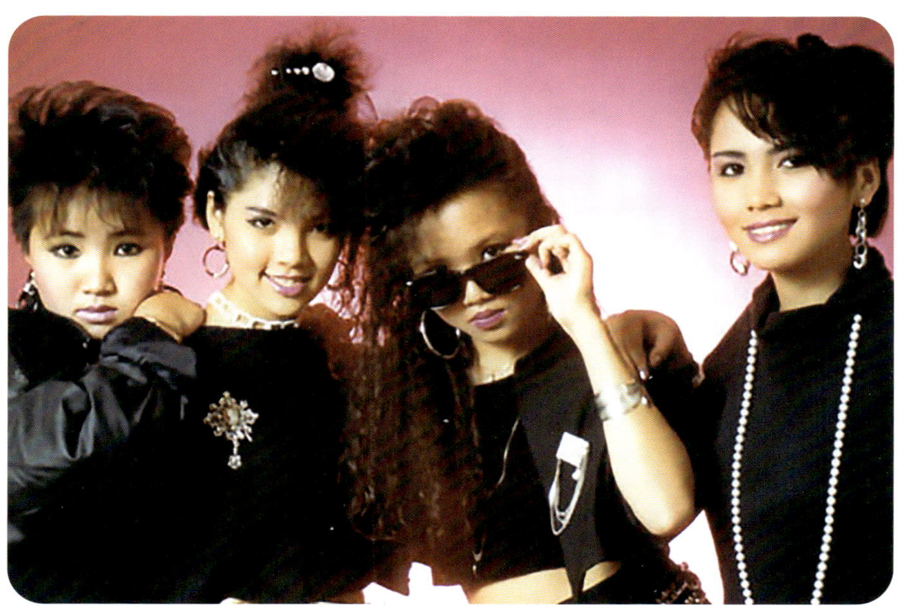

Opposite: Lynda Trang Đài, circa 1985. Right: New Wave girls, circa 1985.

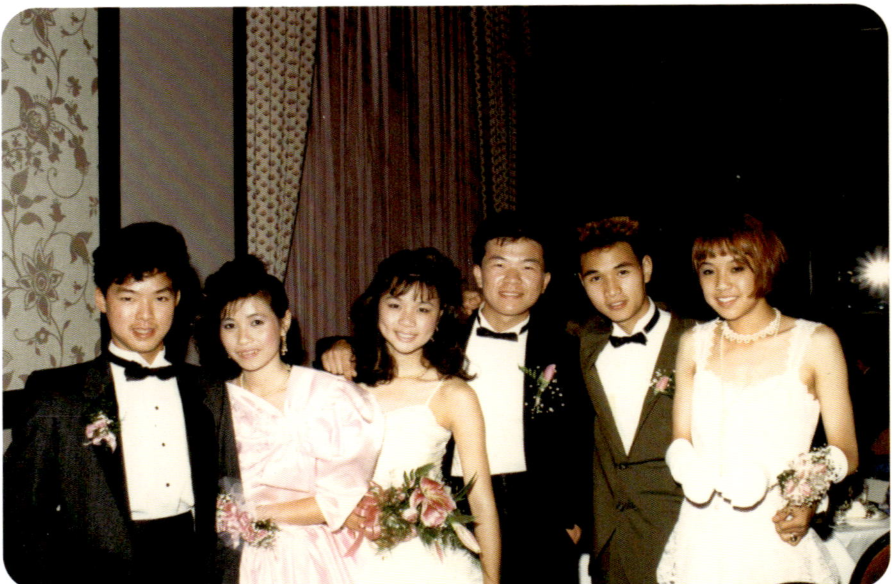

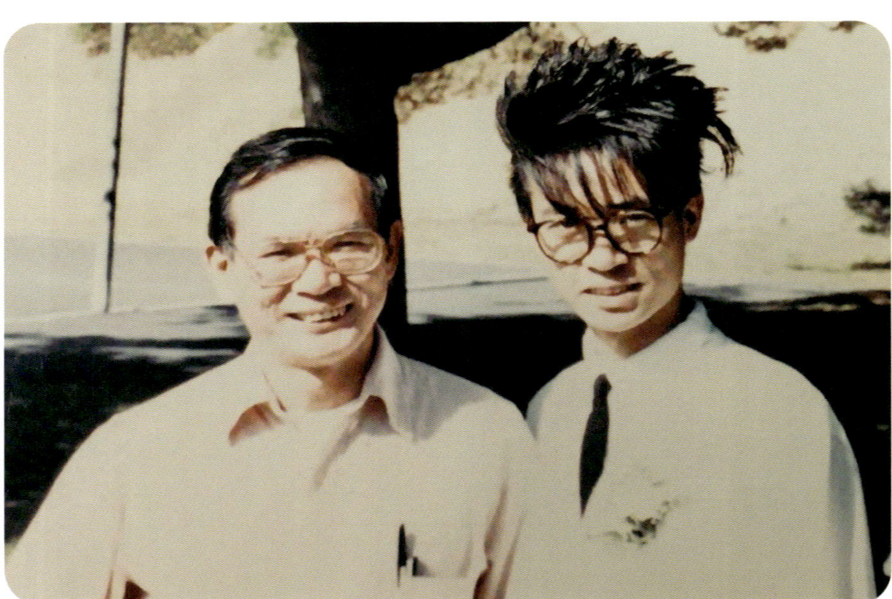

Left: Vietnamese teenagers at prom, 1987. Below: Ian Nguyen, with full New Wave hair, poses with his father, Nguyễn Mộng Giác. Opposite: Thao Ha, Houston, Texas, circa 1980s.

the broader cultural landscape of their communities. By blending elements from European music scenes with aspects of American and Vietnamese traditions, they created a dynamic subculture that was as much about personal expression as it was about collective identity. This evolving youth culture in the 1980s became the foundation of Vietnamese American identity in Southern California and beyond. It was a powerful affirmation in a world where young people often felt marginalized.

CREATIVE REBELLION

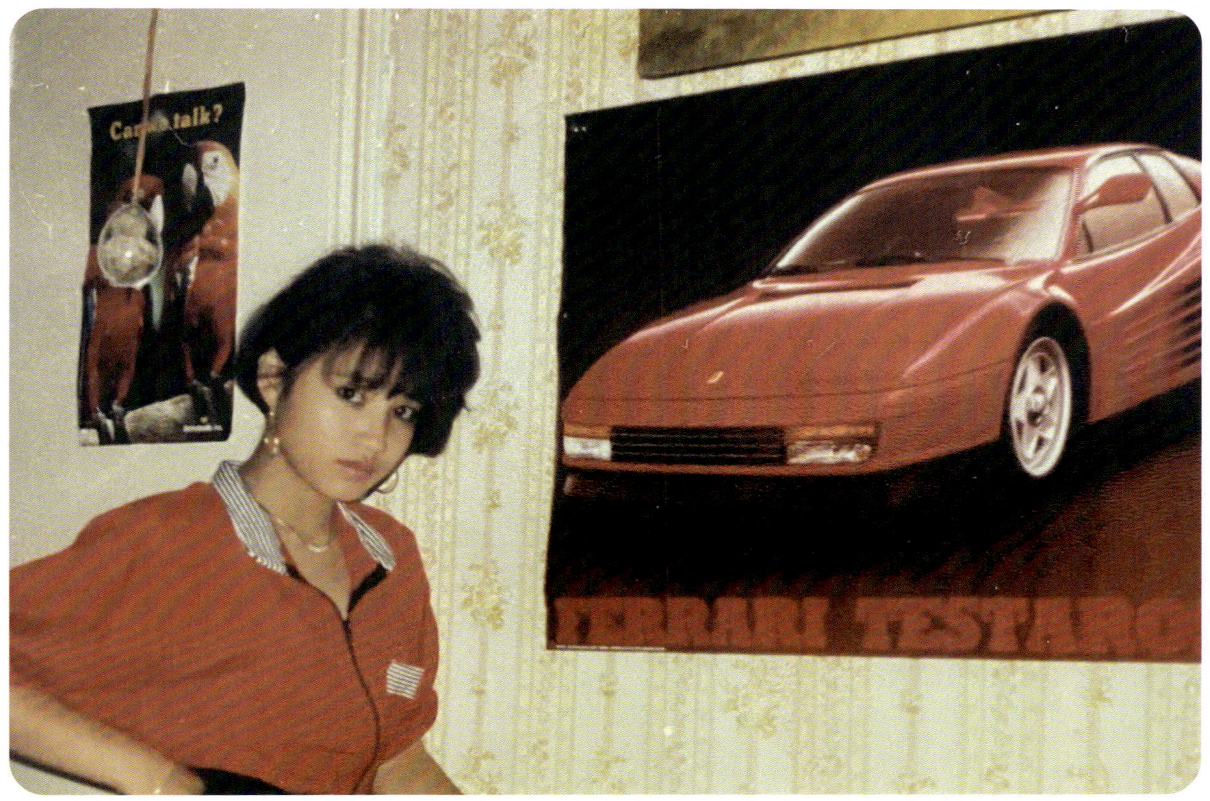

Thao Ha

Ah, the 1980s! As a Vietnamese American youth during that era, rebellion wasn't just a word; it was a blazing fire that fueled a refugee revolution. We called that revolution New Wave. My friends and I weren't just seeking to assert who we were—we were ripping apart the mold society tried to impose upon us. I've always been a contrarian, restlessly searching for a sense of self. In a refusal to conform, coming of age meant more than merely challenging societal norms; it was about pushing the boundaries of norms; our identities busted through cultural walls that were built on the expectations of obedience and submission. From the clothing we wore to the tracks we played at house parties, New Wave was a shared statement. Yet our rebellion wasn't just a protest, but rather, a symphony and a dance of liberation. In those moments, we weren't just shaping our culture; we were sculpting a transformative world, one where being Vietnamese American was a celebration of resilience and individuality.

After fleeing Vietnam in 1975, my family settled in Houston, Texas, in the late 1970s. We planted our roots in a modest ranch-style home in the working class suburb of South Belt. By the 1980s, the neighborhood had become a popular destination for hundreds of Vietnamese refugee families. I entered middle school in 1986, and there was no shortage of Vietnamese kids in school to kick it with. I had scored starting spots on several girls' sports teams, which was a lot of fun, but the real fun was after morning practice. It was in the locker room where I changed out of practice shorts and t-shirts into baggy black pants and fitted black tops. I switched out my sneakers for black, pointed-toe lace up booties. I pulled the teal Aqua Net can from my gym bag and sprayed my bangs

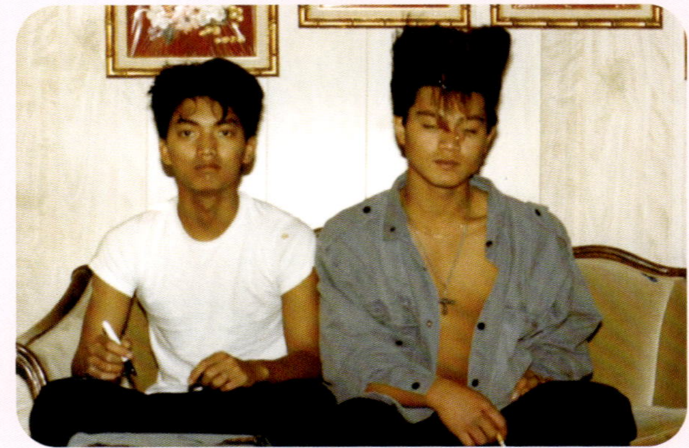

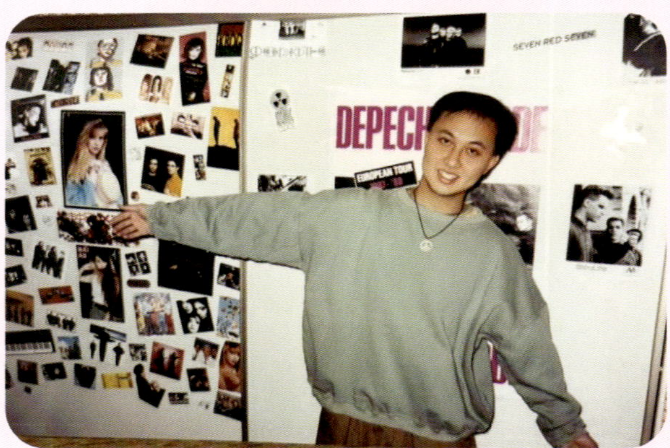

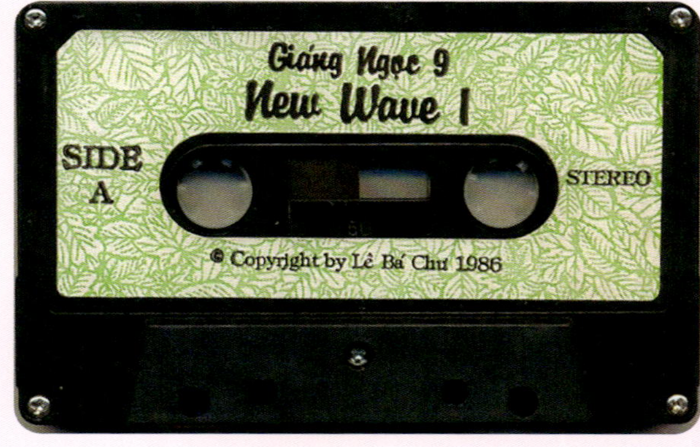

Community photos, 1980s.

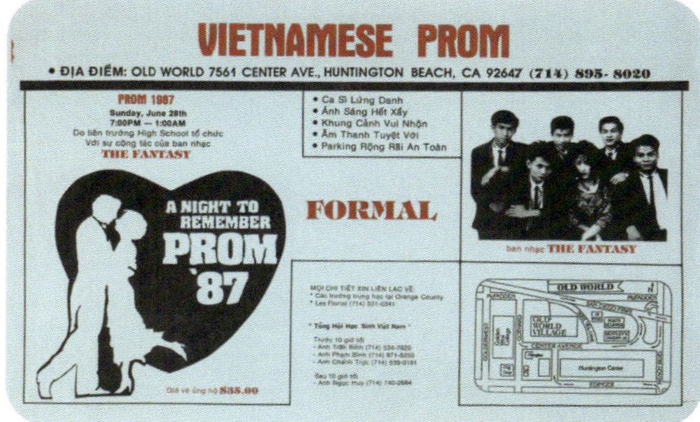

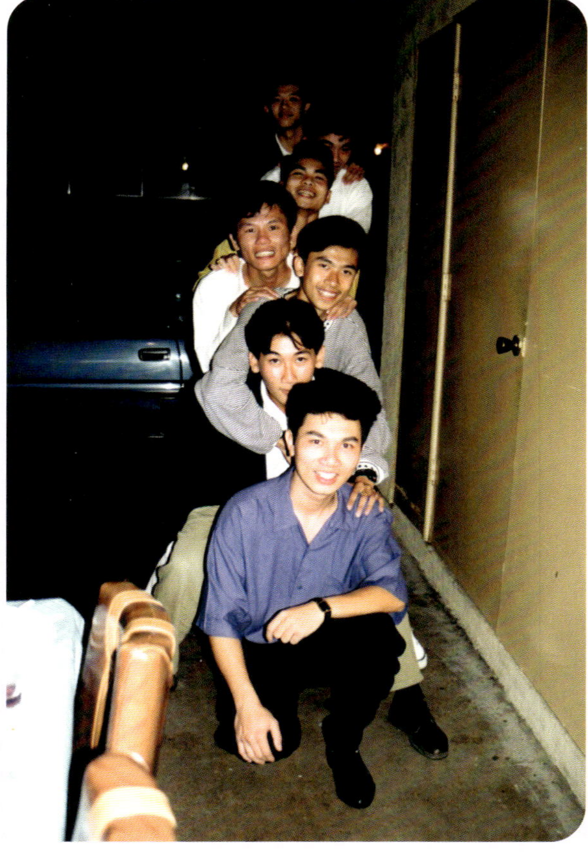

Community Photos, 1980s.

high into the sky. Black eyeliner and bubblegum-pink lipstick completed the look. It was the look of New Wave. Outside the classrooms, I clustered with the Vietnamese boys and girls who shared my aesthetics and demeanor. The hallways were charged with the air of rebellion as we scurried along, late to class because the bell had rung. We regularly lost track of time while we schemed our after-school shenanigans, escapades that included getting picked up by the high school-age Vietnamese New Wavers in second-hand Nissans and Toyotas, so we could jam out in the park or hit the malls and arcades. We heard some of them were gangbangers, but we didn't judge. We felt connected to each other, a shared experience of searching for friendships and community.

Not only did we find commonality in the love of New Wave styles and music, we spoke the same language and ate the same food. We had similar struggles with being bullied and trying to get along with our parents. Those bonds held us together as we navigated the disparate expectations of assimilation into dominant culture while adhering to the roots of our own.

Amid the swirling lights of house party dance floors and the rhythmic pulse of Bad Boys Blue, Modern Talking, C.C. Catch, and Joy, my friends and I discovered more than just music. Our outbursts of laughter, singing, and dancing were an outlet for teenage angst, set against the backdrop of a tumultuous socio-political history. We came from families who were cast into a foreign land with promises of a new beginning, yet we bore the weight of the struggle for acceptance, as well as the scars of a history rife with conflict and displacement. In those rhythms, coupled with our distinct modes of fashion, we found an expression that wove the intricate threads of our past into the vibrant tapestry of our uncertain future.

Sure, there were pop hits on the radio, but the syncopated rhythms and pulsating bass lines of Europop were more than just notes on a staff; they were a fresh, upbeat, and invigorating sense of who we were. We were Vietnamese Americans, and we were New Wavers. When we met others like us at the Vietnamese American club, Queen Bee, New Wave became our anthem. We became badasses, not backing down to the bullies and the racists. Cruising in our rides with aftermarket Alpine sound systems, lyrics like "You're my heart, you're my soul," propelled us to throw our hands up and scream out of tinted windows at our nemeses, "Viet Pride, Baby! Fuck you! We're Vietnamese!"

As Vietnamese American communities continued to grow, the time was ripe for Vietnamese American pop icons and media to take center stage. My friends and I harnessed the transformative potential of cassette tapes, mixtapes, and CDs. In this era, artists like Anh Tài Band and Lynda Trang Đài were more than musicians; they became emblematic

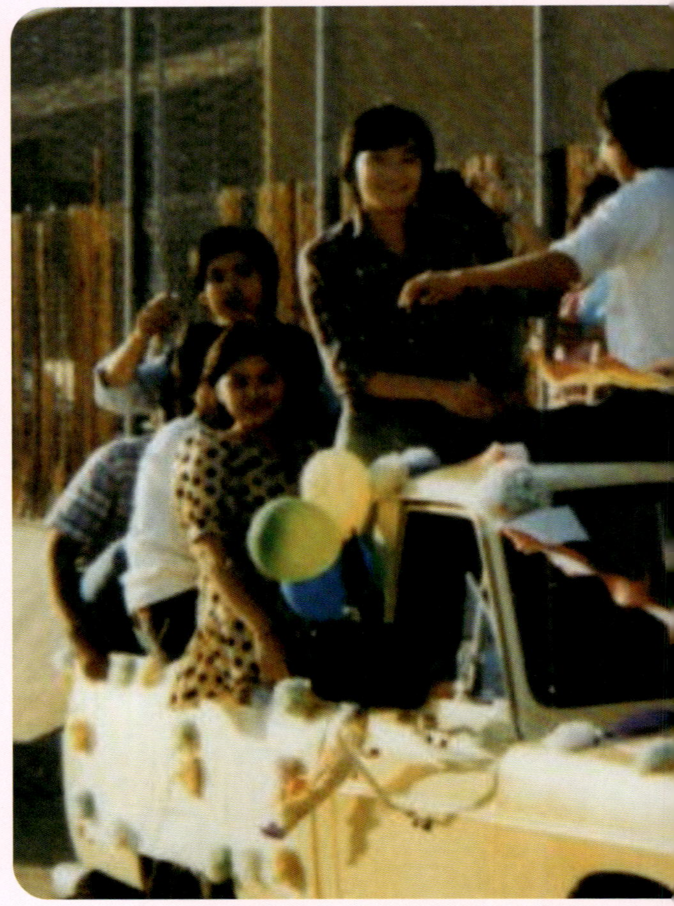

Above: Members of Hollywood High School's Vietnamese Club ride in a decorated truck at homecoming. Opposite: Big hair and shoulder pads were a hallmark of New Wave style.

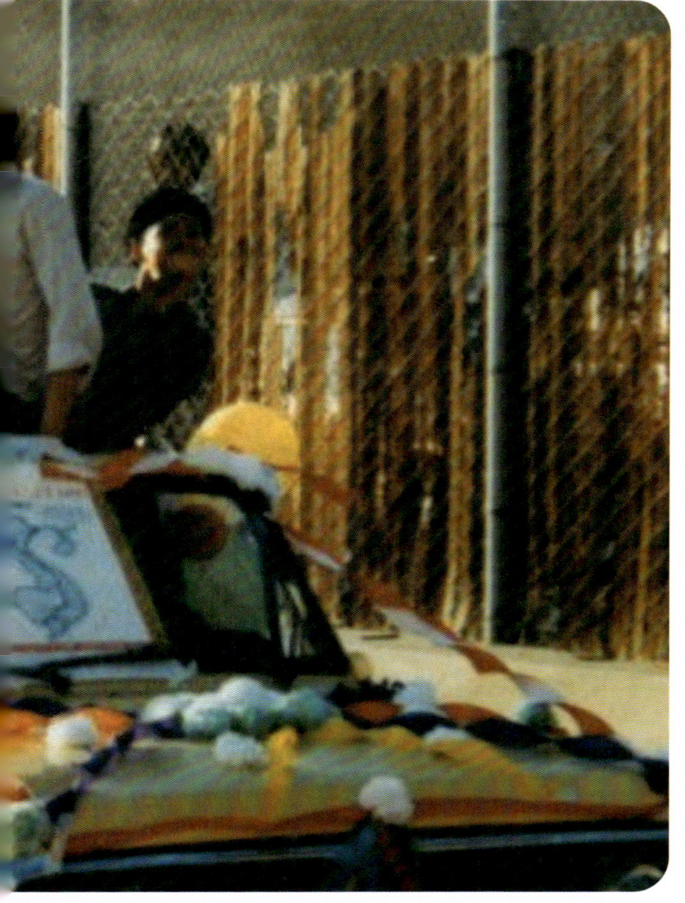

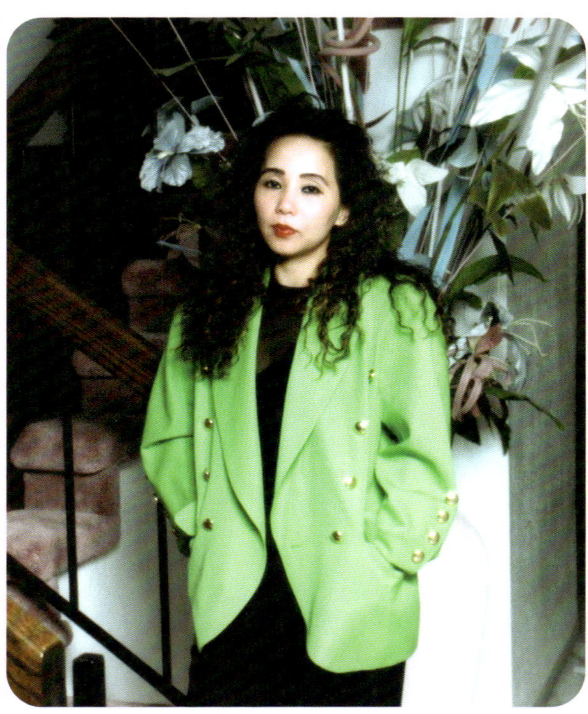

cultural trailblazers of a new generation. Their New Wave covers were audio treasures, but their music was more than recordings; they were the embodiment of thought and expression that was uniquely Vietnamese American. My parents rented VHS tapes of *Paris By Night*, and for me, they became portals to a world of possibilities.

Lynda Trang Đài's appearances were not just performances; they were cultural catalysts, igniting an explosion of New Wave style and setting off a revolution across the Vietnamese diaspora. I'll never forget my mother's gasp when we watched "LTD" strut across the stage in a body tight suit, with one full legging and the other just "her underwear." I thought it was bold and cool. Her presence drew me into a realm where individuality was celebrated and traditional constraints began to crumble. My friends talked about the outfit at lunch in the cafeteria. We wondered if the shops in Houston's Little Saigon sold such risqué outfits, and who among our group would dare to wear and dare to bare.

New Wave music and fashion weren't just fleeting trends. My friends and I stayed loyal to it while also mixing our playlist with mainstream radio hits of the 1980s and 1990s. Through the power of CDs and DVDs, Vietnamese American music and style gave birth to V-pop, a genre that bridged the traditional melodies of heritage with the electrifying sounds of the contemporary world. Lynda Trang Đài transformed herself while still a fixture on *Paris By Night*, but it was Shere Thu Thuy who graced the screen on MTV. I watched hours of music videos waiting to catch a glimpse of her music video. It wasn't just a spectacle, though. To me, we made it in pop culture. Beyond the spotlight, New Wave thrived in our homes, our cars, our playlists, our nightclubs, our clothing shops, and our music stores. New Wave became ubiquitous, etching its presence into the very fabric of my everyday life.

New Wave is nostalgic, but the lifestyle wasn't just a moment in time; it was a cultural evolution that defined what it meant for me and so many others to be Vietnamese American in the early years of our resettlement. It empowered my generation to embrace our unique identities, celebrate our roots, and, in the process, create a tapestry of resilience, rebellion, and cement an enduring legacy. New Wave concerts in recent years brought my generation out in droves. We danced to the music, reliving the memories and cheering to the joy of our youth. While the New Wave era is of the past, it is also a timeless emblem of a vibrant, dynamic, wild, and ever-evolving part of Vietnamese American history. It left an indelible mark of identity on a significant number of us in that generation.

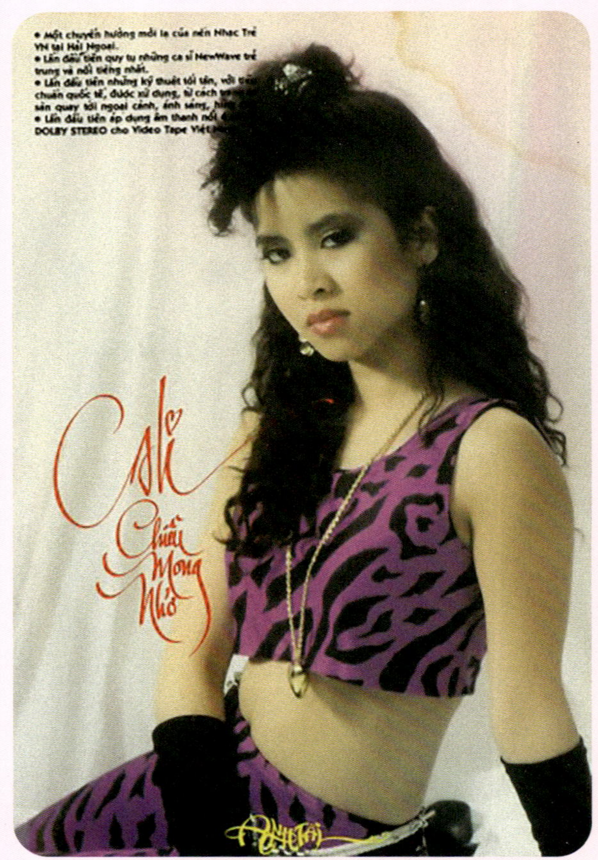

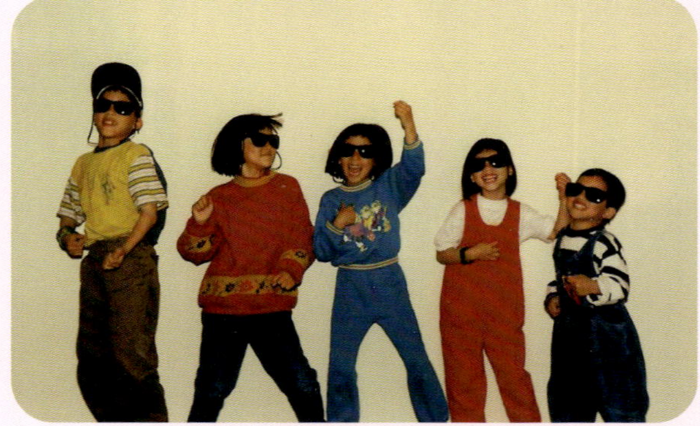

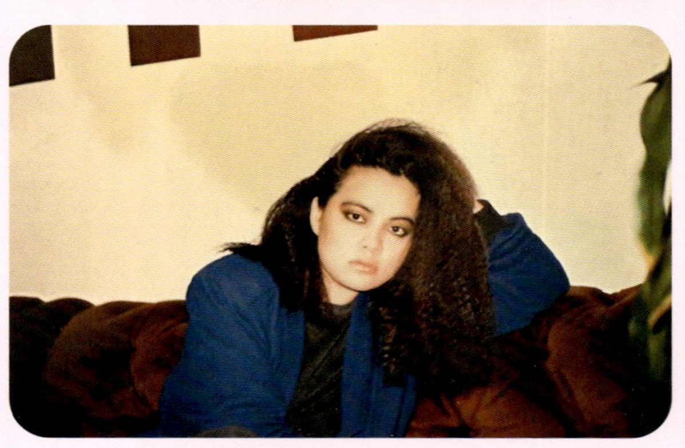

Top: New Wave cassette tape. Center and below: Community photos provided by Quynh-Mi Mimi Walker, circa 1980s.

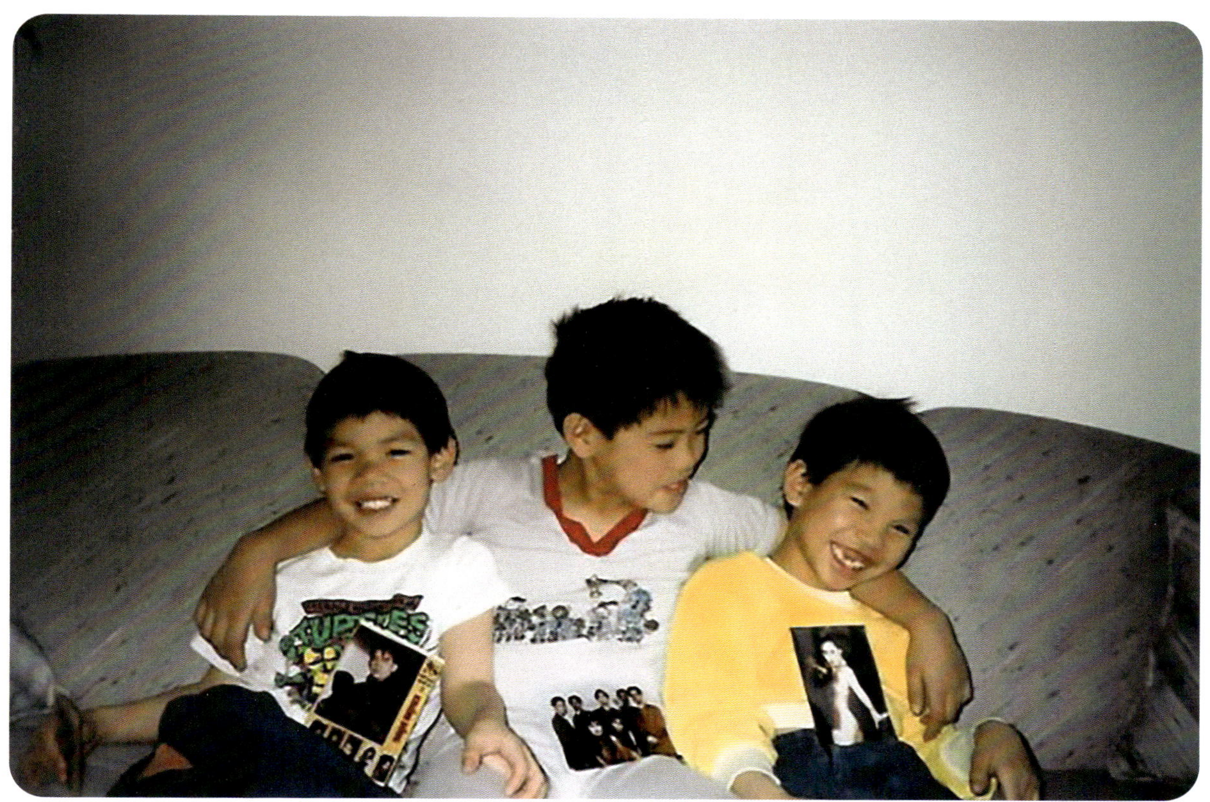

My parents would often host dance parties in our empty, unfinished basement with friends and family from all over the state of Colorado. As proud new owners of a brand new home in the 1980s, this was a sign of success for them. A family friend would bring a disco ball and they would play New Wave mixtapes they created and dance to Vietnamese renditions of Modern Talking and C.C. Catch songs. On weekends they would leave my brothers and I at my aunt's house and would go "nhay dam" into the wee hours of the early morning. I distinctly remember them coming home to kiss us goodnight while we were sleeping, reeking of smoke and alcohol. In hindsight, my parents met at a night club and I believe their nights out were an escape from having to become adults and having families so early in their lives. Why else would all the parents leave us kids at home to fend for ourselves?

A family friend took this photo after their night out. I'm pictured here in the yellow sweater with my cousin and little brother, with photos of the performing artists from the night before. I was obsessed with Lynda Trang Đài, so our family friend got me an autographed photo and a bracelet that Lynda had thrown out into the audience. For my fifth birthday, my aunt gifted me a copy of Anh Tài's Cali Chieu Mong Nho VHS tape, and for me, this was the epitome of Vietnamese New Wave music. I would rewatch it over and over until the tape wore out and turned to static, especially Lynda Trang Đài's video for "Burning Up." As a kid, I would mimic her every move and reenact the video. When I think about it, it was very expressive and sexual and probably helped me express my own sexuality and identity. If you ask any gay guy who his female idol was when they were young, they would probably say Madonna but for me, it was Linda Trang Đài. I still listen to Vietnamese New Wave today, it connects me to my parents and brings me back to my childhood when my worries were far away.

– Mitchell Dao

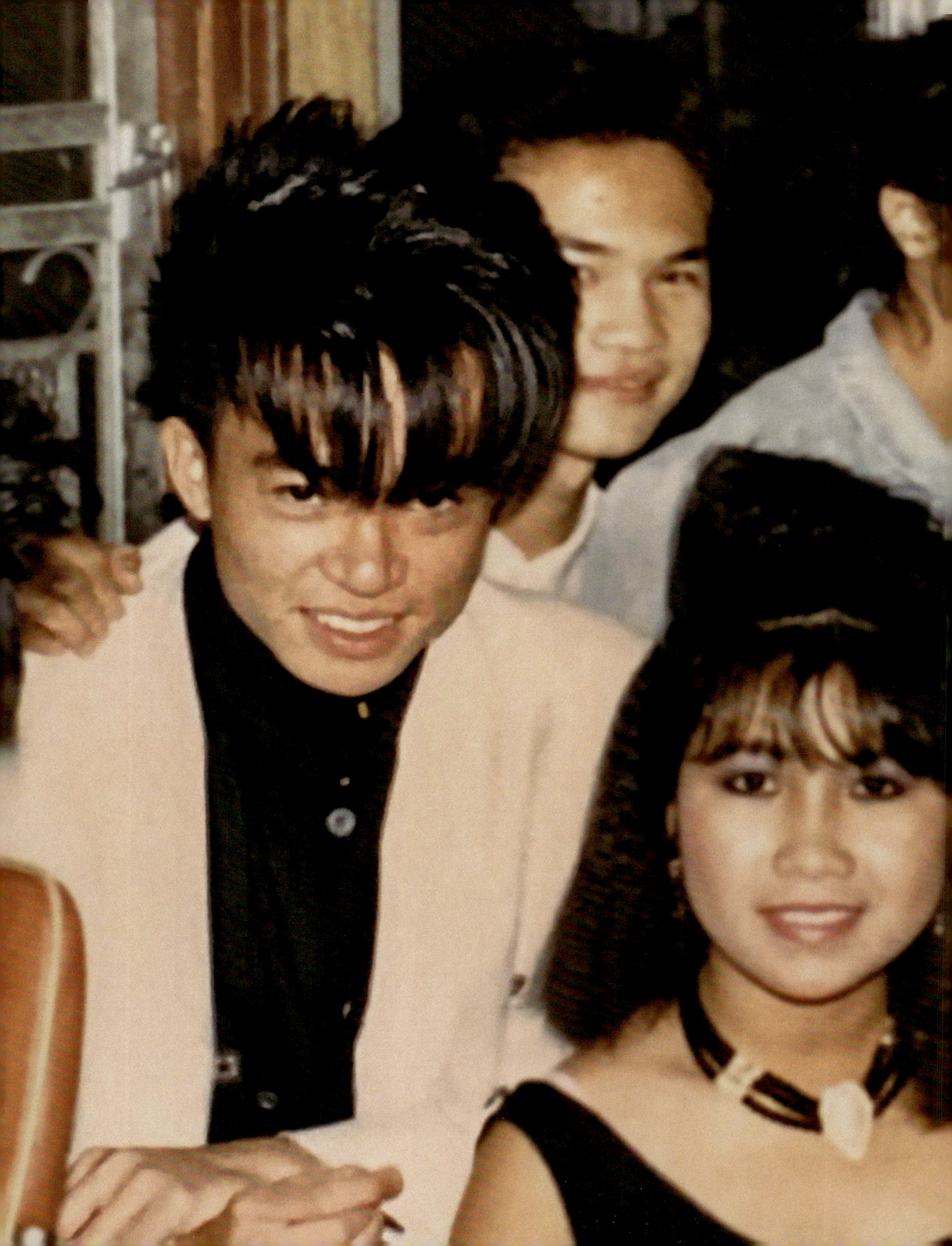

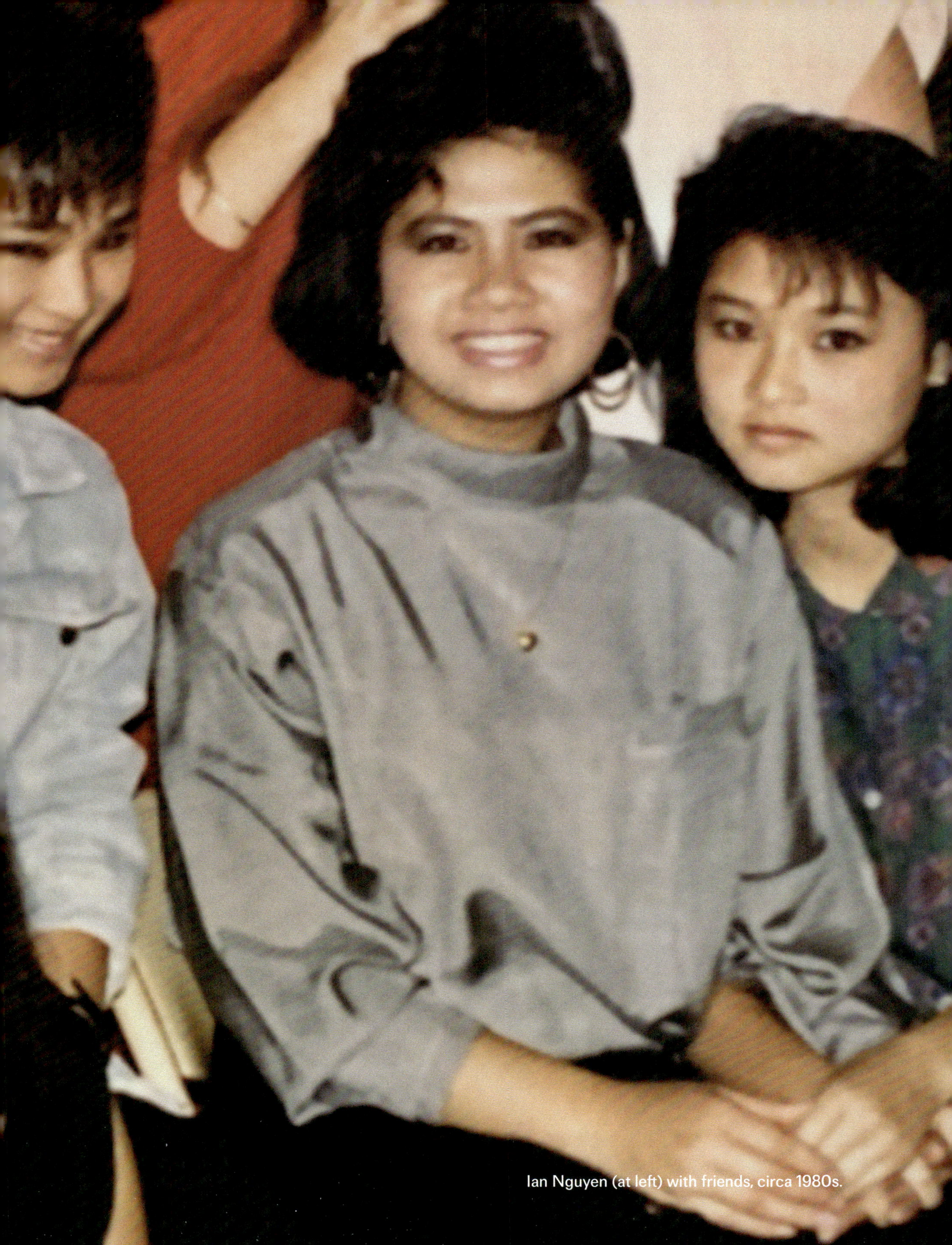

Ian Nguyen (at left) with friends, circa 1980s.

Giáng Ngọc 25 TOP NEW WAVE

Tiếng hát Lynda Trang Đài
TOP NEW WAVE

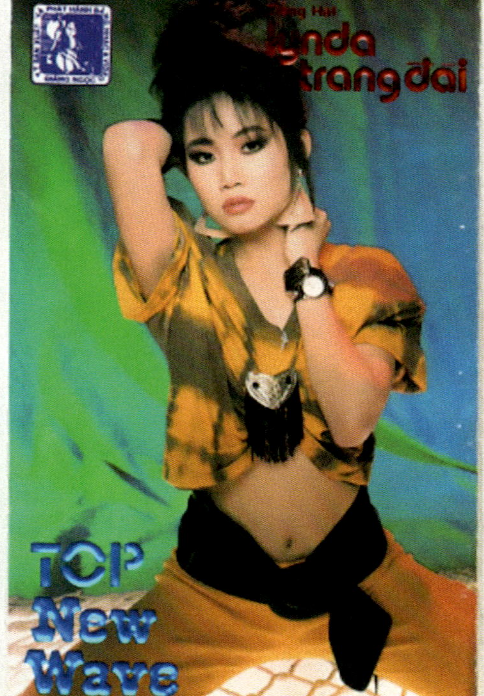

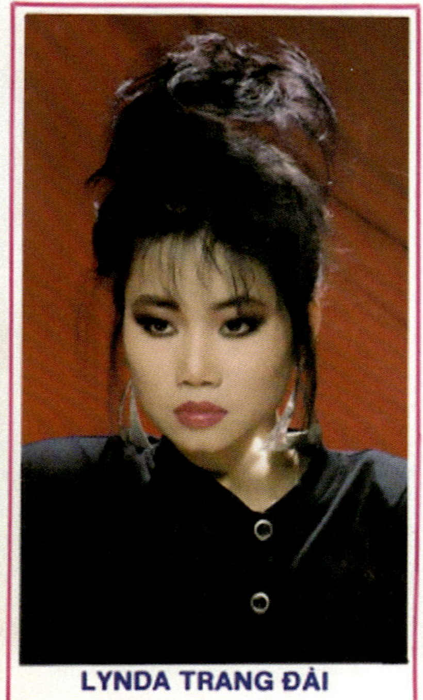

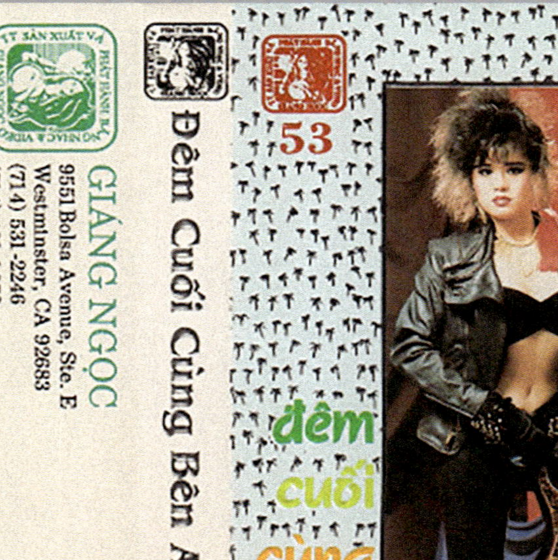

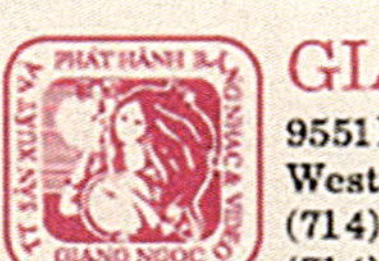

GIÁNG NGỌC
9551 Bolsa Avenue, Ste. E
Westminster, CA 92683
(714) 531-2246
(714) 491-1672

- Giáng Ngọc 32: *Heartflash Tonight*
- Giáng Ngọc 33: *Sao Rơi Trên Biển*
- Giáng Ngọc 34: *Chiều Lá Đổ*
- Giáng Ngọc 35: *Hoa Biển*
- Giáng Ngọc 36: *Magic For Love*
- Giáng Ngọc 37: *Nguyệt Ánh & Việt Dzũng*
- Giáng Ngọc 38: *Ngọc Lan 2 (Người Yêu Dấu)*
- Giáng Ngọc 39: *Bên Nhau Ngày Vui*
- Giáng Ngọc 40: *Tình Yêu Ơi Tình Yêu*
- Giáng Ngọc 41: *Lady Lai (New Wave)*
- Giáng Ngọc 42: *Điệu Buồn Dang Dở*
- Giáng Ngọc 43: *Chiều Vàng (nhạc tiền chiến)*
- Giáng Ngọc 44: *Chiều Trên Đồi Thông*
- Giáng Ngọc 45: *Tuấn Vũ 3 (gặp nhau)*
- Giáng Ngọc 46: *Xuân Hợp Mặt*
- Giáng Ngọc 47: *Hờn Trinh Nữ 2*
- Giáng Ngọc 48: *Phượng Mai - Tuấn Vũ*
- Giáng Ngọc 49: *China Boy (Trung Nghĩa New Wave 3)*
- Giáng Ngọc 50: *Cay Đắng Bờ Môi*
- Giáng Ngọc 51: *Những Ngày Thơ Mộng*
- Giáng Ngọc 52: *Tình Ngoại Ô*
- Giáng Ngọc 53: *Đêm Cuối Cùng Bên Anh*
- Giáng Ngọc 54: *Tiếng Hát Khói Sương*

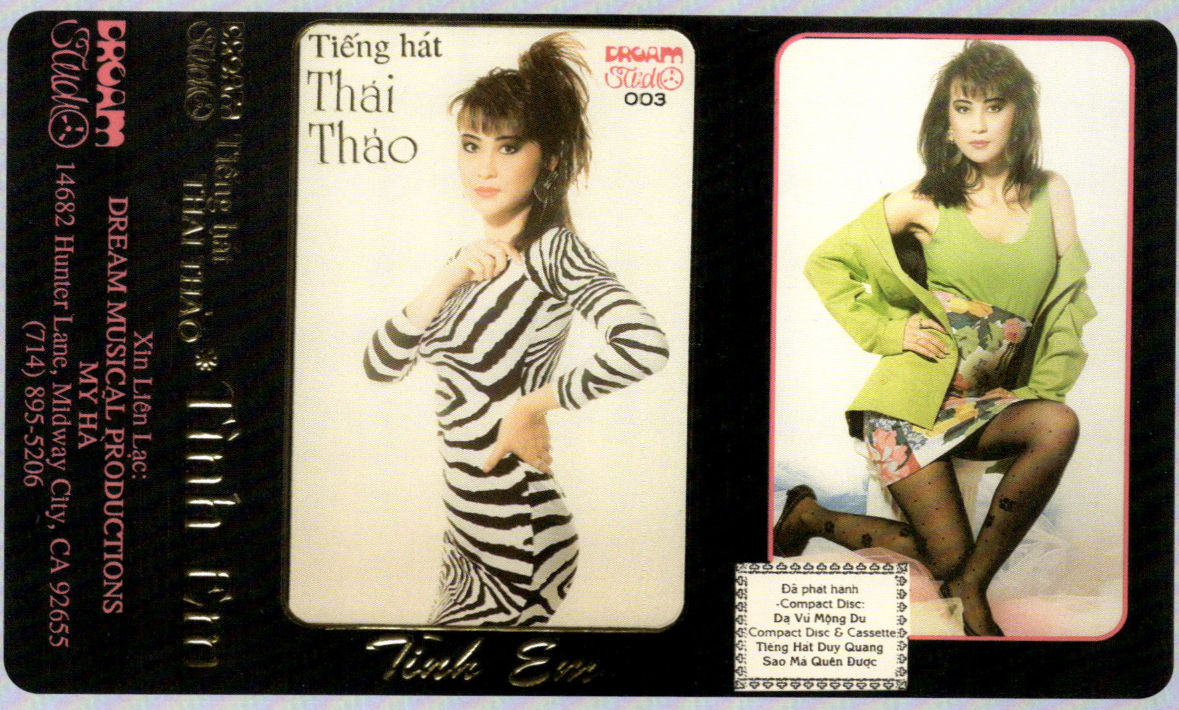

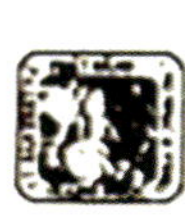

GIÁNG NGỌC 67

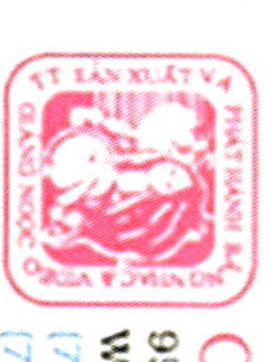

GIÁNG NGỌC
9551Bolsa Avenue, Ste. E
Westminster, CA 92683
(714) 531-2246
(714) 491-1672

Nhạc Tình Mùa Thu

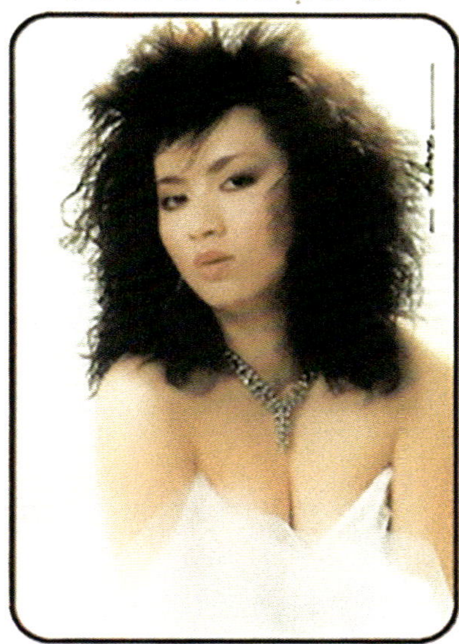

nhạc tình Mùa Thu

67

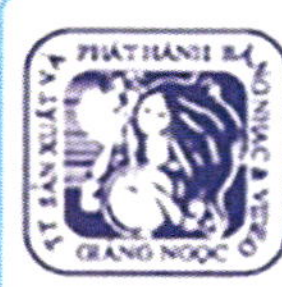

GIÁNG NGỌC
9551Bolsa Avenue, Ste. E
Westminster, CA 92683
(714) 531-2246
(714) 491-1672

- Giáng Ngọc 49: China Boy (Trung Nghĩa New Wave 3)
- Giáng Ngọc 50: Cay Đắng Bờ Môi (Hương Lan, Thanh Phong, Thanh Tuyền)
- Giáng Ngọc 51: Những Ngày Thơ Mộng
- Giáng Ngọc 52: Tình Ngoại Ô (Giao Linh, Tuấn Anh, Tuấn Vũ)
- Giáng Ngọc 53: Đêm Cuối Cùng Bên Anh
- Giáng Ngọc 54: Tiếng Hát Khổi Sương
- Giáng Ngọc 55: Đôi Mắt Người Xưa Giao Linh & Tuấn Vũ
- Giáng Ngọc 56: Ngọc Lan 3 (L'amour - Tình Ta)
- Giáng Ngọc 57: Magic 3 (Still Loving You)
- Giáng Ngọc 58: Thuyền Viễn Xứ (Tiếng hát Lệ Thu)
- Giáng Ngọc 59: Red Summer (New Wave Hè 88)
- Giáng Ngọc 60: Trúc Đào (Tiếng hát Phượng Mai)
- Giáng Ngọc 61: Hận Tình Trong Mưa (Phượng Mai, Tuấn Anh, Tuấn Vũ)
- Giáng Ngọc 62: Ngỏ Ý (Giao Linh, Tuấn Vũ, Anh Vũ)
- Giáng Ngọc 63: Từ Ngày Yêu Em
- Giáng Ngọc 64: Nắng Thủy Tinh
- Giáng Ngọc 65: Như Một Nụ Hồng
- Giáng Ngọc 66: Giao Linh - Phượng Mai
- Giáng Ngọc 67: Nhạc Tình Mùa Thu

New Wave cassette covers, 1980s.

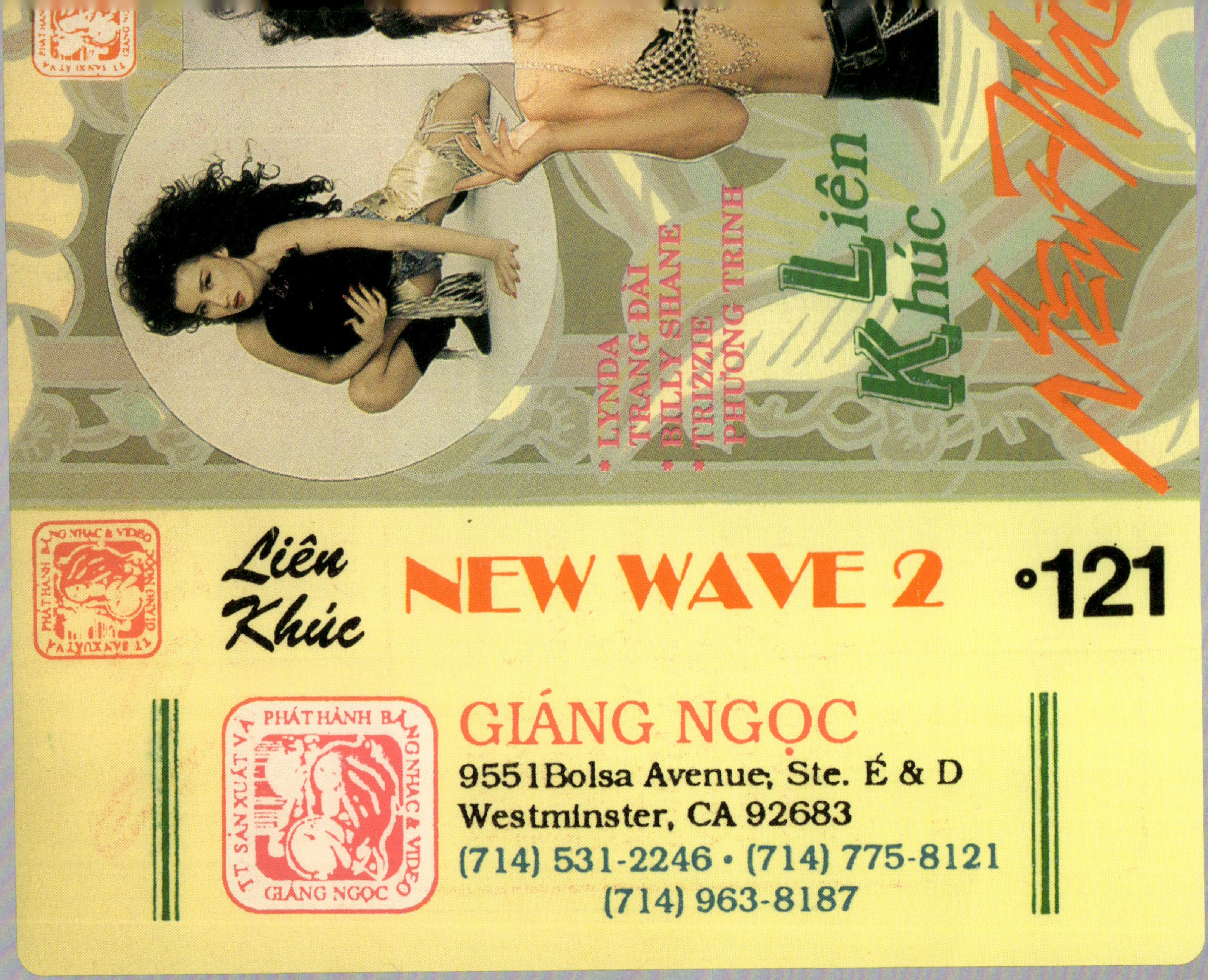

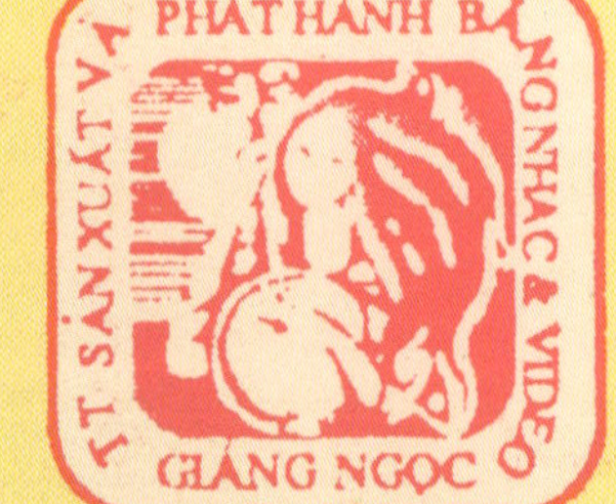

* LYNDA
TRANG ĐÀI
* BILLY SHANE
* TRIZZIE
PHƯƠNG TRINH

Liên Khúc

New Wa

Liên Khúc

NEW WAVE 2

•121

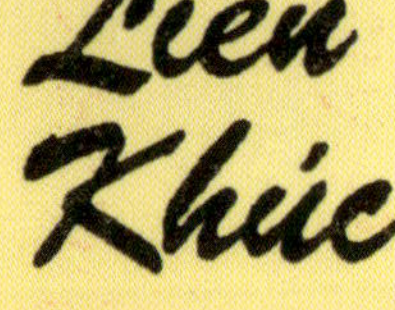

GIÁNG NGỌC
9551Bolsa Avenue, Ste. É & D
Westminster, CA 92683
(714) 531-2246 • (714) 775-8121
(714) 963-8187

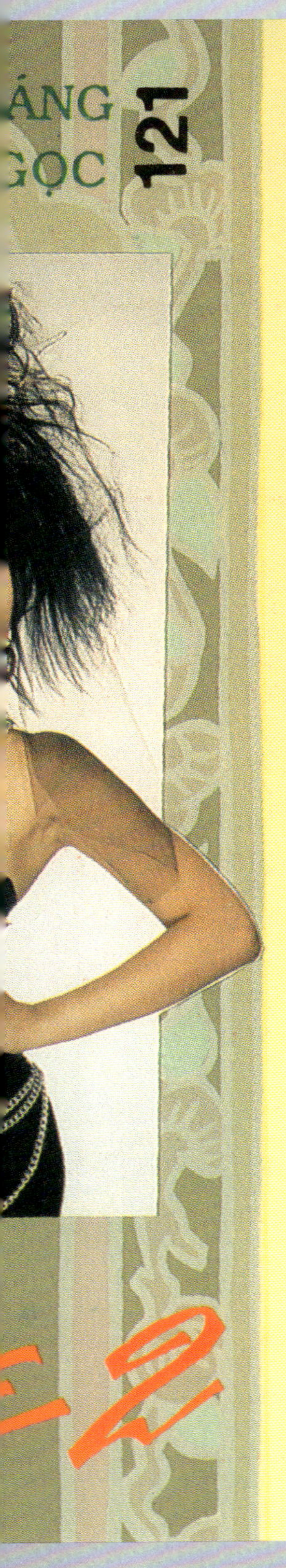

GIÁNG NGỌC

9551 Bolsa Avenue, Ste. E&D
Westminster, CA.92683
(714) 531-2246 (714) 775-8121
(714) 963-8781 & 1-800-266-3741

Giáng Ngọc 096: *Crazy For You*
Giáng Ngọc 097: *Tình Sầu Biên Giới*
Giáng Ngọc 098: *Tôi Đi Giữa Hoàng Hôn*
Giáng Ngọc 099: *Hoa Sứ Nhà Nàng*
Giáng Ngọc 100: *Dạ Vũ Bebop Cha Cha*
Giáng Ngọc 101: *Trong Tầm Mắt Đời*
Giáng Ngọc 102: *Lost in Your Eyes*
Giáng Ngọc 103: *Mảnh Tình Thương*
Giáng Ngọc 104: *Bên Đời Hiu Quạnh*
Giáng Ngọc 105: *Nhạc hòa tấu Khiêu Vũ*
Giáng Ngọc 106: *Thiên Trang Đặc Biệt*
Giáng Ngọc 107: *Hãy Yêu Nhau Đi*
Giáng Ngọc 108: *Khúc Hát Ân Tình*
Giáng Ngọc 109: *Người Đi Qua Đời Tôi*
Giáng Ngọc 110: *Dấu Chân Kỷ Niệm*
Giáng Ngọc 111: *Dân Ca Ba Miền*
Giáng Ngọc 112: *Tình Lỡ*
Giáng Ngọc 113: *Liên Khúc Tình Ta*
Giáng Ngọc 114: *Bao Giờ Biết Tương Tư*
Giáng Ngọc 115: *Cánh Nhạn Hồi Âm*
Giáng Ngọc 116: *Trộm Nhìn Nhau*
Giáng Ngọc 117: *Liên Khúc New Wave*
Giáng Ngọc 118: *Em Đi Trong Chiều*

Lynda Trang Đài (standing) and Trizzie Phương Trinh on the cover of *New Wave 2* from Giáng Ngọc Productions.

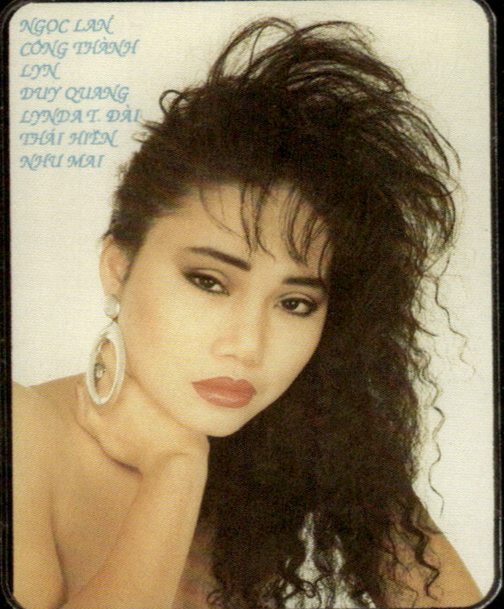
STAR ☆ PRODUCTIONS
NGỌC LAN
CÔNG THÀNH
LYN
DUY QUANG
LYNDA T. ĐÀI
THÁI HIỀN
NHƯ MAI
NÀNG TRUNG HOA XINH ĐẸP
STAR ☆ PRODUCTIONS
NÀNG TRUNG HOA XINH ĐẸP
Mọi chi tiết xin liên lạc:
STAR ☆ PRODUCTIONS
P.O. BOX 3391
Costa mesa, CA 92626
Tel: (714) 964-8529

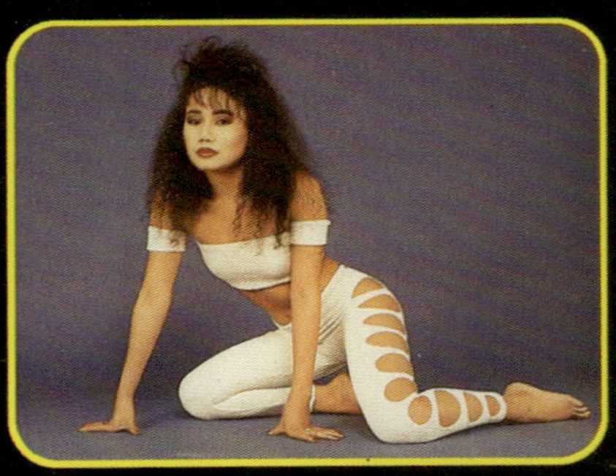
CA SĨ LYNDA TRANG ĐÀI
"UPCOMING RECORD"
CRAZY LOVE
ORIGINAL SONGS
Những nhạc khúc tuyệt vời đầu tiên được thực hiện qua hình thức dĩa nhạc của LYNDA TRANG ĐÀI (Original) Phát hành sau Tết Âm Lịch.

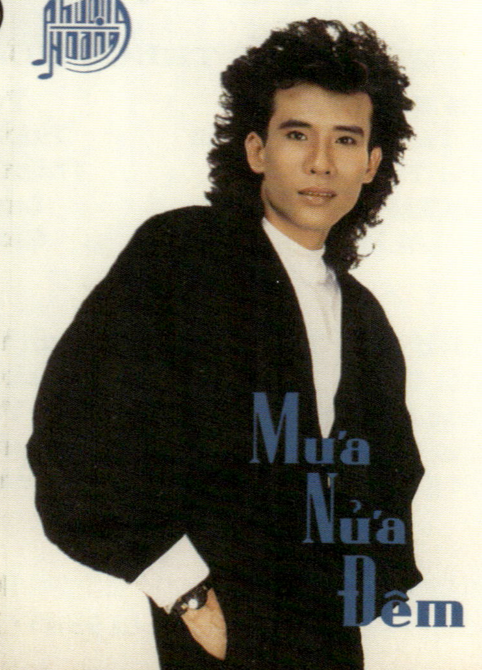
Mưa Nửa Đêm
PHƯỢNG HOÀNG 11
PHUONG HOANG PRODUCTIONS • 714-839-6481
A
Mưa Nửa Đêm
Để Trả Lời 1 Câu Hỏi
Đêm Tâm Sự
Đò Chiều
Hai Lối Mộng
B
Chiều Cuối Tuần
Thói Đời
Bông Cỏ May
Đêm Gác Trọ
Bông Nhỏ Dường Chiều
TRUNG TÂM PHÁT HÀNH BĂNG NHẠC PHƯỢNG HOÀNG
Hân Hạnh Giới Thiệu
PH1: Chuyện Tình Không Hối Tiếc
PH2: Chuyện Tình Không Suy Tư
PH3: Ai Lên Xứ Hoa Đào
PH4: Giao Linh: Tâm Sự Với Anh
PH5: Dạ Vũ Phượng Hoàng
PH6: Người Mang Thương Nhớ
PH7: Tình Khúc Đổ Lễ
PH8: Điệp Khúc Thương Dau
PH9: Nắng Xanh
PH10: Hai Âu Phi Xứ
PH11: Mưa Nửa Đêm
PH12: Chuyện Chúng Mình
PH13: Phượng Hoàng Xuân
PH14: Quê Hương Mời Gọi
PH15: Tuấn Vũ 90: Yêu 1 Mình
PH16: Kiều Nga 90: Những Nụ Tình Xanh (Tous Les Garcons Et Les Filles)
PH17: Tuấn Vũ: Tiếng Hát Đế Dời
PH18: Dạ Vũ Đêm Hoa Đăng
PH19: Thương Hoài Ngàn Năm

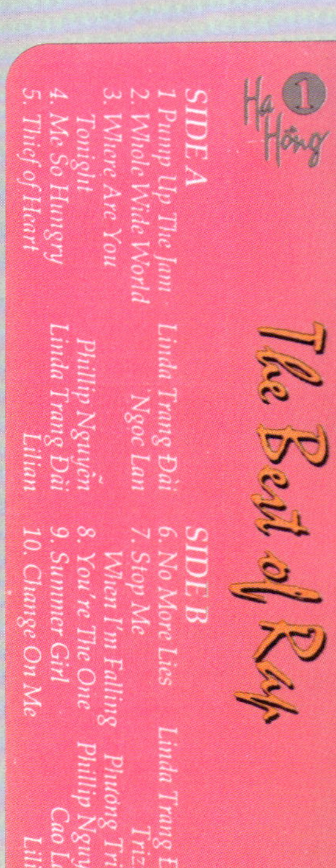

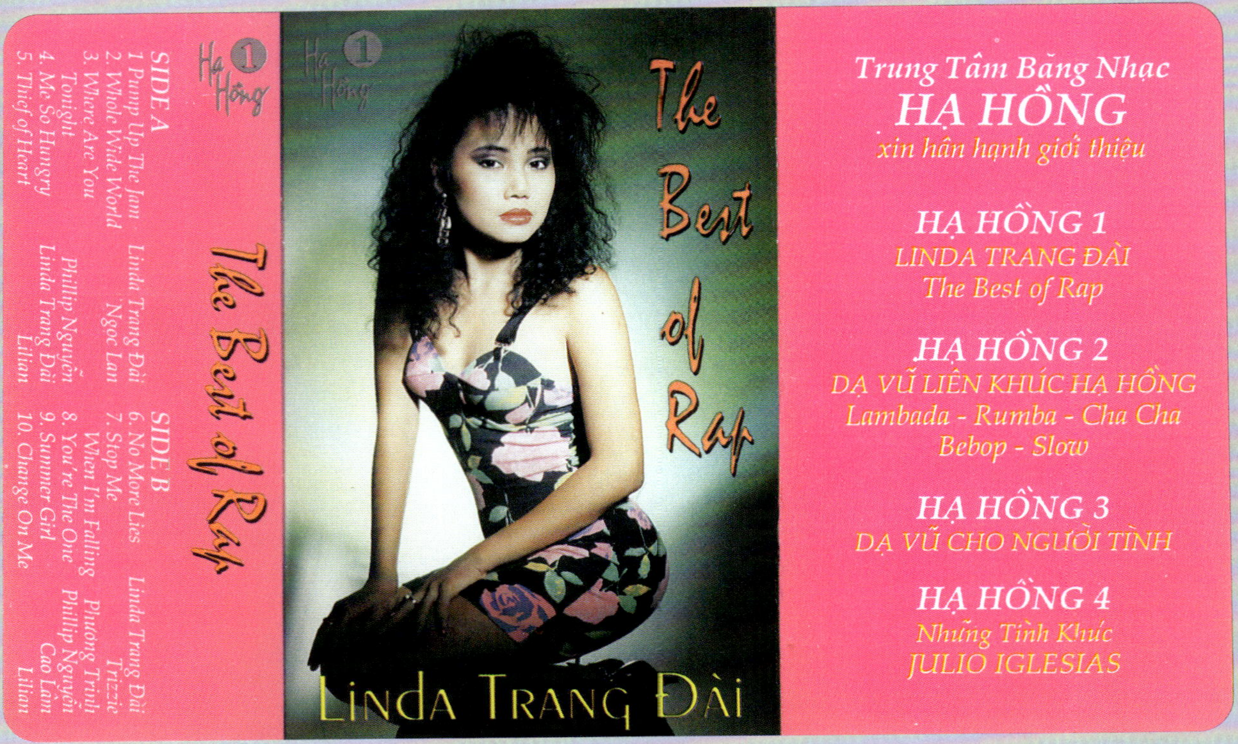

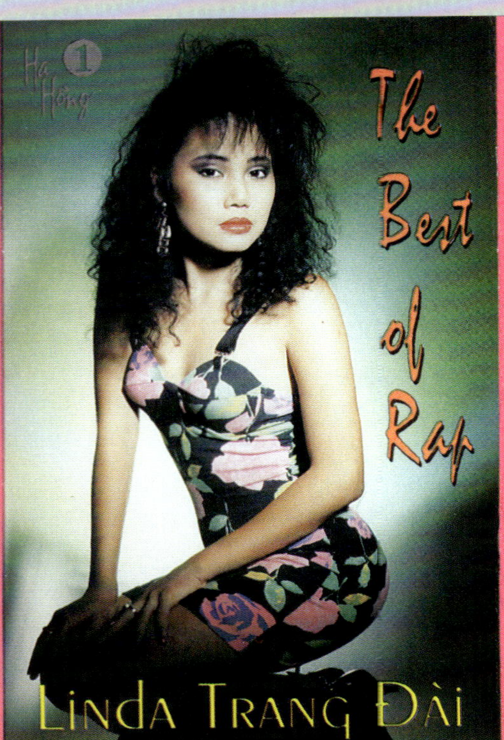

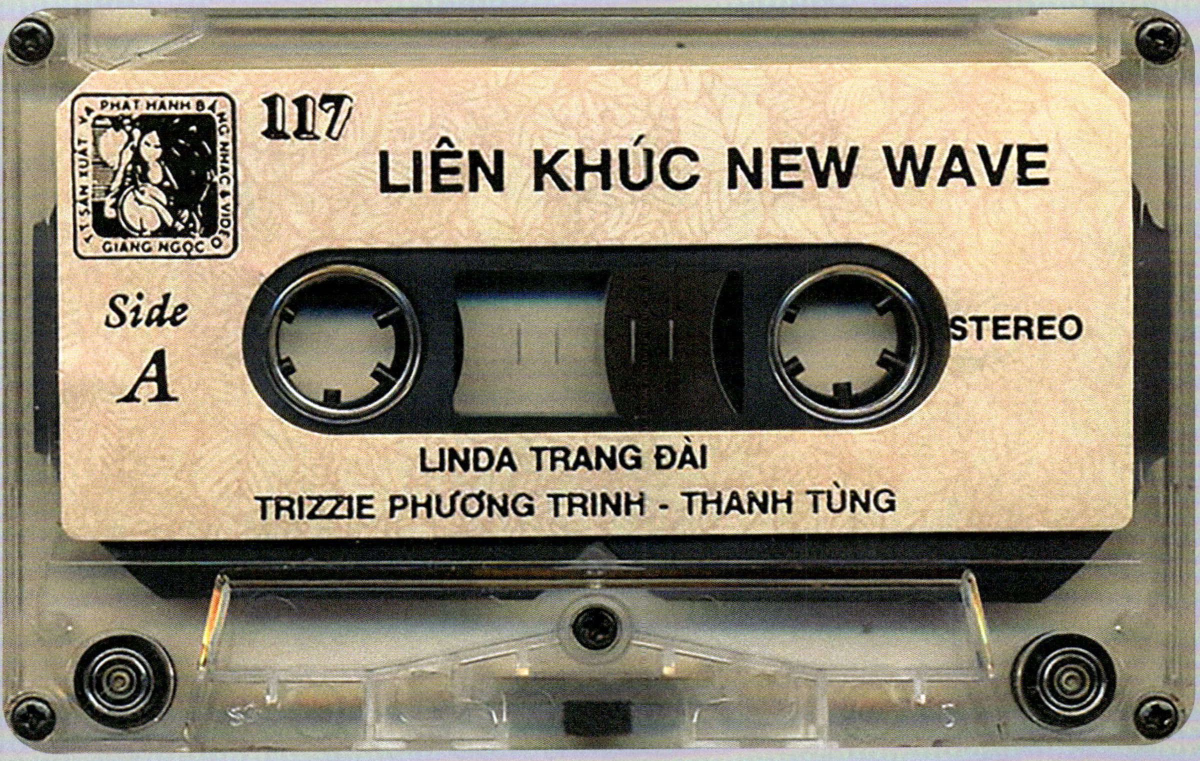

New Wave cassette and covers, 1980s.

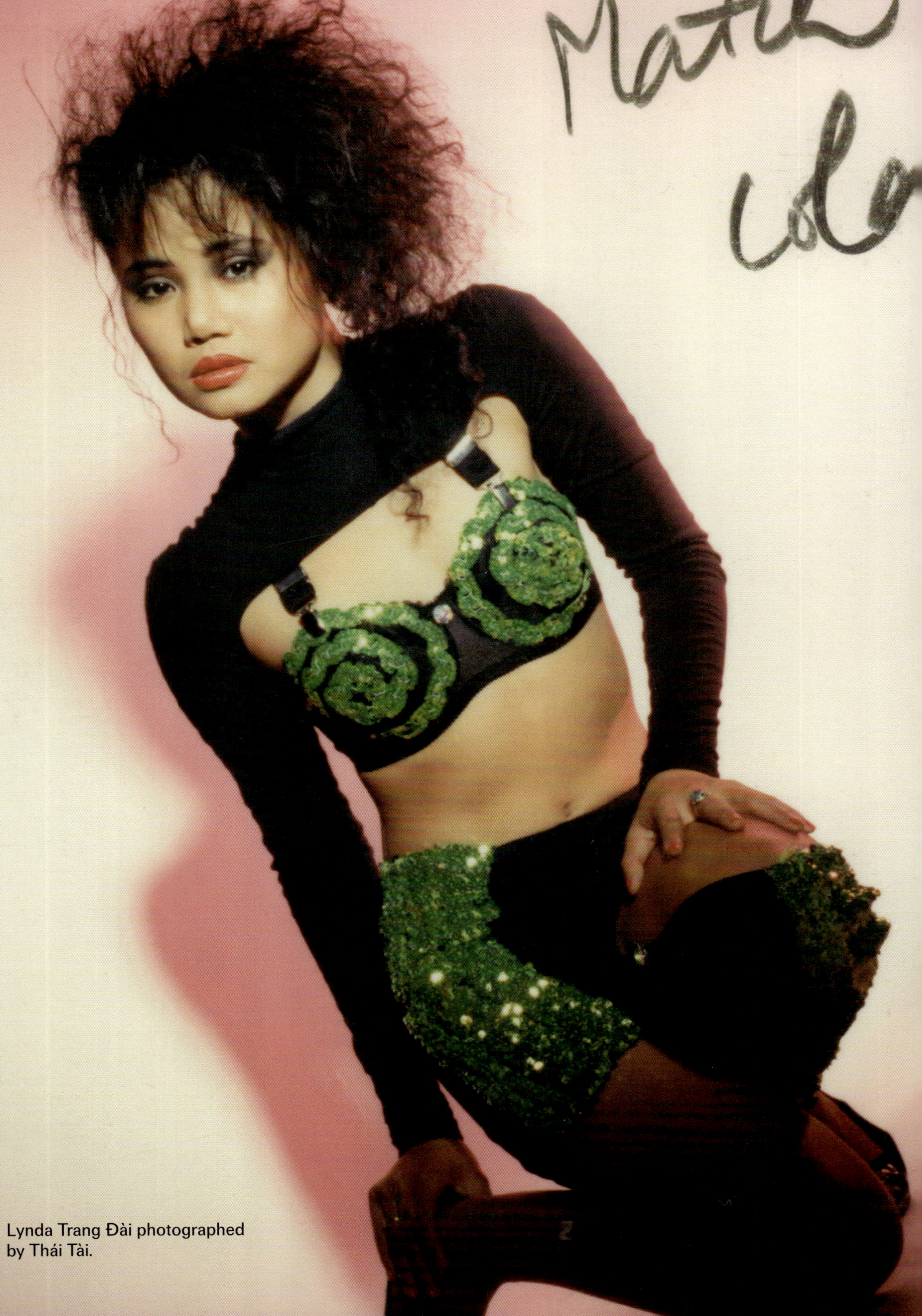

Lynda Trang Đài photographed by Thái Tài.

THE BIRTH OF NEW WAVE

The birth of New Wave music marked a pivotal moment for Vietnamese American youth in the 1980s. This genre, characterized by its eclectic mix of electronic beats and futuristic sounds, sparked an explosion of curiosity and creativity among these young individuals. New Wave wasn't typically found on mainstream radio stations nor heavily featured on MTV, which predominantly showcased pop and rock from American and British bands. This scarcity made the music all the more appealing to Vietnamese American teens, who were eager to distinguish themselves from both their American peers and the traditional expectations of their immigrant community.

To satisfy their craving for Eurodisco and other New Wave sounds, these teens turned to local record shops. These stores became cultural havens where albums by artists like C.C. Catch, Modern Talking, Sandra, and Bad Boys Blue were discovered—often miscategorized under "UK New Wave" due to the lack of a specific section for this burgeoning genre. With the high cost of records, bootlegged mixtapes quickly became emblematic of the era. These compilations, meticulously curated and exchanged among friends, were more than just collections of music; they were passports to a new realm.

As New Wave music gained momentum, it fostered a unique subculture among Vietnamese American youth. Record stores flourished, offering an ever-growing selection of cassettes, CDs, and even laser disks, catering to the diverse tastes of an eager fanbase. These music hubs became the ground zero of a burgeoning youth movement, where teenagers gathered not just to buy music but to connect over shared tastes and experiences.

This era of musical exploration and identity formation through New Wave not only defined a generation but also left a lasting imprint on the cultural landscape of the Vietnamese diaspora in America. As these teens grew into adults, the echoes of New Wave continued to influence their artistic and personal expressions, cementing this genre as a defining feature of their youth and a bridge to their future.

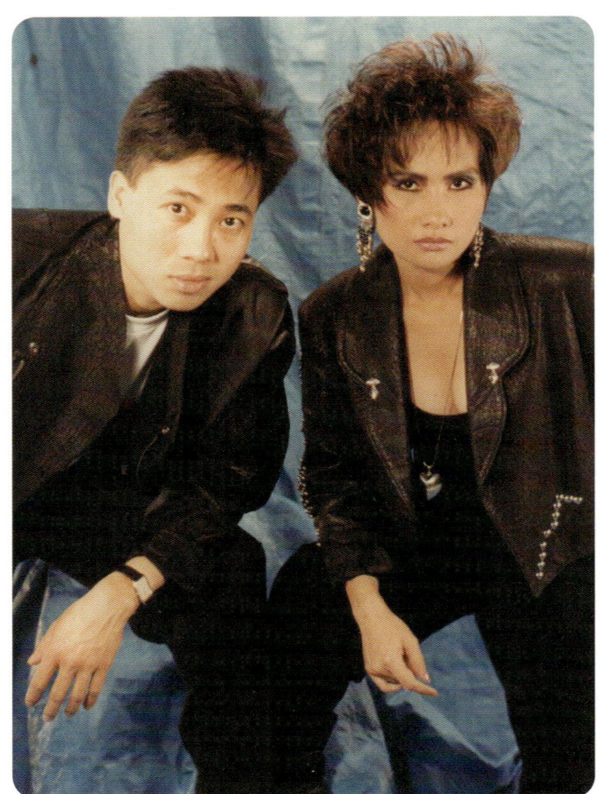

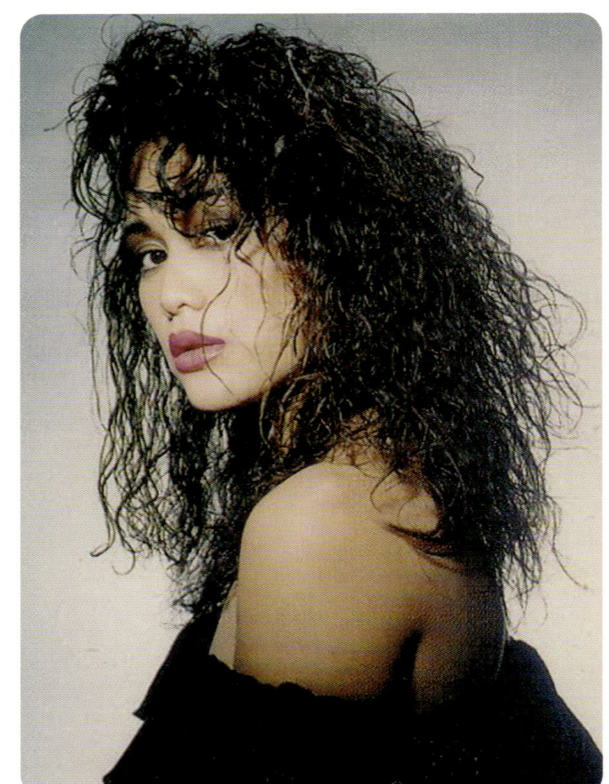

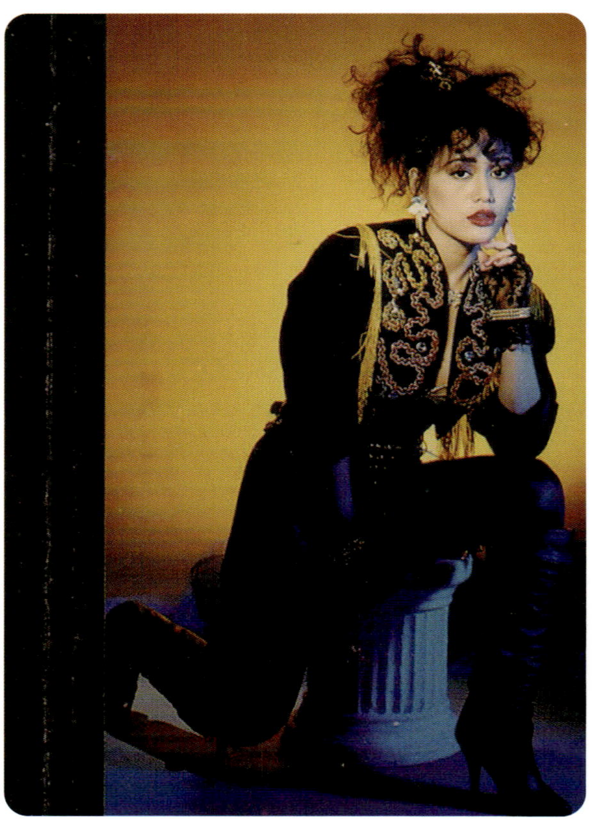

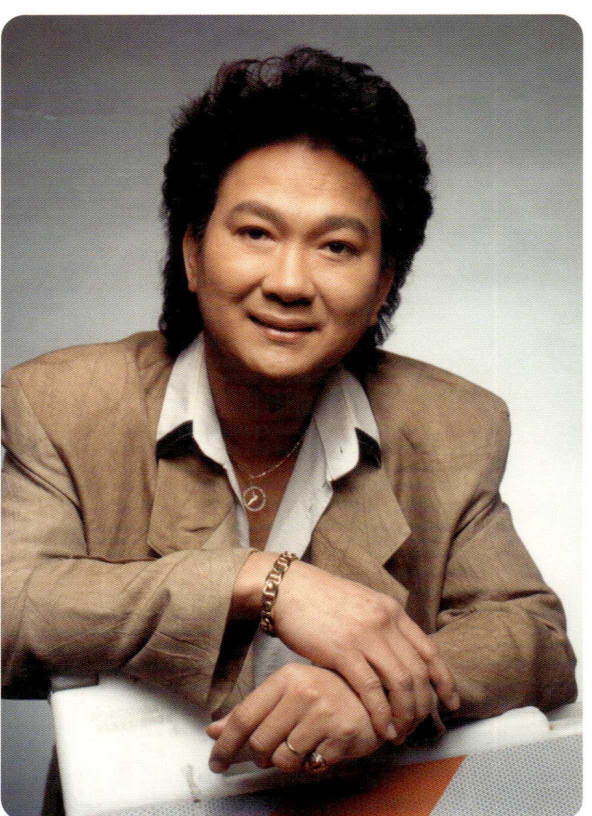

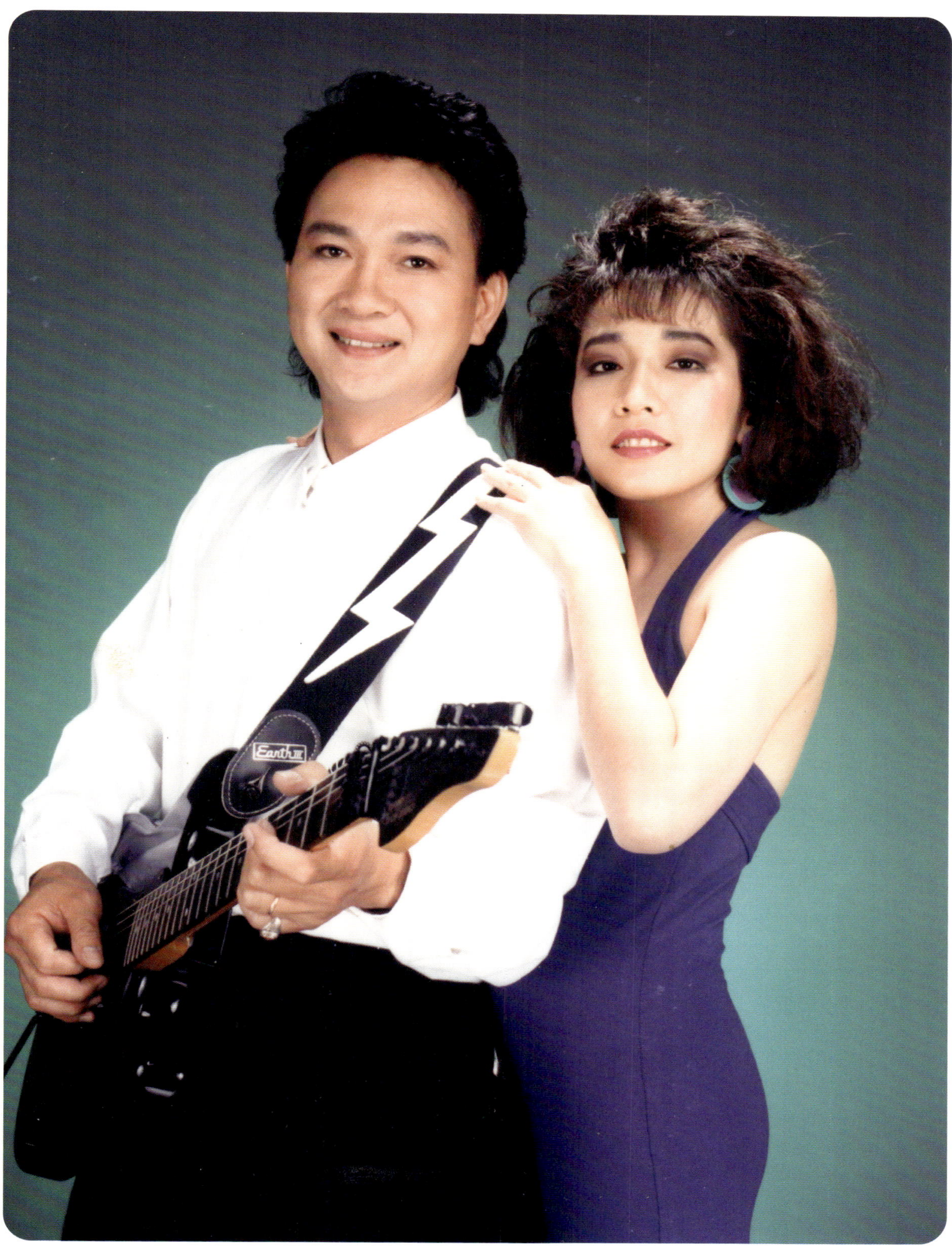

New Wave artists, photographed by Thái Tài.

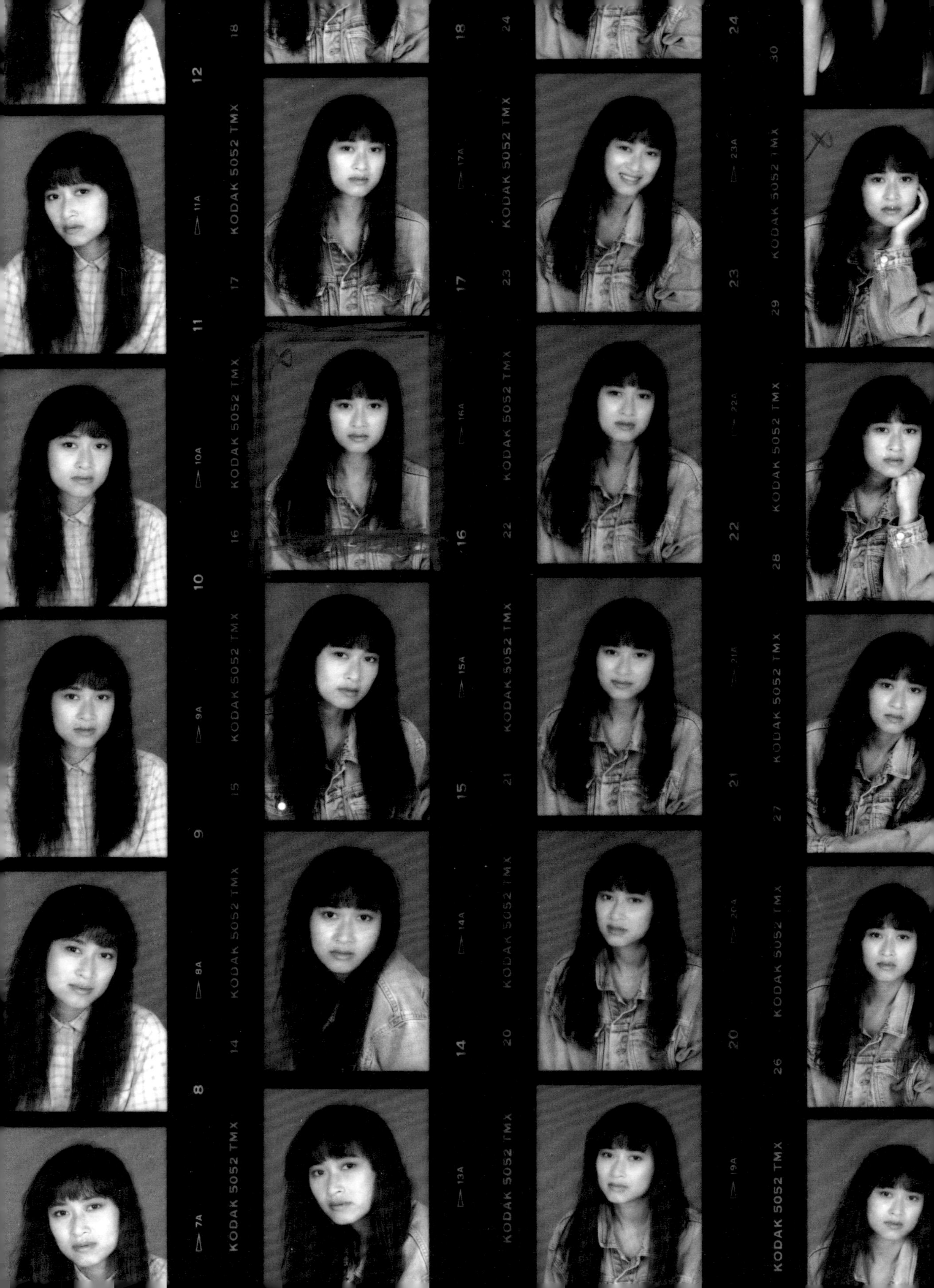

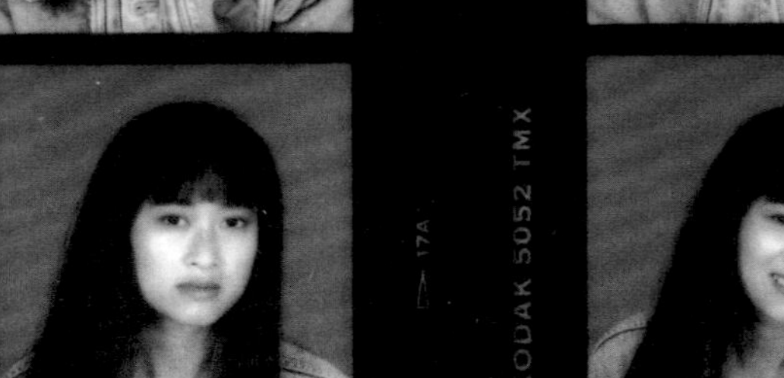
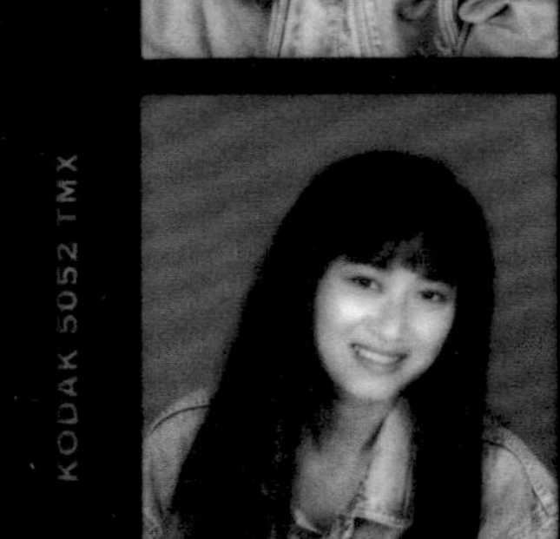
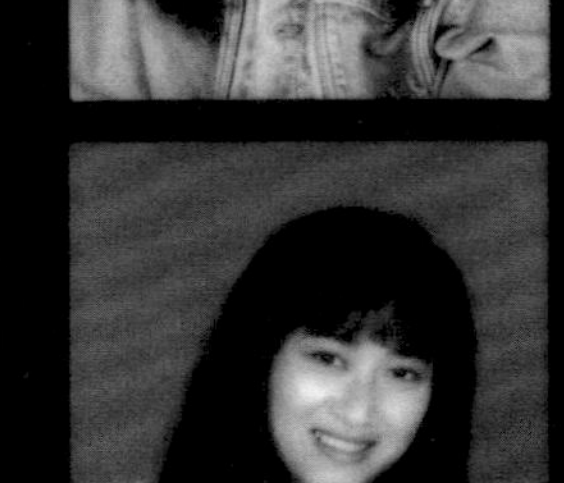

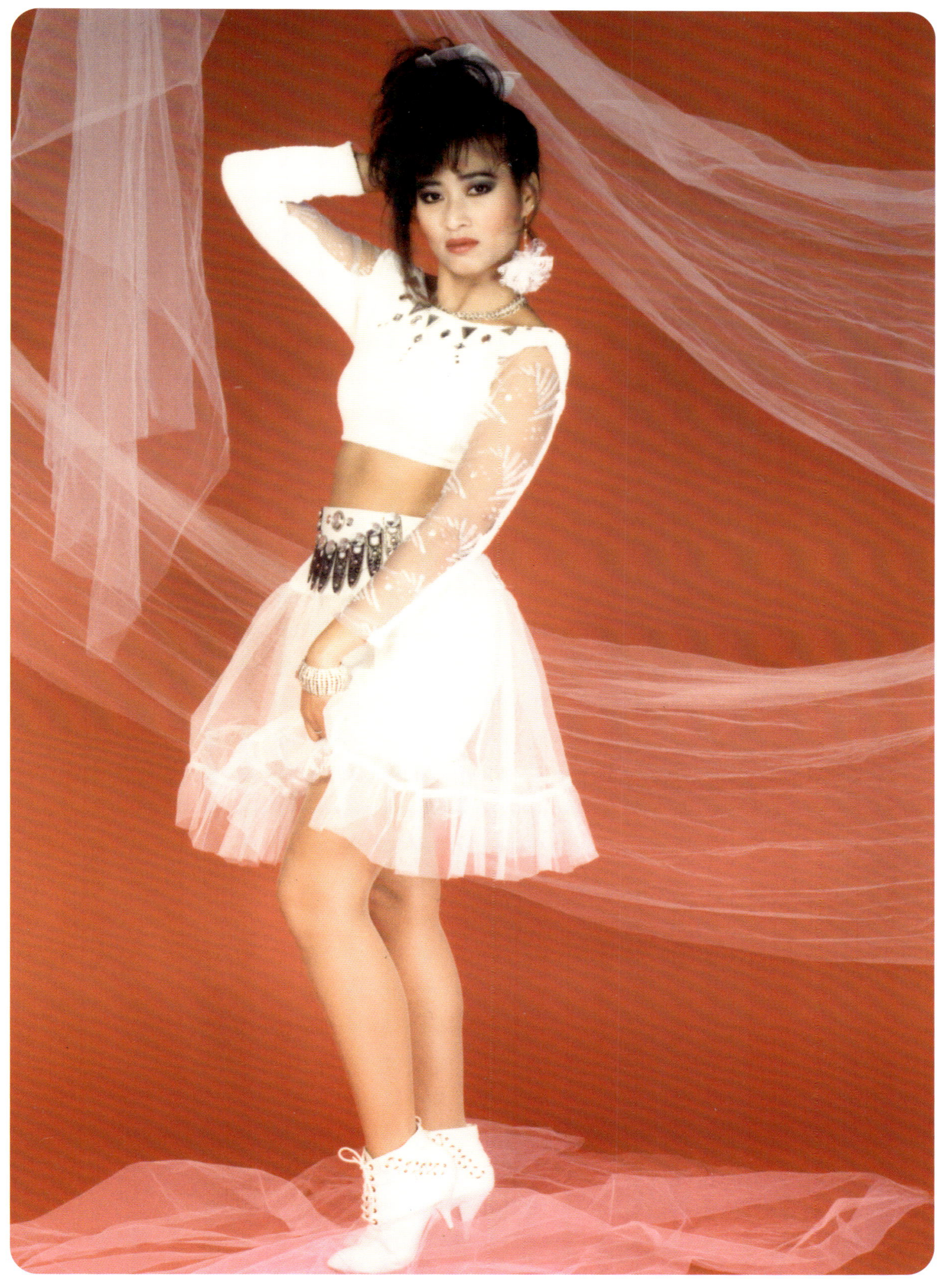

Portrait and proofs of singer Thuý Vi, photographed by Thái Tài.

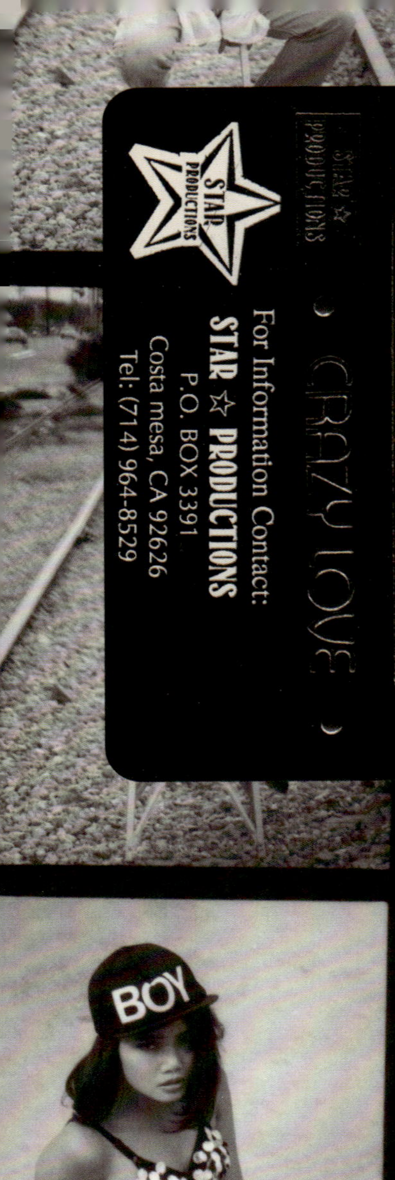

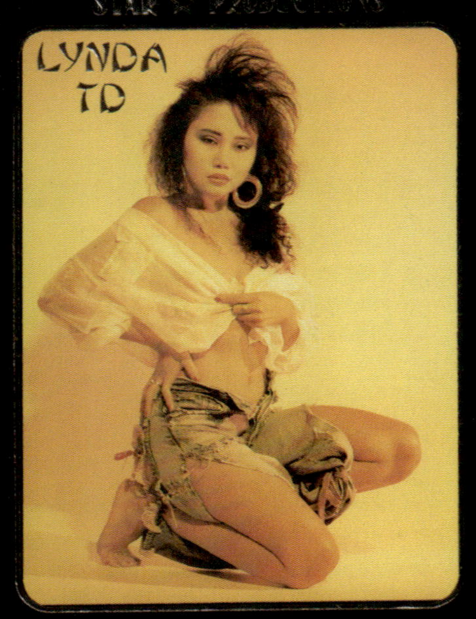

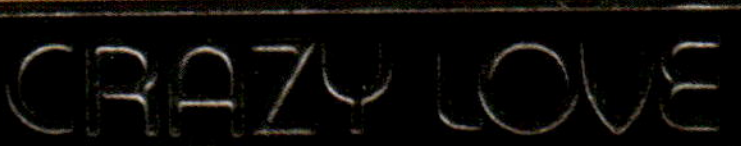

ORIGINAL SONGS

ORIGINAL SINGER

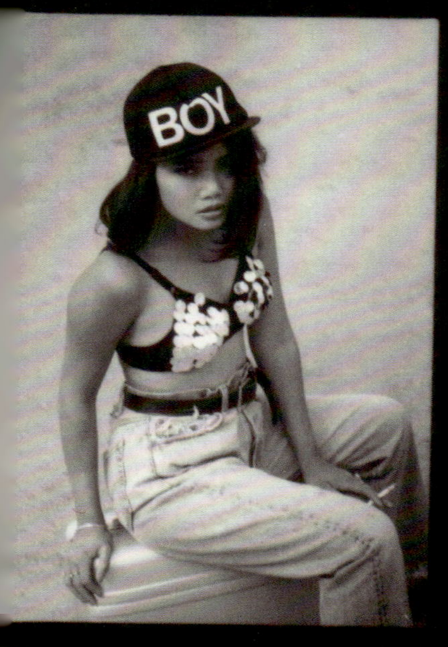

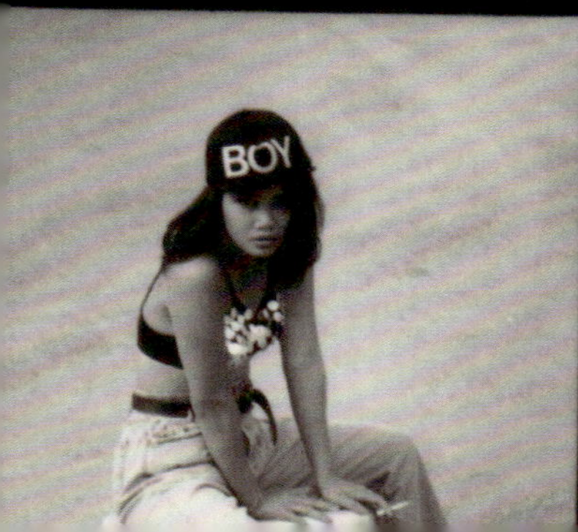

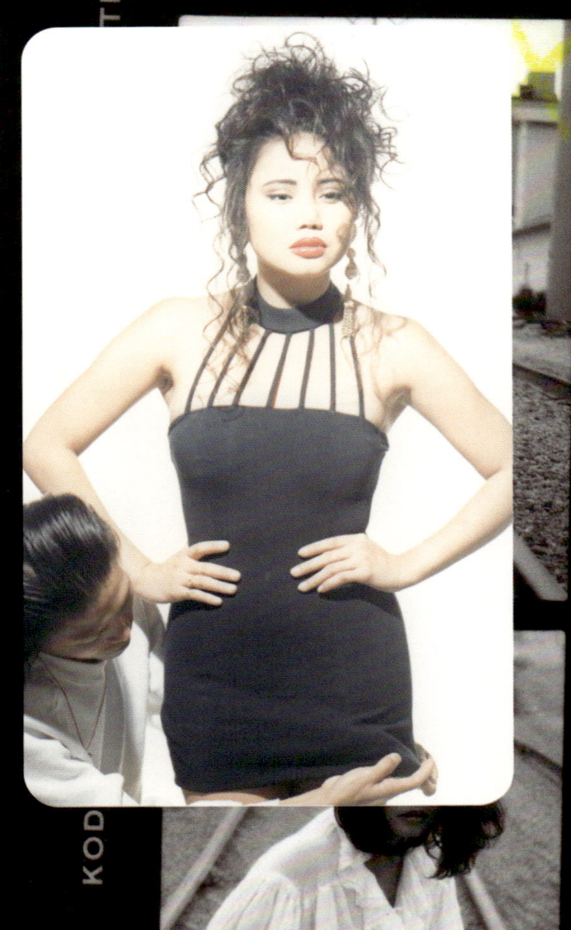

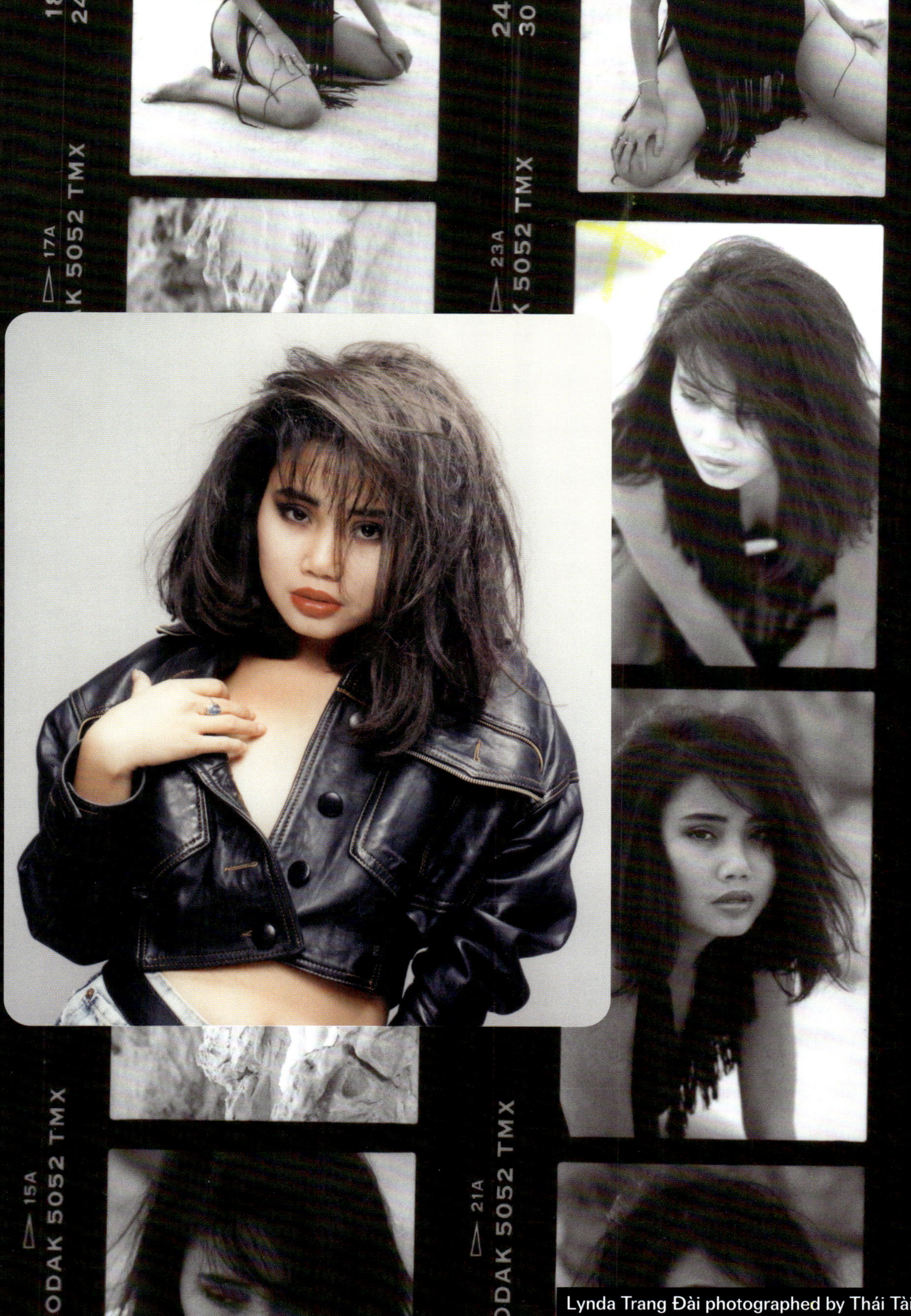

Lynda Trang Đài photographed by Thái Tài.

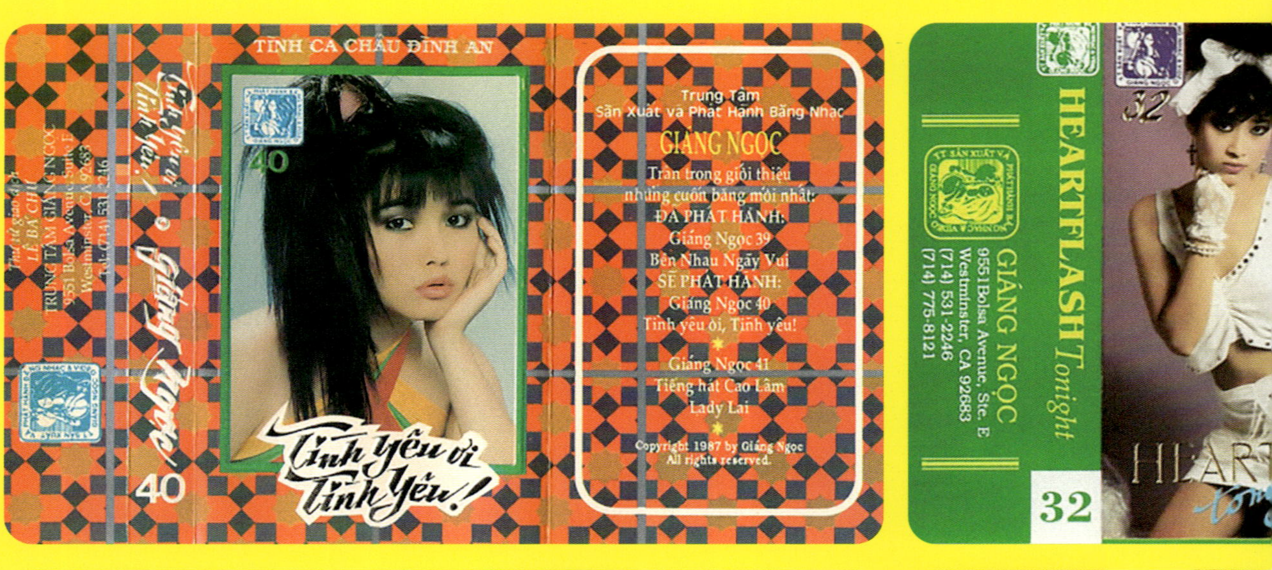

TÌNH CA CHÂU ĐÌNH AN
40
Tình yêu ơi Tình yêu!
Trung Tâm
Sản Xuất và Phát Hành Băng Nhạc
GIÁNG NGỌC
Trân trọng giới thiệu
những cuốn băng mới nhất:
ĐÃ PHÁT HÀNH:
Giáng Ngọc 39
Bên Nhau Ngày Vui
SẼ PHÁT HÀNH:
Giáng Ngọc 40
Tình yêu ơi, Tình yêu!
Giáng Ngọc 41
Tiếng hát Cao Lâm
Lady Lai
Copyright 1987 by Giáng Ngọc
All rights reserved.
HEARTFLASH Tonight
GIÁNG NGỌC
9551 Bolsa Avenue, Ste. E
Westminster, CA 92683
(714) 531-2246
(714) 775-8121
32

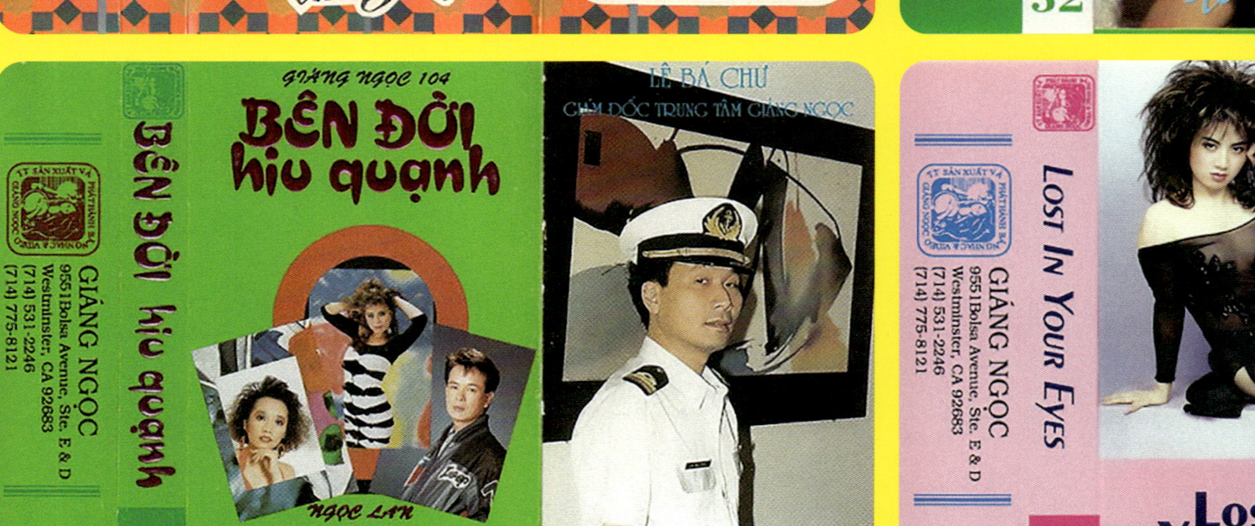

GIÁNG NGỌC 104
BÊN ĐỜI hiu quạnh
NGỌC LAN
KIỀU NGA
ĐỨC HUY
GIÁNG NGỌC
9551 Bolsa Avenue, Ste. E & D
Westminster, CA 92683
(714) 531-2246
(714) 775-8121
104
LÊ BÁ CHƯ
GIÁM ĐỐC TRUNG TÂM GIÁNG NGỌC

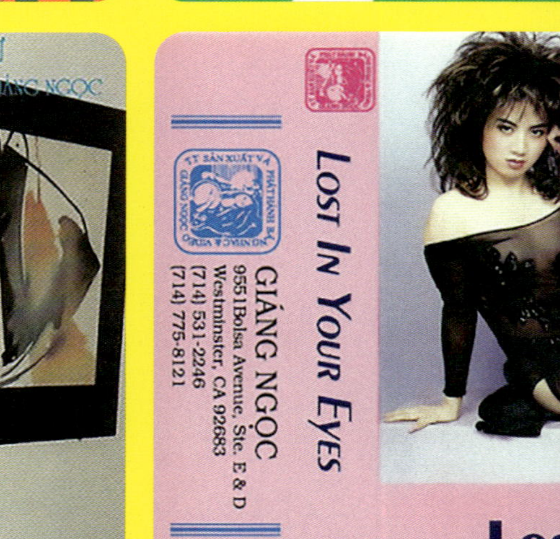

LOST IN YOUR EYES
GIÁNG NGỌC
9551 Bolsa Avenue, Ste. E & D
Westminster, CA 92683
(714) 531-2246
(714) 775-8121
102

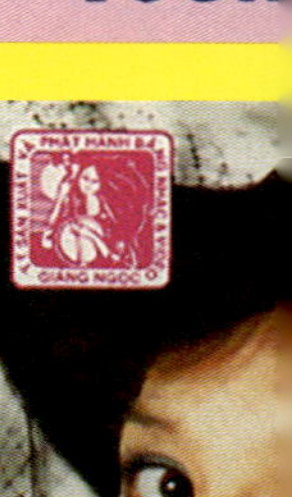

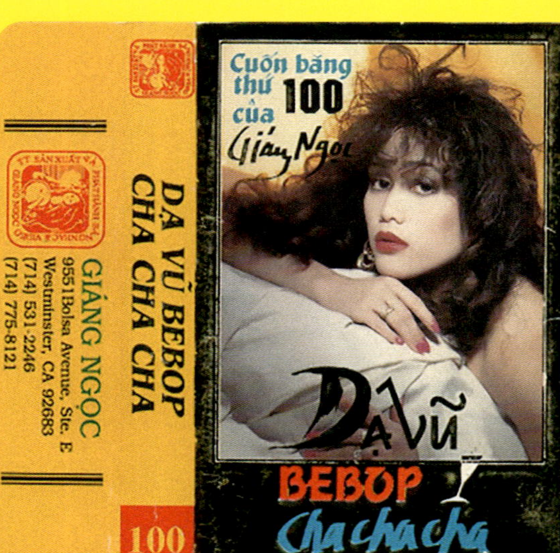

DẠ VŨ BEBOP CHA CHA CHA
GIÁNG NGỌC
9551 Bolsa Avenue, Ste. E
Westminster, CA 92683
(714) 531-2246
(714) 775-8121
100
Cuốn băng thứ 100 của Giáng Ngọc
Dạ Vũ
BEBOP
Cha cha cha

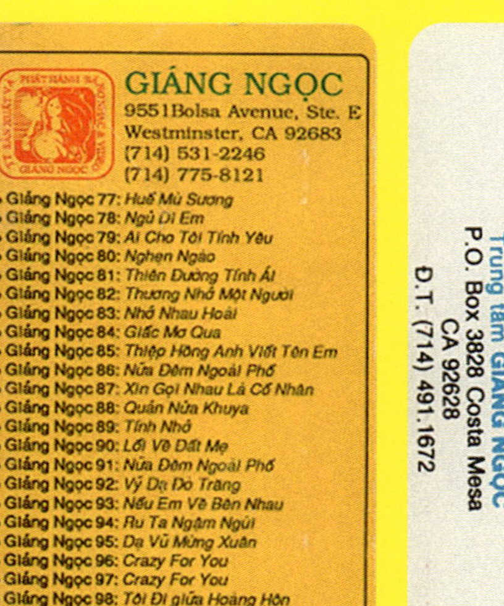

GIÁNG NGỌC
9551 Bolsa Avenue, Ste. E
Westminster, CA 92683
(714) 531-2246
(714) 775-8121
• Giáng Ngọc 77: Huế Mù Sương
• Giáng Ngọc 78: Ngủ Đi Em
• Giáng Ngọc 79: Ai Cho Tôi Tình Yêu
• Giáng Ngọc 80: Nghẹn Ngào
• Giáng Ngọc 81: Thiên Đường Tình Ái
• Giáng Ngọc 82: Thương Nhớ Một Người
• Giáng Ngọc 83: Nhớ Nhau Hoài
• Giáng Ngọc 84: Giấc Mơ Qua
• Giáng Ngọc 85: Thiệp Hồng Anh Viết Tên Em
• Giáng Ngọc 86: Nửa Đêm Ngoài Phố
• Giáng Ngọc 87: Xin Gọi Nhau Là Cố Nhân
• Giáng Ngọc 88: Quán Nửa Khuya
• Giáng Ngọc 89: Tình Nhỏ
• Giáng Ngọc 90: Lối Về Đất Mẹ
• Giáng Ngọc 91: Nửa Đêm Ngoài Phố
• Giáng Ngọc 92: Vỹ Dạ Đồ Trăng
• Giáng Ngọc 93: Nếu Em Về Bên Nhau
• Giáng Ngọc 94: Ru Ta Ngậm Ngùi
• Giáng Ngọc 95: Dạ Vũ Mừng Xuân
• Giáng Ngọc 96: Crazy For You
• Giáng Ngọc 97: Crazy For You
• Giáng Ngọc 98: Tôi Đi giữa Hoàng Hôn
• Giáng Ngọc 99: Hoa Sứ Nhà Nàng
• Giáng Ngọc 100: Dạ Vũ Bebop-Cha Cha Cha

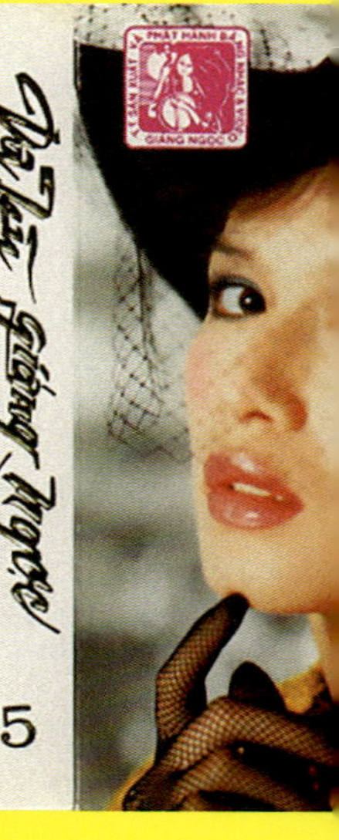

Dạ Vũ Giáng Ngọc
Thư từ giao dịch
LÊ BÁ CHƯ
Trung tâm GIÁNG NGỌC
P.O. Box 3828 Costa Mesa
CA 92628
Đ.T. (714) 491.1672
5

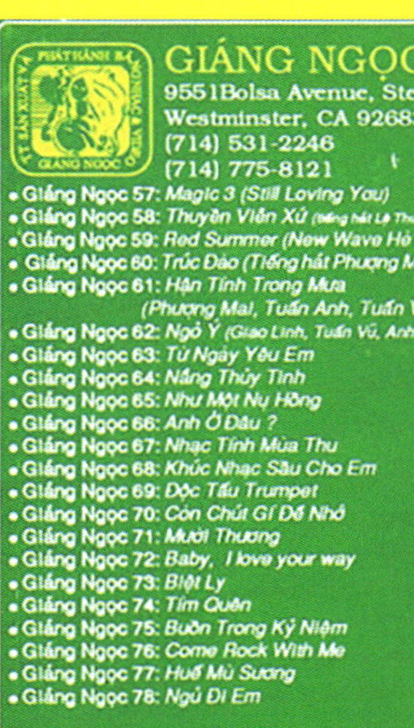

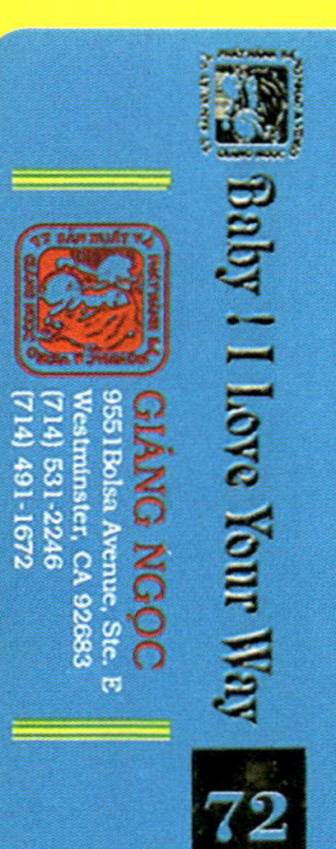

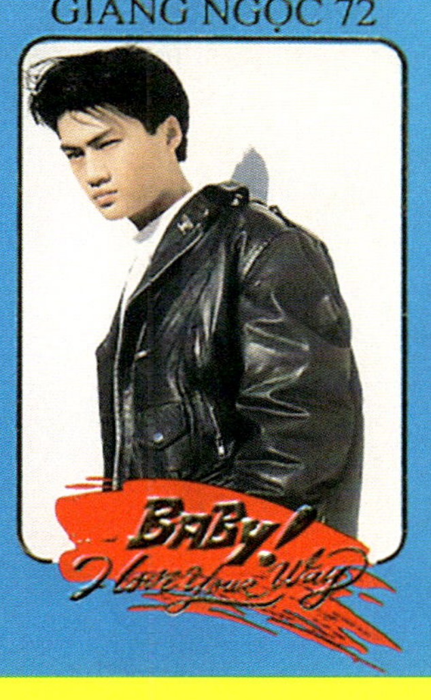

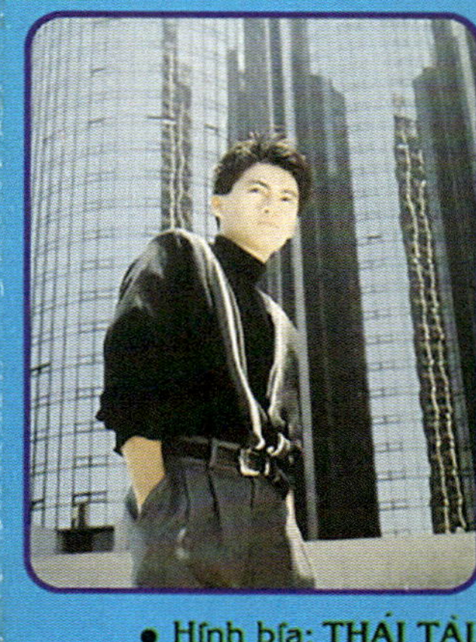

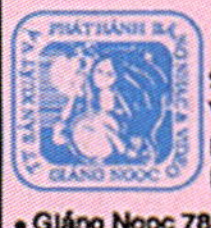

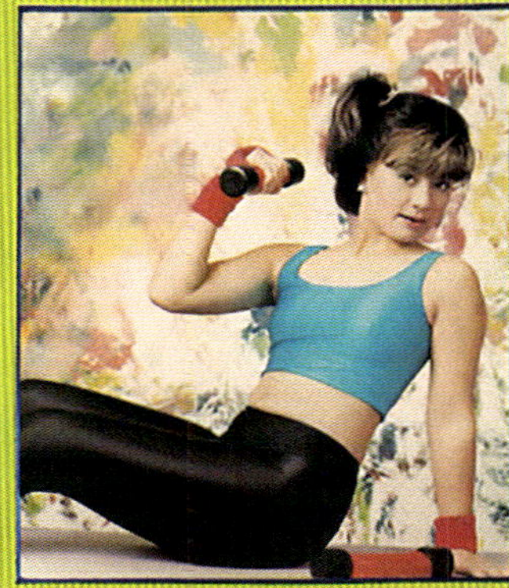

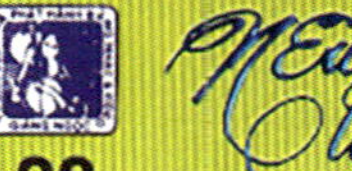

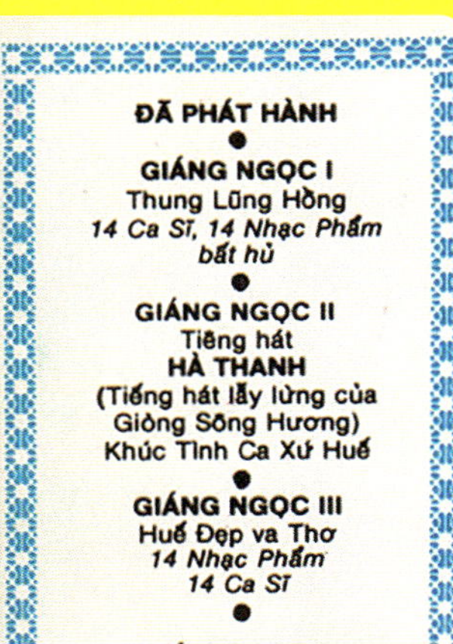

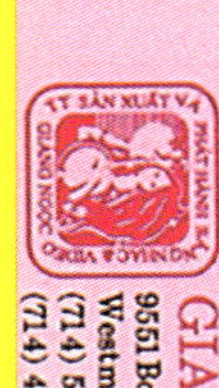

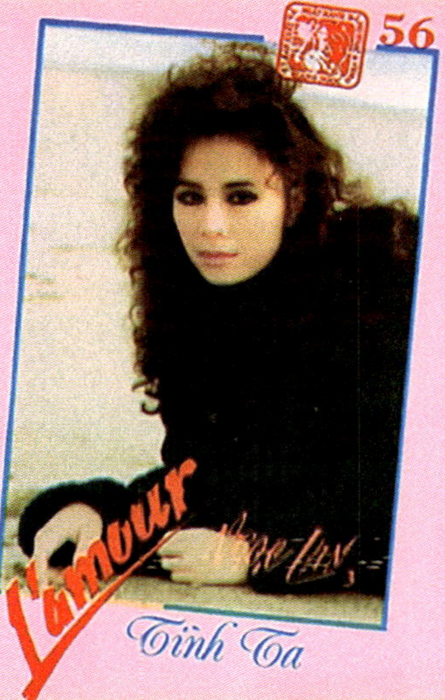

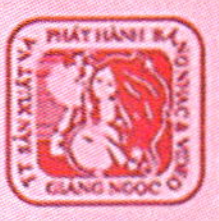

New Wave cassette covers, 1980s.

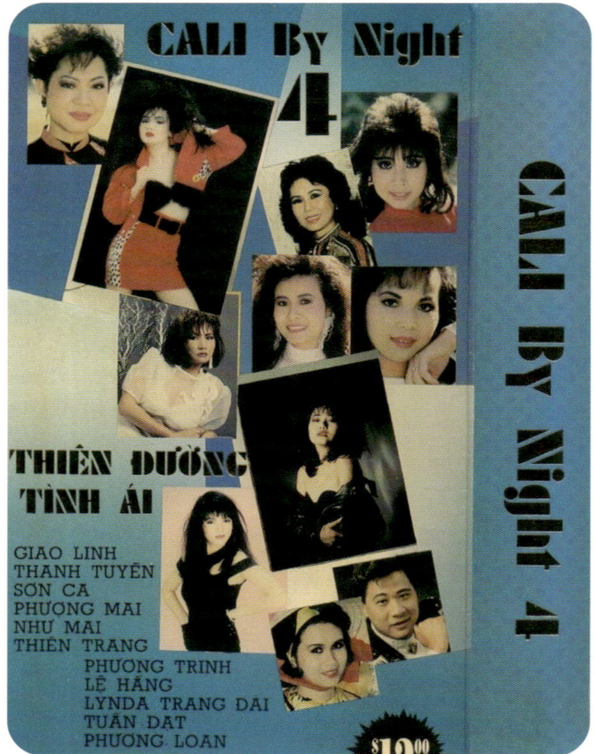

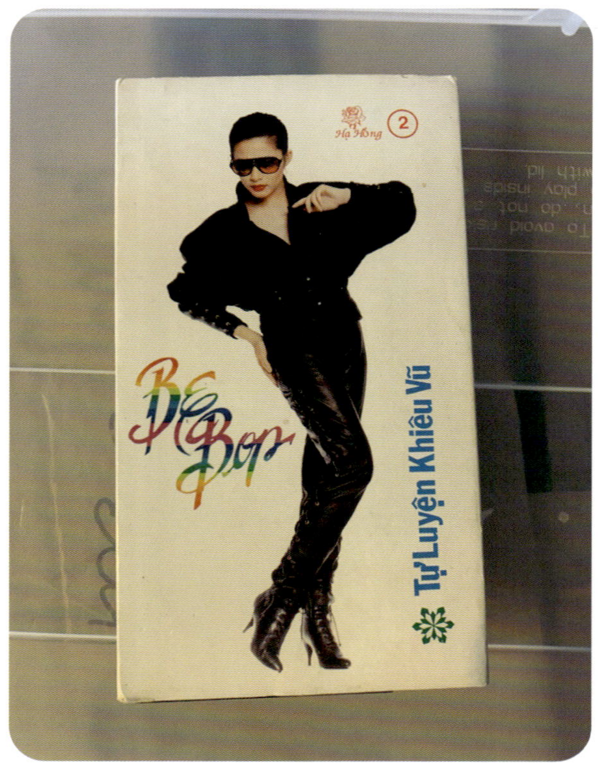

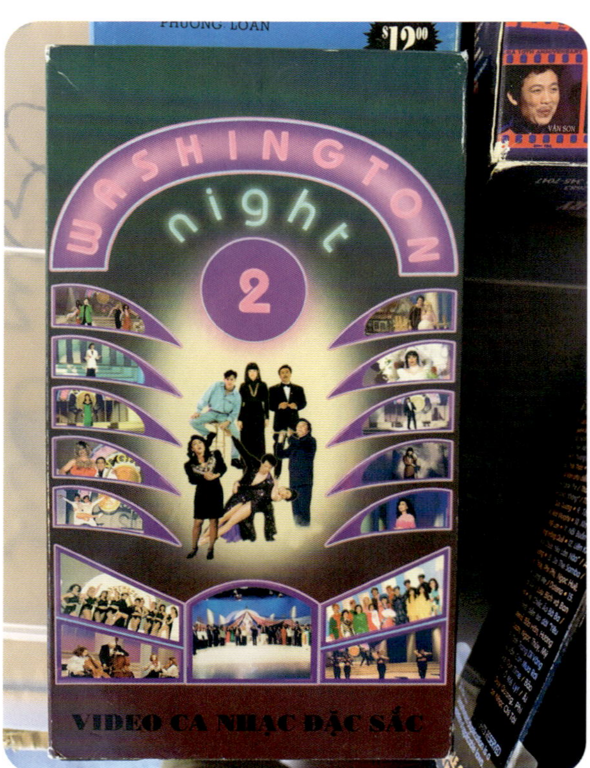

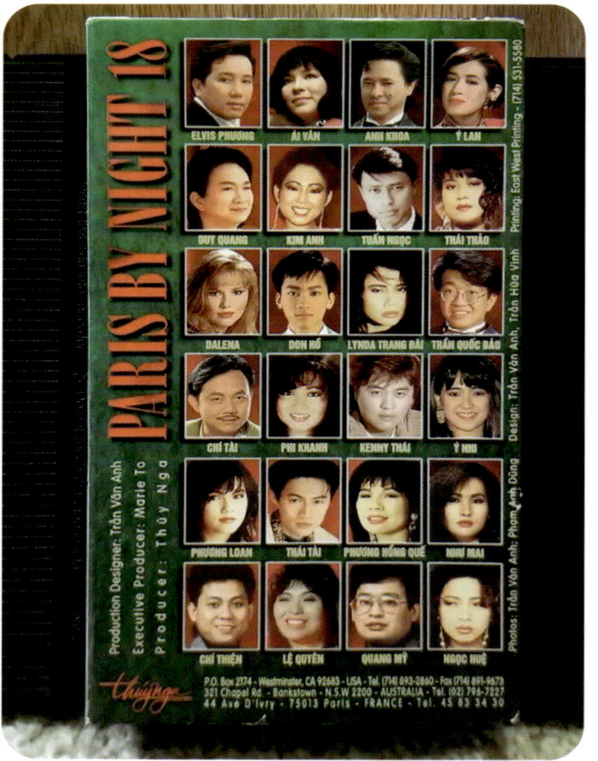

Community archive of VHS tapes.

JUMP IN MY CAR

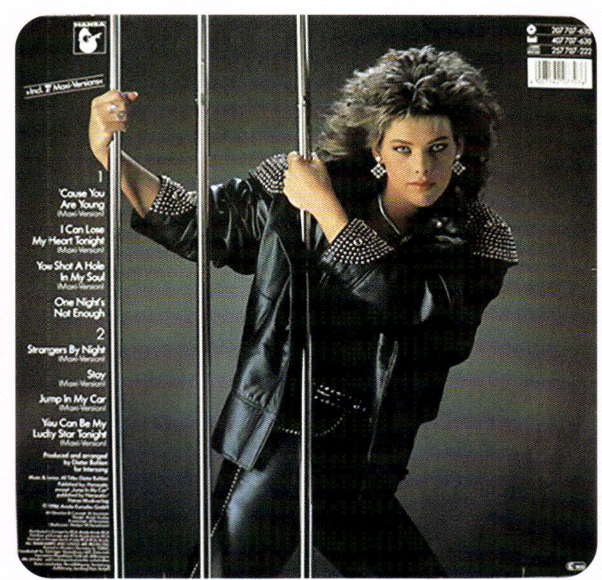

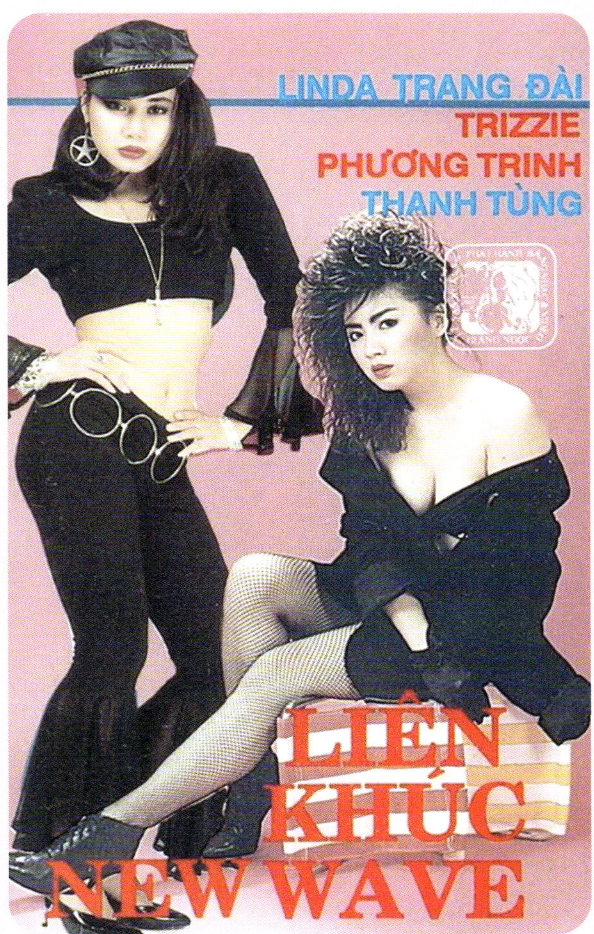

LAN DUONG

Above, left: Lien Khuc New Wave cassette.
Above, right: C.C. Catch album cover.

Jump in my car, I want some fun
Baby, when the working day is done
You are my everything, you give me more
You fill my dreams

C.C. Catch, "Jump in my Car" (1986)

When I think about the birthplace of Vietnamese New Wave—Little Saigon in Orange County—this place, at this time, was pure fantasy for me. Like the sun and palm trees promised me when we made the trek from the East to the West Coast in 1981, I imagined that Orange County, where Vietnamese American pop media culture emerged, promised a "something else" outside of the orange groves and dusty roads of San Jose, where I grew

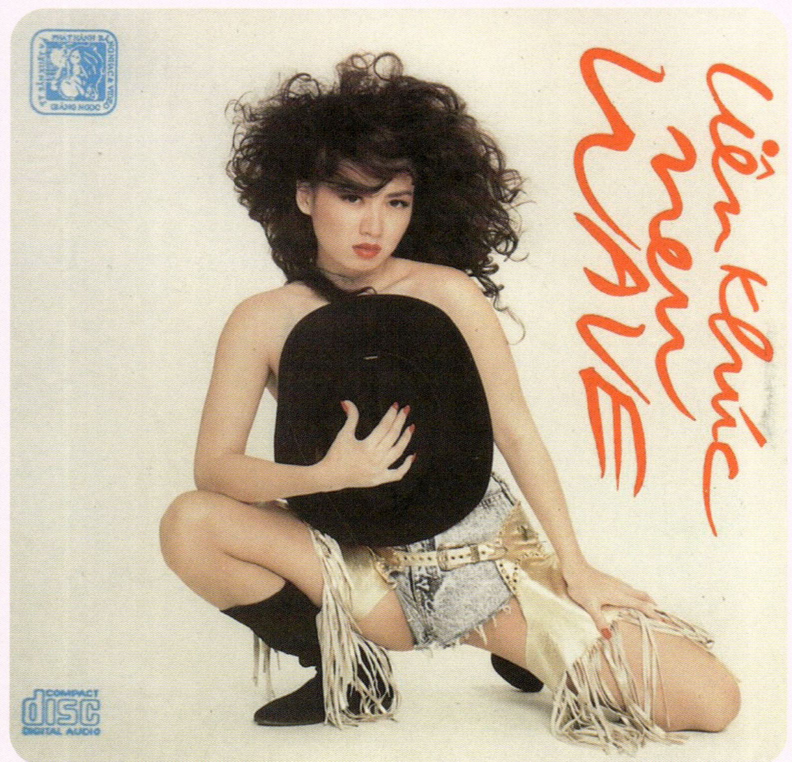

up. During a time of cassette tapes, video tapes, and music concerts, a Vietnamese American subculture formed its own archive of images, feelings, and meaning, and I wanted to be a part of it.

When C.C. Catch's song, "Jump in My Car" came out, it was my first year at Yerba Buena High School, where I learned to inhale Aqua Net, and paired my best brooches with the blackest blouse I could find in my sisters' closets. With teased hair resting on my shoulders like cotton candy, my Vietnamese girlfriends and I, all of us refugees of the war just eleven years earlier, waited on the school's sloping hills, our white pumps digging into the freshly cut grass, to hang out with our homeboyz. We jumped in the cars that bumped to the baddest beats and talked

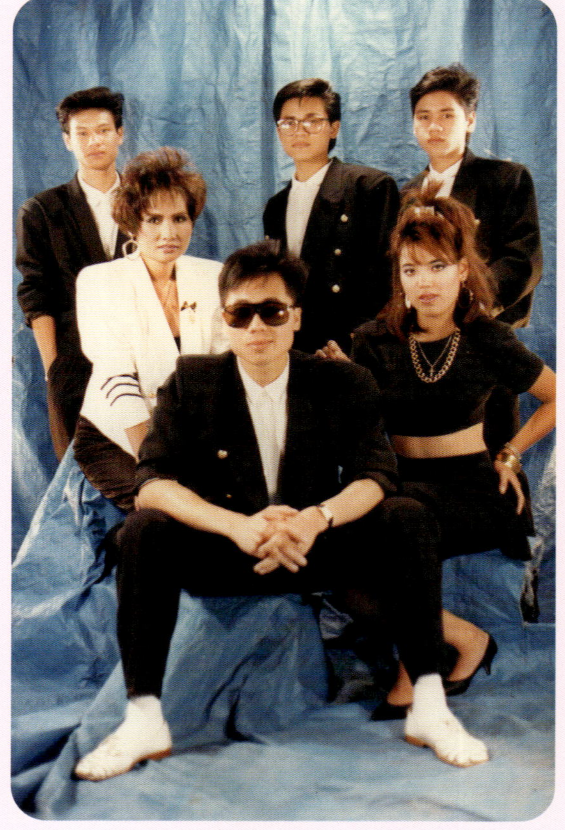

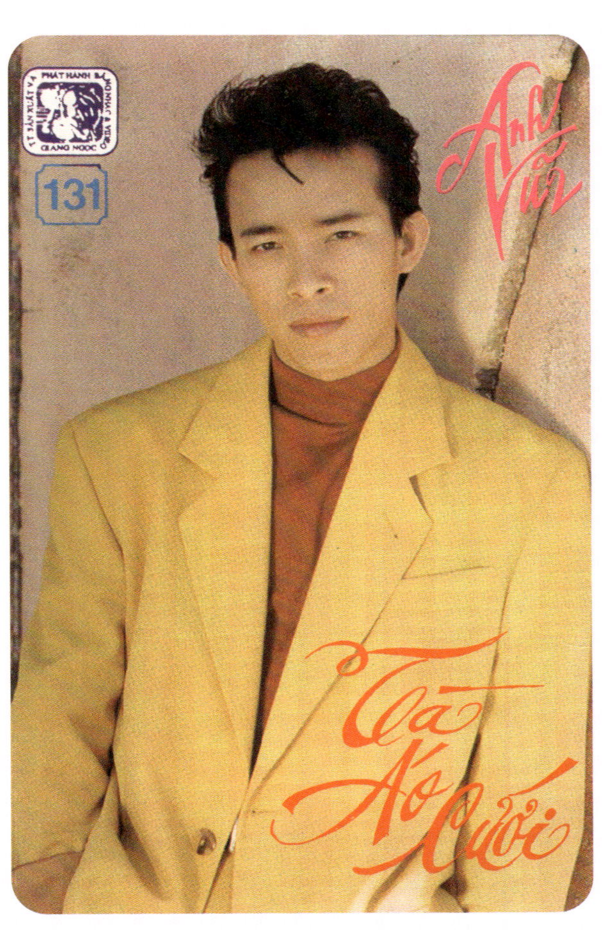

Above, and opposite above: Album covers from Giáng Ngọc Productions. Opposite, below: New Wave portrait by Thái Tài.

to the boys with the highest hair (who we affectionately called "rooster heads"). C.C. Catch's flirty song, with its hint of sex and danger and a particular kind of wild, was the song that jump-started my love for New Wave's incorrigible style, music, and fashion—and its possibilities.

I threw myself into New Wave's geometric hairstyles, soft baggy clothes, and pointy shoes for a reason. Remade in OC, New Wave contoured my way of being for a long time; it was a pathway to a sonic joy and to a sociality that allowed me to feel connected, even in the disconnections that were so much a part of my adolescence. This is what links Vietnamese American generations and the cities that we sought to remake.

Most of all, Vietnamese New Wave mirrored refugees' desires to see and move our bodies differently than the ways that we had always been captured—still—in the American story about the Vietnam War, told and retold in its popular culture, film, and media as victims and losers of the war, and then gangsters and model minorities. With the fiftieth anniversary of the fall of Saigon in 2025, we will relive in mainstream and nationalistic discourse, our memories of trauma and displacement. But at the same time, we must also recognize the ways we upheld joy in a formative time of our lives.

For me, then and now, Vietnamese New Wave will always be about jumping in cars and shuffling to our own beats.

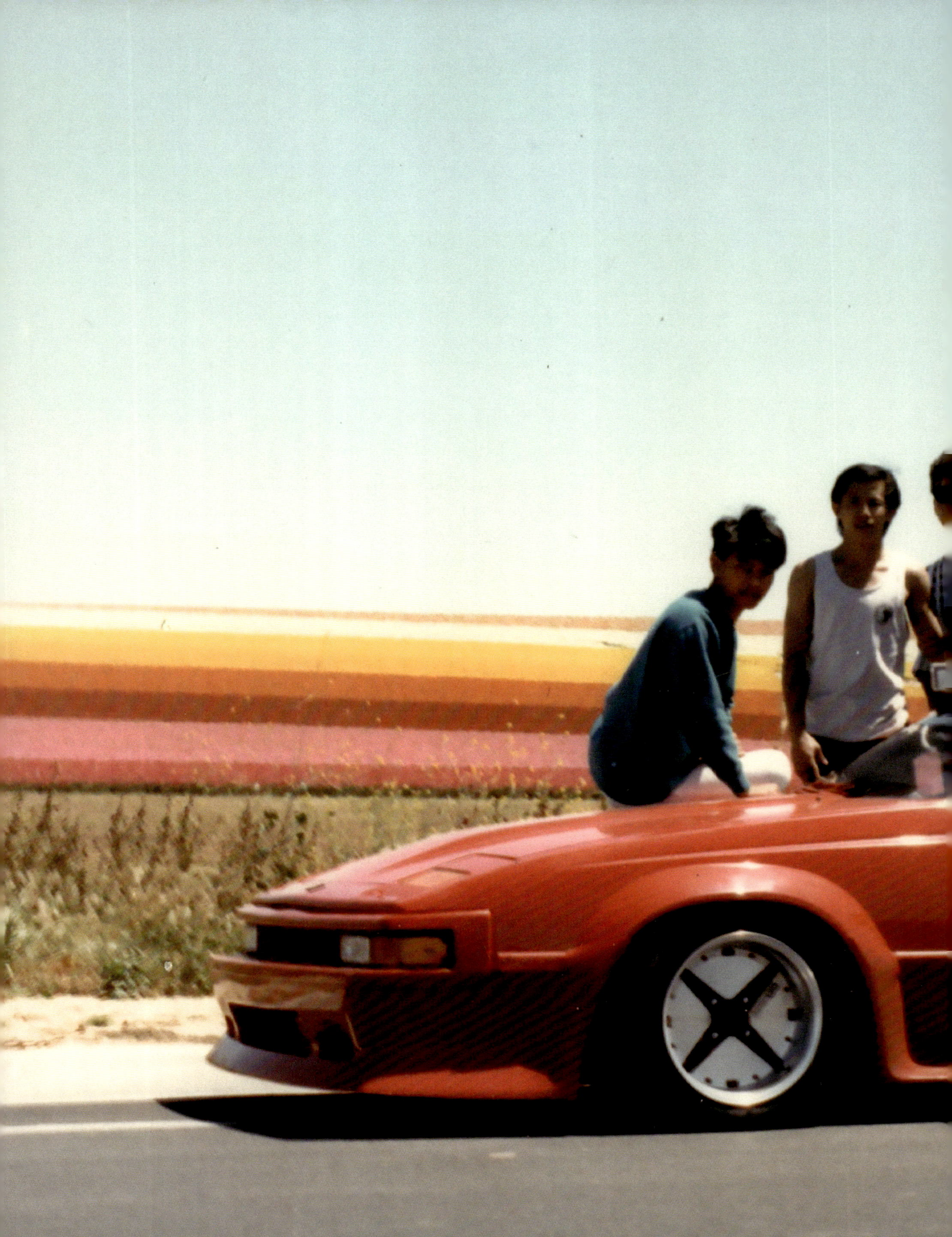

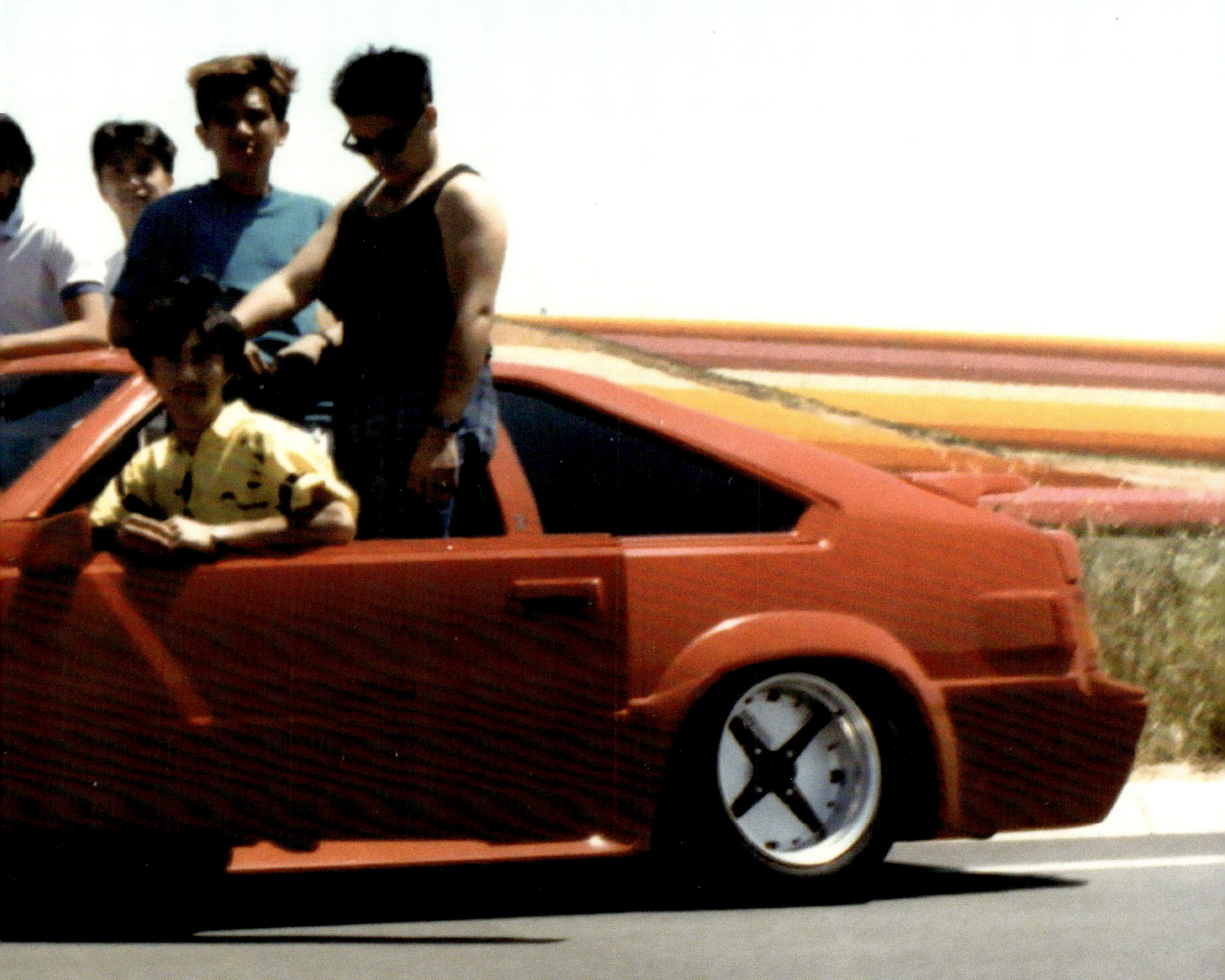

Teens cruising past the flower fields in Carlsbad, California, circa 1987.

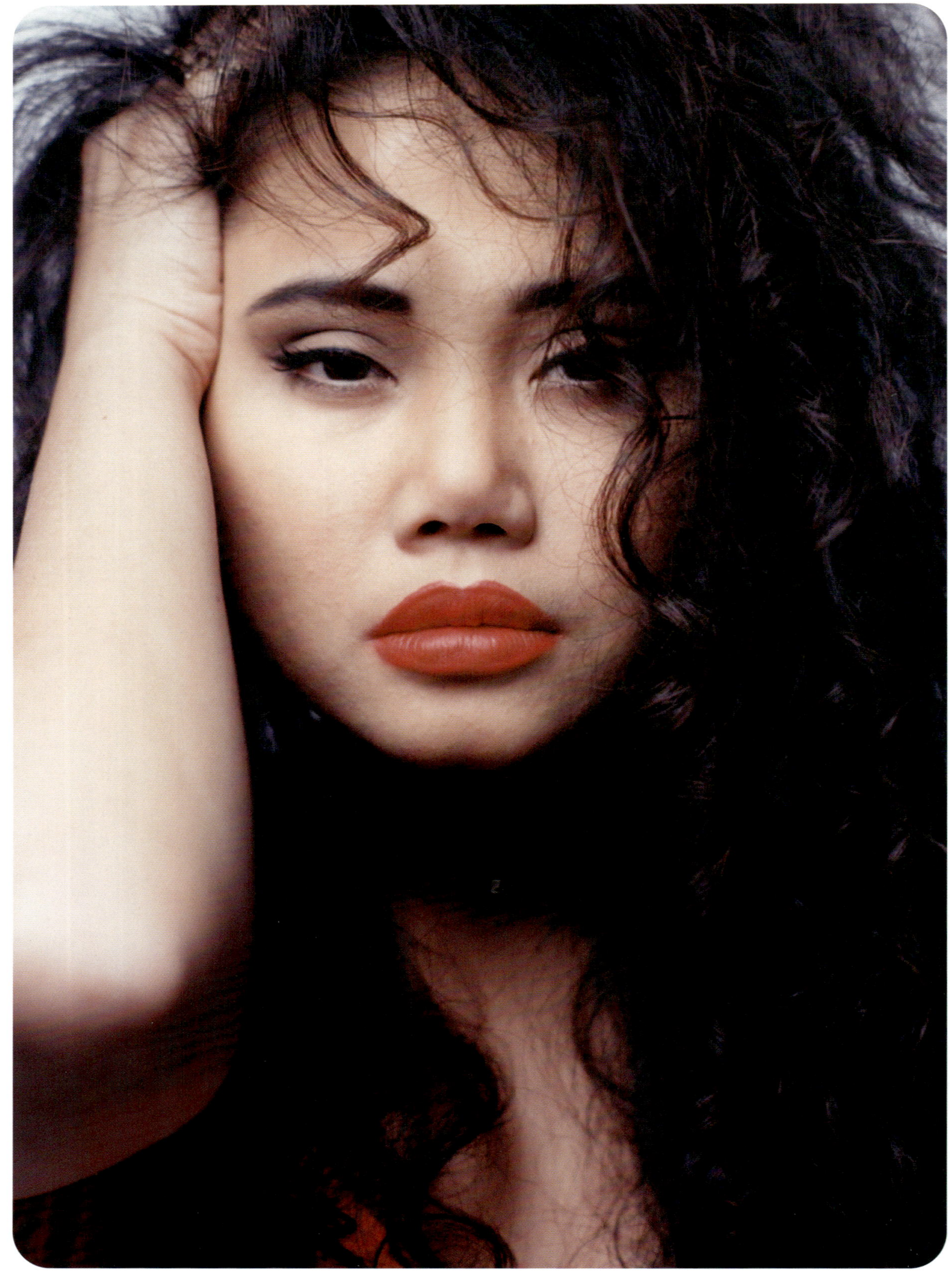

THE BOOM: NEW WAVE GROWS

As New Wave and Eurodisco's popularity soared among Vietnamese American youth in the 1980s, its influence didn't just resonate through headphones and mixtapes—it began to transform the Vietnamese American music landscape itself. Pioneering artists like Anh Tài Band and Lynda Trang Đài emerged, blending Eurodisco's catchy beats with Vietnamese musical nuances. Their electric performances captivated audiences, fostering widespread acceptance and paving the way for what would later become known as V-pop.

Lynda Trang Đài became a cultural icon, her appearances on *Paris By Night* and her nightclub performances catalyzing an explosion of interest in New Wave style. This surge in popularity helped integrate Eurodisco elements into traditional Vietnamese music, sparking a stylistic revolution that resonated across generational lines. Lynda's iconic and sexy performances on *Paris By Night* and her provocative presence in nightclubs across the diaspora became hallmarks of the era. Her music and style did more than just fill dance floors; they set fashion trends and influenced artistic expressions throughout the Vietnamese American community. Singing in both Vietnamese and English, she captivated audiences far and wide. Small clothing retailers began stocking outfits that mirrored her flashy stage ensembles, and her impact was visible in archival photos and album covers that became staples across the community, integrating V-pop into the everyday cultural tapestry. This diaspora music surged in popularity to such an extent that it sparked a thriving black market back in Vietnam. People were eager to get their hands on the latest fashions and hear the bilingual New Wave tracks being covered, demonstrating the broad appeal and cultural influence of Lynda's performances.

Following in Lynda's footsteps, artists such as Trizzie Phương Trinh, Thái Tài, Henry Chuc, and Tommy Ngo continued to innovate and popularize the V-pop genre. These artists built on the foundations laid by predecessors like Ngoc Lan, Thai Hien, and Thai Thao, as well as bands like the Magic and the Dreamers, who had melded Western musical styles with Vietnamese themes.

Initially, many in the older generation were skeptical of these new musical expressions, viewing them as too detached from traditional Vietnamese culture. However, as the commercial potential of V-pop became apparent, previously hesitant

Lynda Trang Đài photographed by Thái Tài.

elders began to embrace and even exploit this burgeoning scene. Record producers and show organizers, once dismissive of New Wave and electronic influences, swiftly moved to capitalize on the young talent, seeing an opportunity to tap into the lucrative market of transnational Vietnamese music.

The resulting fusion—V-pop—combined traditional Vietnamese elements with the upbeat, synthesized rhythms of New Wave. It became a dominant force in the mainstream Vietnamese music scene. This musical evolution did more than update old tunes—it inspired a new generation of performers. Young Vietnamese American artists, who grew up under the dual influence of their cultural heritage and the burgeoning New Wave scene, began to experiment more boldly with both music and performance styles.

As V-pop continued to evolve, it not only solidified the legacy of New Wave and Eurodisco within the Vietnamese American community but also highlighted the complex intergenerational dynamics at play. Elders who had once resisted the new musical trends now found themselves at the forefront of producing covers of these popular tracks, promoting and profiting from the very innovations they had criticized, showcasing the transformative power of these genres on the cultural and economic landscapes of the diaspora.

Below: Thao Ha matches her shirt to her car poster. Opposite, above: New Wave teens, circa 1980s. Opposite, below: Singer Thuý Vi, photographed by Thái Tài.

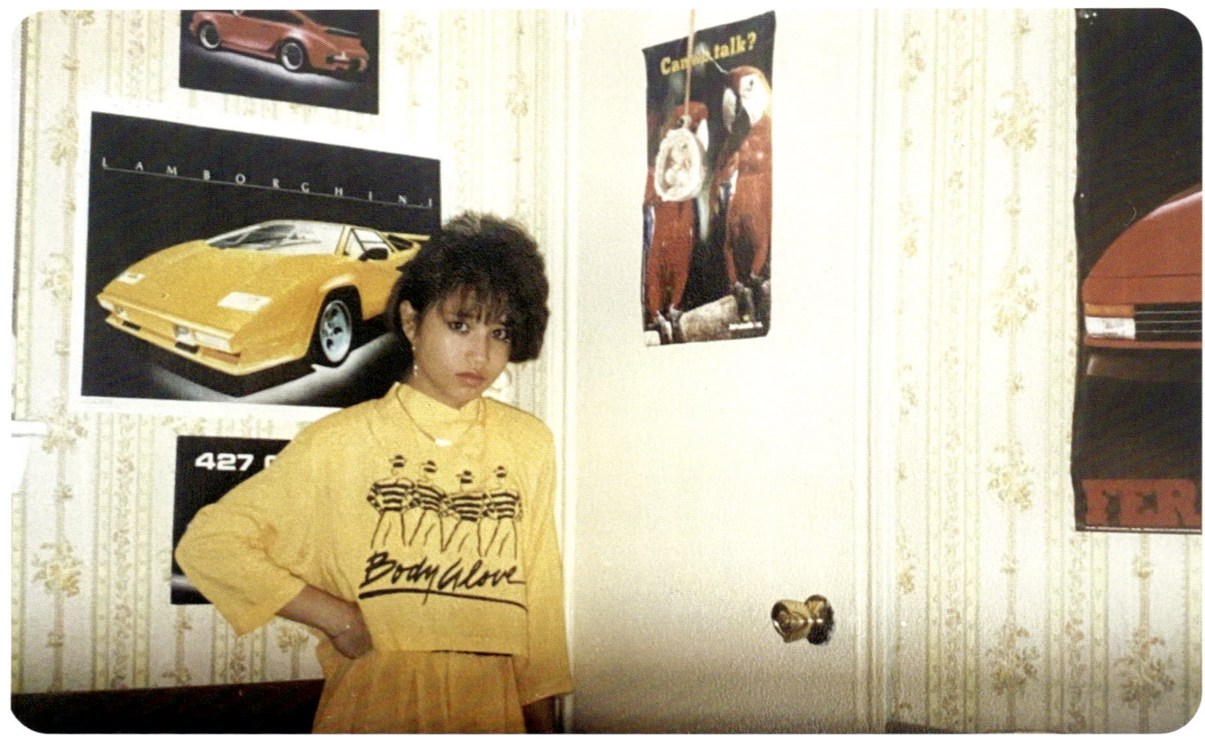

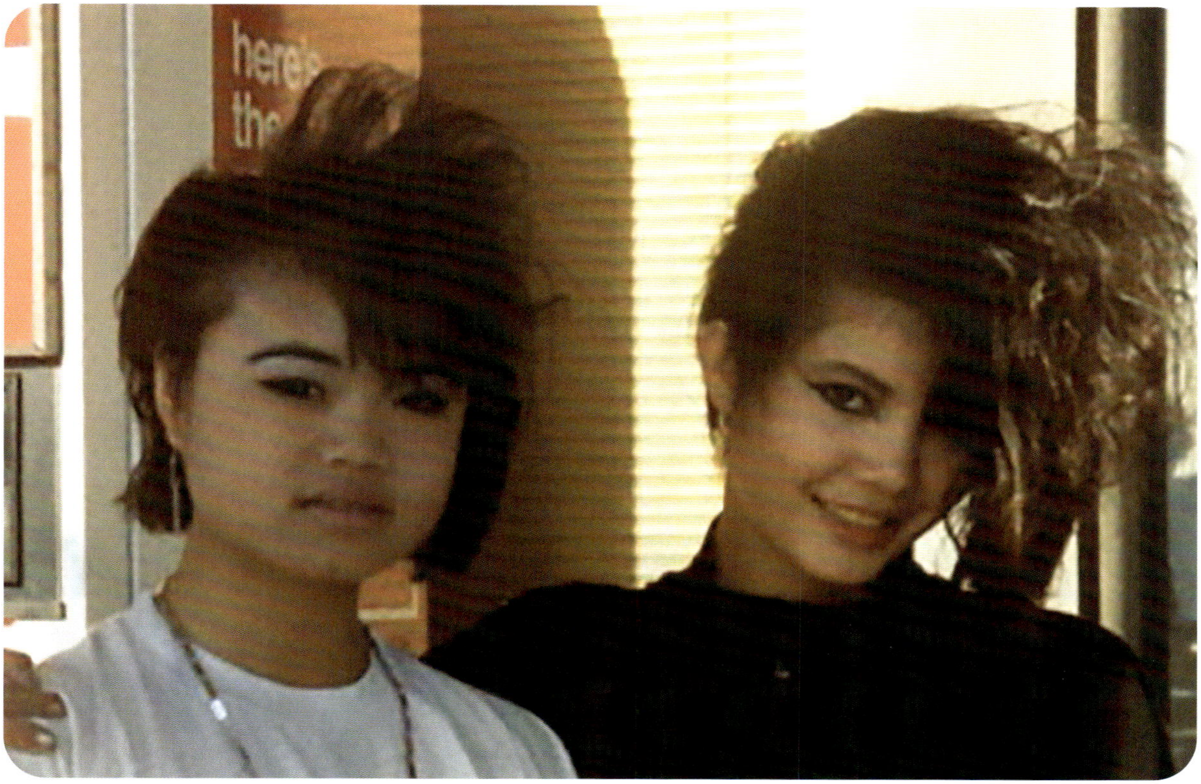

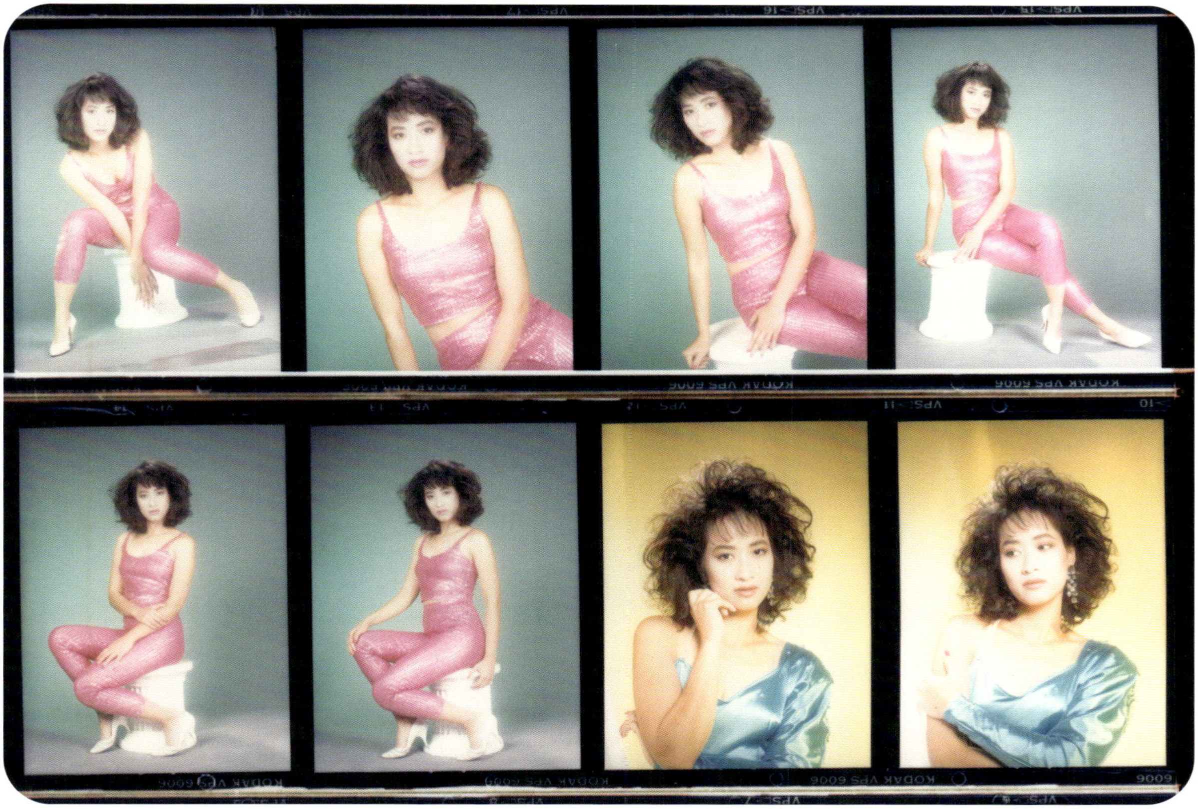

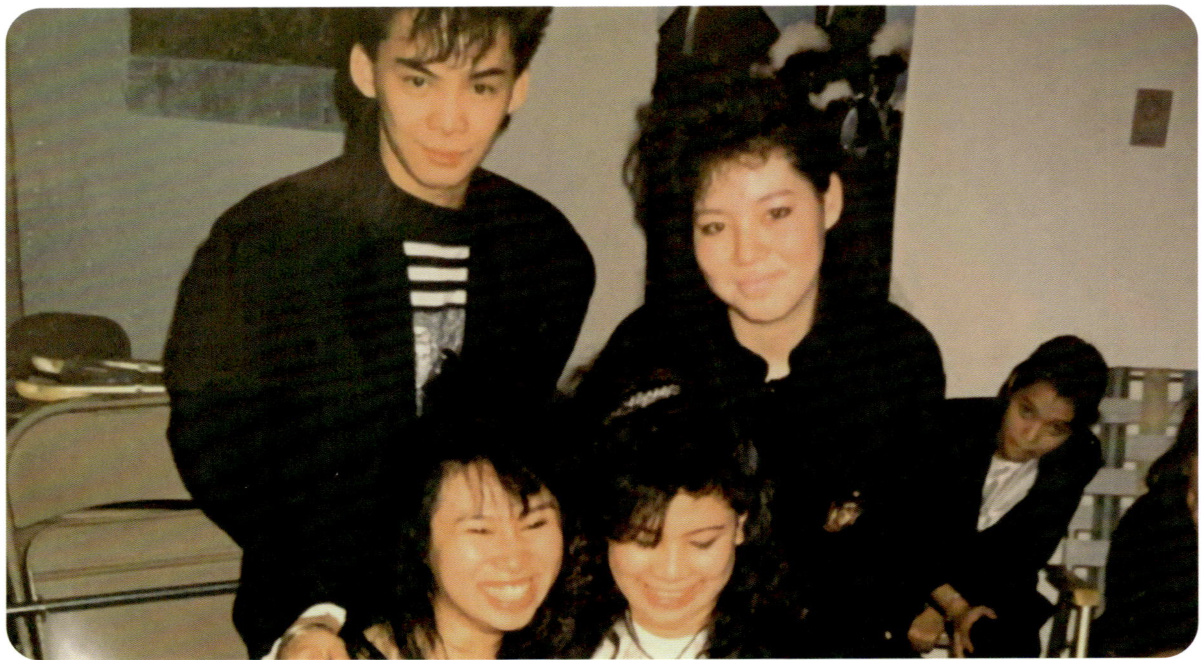

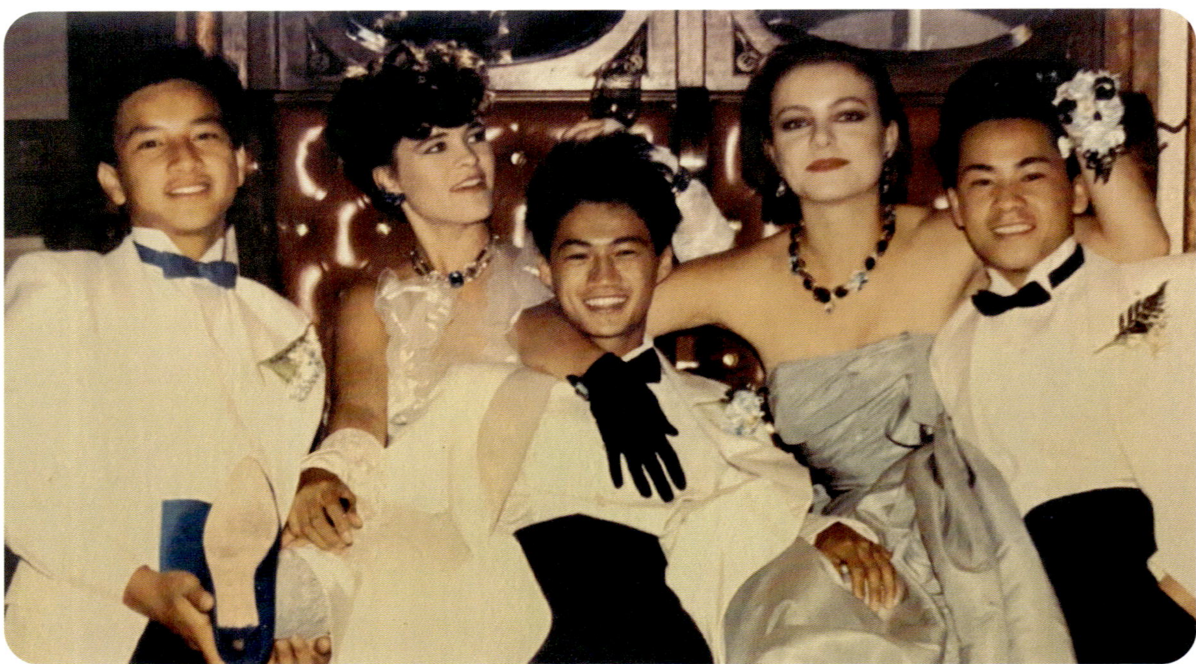

Above: community photo of New Wave teens, circa 1980s. Below: Thái Tài (center) at prom. Opposite: Thúy Võ Đặng, upstate New York, 1984.

A WHOLE MOOD

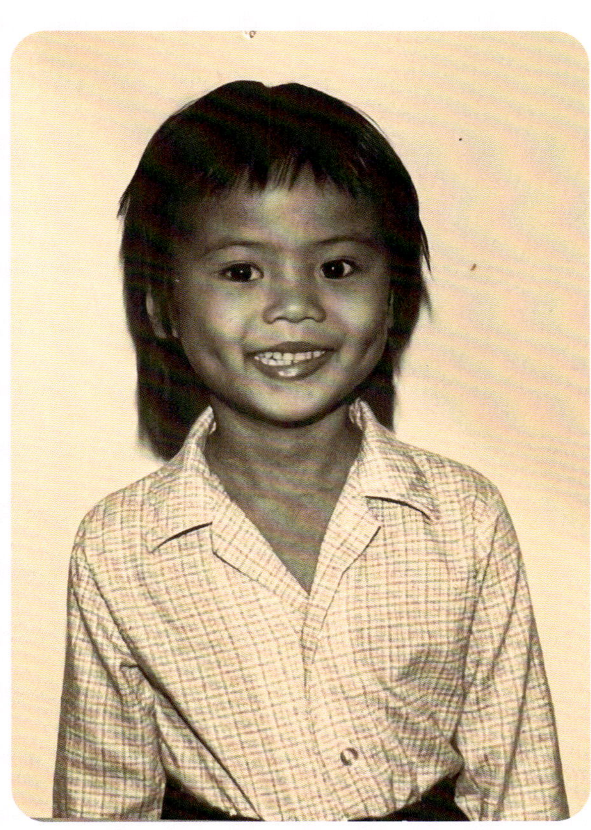

Thúy Võ Đặng

It was not the fair-skinned, hair-teased-to-there German-Dutch pop singer C.C. Catch who prompted a generation of Vietnamese youth to "jump in my car" or told us to #yolo before hashtags became a thing. It was Lynda Trang Đài, Thái Tài, Trizzie Phương Trinh, Tuấn Anh, and others. Yet, all the same, C.C.'s catchy songs served as an anthem for a generation of Vietnamese Americans in an era when we needed this reminder:

'Cause you are young
You will always be so strong
Hold on tight to your dreams, hold on.
You are right, don't give up—(baby, baby, babe)

When Vietnamese Americans heard such lyrics by C.C. Catch, Modern Talking, Bad Boys Blue, and others remixed and performed by our own pop icons in the 1980s, Euro Disco became a part of Vietnamese American culture. In this moment, a "new wave" was pushing against the currents of postwar loss, grief, and trauma. That wave consisted of synthesized beats, house parties, bold fashion, and hair…a whole mood.

While I was not quite the appropriate age to wholeheartedly embrace the rebellious aesthetic of Vietnamese New Wave, I saw enough to know it was something unique, cool, and distinctly "ours." As a refugee kid with plenty of older siblings, I lived vicariously through their experiences and simultaneously soaked in the beats that blasted from their souped up car's stereo system. I also watched with endless fascination the *Paris By Night*, ASIA Entertainment, and Văn Sơn music videos that were always playing in the homes of just about every Vietnamese family we knew in Southern California. The soundtrack of Vietnamese America in the 1970s through the '90s is surely a motley mix of *tân nhạc* and Vietnamese New Wave.

The 1980s and '90s were a challenging time for youth in the diaspora. On the streets and in schools, many young Vietnamese faced discrimination and a general lack of understanding and support. Some of us responded to the harshness of American society's demands for linguistic and social assimilation by trying to do just that. We abided by our elders' admonishments to work hard, learn English quickly, keep our heads down, and excel in school so we could uplift our families. Some sought belonging and safety by joining or forming gangs, empowering themselves as their social world was precarious and inhospitable. While trying to find our place in America, some of us experienced immense loss such as the loss of language or, tragically, the loss of our loved ones separated by the vastness of the Pacific ocean and enforced by US postwar embargoes and sanctions on Vietnam. Vietnamese youth who were unaccompanied when resettled in America, and even those with families, continued to struggle with suturing the

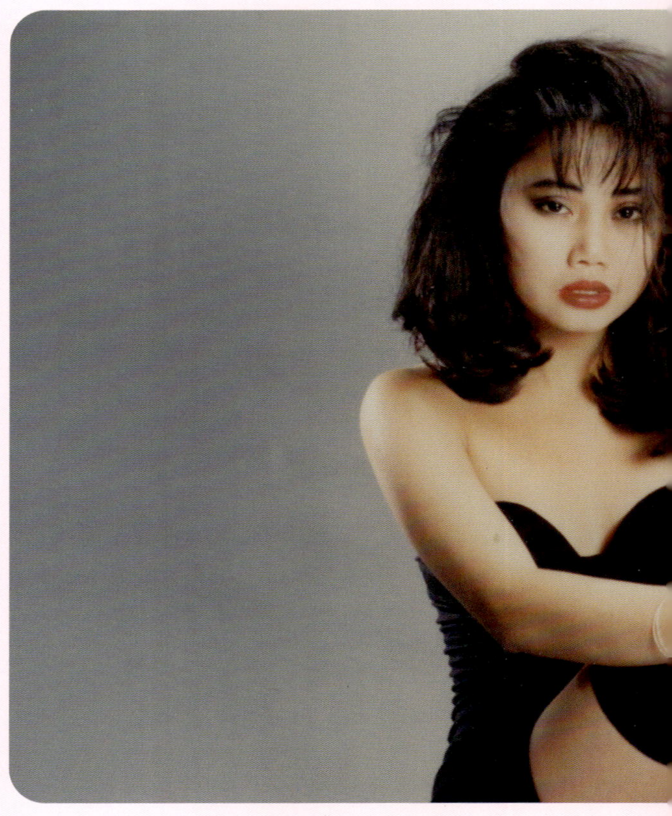

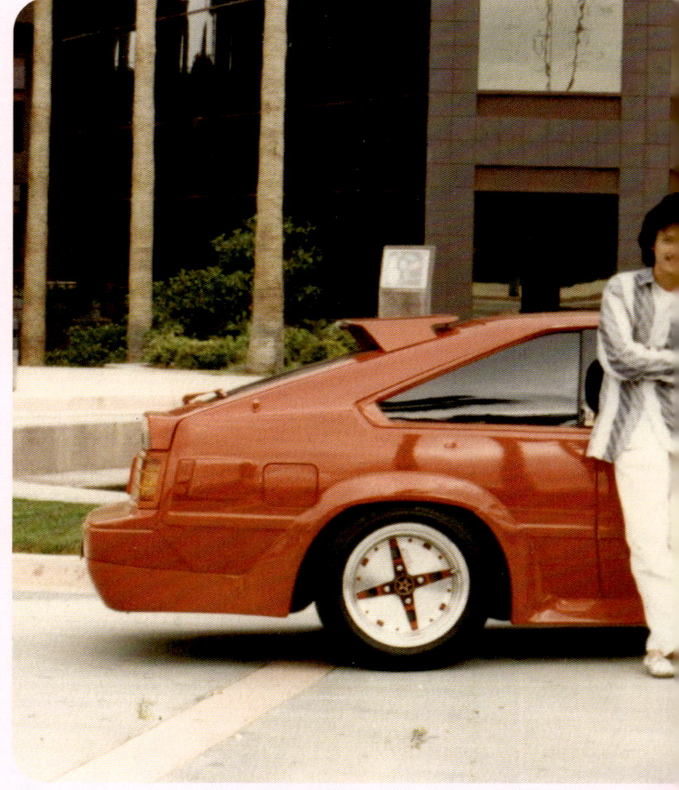

pieces of our fragmented lives.

The siren call of New Wave music and culture was just the balm our souls needed at this tumultuous moment in Vietnamese American history. Set adrift in a new land, and having experienced great loss, a generation of us found an outlet for expression, a means of coming together in celebration and, perhaps, rebellion against the unfairness of it all. Vietnamese New Wave was born out of a moment that may never be replicated again in the story of the Vietnamese diaspora, but its sounds and significance remain for future generations to remix and retell.

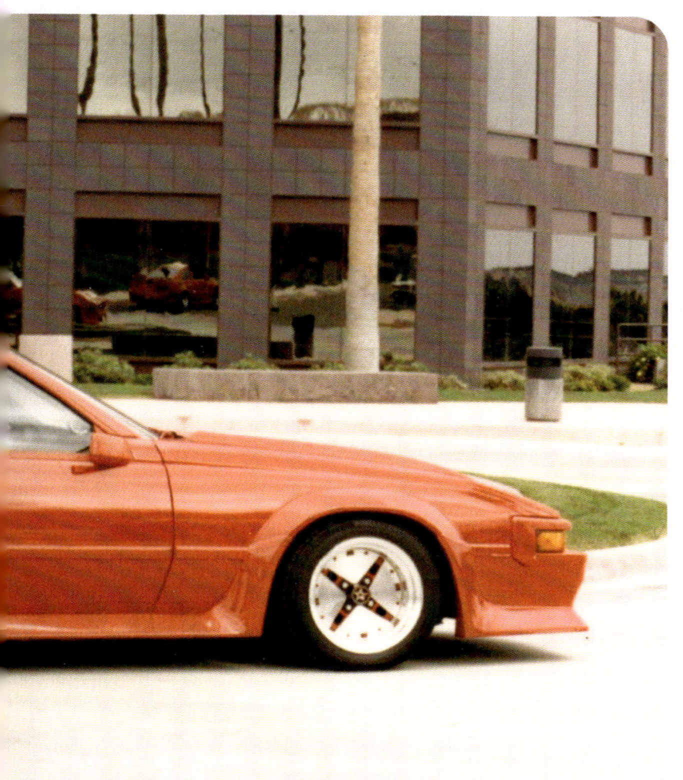

Above: Lynda Trang Đài, photographed by Thái Tài. Left: New Waver Hank Wu.

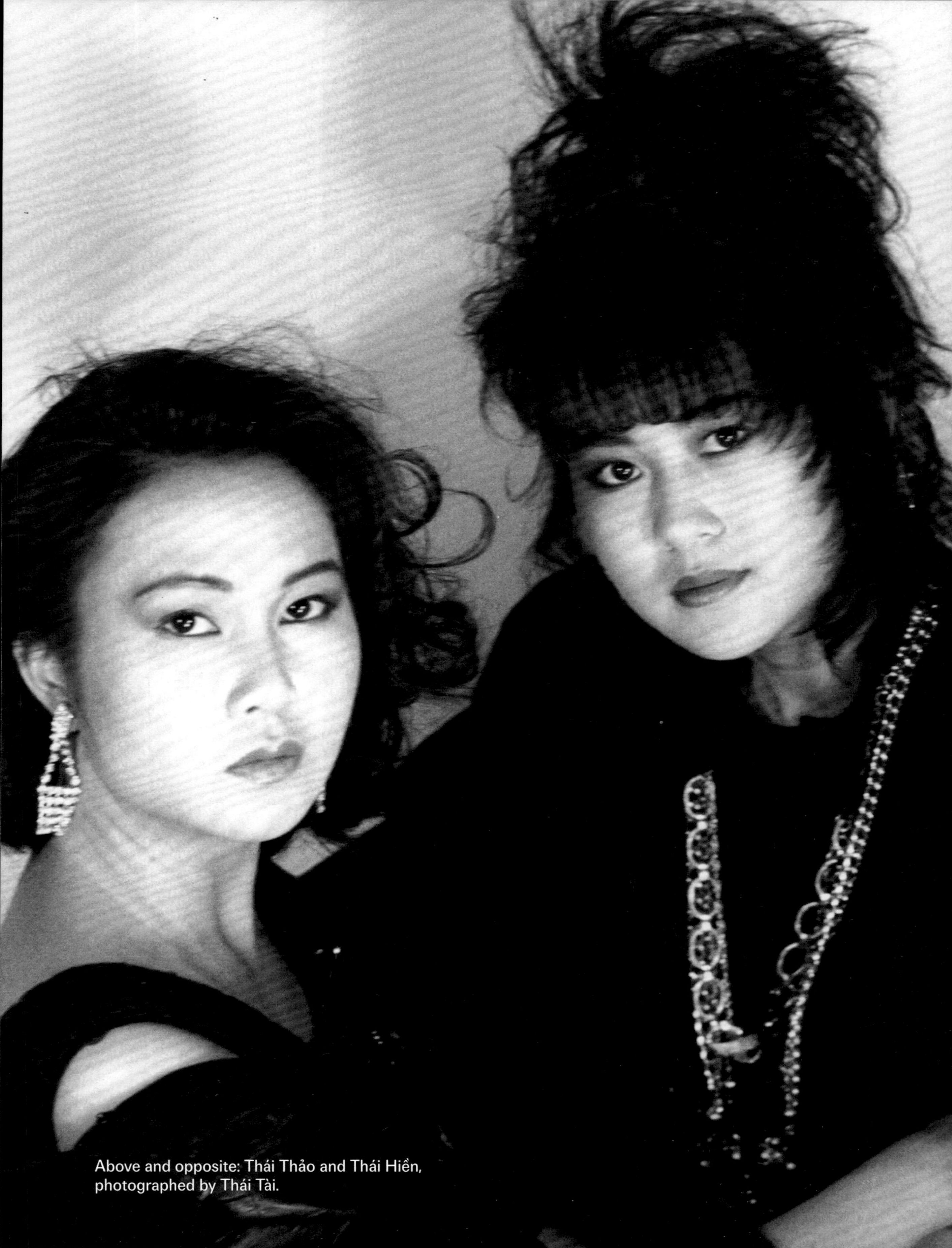

Above and opposite: Thái Thảo and Thái Hiền, photographed by Thái Tài.

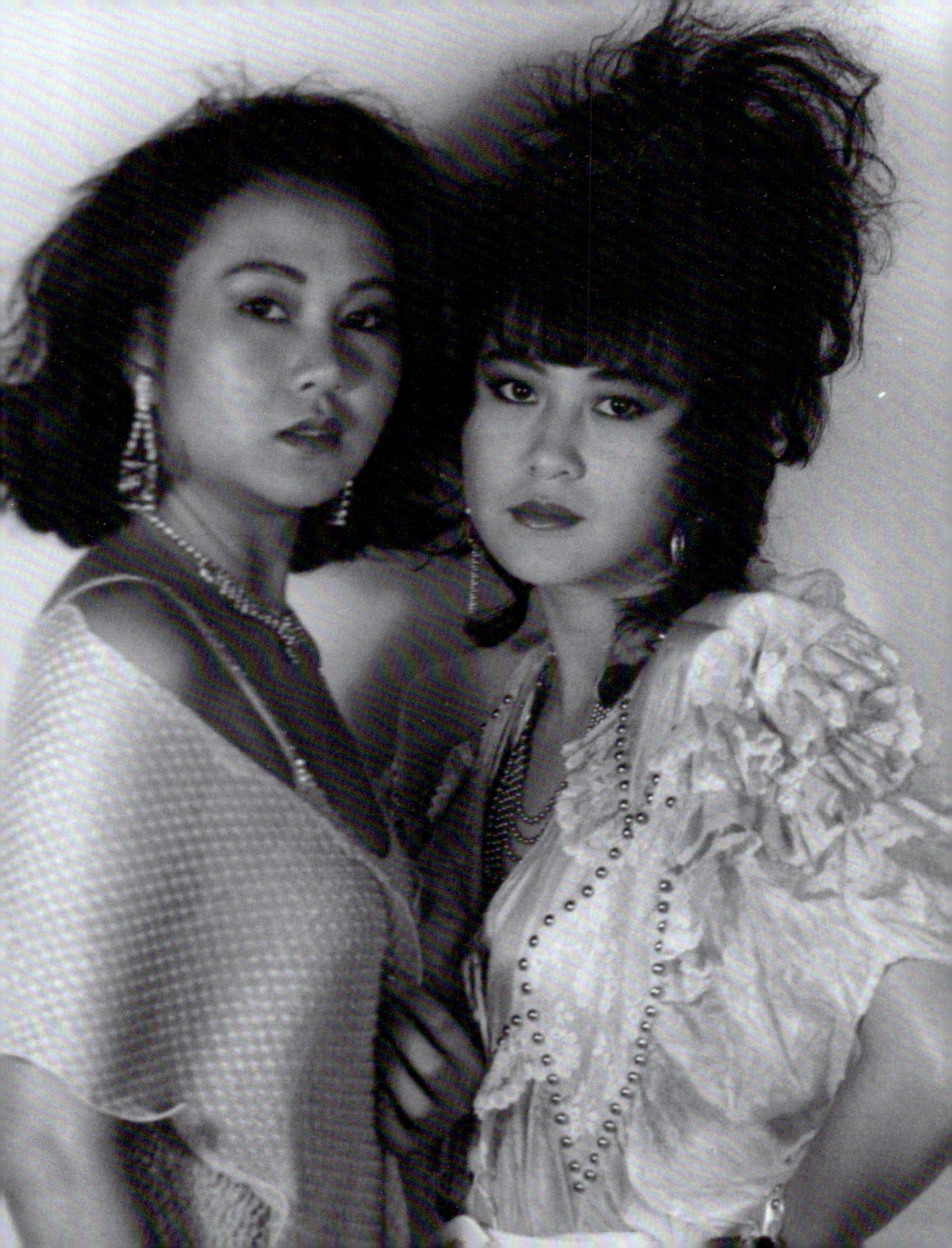

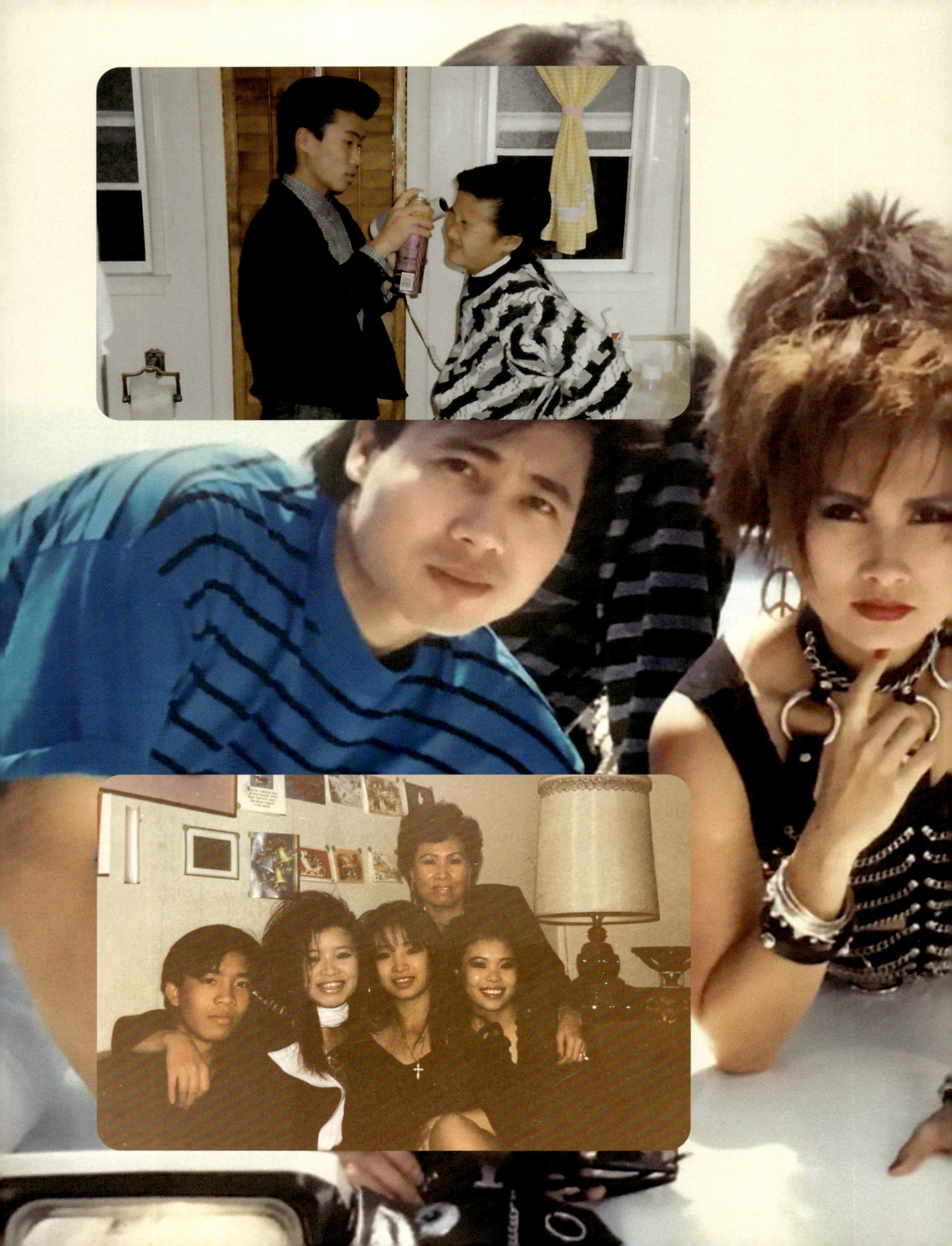

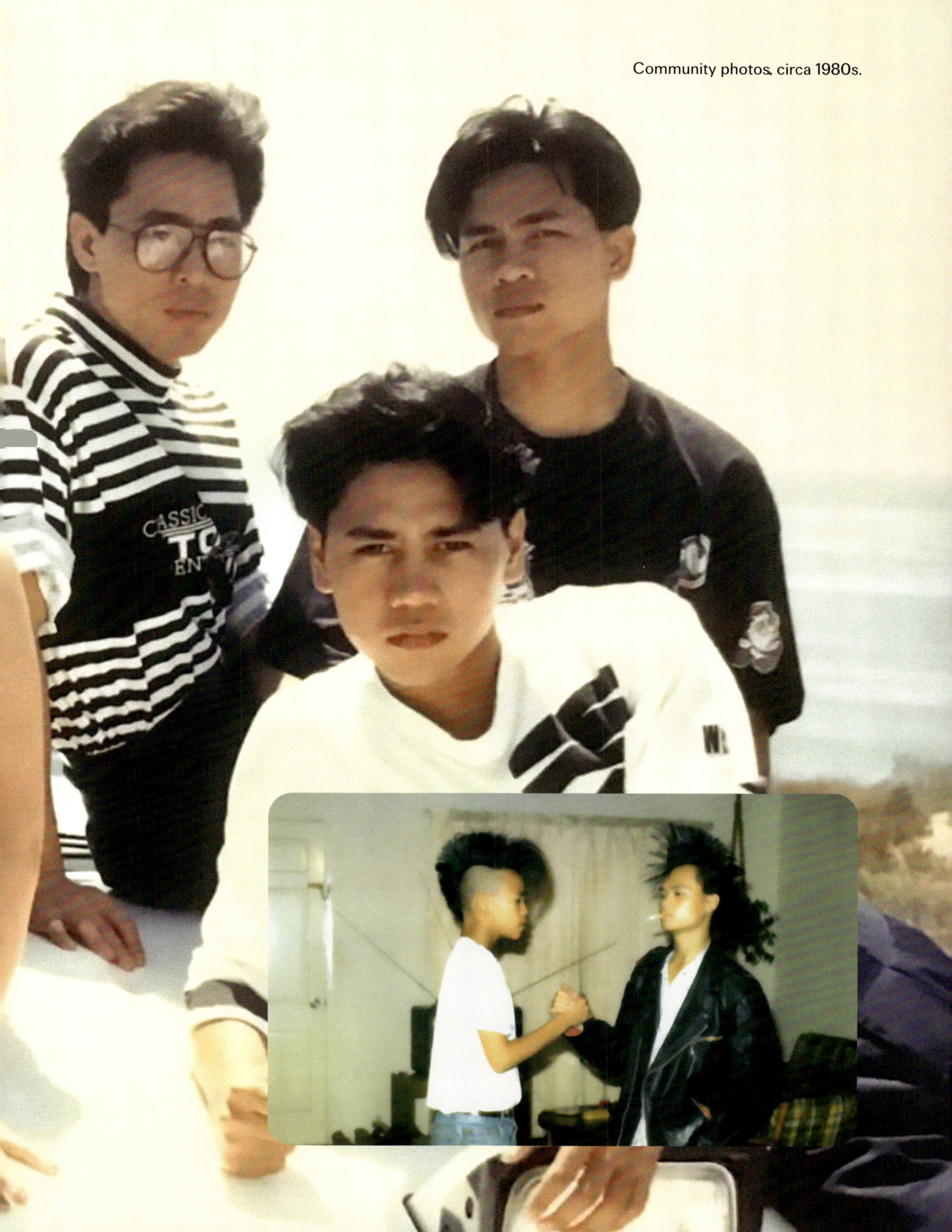

Community photos, circa 1980s.

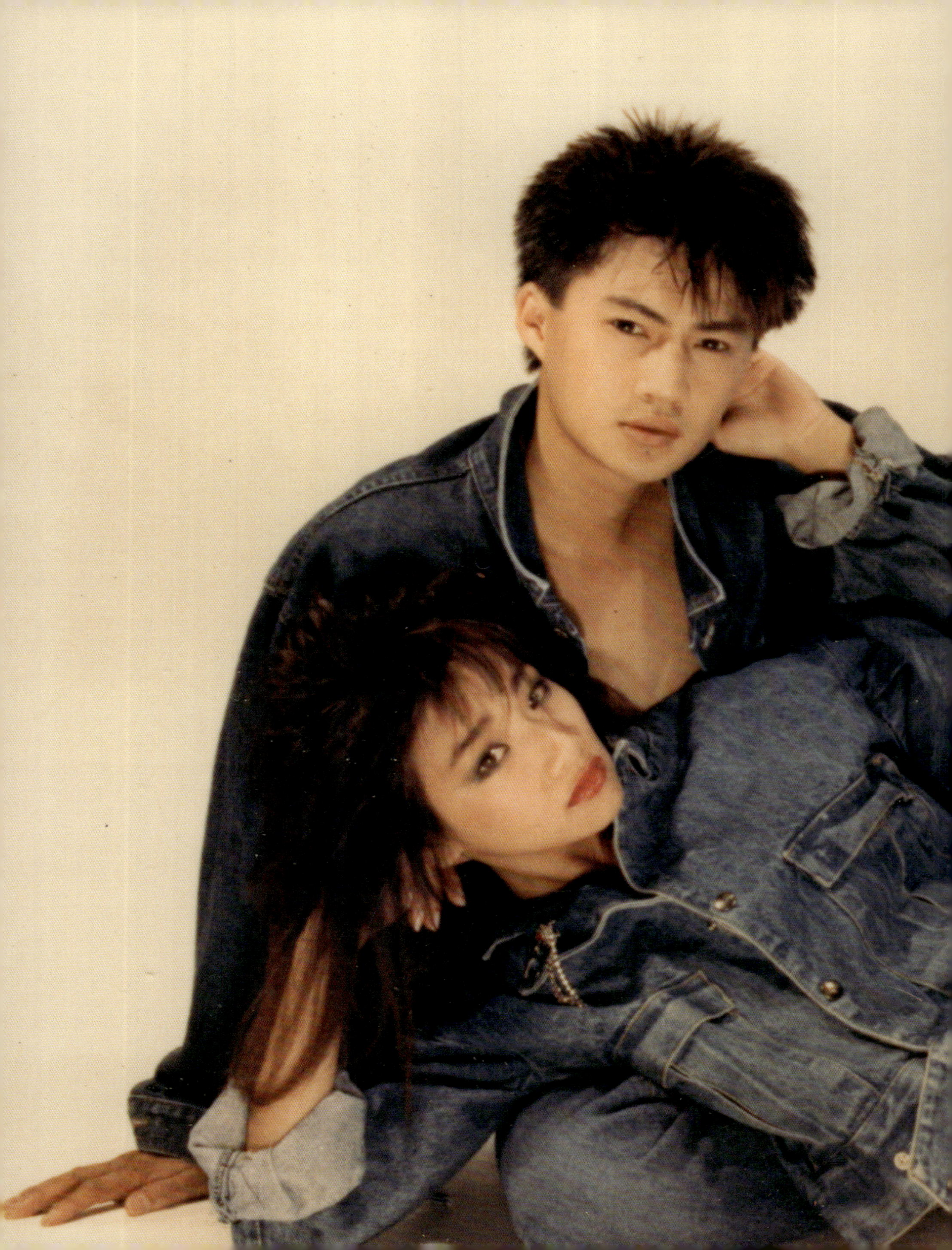

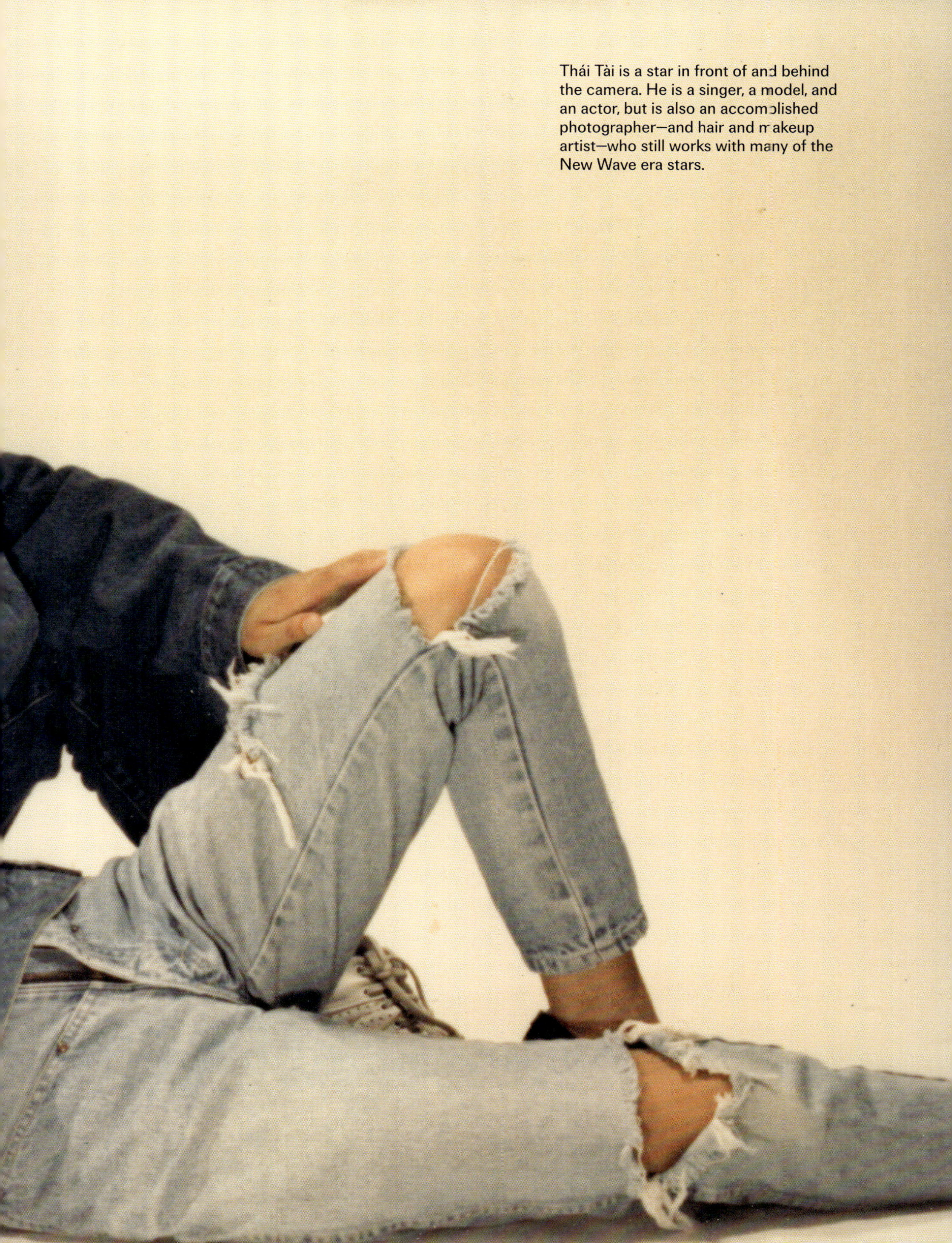

Thái Tài is a star in front of and behind the camera. He is a singer, a model, and an actor, but is also an accomplished photographer—and hair and makeup artist—who still works with many of the New Wave era stars.

Thành phố Hồ Chí Minh, Wednesday, January date 16th 1993 no (one)

Dear Thái Tài

I'm sorry! Nếu anh nhận được lá thư trước thì cho em xin lỗi. Vì trước đó em có gửi thư cho anh để tỏ lòng hâm mộ đồng thời xin anh hai tấm hình (hai kiểu đẹp I) và chữ ký. Nhưng em đã viết lộn địa chỉ. Thay vì "Los Angeles" nhưng em viết "Los Angelex" không biết có sao không? Dù sao đi nữa cũng không sao, em viết lại lá thư này gửi đến anh như bao khán thính giả hâm mộ. Tuy nhiên thư của em hơi đặc biệt là trong đó có gửi kèm theo tình cảm của người ~~anh~~ em đối với người anh. Không hiểu sao em thường ước:

"I wish you could be my brother and I could be your young brother," và cũng từ đó em có tình cảm như em đã là em trai của anh và ngược lại. Từ lúc gửi thư cho anh tuy có sai địa chỉ nhưng em vẫn mong chờ thư hồi âm. Mỗi lần nhận được thư thì em hy vọng là thư của anh nhưng nào đó chỉ là thư của bạn em và bạn của má em. Nhiều lần đã làm cho em thất vọng. Nếu anh ở vị trí của em anh sẽ hiểu thôi không nói đến đó chứ rồi, bây giờ em sẽ đi sâu vào vấn đề hơn của người hâm mộ đối với người mình hâm mộ. Trước khi trở thành ca sĩ anh làm gì? Anh là ca sĩ bao nhiêu năm? Tên thật của anh là gì? Một lần nữa xin lỗi anh là hiện nay anh bao nhiêu tuổi? Có gia đình chưa? Có em trai or gái không? Em có xứng đáng làm em trai anh không? Nói thiệt nhe, em chỉ là con của một gia đình lao động nghèo thôi đó. Có phải ước mơ của em thật quá đáng, thật cao không? Sắp tới anh sẽ hát cho chương trình Hải Âu, Thúy Nga or chương trình của Ng~ Cao Kỳ Duyên? Bài gì? Anh có thể hát một bài để tặng cho người em trai ở xa không? Ví dụ như em là em trai của anh và anh hát để tặng em được không? Có lẽ anh không đáp lại nguyện vọng của em. Riêng em, em vẫn không hoài bỏ ước mơ đó và em có thể viết thư cho anh được không? Và anh, nếu rảnh có thể viết thư cho em được không? Nhưng bắt buộc anh phải viết thư hồi âm và gửi cho em hai tấm hình nhe! Thôi thư cũng dài, thư sau sẽ viết dài hơn. Nhân dịp tết quí dậu 93 sắp tới em chúc anh hưởng một năm mới vui vẻ, khoẻ, được vạn sự như ý và thành công trong mọi công việc và nhất là trở thành một ca sĩ nổi tiếng nhất!

Em trai của anh

Vphong

Võ Thanh Phong

Tái bút:

Em mới có 16 tuổi, tuổi con rắn
sinh ngày 1-1-1977 (âm lịch)
tức ngày mùng 1 tết. Rất thông minh!
Thằng bạn nó lấy cuốn album hình
đi Mỹ rồi nên em không có hình.

WATERMAN

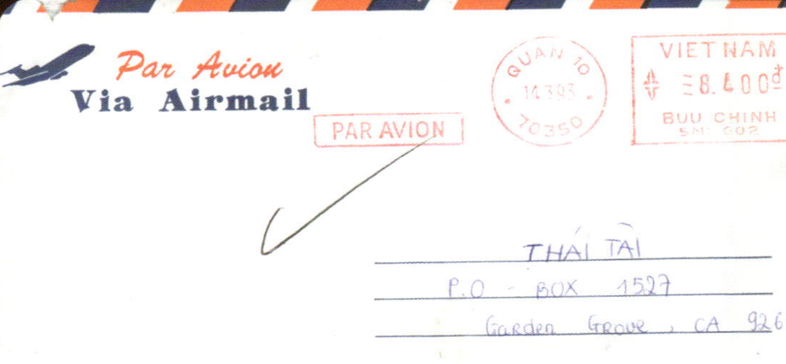

Thái Tài received fan mail from all over the world, including this letter from Vietnam.

CHÚC MỪNG

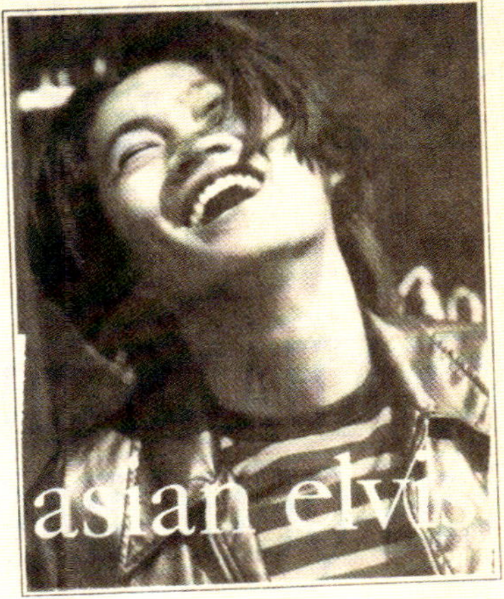

Nhận được tin vui:
Nam Ca Sĩ THÁI TÀI
Sẽ khai trương Studio mới
LOOP ONE STUDIO
tại 12821 Westminster Ave. #N
Garden Grove, CA 92841
Tel: (714) 901-3905
hân chúc Thái Tài khai trương hồng phát
hồng phát đại hồng phát.

Trần Thị Diễm Phúc và Diễm / Việt Dzũng & Hoàng Anh (Faces In Photo) / Lê Bá Chư
Chí Thiện Minh Phượng / Minh CD Loop One cùng gia đình / Kenny Khánh Châu / Christian
Kathy Huệ / Khuê / Hùng Trang / Don Ho / Lâm Thúy Vân / Linda & Tommy Ngô / Mạnh Quỳnh
Trần Quốc Bảo / Duy Thanh / Ma Nữ Đa Tình / Calvin Tuấn / Danny Tuấn / Lay Minh
Cùng các thân hữu và bằng hữu.

Diễm trang 81

CHAPTER 4

THE ONLY CONSTANT IS CHANGE

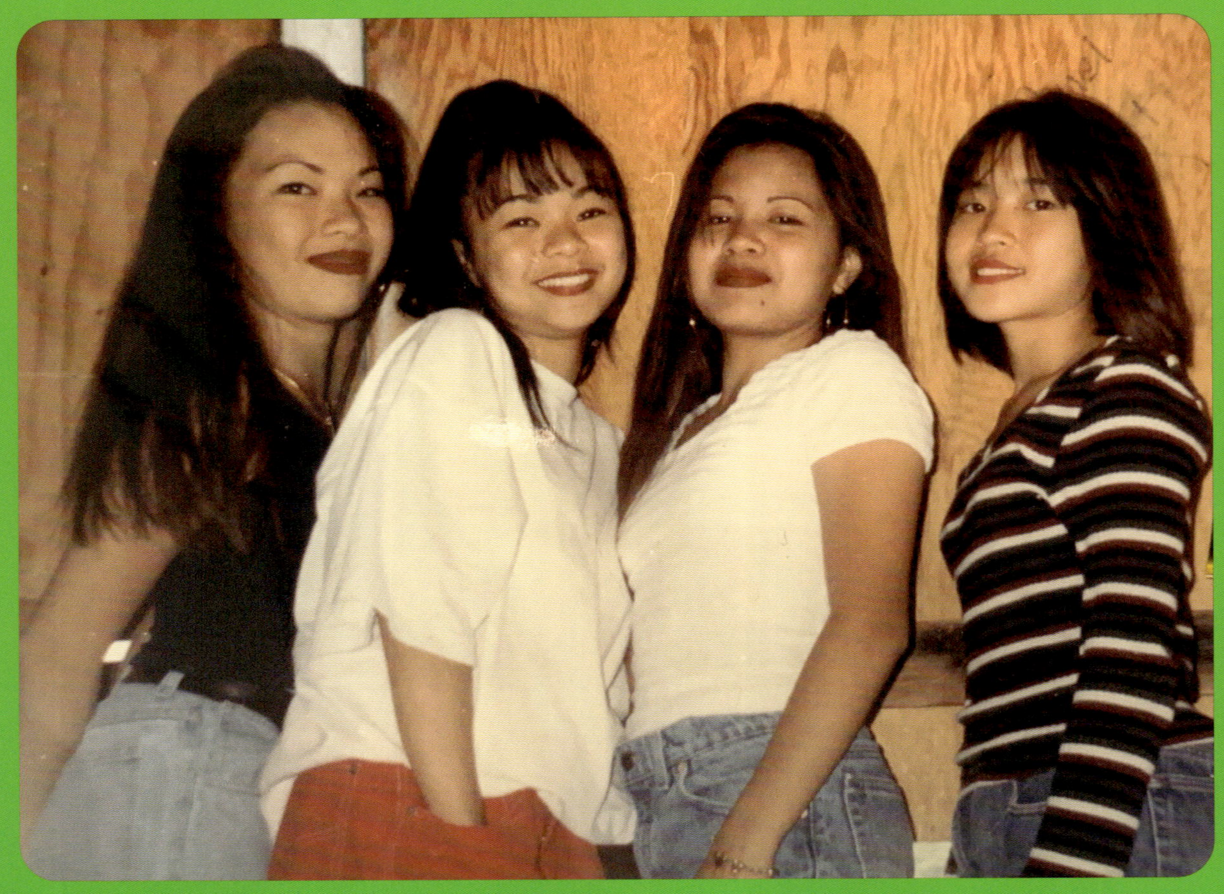

1990s

As the 1980s drew to a close, the influence of V-pop within the Vietnamese American community was undeniable. It had sparked a cultural renaissance, heralding a new chapter in the community's evolution. Understandably, a community rebuilding from the traumas of displacement didn't have the wherewithal to invest in nurturing new forms of music from their youth. This stagnation led to a decline in the genre's popularity, despite its initial success. The failure to evolve musically reflected broader challenges within the community, struggling to balance the preservation of cultural roots with the need to foster fresh, creative expression among its young people.

The Vietnamese American community began to experience a subtle yet profound cultural shift as the 1990s dawned. The older generation of "OG" New Wave listeners, who had once embraced the genre as a defining part of their eclectic identity, now found themselves in more mundane and domesticated settings. These animated punks were now in the '90s, hanging up their old outfits for a more understated style. The electric energy of New Wave music began to wane, gradually blending into the background as generic pop music dominated the airwaves.

This transition marked the end of an era. For many within the Vietnamese American community, New Wave represented a time of youthful rebellion and creative exploration, a stark contrast to the increasingly commercialized landscape of the 1990s, and demands of adult life.

Yet, as the decade unfolded, it became clear that the landscape of Vietnamese American culture was evolving. New generations brought different experiences and influences, reshaping the community's cultural fabric. The music that once resonated so deeply with the first wave of V-pop fans was giving way to new sounds and new attitudes. This was not just a shift in musical taste but a broader transformation: how cultural identity was expressed and experienced.

It reflected broader changes within the community as well—changes in socio-economic conditions, generational priorities, and the continuous blending of cultural influences that challenged the traditional norms. As these dynamics shifted, so too did the personal identities of those who called the Vietnamese American community home. They were navigating a complex emotional landscape, looking to find a balance between the cherished heritage of their past and the unfolding realities of their present.

Elizabeth Ai and friends in the 1990s.

In this context, the fading of New Wave's prominence was symbolic of the inevitable passage of time and the ever-changing nature of cultural identity. It underscored a fundamental truth: that communities and individuals within them are always in flux. The only constant is change.

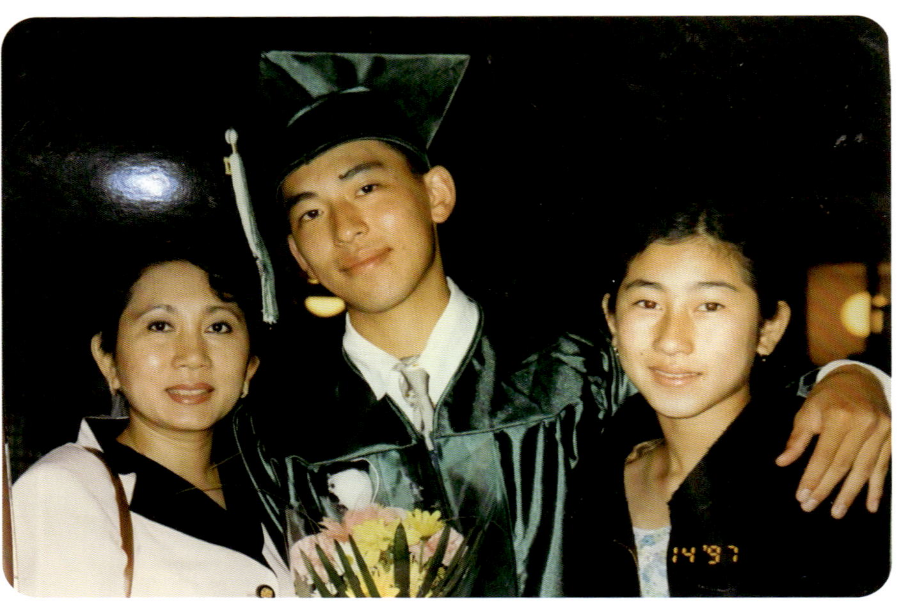

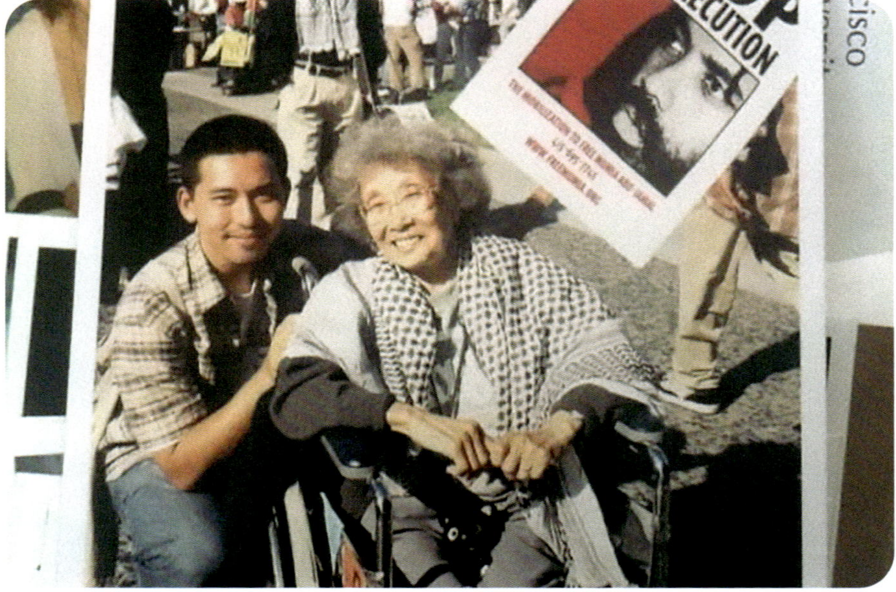

Above: Michael Tran's high school graduation photo in San Jose.
Left: Michael Tran with political activist Yuri Kochiyama.

THINGS COME TO AN END

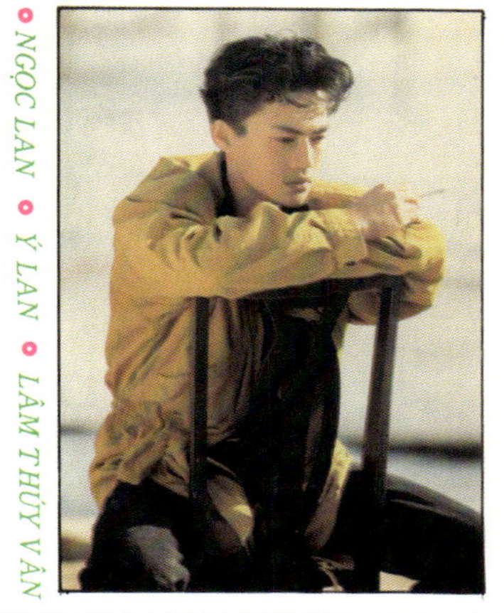

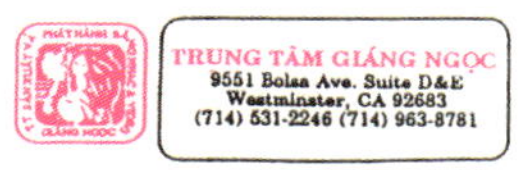

Cassette tape for Thái Tài's *Oh Mon Amour*.

Eric Nguyen

Some of my earliest memories are watching *Paris by Night* with my parents and falling in love with the slow, maudlin *nhạc vàng* of Hương Lan, Thanh Tuyền, Elvis Phương. There's a video of me standing on my parents' bed with a round brush in my hand. Putting on a sad face—the biggest frown you've ever seen on a child, eyes nearly closed from all the tears—I mimicked Thanh Tuyền's rendition of "Buồn Nào Hơn Đêm Nay." *Buồn* means sad, and boy, was I *buồn* as I sang about my lover being away in another land, maybe because of war, maybe something else. I was four years old, and I was selling it. And my parents—well, they were eating it up, if their amused giggles behind the camera were to be believed. They seemed proud, even, that I knew the words to this Vietnamese song, a kind of respite in an America where everybody spoke English. But that could only last so long.

Everything changed when I saw Lynda Trang Đài.

At first, it looked like one of my mom's aerobic exercise shows. A light brightens onto four svelte women arranged in a square. Some upbeat music starts playing, and they begin to move, taking steps to the rhythm as they gaze into the camera with concentrated intent. They're all wearing tight black yoga pants and crop tops in neon colors.

Except one.

The girl at the center of it all wears leather chaps with fringe, a black crop top, a chain around her neck, and biker gloves. To my surprise, the words she sings are in Vietnamese. This wasn't one of my mom's workout shows. No, this was something different.

Effortlessly, this girl glides across the screen. As the women in back did their synchronized choreography, this one didn't seem to care: she danced to the beat of her own drum. Later, I would learn there was a word for this: cool.

I looked over at my parents.

"Kids these days," they were mumbling. Where were the *áo dais*? The forlorn gazes? The lyrics about pure love? The modesty? Her name wasn't even Vietnamese. What kind of name was Lynda anyway? I think that was when we started separating, my parents and I. They were old, traditional, so uncool. Meanwhile, I was falling head over heels for Lynda.

The next time my parents took the long ride to Virginia, where the closest Vietnamese shopping center was located, I knew exactly which store I wanted to go to. After my parents bought snacks at the bakery, and remedies at the herbalist, we made our way to the music shop. There, display cases of cassettes, CDs, and laser discs surrounded the perimeter of the store. Meanwhile, a karaoke video played on a giant screen behind the cash register. It was here that I searched for cassettes of Lynda. And then there was Tommy Ngô, her boyfriend at the time; Don Hồ, who danced like he was washing a car; and Thái Tài, a handsome man with pouting

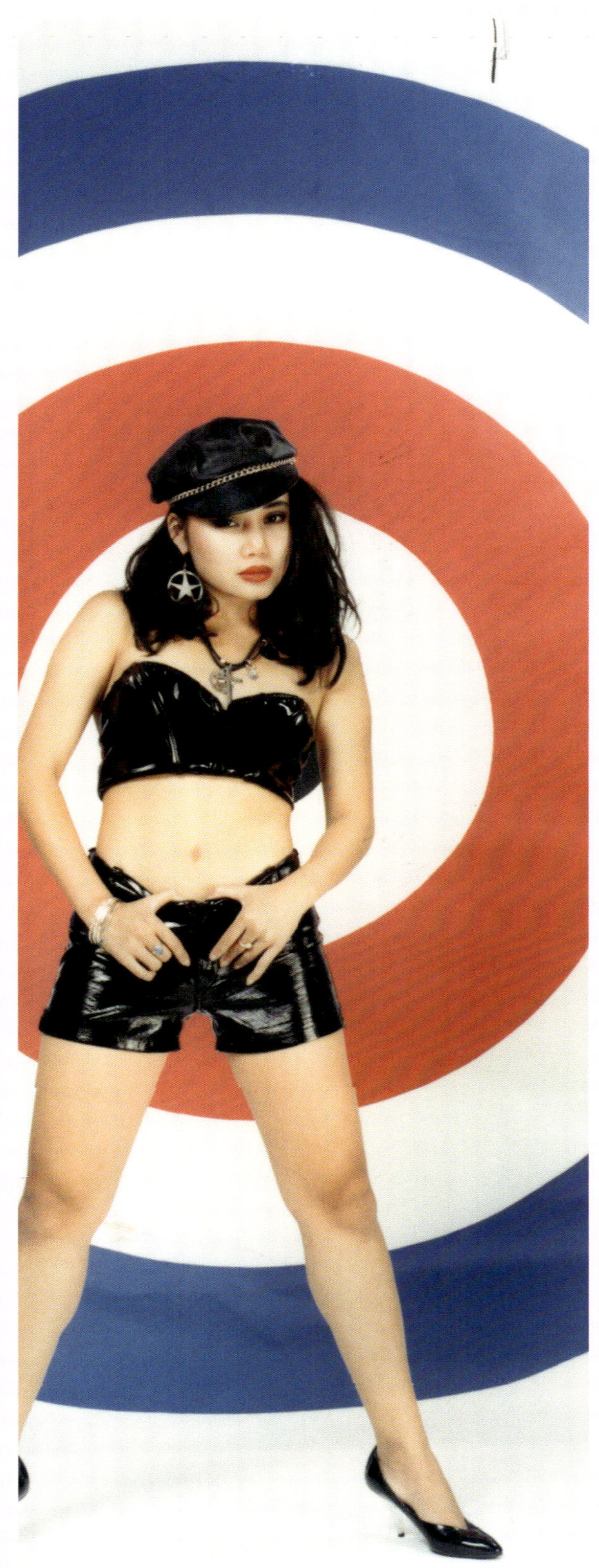

lips and flawlessly gelled hair. (I am sure Thái Tai was my first crush.)

My parents hated this music. It was too sexy, they'd complain, too American. Maybe it was because many times these were American songs, covers reimagined with the electronic danceability of the 1990s and rewritten with Vietnamese verses. Instead of folksy acoustics, these songs relished in the artificial tones of keyboards and the distinct beats of electronic drums. The sound of the songs conjured images of smoky nightclubs with neon lights, not the countryside of the Vietnam I never knew.

Still, my parents gave in, and every time we went shopping, they'd let me buy a cassette. As a Vietnamese American kid growing up in a community that did not look like me, these cassette tapes felt significant. They were something no one else knew about, and it was like I was in on a secret. They also made me feel so proudly Vietnamese, despite what my parents said. I would accumulate a desk drawer of cassette tapes, all Vietnamese, until a copy of Madonna's *The Immaculate Collection*, accidentally ordered through one of those Columbia House Music Club catalogs, found its way there.

And that was the beginning of the end.

There was more Madonna. She was not only on the radio on the car ride to Virginia; she was now inside the house. Soon cassette tapes were replaced by CDs. My first CD was the *Space Jam* soundtrack, followed by the Spice Girls' debut album, *Spice*. Suddenly, my New Wave cassette tapes started to sound old. And the last thing a kid wanted to be was old.

Sequestered into Vietnamese music shops in mall outlets and a forgotten desk drawer, Lynda and gang were no match, and they, too, went the way of cassette tapes.

Now that I'm my parents' age when they were raising three kids and making shopping trips to the Vietnamese strip mall, CDs, too, are gone. In the years between, I abandoned them for MP3 downloads and, today I listen to music streams on Spotify. Despite promising millions of songs at the touch of a button, their catalog is still meager. There are a few Lynda albums but no Thái Tài.

In bouts of nostalgia, I look up these artists on eBay. People are selling cassettes and CDs at exorbitant prices. If I kept my collection, I could have made a good amount of money now, or perhaps I would have a box full of memories, something that I can hold in my hands, something that was once important to me.

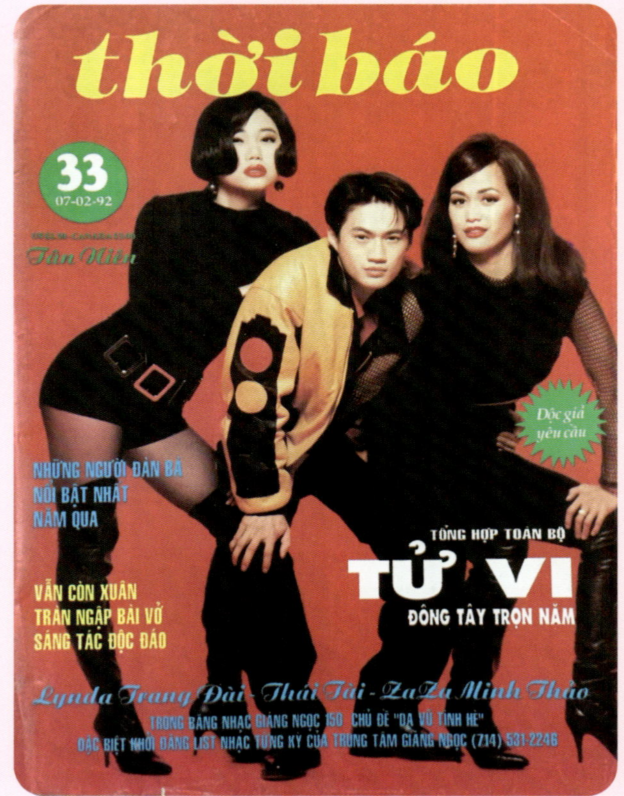

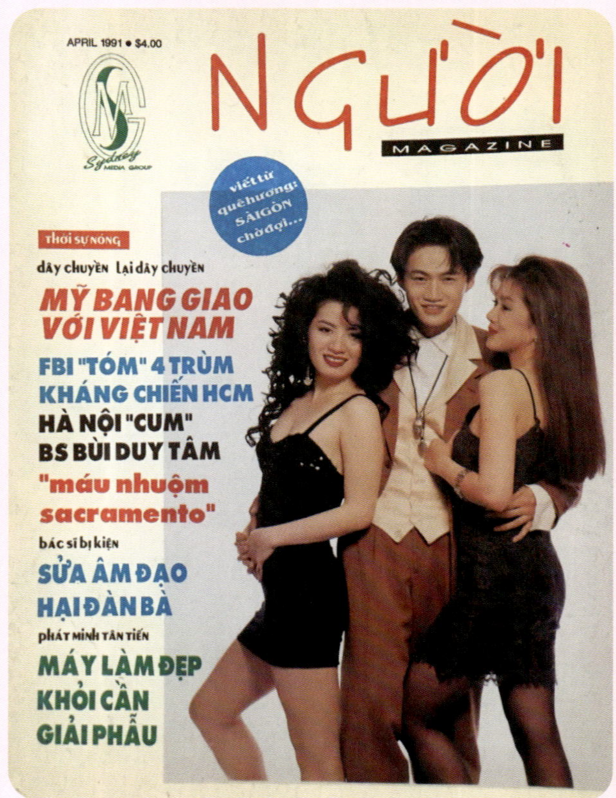

Magazine covers featuring Thái Tài.

As the turn of the millennium approached, the pulse of New Wave music that had once been blaring out of car speakers down Bolsa Avenue in Little Saigon began its slow descent into silence. The Digital Age ushered in new technologies that transformed how music was consumed, and unfortunately, also facilitated a surge in music piracy. The ease of downloading and sharing music files illegally meant that tapes and CDs, once cherished and coveted artifacts in record stores, gathered dust on shelves.

The distinctiveness and rebellious spirit of New Wave, which had marked an era of cultural flourishing and identity formation, faded into obscurity, replaced by the relentless churn of pop hits and radio-friendly tunes that dominated the new century. As the 2000s progressed, the impact of digital piracy and the shifting music industry landscape became more pronounced. Record shops and cultural hubs that had been bustling centers of community interaction and musical exploration, such as the Asian Garden Mall in Little Saigon, now stood quieter. These places, once teeming with life during the heyday of New Wave, began to resemble ghost towns as the youth moved on and away, choosing to live and establish their lives elsewhere.

This shift was not merely a change in musical taste but reflected a larger change within the community itself. The venues that had once hosted raucous gatherings reflected the broader cultural transitions occurring across generations of Vietnamese Americans. Yet, amidst the decline of New Wave, the seeds of a new chapter were being sown. A younger generation, raised at the intersection of their Vietnamese heritage and the diverse influences of American culture, was beginning to make its mark. This new era was not defined by a single musical genre but was characterized by a more eclectic and integrated approach to cultural expression. As the community navigated the complexities of identity in a rapidly globalizing world, they were redefining what it meant to be Vietnamese American in the face of changing times.

As the once bustling hubs like the Asian Garden Mall began to echo with the silence of a bygone era, the youth who had filled these spaces matured into adulthood. This transition from the rebellious fervor of adolescence to the pragmatic realities of adult life mirrors the rise and fall of New Wave music. The dynamic energy and boundless creativity of youth, once expressed through electrifying music and rebellious fashion, gradually gave way to the sobering demands of adult responsibilities. Dreams once vivid with the sounds of New Wave beats are now tempered by the necessities of career, family, and community obligations.

The chapter of youthful rebellion and cultural exploration concludes with a bittersweet acknowledgment of life's inevitable progressions. The cultural vibrancy once dominated by the distinct sounds of V-pop and New Wave yields to the broader, more encompassing rhythms of mainstream American life. Yet, amidst these changes, the core essence of the Vietnamese American identity remains steadfast. Rooted in the resilience and enduring spirit of their community, this identity is unified not just by a shared heritage, but by the collective experiences that have shaped each generation.

And though the era of New Wave may have receded into the annals of history, its legacy endures. It lives on in the hearts and minds of those who once danced to its rhythms, forever influencing the cultural landscape of the Vietnamese American community. As these adults navigate their dual identities, they bring forward the lessons from their youth, shaping not only their lives but also influencing the evolving narrative of their community in America as they pass on their experiences and hopes to the next generation.

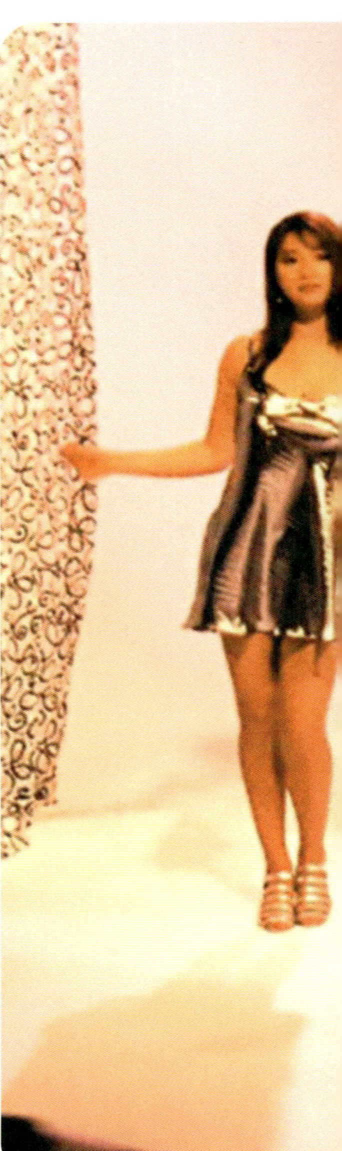

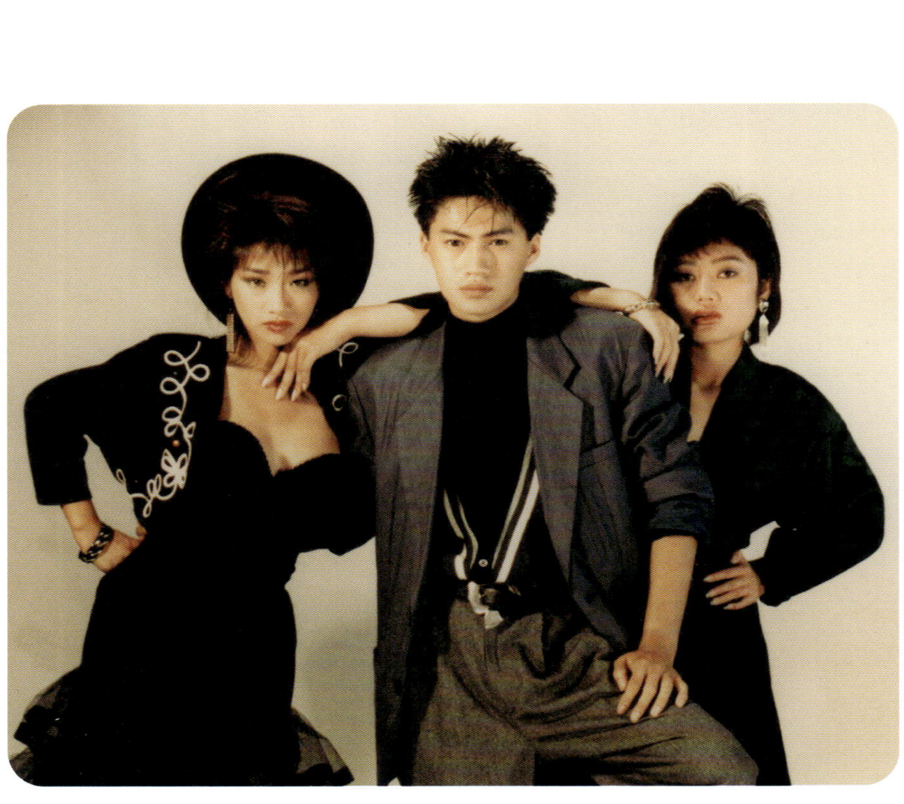

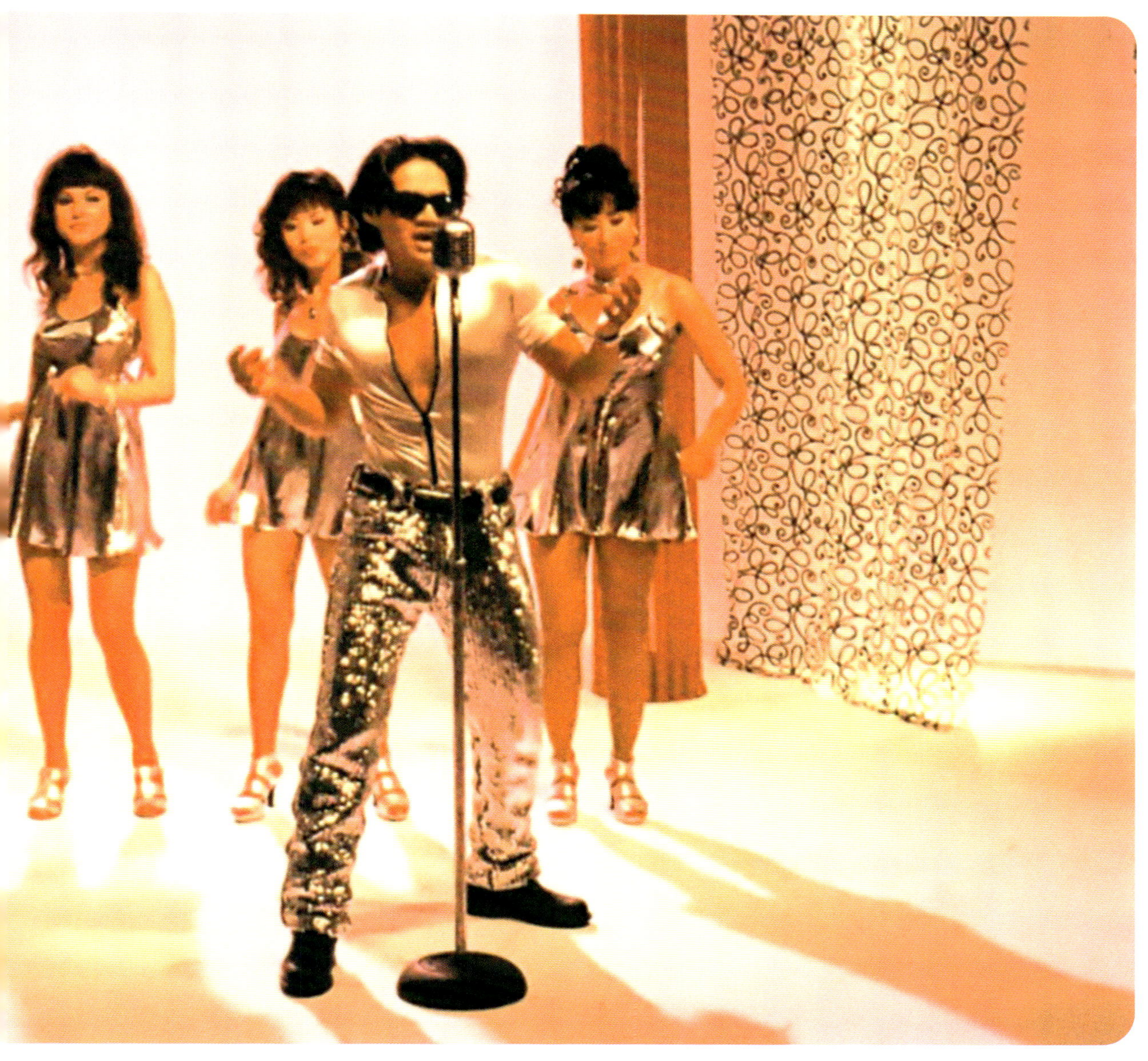

Opposite and above: Thái Tài's career continued into the 1990s, and his style changed with the times.

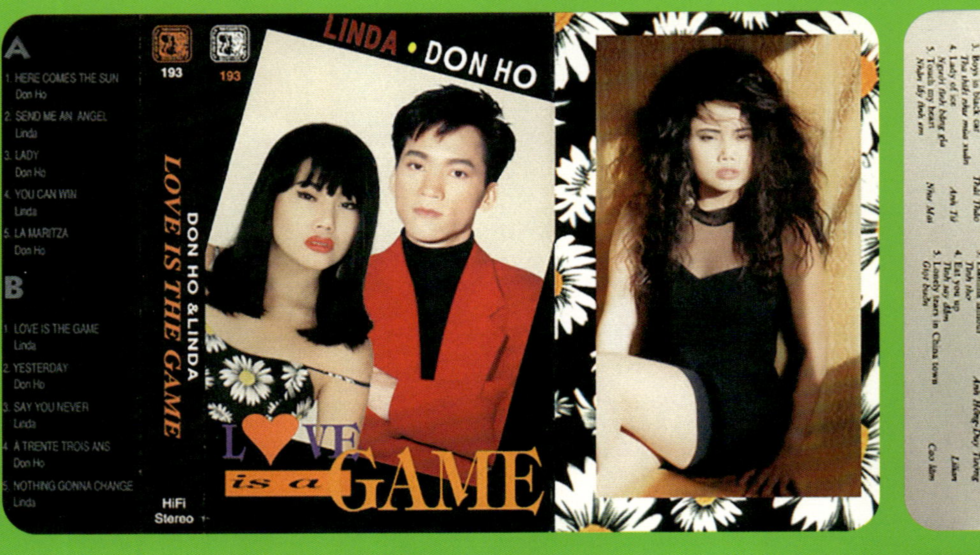

LINDA • DON HO
193
A
1. HERE COMES THE SUN
Don Ho
2. SEND ME AN ANGEL
Linda
3. LADY
Don Ho
4. YOU CAN WIN
Linda
5. LA MARITZA
Don Ho
B
1. LOVE IS THE GAME
Linda
2. YESTERDAY
Don Ho
3. SAY YOU NEVER
Linda
4. A TRENTE TROIS ANS
Don Ho
5. NOTHING GONNA CHANGE
Linda
LOVE IS THE GAME
DON HO & LINDA
LOVE is a GAME
HiFi
Stereo

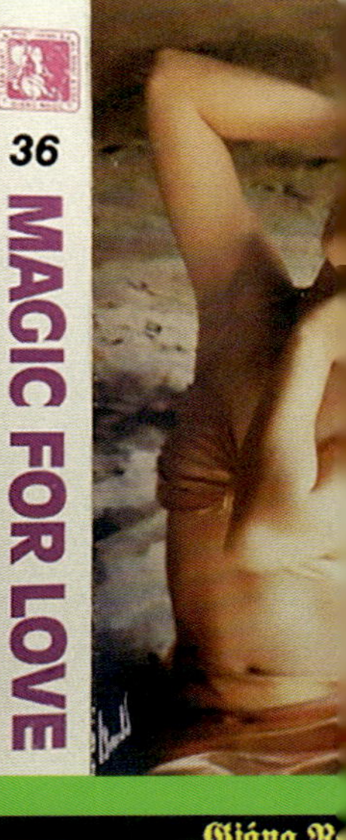

36
MAGIC FOR LOVE

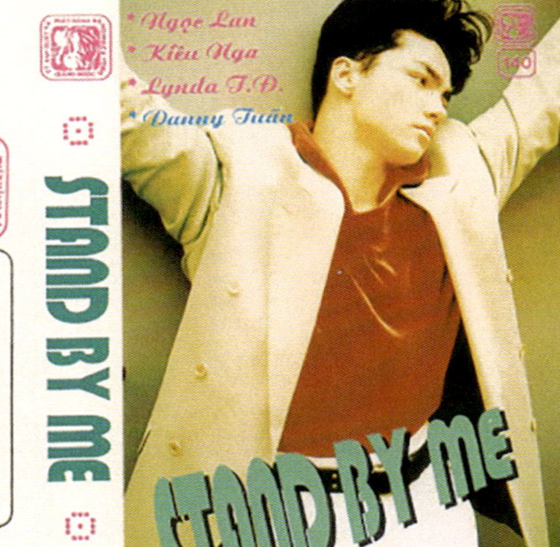

* Ngọc Lan
* Kiều Nga
* Lynda T.Đ.
* Danny Tuấn
STAND BY ME
TRUNG TÂM GIÁNG NGỌC
9551 Bolsa Ave. Suite D&E
Westminster, CA 92683
(714) 531-2246 (714) 963-8781
140
STAND BY ME

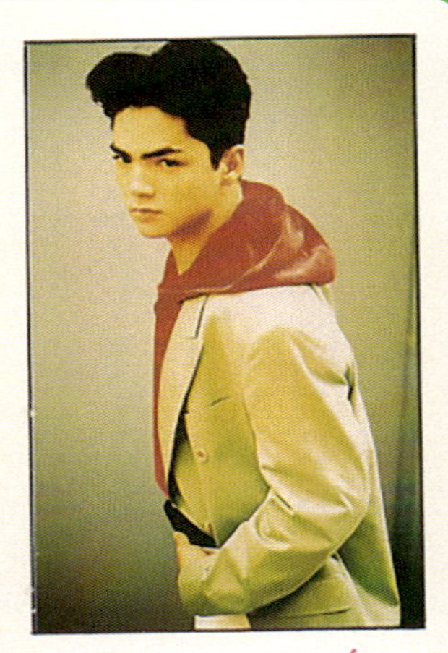

* Ca sĩ DANNY TUẤN

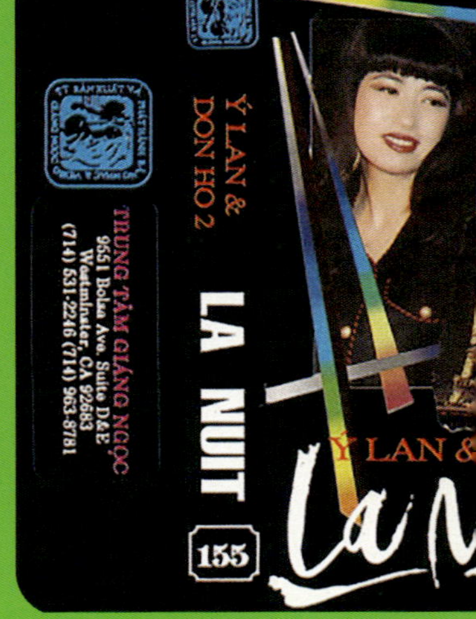

Giáng Ng
Ý LAN & DON HO 2
LA NUIT
TRUNG TÂM GIÁNG NGỌC
9551 Bolsa Ave. Suite D&E
Westminster, CA 92683
(714) 531-2246 (714) 963-8781
155
Ý LAN &

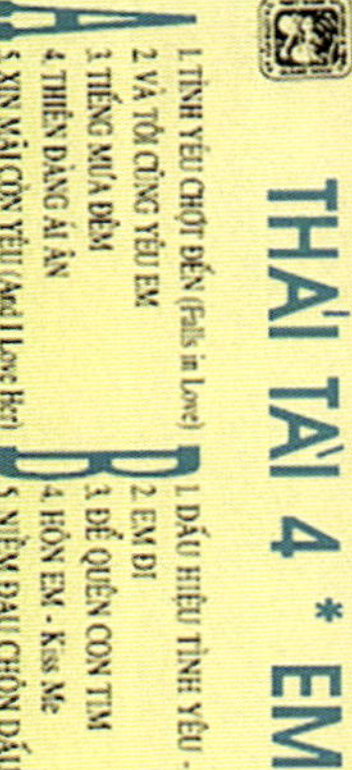

A
1. TÌNH YÊU CHỢT ĐẾN (Falls in Love)
2. VÀ TÔI CŨNG YÊU EM
3. TIẾNG MƯA ĐÊM
4. THIÊN ĐÀNG ÁI ÂN
5. XIN MÃI CÒN YÊU (And I Love Her)
B
1. DẤU HIỆU TÌNH YÊU - Knock Three Times
2. EM ĐI
3. ĐỂ QUÊN CON TIM
4. HÔN EM - Kiss Me
5. NIỀM ĐAU CHÔN DẤU
THÁI TÀI 4 * EM ĐI
182

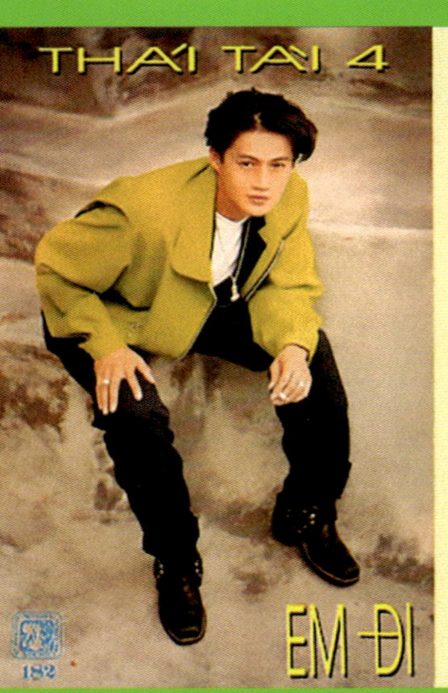

THÁI TÀI 4
EM ĐI
182

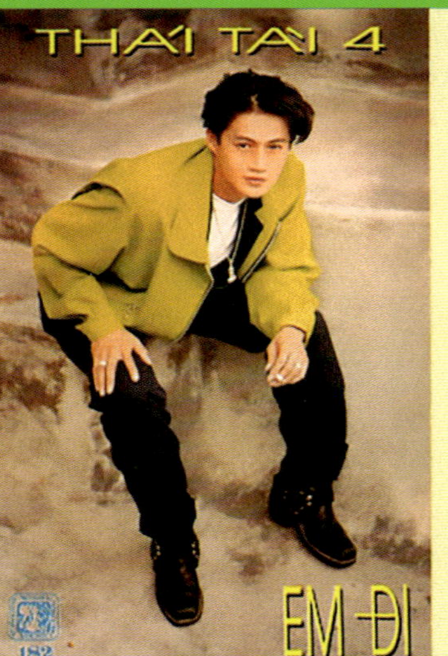

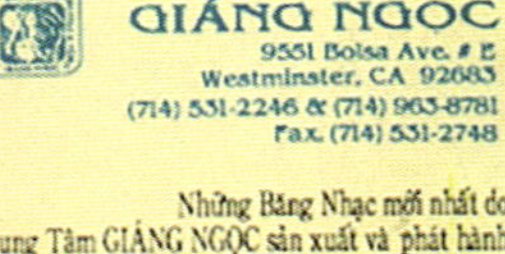

GIÁNG NGỌC
9551 Bolsa Ave. # E
Westminster, CA 92683
(714) 531-2246 & (714) 963-8781
Fax. (714) 531-2748
Những Băng Nhạc mới nhất do
Trung Tâm GIÁNG NGỌC sản xuất và phát hành
Giáng Ngọc 176
BEBOP - CHA CHA
Giáng Ngọc 177
CUỐI CÙNG CHO MỘT TÌNH YÊU
Giáng Ngọc 178
ĐÊM BUỒN TỈNH LẺ
Giáng Ngọc 179
MERCEDES BOY
Giáng Ngọc 180
THÀNH PHỐ MƯA BAY
Giáng ngọc 181
TÌNH SAY

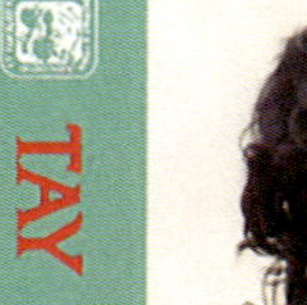

Side a:
1. HẠNH PHÚC BUỒN — THÁI CHÂU
2. TAY NGỌC — LAN THANH
3. EM CHỜ HẸN — DON HO
4. MỘT NGÀY CHO TÌNH YÊU — LAN THANH
5. ĐÊM HOÀNG LAN — HOÀNG T. TÂM
Side b:
1. XUÂN KHÚC — LAN THANH
2. HƠN KHỞI THƯỚC — THÁI CHÂU
3. GIỌT LỆ TÌNH — HẢI LÝ
4. THÁNG 6 TRỜI MƯA — HOÀNG T. TÂM
5. TÓC BUỒN — LAN THANH
TAY NGỌC
Tình Ca Hoàng Thanh Tâm
165

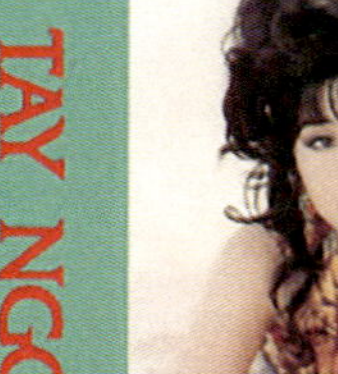

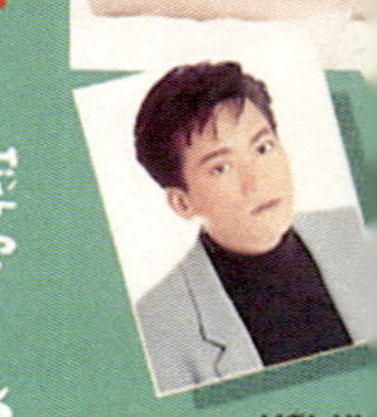

VỚI NH

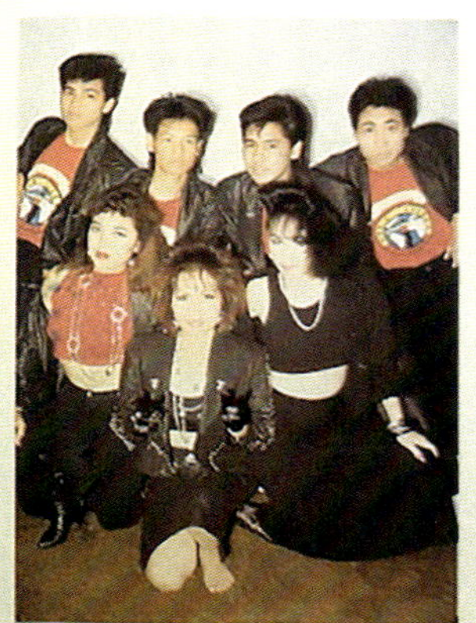
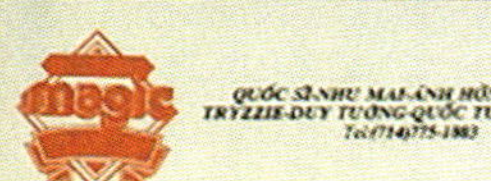
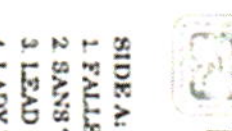
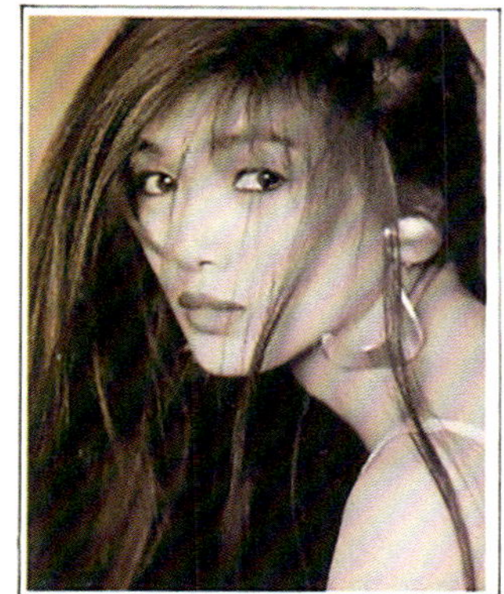
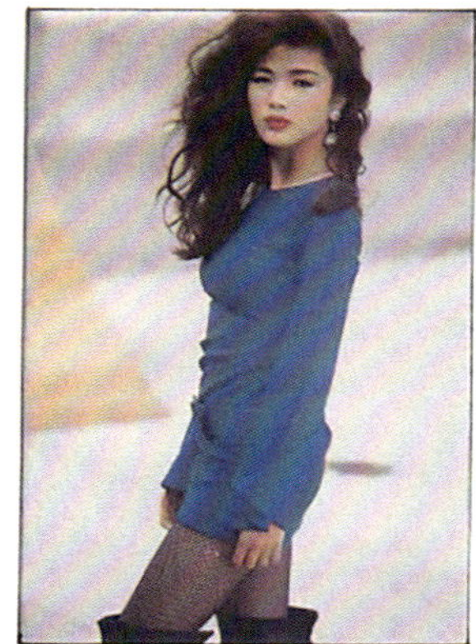
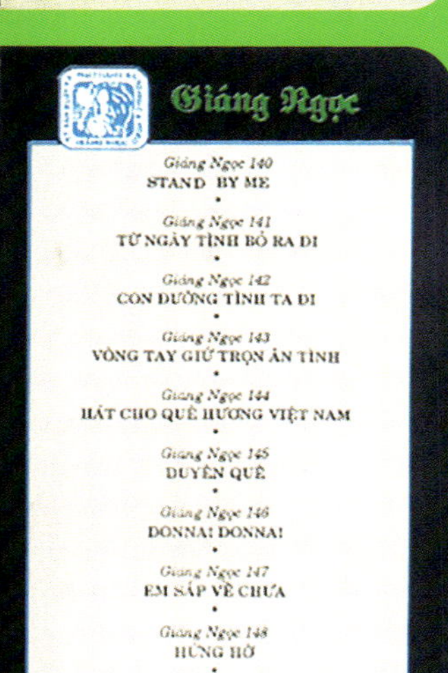
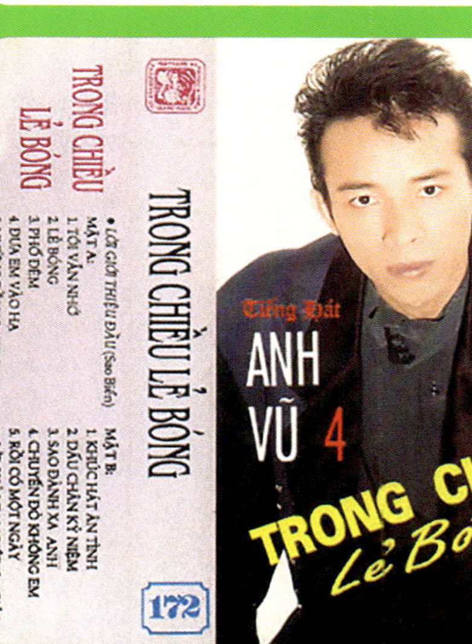
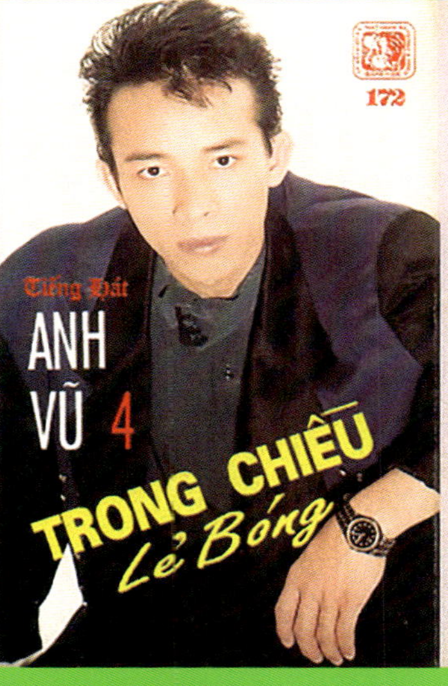
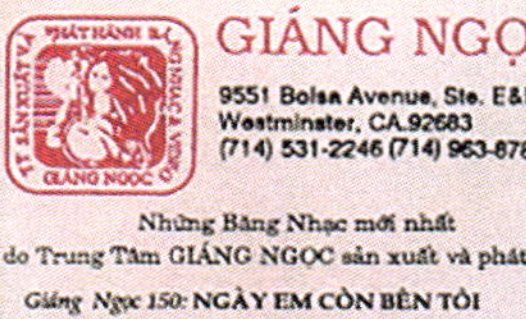
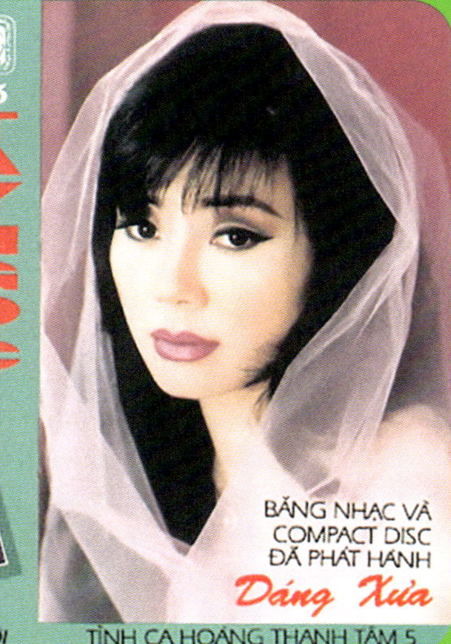
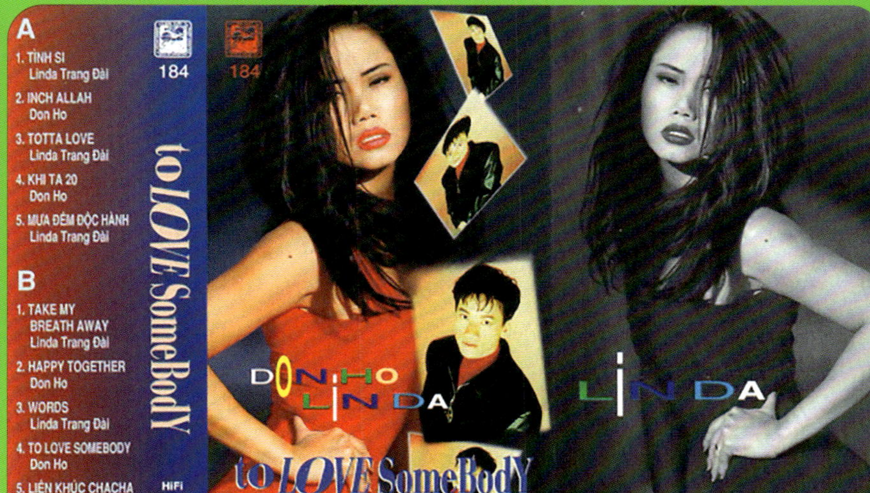

Cassette tapes from Giáng Ngọc Productions, after the New Wave era began to fade.

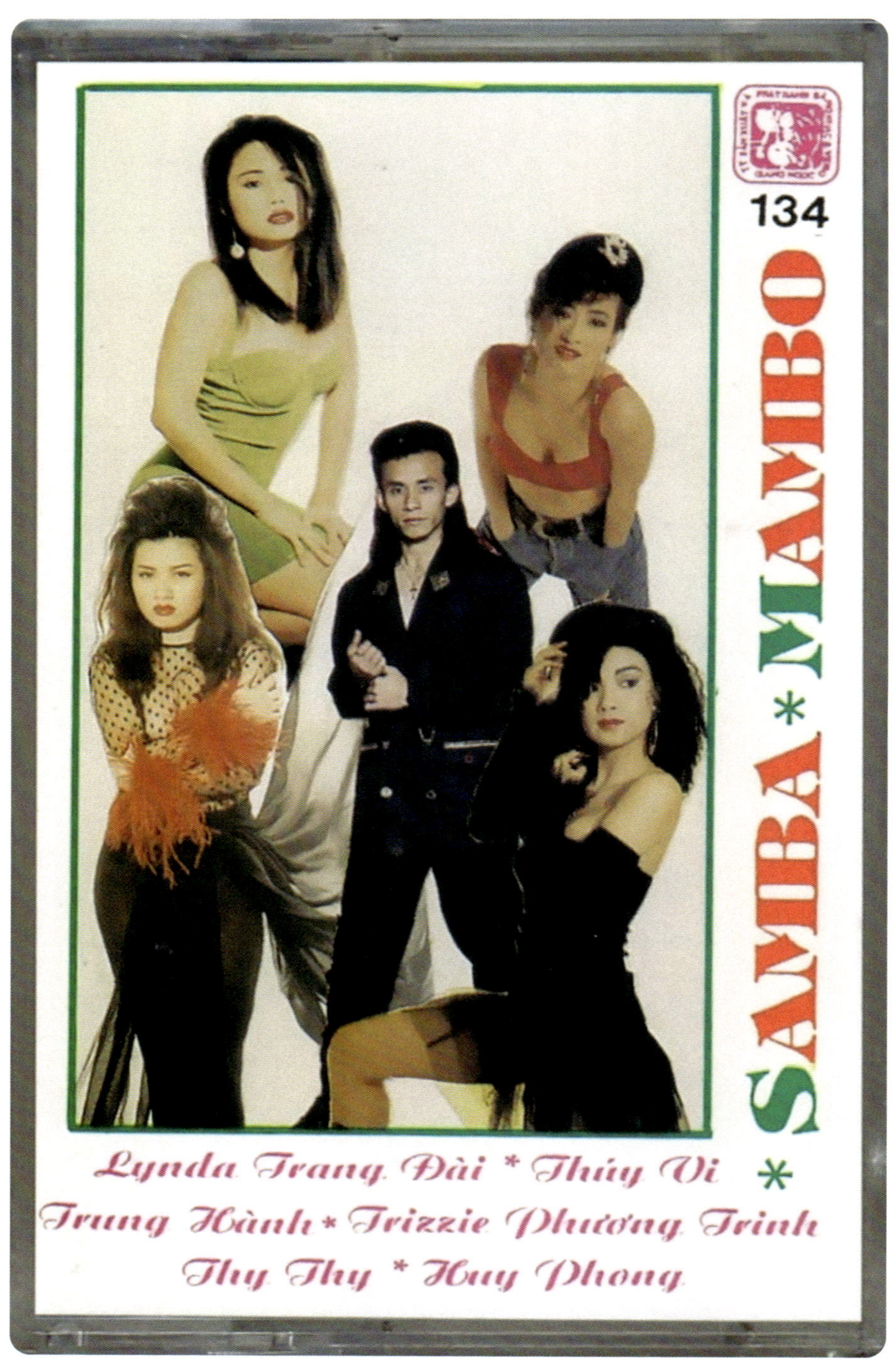

As time moved on, New Wave artists experimented with different genres to stay on trend.

MAKE SURE YOU BRING CASH

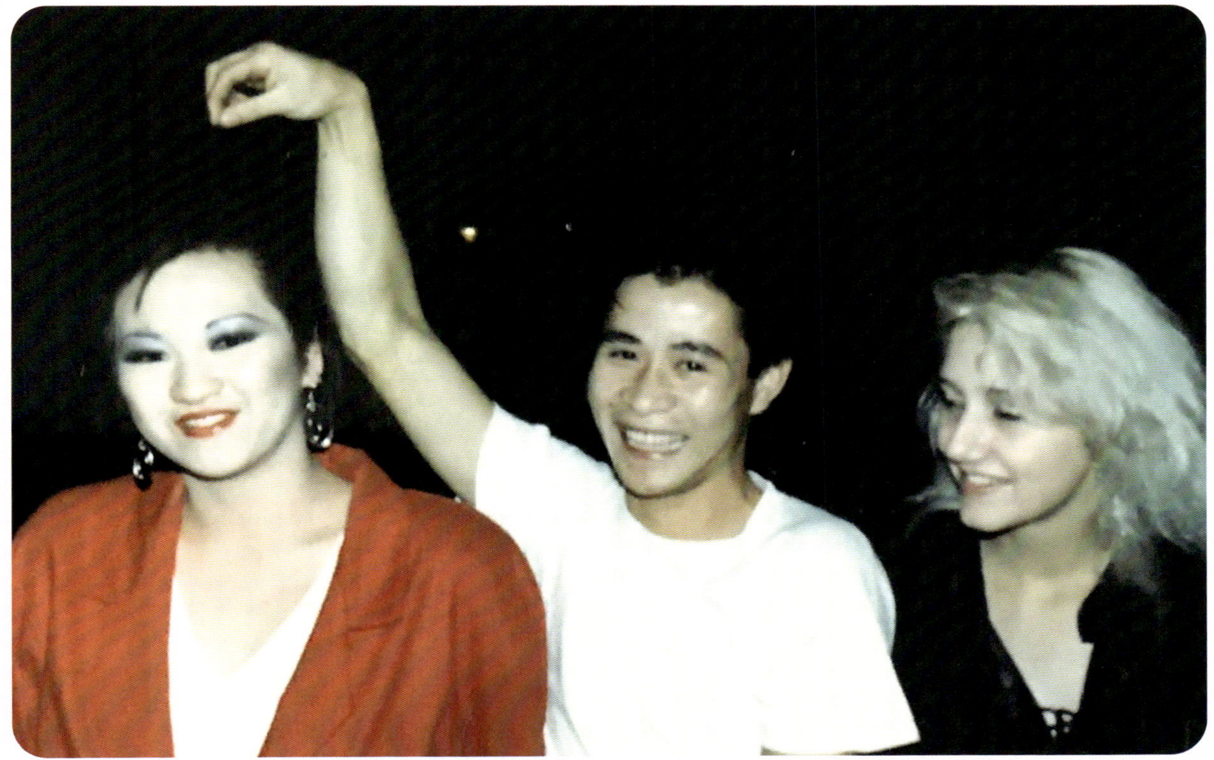

Carolyn Huynh

The father of the bride, Paul Tran, had only one request for his first-born daughter's wedding: at some point in the night, play his curated seven-hour Spotify playlist filled with ninety-six New Wave and Classic Rock hits. Paul hadn't outright threatened his daughter and future son-in-law to ensure that his playlist, aptly titled "Father of the Bride Favorites," be prioritized, but it was heavily insinuated. On top of her other duties, the bride,

Paul Tran and his friends in the 1980s.

Catherine Tran, applied pressure to the DJ to make her father's wish come true, because she knew how much it would mean to him to hear New Wave play at her wedding.

As the eldest Vietnamese daughter, Catherine understood that her wedding wasn't about herself, or her fiancé, it was about the family, always. And nothing would make her family happier than hearing the soundtrack of their youth, to dance at the first daughter's wedding (and she was the first to get married!) to the sounds of New Wave staples such as Depeche Mode, Pet Shop Boys, Eurythmics, and more. Along with the random Enrique Iglesias, Ricky Martin, and Pitbull song thrown in, of course.

Because what was more of a full circle moment than watching the next generation dance to that same quirky synth pop that brought them so much comfort when the only identity they had was being immigrant refugees? What would be more on the nose than listening to Billy Idol's "White Wedding" at Catherine Tran's Little Saigon wedding?

Against the backdrop of a strict Catholic junior high, Catherine and I became friends in the way only girlhood can bring two girls together: huddling in large groups with other Asian girls during lunch and shyly revealing who our crush was. As the only Buddhist girl in Catholic school, I was grateful I had someone to lean on. Beyond any fake piety we had to put on in front of the stone-faced nuns

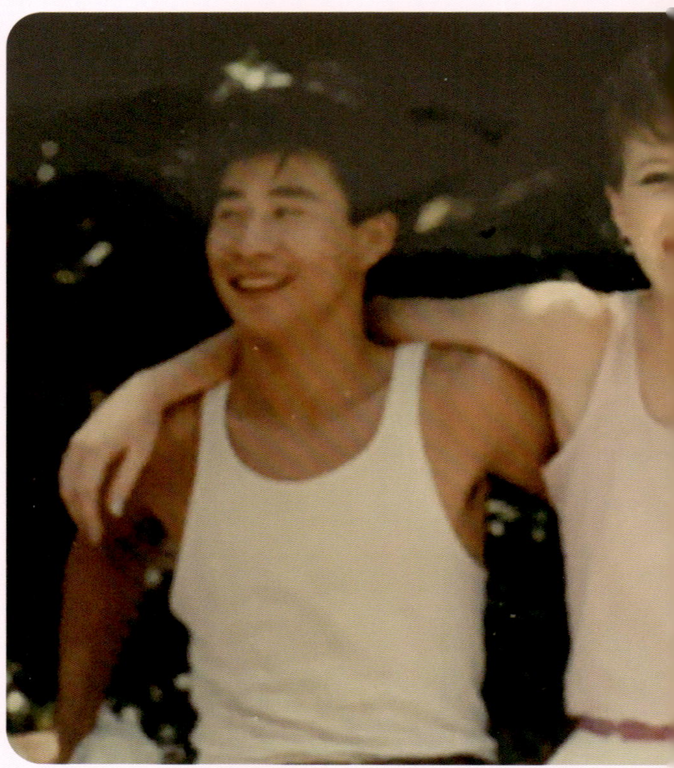

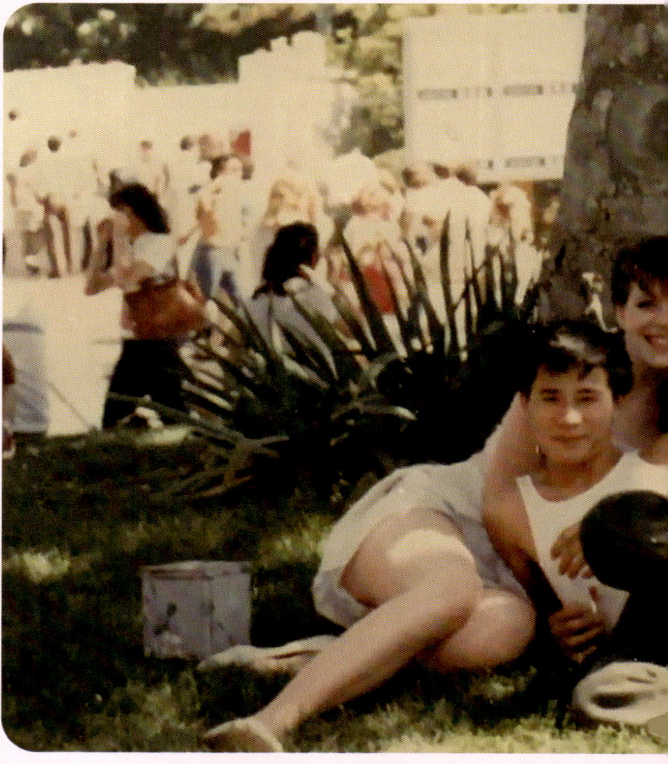

Paul Tran and friends, 1980s.

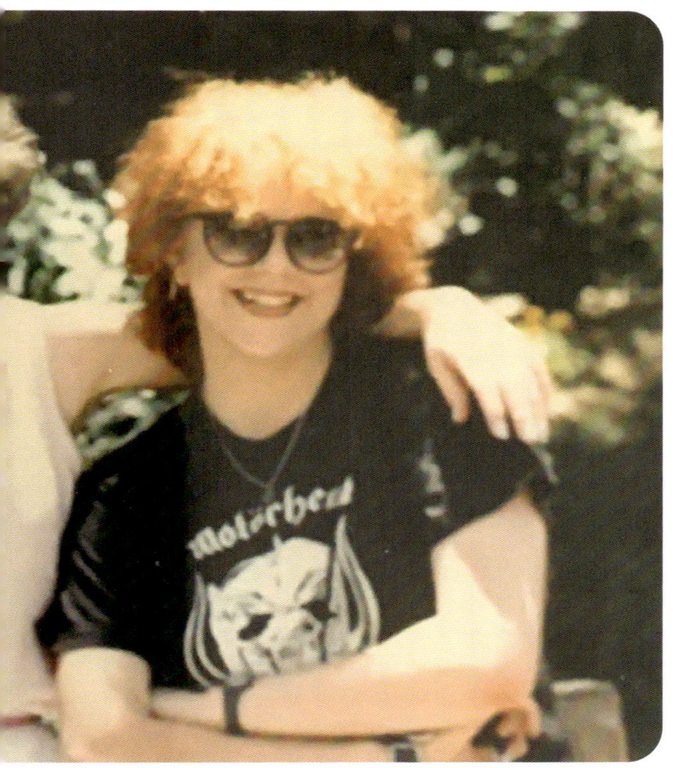

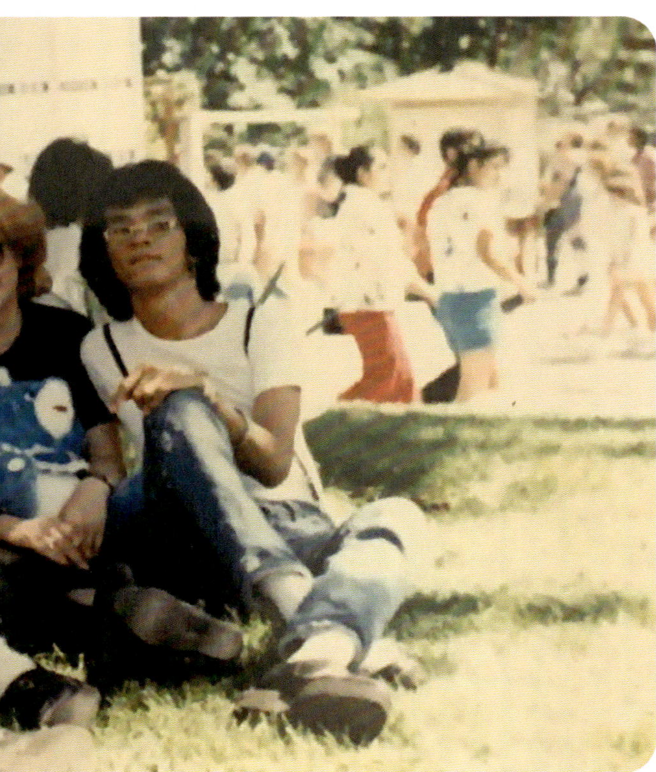

and furrowed-browed priests, Catherine saw just another scrawny, Vietnamese American girl in need of a friend. After a friendship that spans twenty-two years, and one wine-infused summer living together in Portland, I became a bridesmaid at Catherine's wedding. I happily manned the wine station that night, opening bottles left and right, sweating in my custom red *áo dài*, as the queue formed faster than I could uncork.

Meanwhile, Paul Tran was scurrying around shaking hands, the DJ was setting up, the guests were figuring out their seat placements, and the bride and groom were getting ready for their entrance. Everything looked familiar, yet different, at Diamond Seafood Palace 2 in Garden Grove. (Not Diamond Seafood Palace the first, or Diamond Seafood Palace 3, the second one. It's important to distinguish: otherwise you'll get lost). The white-draped chairs, the translucent flower lights, the waiters wearing white button-ups, the faux-glass chandeliers. It was the picture-perfect Orange County Vietnamese banquet wedding, and as I uncorked faster, I knew that meant people were ready to party. An Orange County Vietnamese wedding in Garden Grove meant that it was going to be one long, drunken, debaucherous night. Intermixed between the seven courses of crab and white asparagus soup and Peking duck, there would be a mix of Hennessey, free-flowing wine, and the dance floor. The guests knew to bring cash, and if their non-Vietnamese significant other didn't, they were quickly taught.

I'd brought $200 with me in cash. This ritual was ingrained in me, just like these familiar spaces. But I wondered how much longer these spaces would be preserved. Would we be the last generation to do banquet-style, seven course meal weddings? Is this how all the aunties and uncles felt when they watched big hair, boxy shoulder pads, and New Wave go out of style? So much of their identity was caught up in that particular style, just like how most of my identity was caught up in these banquet halls. How many more Vietnamese banquet weddings would I be able to attend in my lifetime, where the father requested New Wave? Or would this be the last?

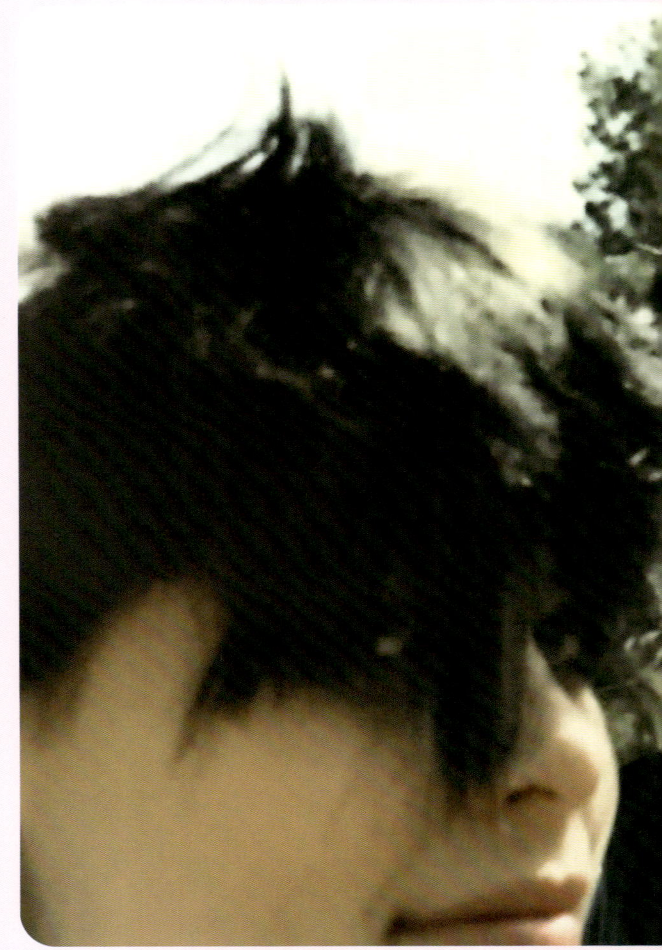

The dance floor opened up. I watched Catherine dance with her husband to their first song as husband and wife. Paul gave a speech. The best man and maid of honor gave speeches. There was a money dance (the groom was Filipino). Between the second and third courses, I remember thinking the playlist slapped hard. Whoever was in charge or had curated the three different playlists knew what they were doing. I watched in awe as all the aunties and uncles began to get up and dance. I missed my father at that moment, grieving for the many unspoken moments between us, wondering if he'd ever get up and dance like that at my own wedding someday. I missed my mother even more, and wondered if she'd

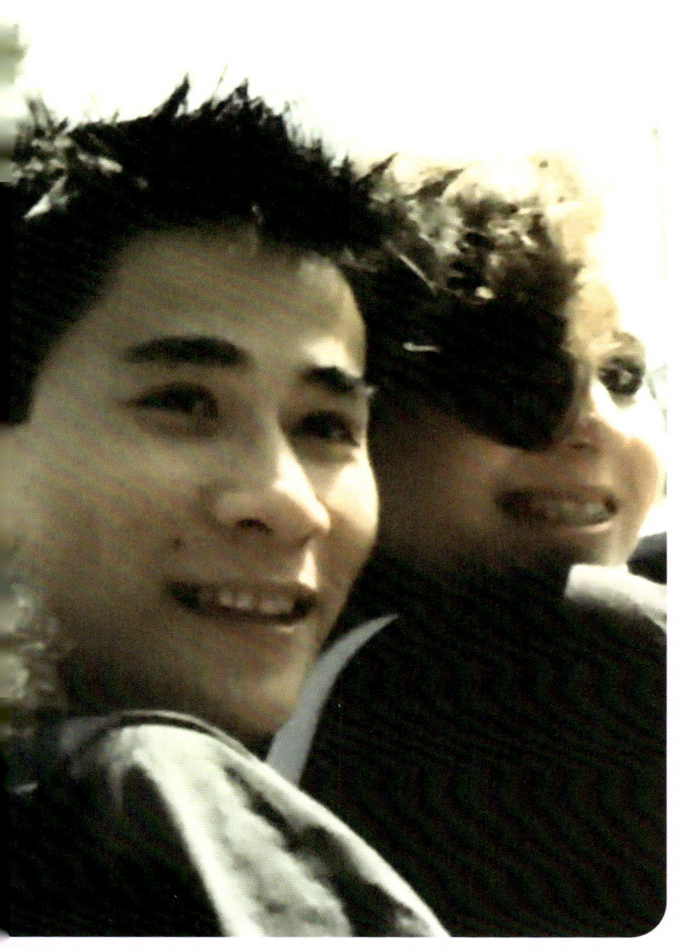

ever danced by herself, alone in her room, in her youth. Someone handed me the money box and told me it was my turn to work the crowd. I quietly slipped in my $200 and began to go around the room, following the bride and groom, as they went around greeting each table, dancing my way to each guest, shaking the box for more cash.

The first song on Paul's playlist was "Poison Arrow" by ABC. The last song was "In the Year 2525" by Visage. I don't know if the DJ played all of his list, some, or just a few songs, but as I watched an elderly Vietnamese man dance, I promised myself that I would do my best to keep preserving these spaces and moments for the next generation. And perhaps one day, if I ever have a daughter, when she grows up, she'll learn to dance to New Order while carrying a money box at her best friend's wedding in Garden Grove. And she'll know to always bring cash.

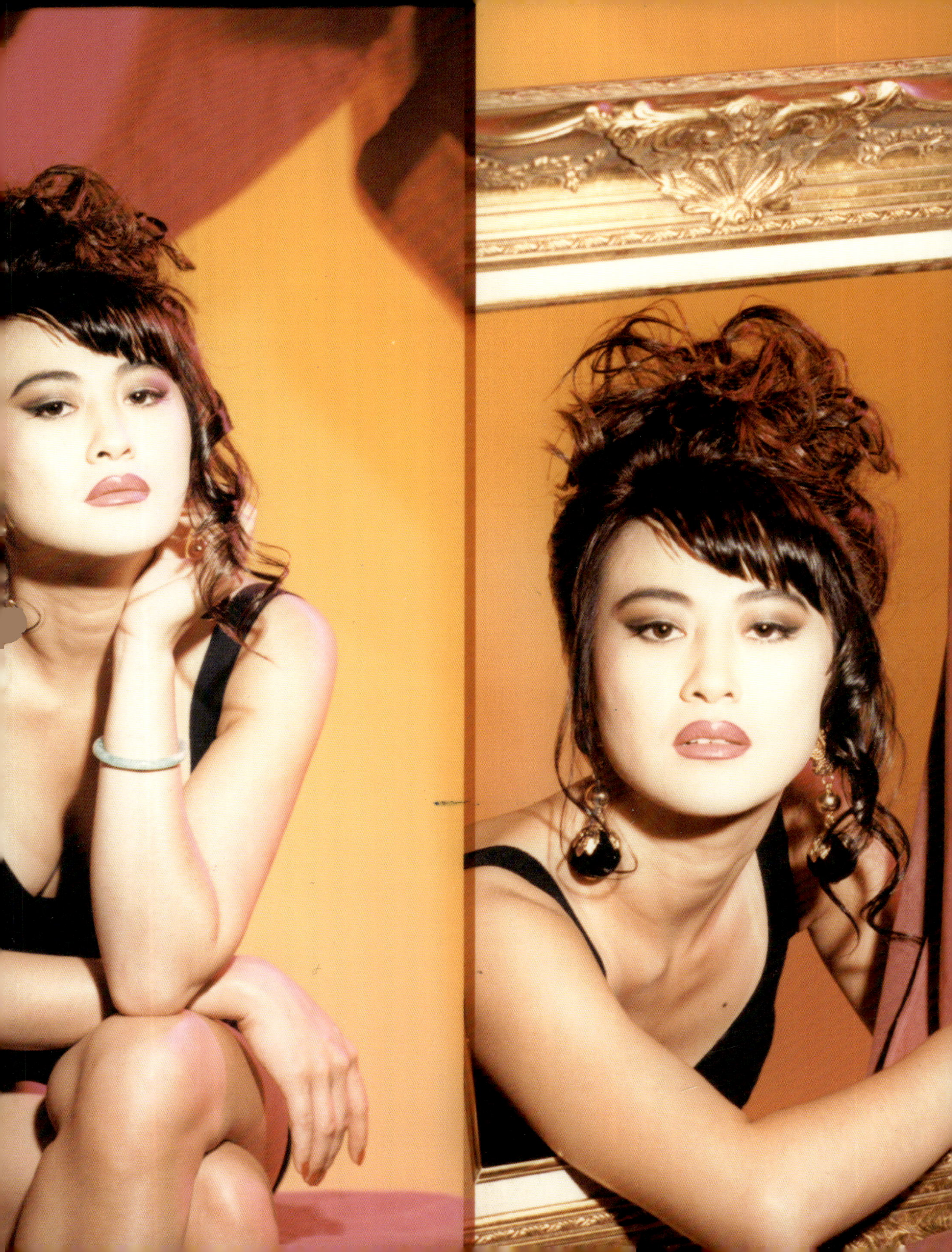

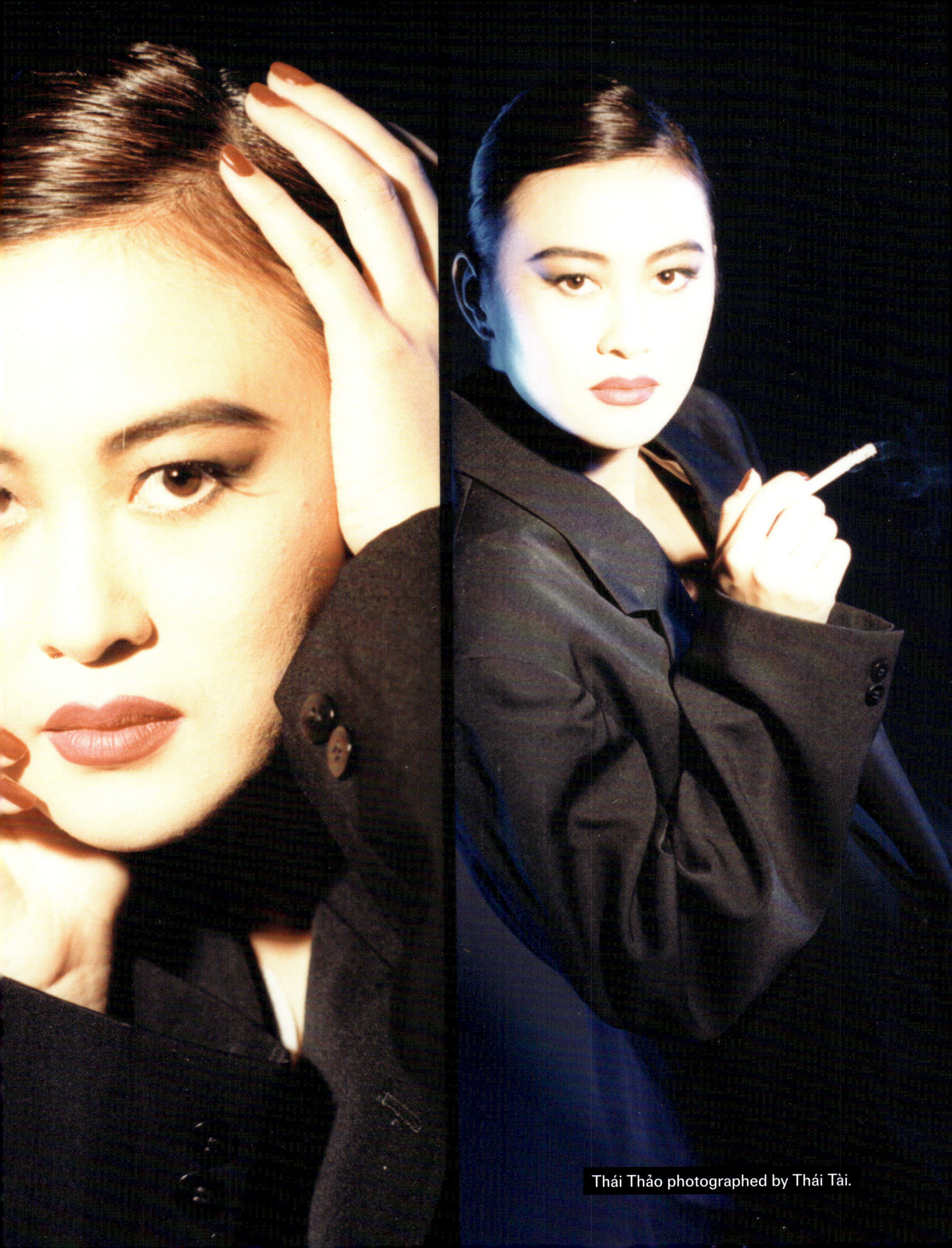

Thái Thảo photographed by Thái Tài.

Orange Co

WHAT GOES ON

Today

A nature film festival for all ages starts at 10 a.m. at the Oak Canyon Nature Center, 6700 E. Walnut Canyon Road, Anaheim. Free. (714) 998-8380.

"A Snow White Christmas," a holiday feast with live music and appearances by Snow White and the Seven Dwarfs and other characters, is being served from noon to 7 p.m. at the Disneyland Hotel, 1150 W. Cerritos Ave., Anaheim. $12.50 to $34.50, $3 for children under 3. (714) 956-6413.

Da Utters, Shiver and **the Belly Rays** play rock at Linda's Doll Hut, 107 S. Adams St., Anaheim. Show time: 8 p.m. Free. (714) 533-1286.

Billy Mitchell plays jazz at 8 p.m. at Randell's, 3 Hutton Centre Drive, Santa Ana. Free. (714) 556-7700.

Echo Love Chamber plays rock at 9 p.m. at Casey's Back Alley Bar & Grill, 1325 N. Tustin Ave., Orange. Free. (714) 538-9683.

The Details play rock at 9 p.m. at the Centerfield Sports Bar & Grill, 17296 Beach Blvd., Huntington Beach. Free. (714) 848-0113.

No-X-It plays rock at 9 p.m. at the Loose Moose Saloon, 8901 Katella Ave., Anaheim. $3. (714) 826-2040.

Upcoming

Eddie Money sings Sunday and Monday at 8 p.m. at the Coach House, 33157 Camino Capistrano, San Juan Capistrano. $29.50. (714) 496-8930.

Winter art camps for ages 6 to 13 take

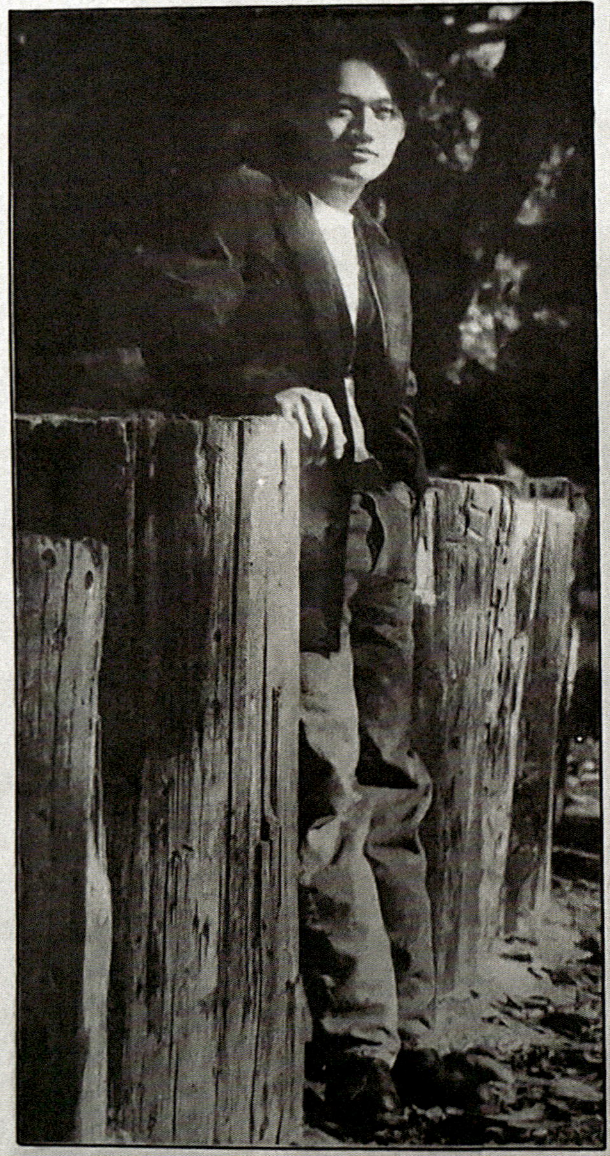

LUIS SINCO / For The Times

"It's like a lot of therapy," says singer and actor Tai Thai about the emotional experience of performing in Oliver Stone's Vietnam epic, "Heaven and Earth." "All these feelings start coming back, all these emotions."

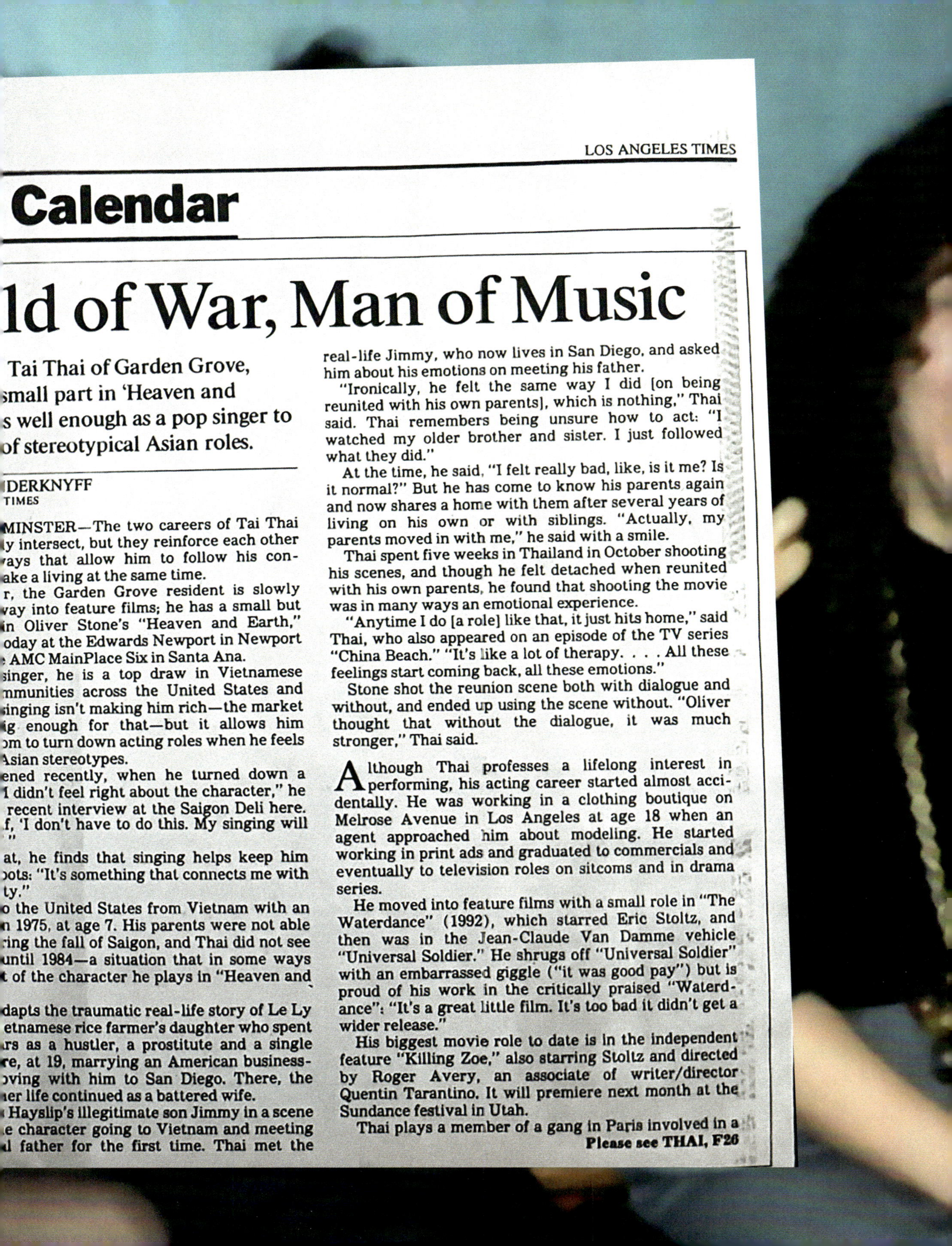

Calendar

ld of War, Man of Music

Tai Thai of Garden Grove,
small part in 'Heaven and
s well enough as a pop singer to
of stereotypical Asian roles.

DERKNYFF
TIMES

MINSTER—The two careers of Tai Thai
y intersect, but they reinforce each other
ays that allow him to follow his con-
ake a living at the same time.
r, the Garden Grove resident is slowly
vay into feature films; he has a small but
in Oliver Stone's "Heaven and Earth,"
oday at the Edwards Newport in Newport
AMC MainPlace Six in Santa Ana.
singer, he is a top draw in Vietnamese
mmunities across the United States and
singing isn't making him rich—the market
g enough for that—but it allows him
om to turn down acting roles when he feels
Asian stereotypes.
ened recently, when he turned down a
I didn't feel right about the character," he
recent interview at the Saigon Deli here.
f, 'I don't have to do this. My singing will
"
at, he finds that singing helps keep him
oots: "It's something that connects me with
ty."
o the United States from Vietnam with an
n 1975, at age 7. His parents were not able
ring the fall of Saigon, and Thai did not see
until 1984—a situation that in some ways
t of the character he plays in "Heaven and

dapts the traumatic real-life story of Le Ly
etnamese rice farmer's daughter who spent
rs as a hustler, a prostitute and a single
re, at 19, marrying an American business-
oving with him to San Diego. There, the
ier life continued as a battered wife.
Hayslip's illegitimate son Jimmy in a scene
e character going to Vietnam and meeting
l father for the first time. Thai met the real-life Jimmy, who now lives in San Diego, and asked him about his emotions on meeting his father.

"Ironically, he felt the same way I did [on being reunited with his own parents], which is nothing," Thai said. Thai remembers being unsure how to act: "I watched my older brother and sister. I just followed what they did."

At the time, he said, "I felt really bad, like, is it me? Is it normal?" But he has come to know his parents again and now shares a home with them after several years of living on his own or with siblings. "Actually, my parents moved in with me," he said with a smile.

Thai spent five weeks in Thailand in October shooting his scenes, and though he felt detached when reunited with his own parents, he found that shooting the movie was in many ways an emotional experience.

"Anytime I do [a role] like that, it just hits home," said Thai, who also appeared on an episode of the TV series "China Beach." "It's like a lot of therapy. . . . All these feelings start coming back, all these emotions."

Stone shot the reunion scene both with dialogue and without, and ended up using the scene without. "Oliver thought that without the dialogue, it was much stronger," Thai said.

Although Thai professes a lifelong interest in performing, his acting career started almost accidentally. He was working in a clothing boutique on Melrose Avenue in Los Angeles at age 18 when an agent approached him about modeling. He started working in print ads and graduated to commercials and eventually to television roles on sitcoms and in drama series.

He moved into feature films with a small role in "The Waterdance" (1992), which starred Eric Stoltz, and then was in the Jean-Claude Van Damme vehicle "Universal Soldier." He shrugs off "Universal Soldier" with an embarrassed giggle ("it was good pay") but is proud of his work in the critically praised "Waterdance": "It's a great little film. It's too bad it didn't get a wider release."

His biggest movie role to date is in the independent feature "Killing Zoe," also starring Stoltz and directed by Roger Avery, an associate of writer/director Quentin Tarantino. It will premiere next month at the Sundance festival in Utah.

Thai plays a member of a gang in Paris involved in a

Please see THAI, F26

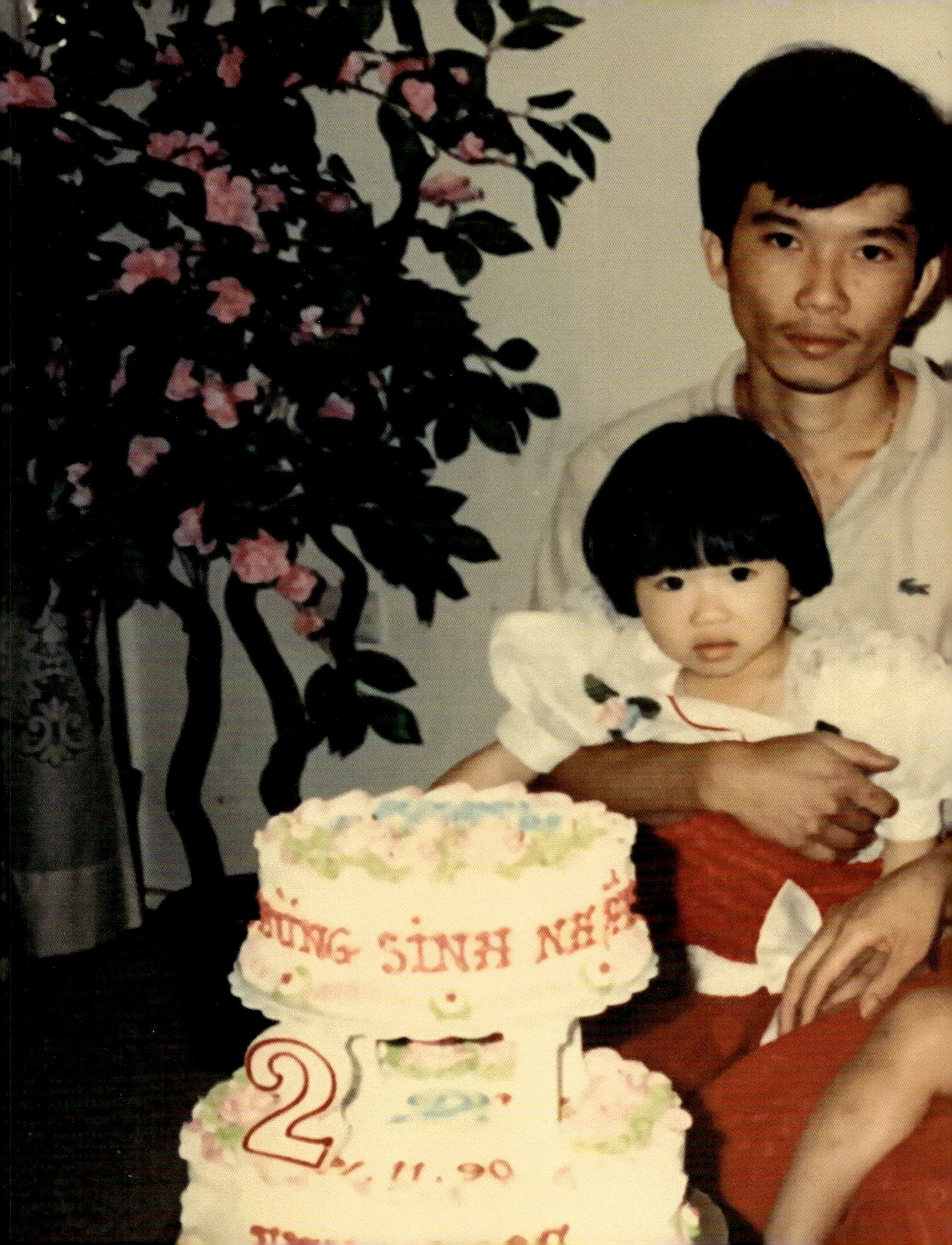
SINH
2
11.90

Vietnamese New Wavers in Australia, 1990.

CHAPTER 5

THE MOTHER OF REINVENTION

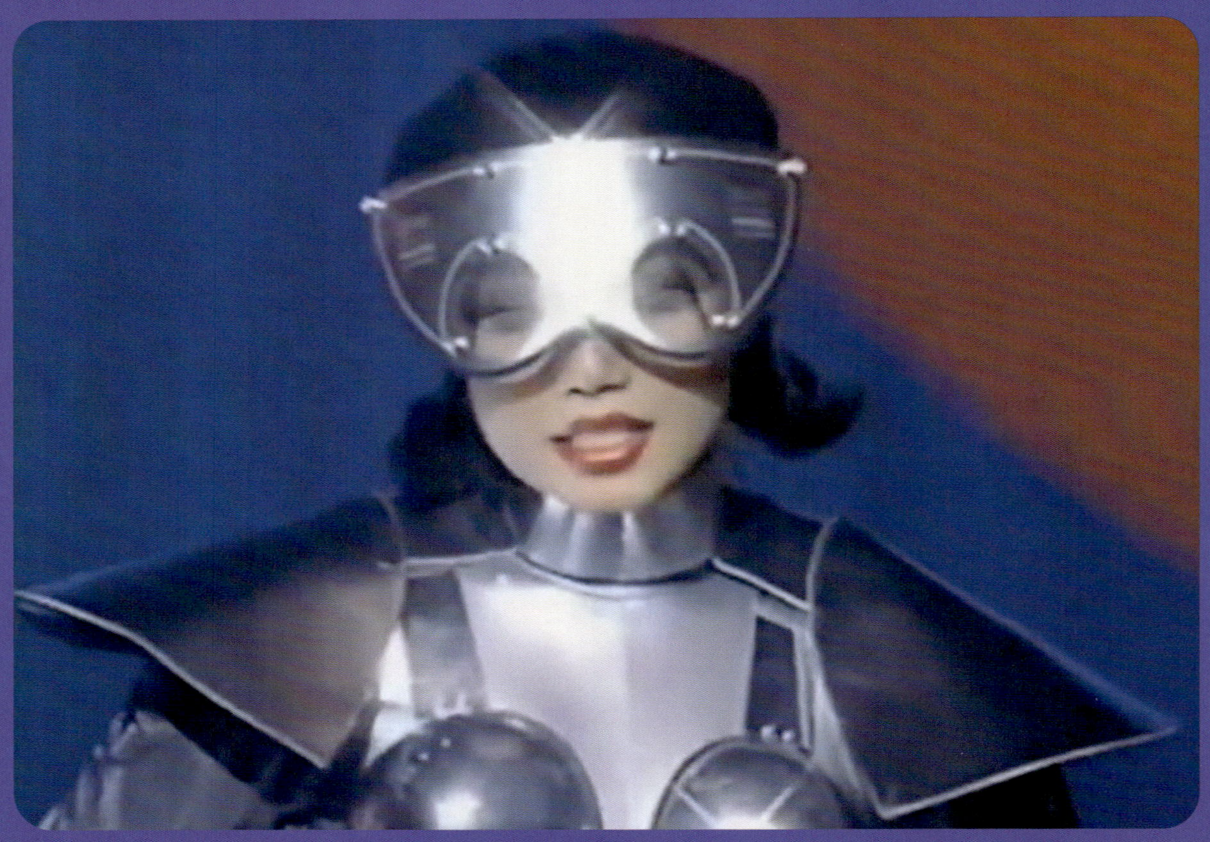

2000s and Beyond

As the 1.5 Generation's exuberance matures into the more measured rhythms of adult life, the power of music and creativity continues to serve as a vital refuge. Though its mainstream popularity has waned, New Wave still resonates throughout the Vietnamese American diaspora, uniting communities across time and space.

The spirit of risk-taking and rebellion that defined the New Wave scene continues to inspire today's generation. Young artists and creatives are challenging the status quo and embracing unconventional paths in pursuit of personal and communal expression. Among them, artists like Thuy, Trace, and Dolly Ave are carving out careers in music as a form of personal healing and community connection. Influenced by her parents' passion for music, Tina Snow Le channels her heritage and her identity as a DJ, using her platform to tell the diverse stories of her community. A creative queer collective known as BUBBLE_T organizes late-night dance parties that not only celebrate the musical icons of their parents' youth but also reclaim and hold space for the cultural vibrancy of New Wave.

Through these varied endeavors, the next generation of Vietnamese Americans is not merely inheriting a cultural legacy; they are actively reshaping and expanding it. By blending the nostalgic elements of New Wave through contemporary expressions and new communities, they ensure their cultural heritage continues to evolve. This dynamic interplay of past and present, tradition and innovation, underscores the community's enduring resilience and creativity—a testament to the powerful role of music and art in the ongoing narrative of identity and belonging.

Constantly evolving, Lynda Trang Đài performs the song *Cyber Queen* on the variety show *Paris by Night*, showing off her new look for the new millennium.

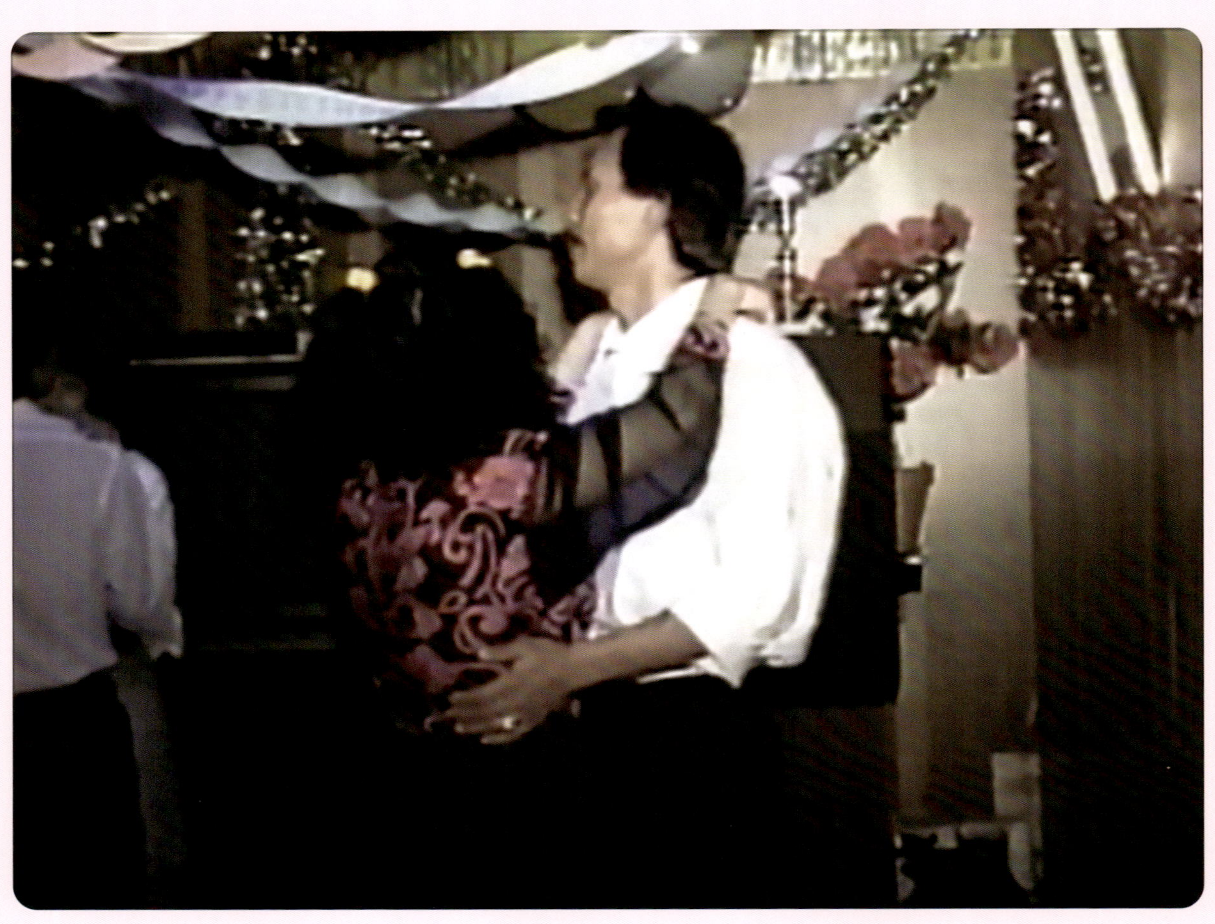

Still from Huỳnh's short film, *Chúng Tôi Nhẩy Đầm ở Nhà (We Dance At Home).*

Opposite: Julia Huỳnh, age five, posing in a purple áo dài in Peterborough, Ontario, Canada.

DANCING THROUGH TIME

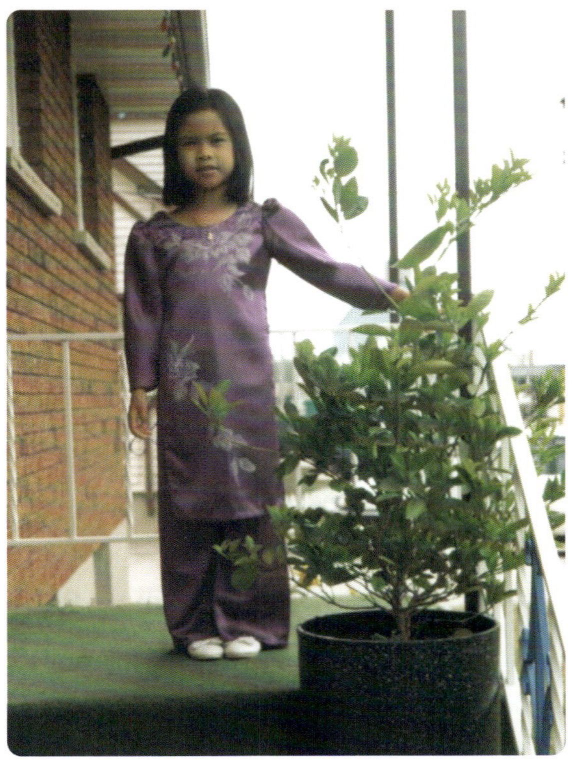

Julia Huỳnh

Remember the journaling prompt in grade school: "What did you do this weekend?" My answer was usually along the lines of "Oh, we had another party!" My parents threw those classic loud Vietnamese parties almost every weekend. Shoes overflowing on top of each other in the foyer. Kids running around, screaming, and laughing. Older kids stuck babysitting the little ones. Dads sitting cross-legged on the floor, helping themselves to the various dishes spread on top of newspapers. Moms gossiping away in the kitchen prepping the dishes. But the party didn't truly start until the karaoke VHS tapes were inserted and the corresponding blue-and-red-labeled microphones were passed around. Couples began to dance, spinning their partners around, hips swaying, arms raised in silky shirts. Each step forward and backward hitting the beat. This was my introduction to New Wave.

As a second-generation Vietnamese Canadian who grew up in a small, predominantly white town, these dance parties at home were the only few times that I was in a space where everyone looked like me. I cherish those gatherings because as we've all gotten older and as life gets busier, it becomes harder for everyone to come together again.

I have always loved to watch my parents dance at home, so much so that I made my own short film about it called *Chúng Tôi Nhẩy Đầm ở Nhà (We Dance at Home)*. I've watched them dance together countless times, mesmerized by their synchronized moves. My dad, an amateur filmmaker in his own right, would edit our home videos to the backdrop of upbeat Vietnamese music. In fact, there's a video of me as a baby bobbing my head to the guitar riffs and synth beats.

I rewatched those videos with curiosity, captivated by my parents' playlist.

"What's that music you and mom are dancing to?" Vietnamese covers of English songs I was somewhat familiar with like "Oh Carol" or Dusty Springfield's "I Only Wanna Be With You." Without hesitation my dad replied, New Wave or Bebop.

I dug through their CD and DVD collections; while my dad had attempted to downsize, there were still at least three boxes full of these colorful CDs. *Doctor New Wave*, *Doctor New Wave 9*, *New Wave 1*, *New Wave 5*, *Fashion Girl*, you name it, he had it.

When I asked my parents why they liked to listen to this type of music, they stated that it made you less sad. It was as simple as that. Not only did this New Wave music and *nhạc xuân* provide fun beats to dance and sing along to, but it allowed a generation of young adults to escape. To simply forget for a moment and enjoy themselves.

Throughout my twenties, I've caught myself yearning to understand what life was like for my parents when they were my age. What did they do for fun? How did they build community? Today, I find myself listening to their music thanks to YouTube and Spotify playlists. In a way, it brings me back to a part of my childhood that was so carefree, where I didn't have to question anything. The music allows me to simply forget, too, and sit with the joy it brings me.

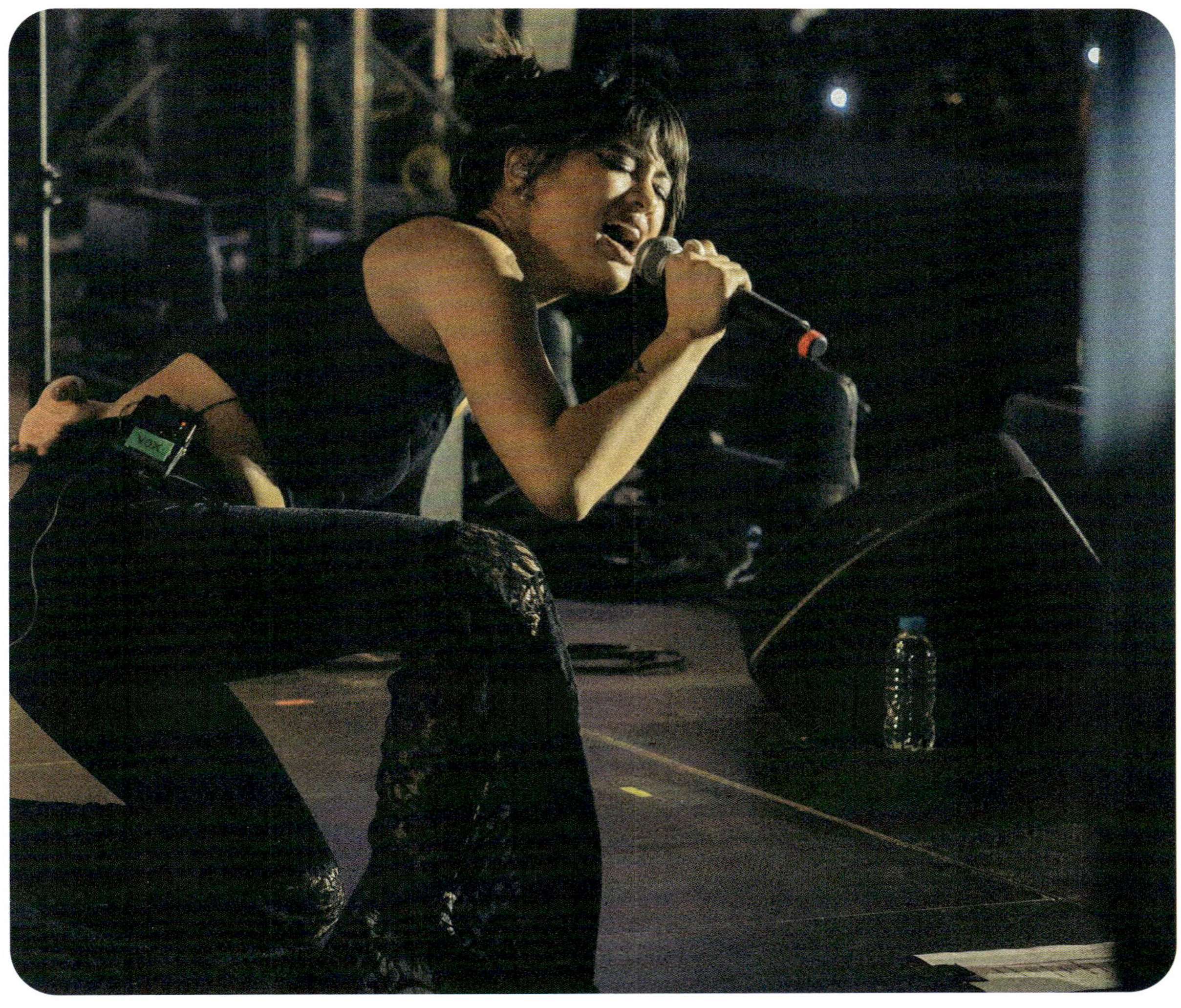

Dolly Ave sings on stage.

"I was thirteen years old residing in Kansas City, Missouri. This was my twentieth house, my second high school transfer, and this strange idea overcame me. I wanted to reinvent myself. Reinventing myself seemed fairly easy in the temporary sense. I've done it countless times. In my short thirteen years of life I have changed schools, taken on new friends, and it became normal to redesign my bedroom with each new canvas. This time I wanted to reinvent my entire existence. I wanted everyone to refer to me as "Dolly Ave." I hated Dolly Nguyen - the life she was born into. I hated that she was born into drugs, poverty, child abuse, government programs. I hated that this young girl had so much imagination for an artistic life, but it was so far from her grasp. Little did I know this alter-ego gave me newfound confidence. This person was energetic, passionate, optimistic, and creative. Dolly Ave saw the world with rose-colored glasses. Her circumstances weren't real. She could be whoever she wanted to be. I reflect now fifteen years later seeing "Dolly Ave" in the most unexpected contexts: *Rolling Stone*, *Harper's Bazaar*, *Billboard*, *Fender*, headlining festivals, the Grammys to name a few. Thirteen-year-old me had a different plan in mind. She didn't know how to fit in the world so she created her own."

– Dolly Ave

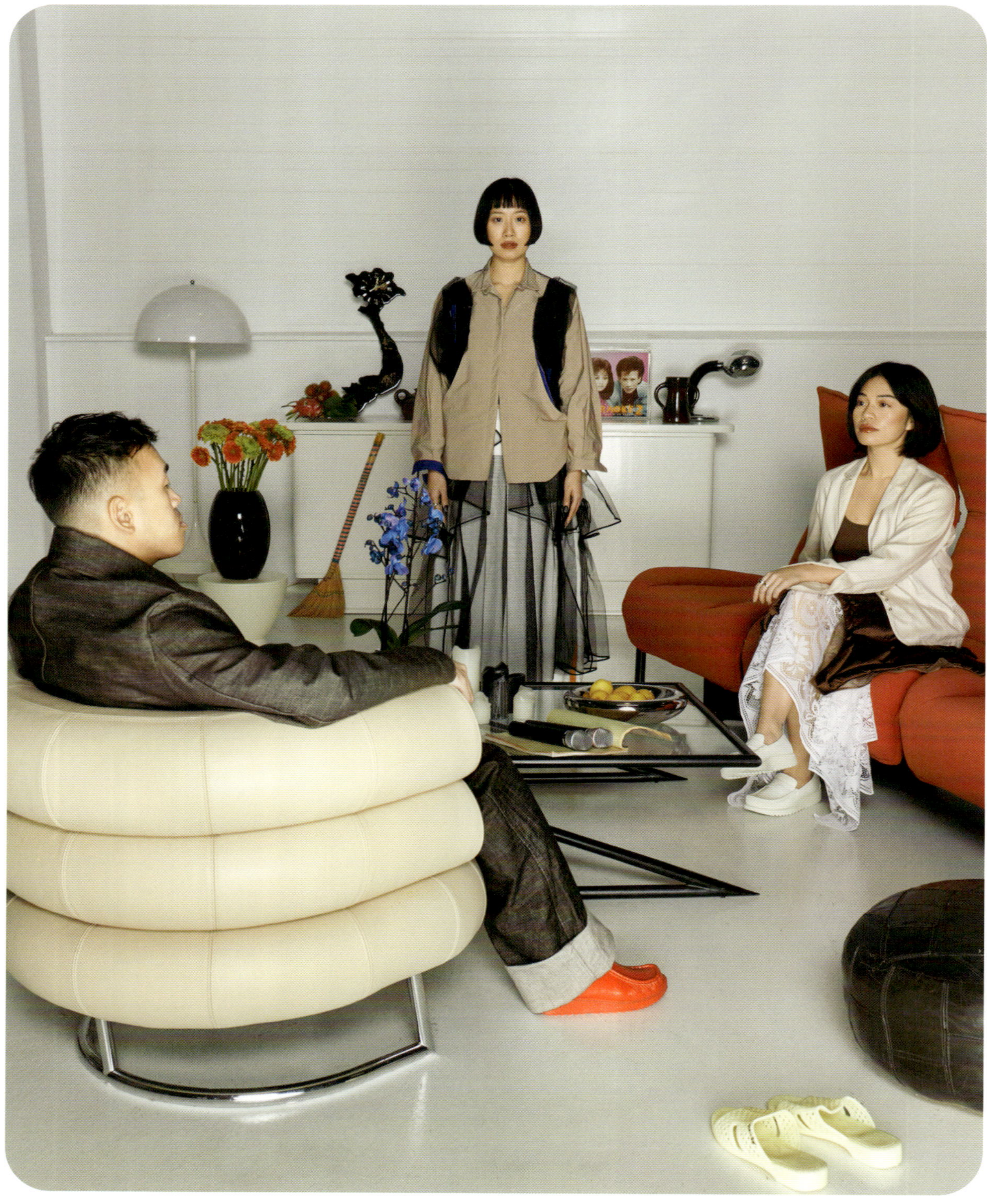

Tessa Yến Nguyễn, co-founder of Saigon Kiss, a multidisciplinary collective of Vietnamese Dutch creatives.

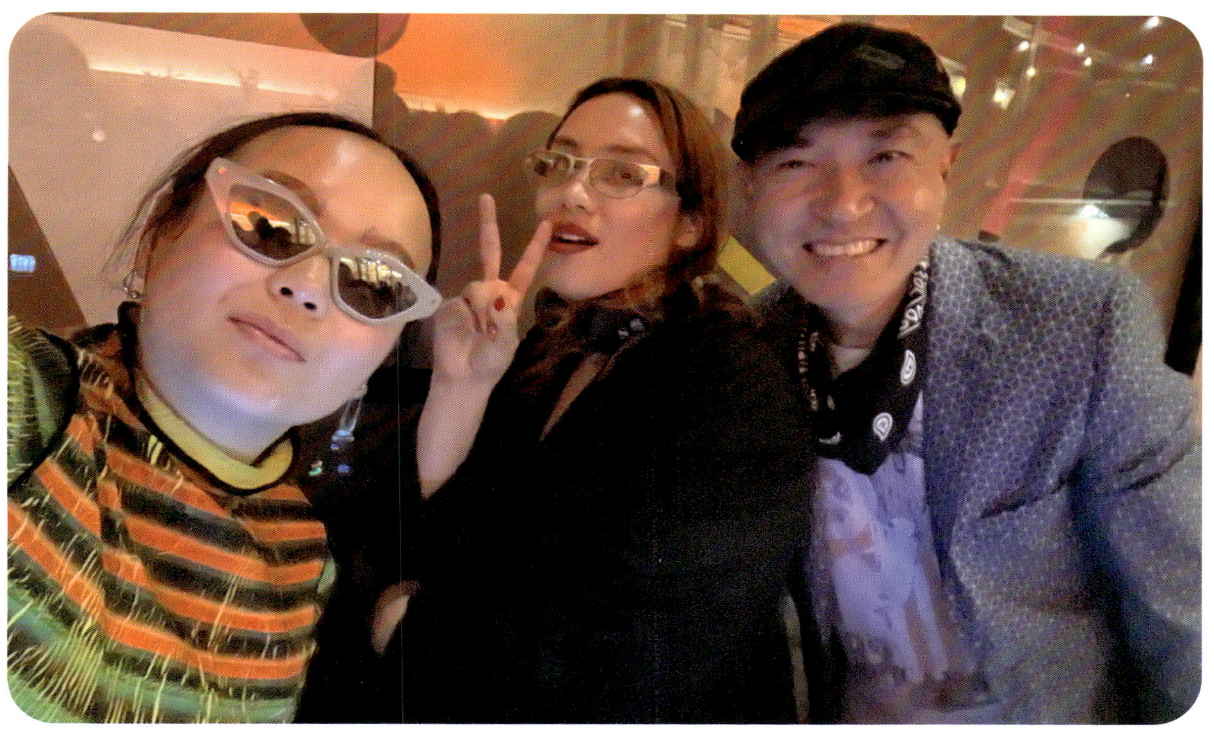

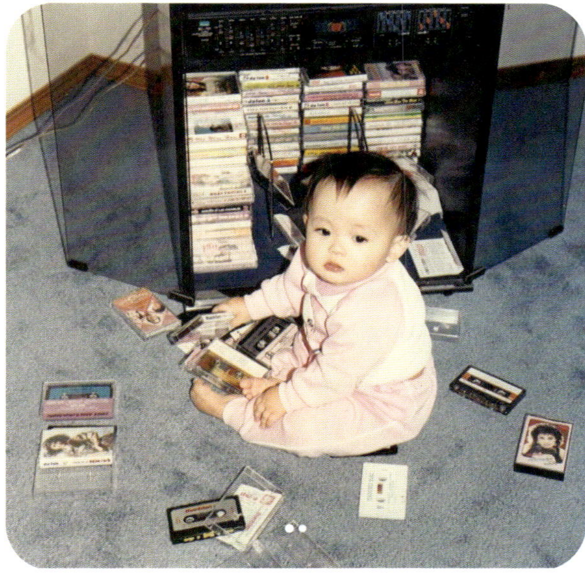

Above: Tina Snow Le (left) with fellow DJs Kim Anh and Ian Nguyen, aka DJ BPM. Left: Tina Snow Le as a baby.

One of my favorite childhood memories is watching music documentaries of artists like George Michael, Air Supply, Bryan Adams, and Janet Jackson with my mom and dad on VHS or DVD. In all of these instances, I saw glimmers of joy in my parents and ông ngoại, having a good time, being themselves. These moments of joy, despite everything that they've gone through, inspired my lifelong passion to bring people together through music and art

— Tina Snow Le

Building on the resilient foundations laid by their predecessors, Generation 2.0+ stands at the forefront of a cultural resurgence within the Vietnamese American community. These children of the first and 1.5 Generation, armed with the legacies of their parents and the revolutionary spirit of New Wave, are breathing new life into the embers of the past. This renewal has sparked a renaissance of New Wave music, through remixes, playlists, and remasters of the old songs, with its pulsating rhythms and infectious melodies echoing louder than ever across new underground parties, community gatherings, and digital platforms alike.

First-generation New Wave enthusiasts, who once felt the wane of their beloved genre, now find themselves reuniting at concerts and house parties with their kids in tow. These gatherings are more than mere nostalgia; they are a celebration of enduring connections and a testament to the timeless appeal of New Wave music. The shared love for this distinctive sound is not only rekindling old friendships but also forging new ones, as younger fans and older aficionados collaborate and create together.

Generations 2.0+ of the Vietnamese diaspora—including Millennials, Gen Z, and even Gen Alpha—are actively exploring and reconnecting with their cultural heritage, both within their local communities and with peers in Vietnam. By fusing traditional Vietnamese New Wave elements with bold, contemporary electronic sounds, they are crafting a unique cultural expression that is entirely their own.

The thrill of rediscovery, combined with the joy of creation, infuses each concert and gathering with a dynamic blend of past and future. As they dance to the rhythms that once moved their parents, Generation 2.0+ is doing more than reminiscing—they are actively and deliberately shaping the future of their community's cultural identity. This revival transcends a simple return to tradition; it is a bold declaration that the spirit of New Wave will continue to flourish and evolve, driven by the passion and creativity of a new generation. What was once an escape has transformed into a celebration.

UN-APOLOGETIC

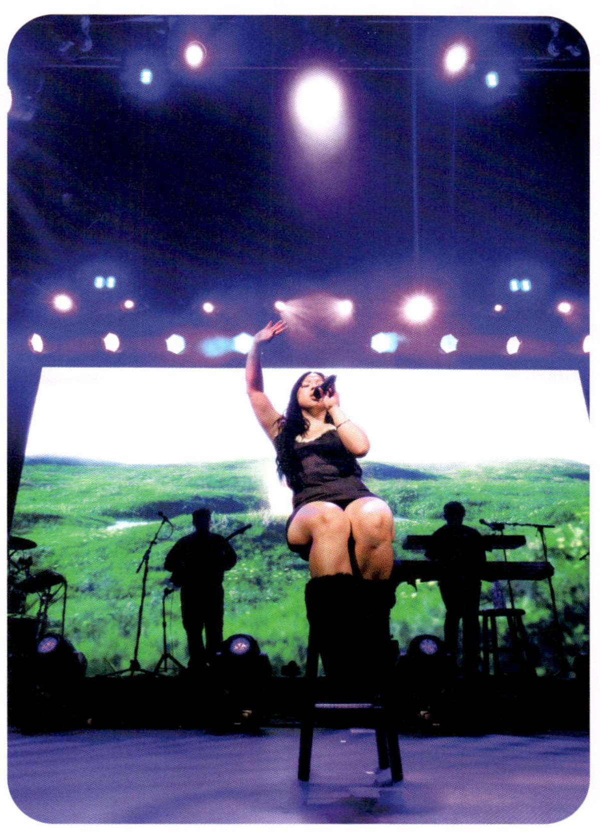

Thuy Tran

Thuy Tran performs on stage.

As a young girl, I never felt like I could fully express myself or get vulnerable around my parents; it just wasn't something I was used to doing. That was until I started on a journey of making music myself. I didn't see anyone who looked like me. It made it hard to see a career in the arts. I'm very proud of myself. I've always been authentic to myself and because of that, so many Vietnamese and other AAPI youth feel like they can also be their true selves.

Music was always an escape for me. It made me feel like I could escape the expectations that came with being the first daughter of two immigrant parents. At first, it was something I hid from them. I was afraid they wouldn't approve or support me. My parents weren't worried until I moved to Los Angeles. They thought I was going to LA to pursue medicine. My parents were confused about why I wasn't enrolled in school, but it pushed me to continue pursuing music despite their doubts. I wouldn't tell my parents about my gigs or talk to them about my music career in fear that they would say something that would make me quit.

Music allowed me to talk about my feelings openly. Growing up I wasn't nurtured to express my feelings, talk about love, and definitely not express my sexuality. Music was my escape. When I saw that other people also related to my music, I knew I had to keep writing about my personal experiences. In the beginning, I didn't want my parents to hear my music or watch my music videos. Now, as I've become more confident in myself, I'm less apologetic. My parents have to accept me.

Throughout this journey, and seeing how my parents went from concerned to now proud of me, I've learned that music was somehow always the glue between them and me. I believe that by being vulnerable, fearless, and authentic to myself, I've not only helped other people through some hard times, but it also ended up being a way for me to connect with my own parents. It led me to see that they've always wanted what was best for me, and if what was best for me also made me happy, they too could be happy for me.

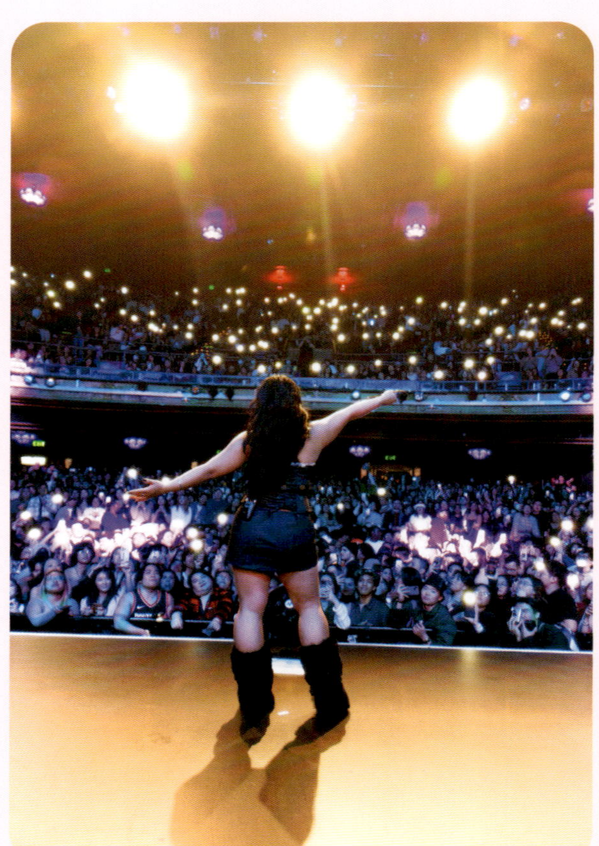

Right: Thuy Tran sings to a crowd.
Below: Thuy Tran (left) as a baby.

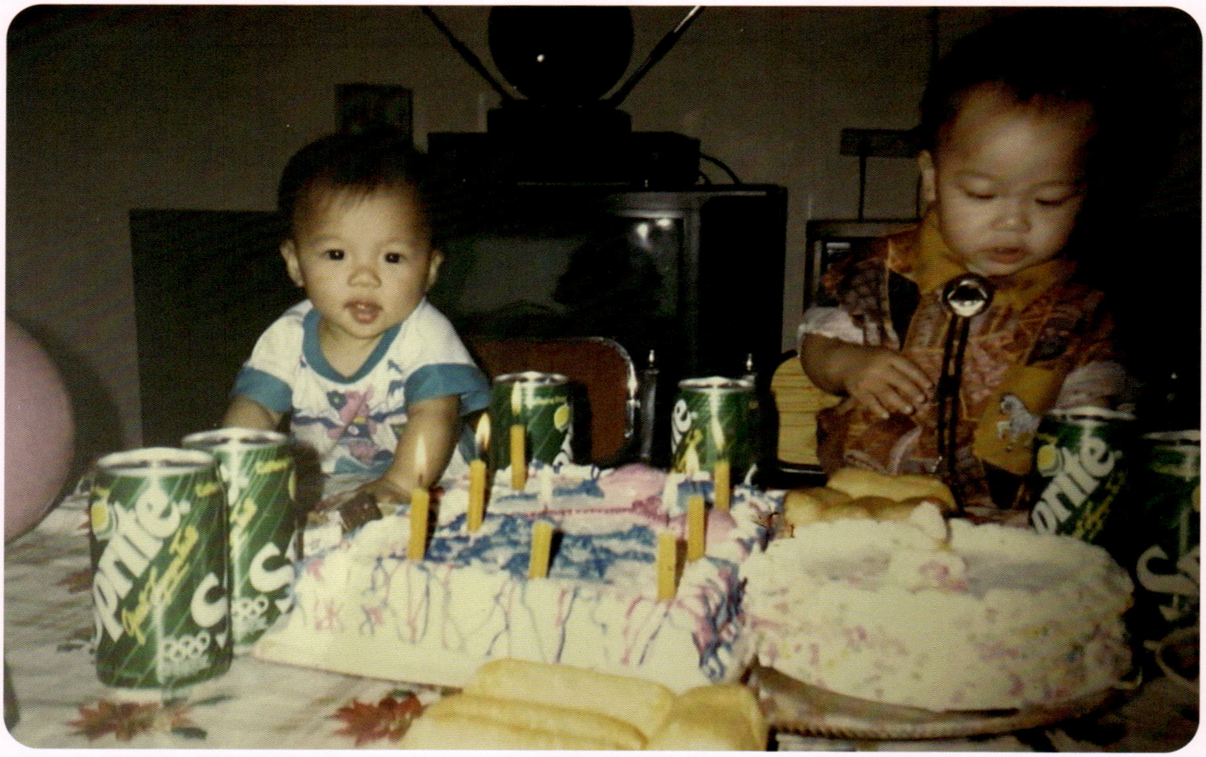

CREATING COMMUNITY

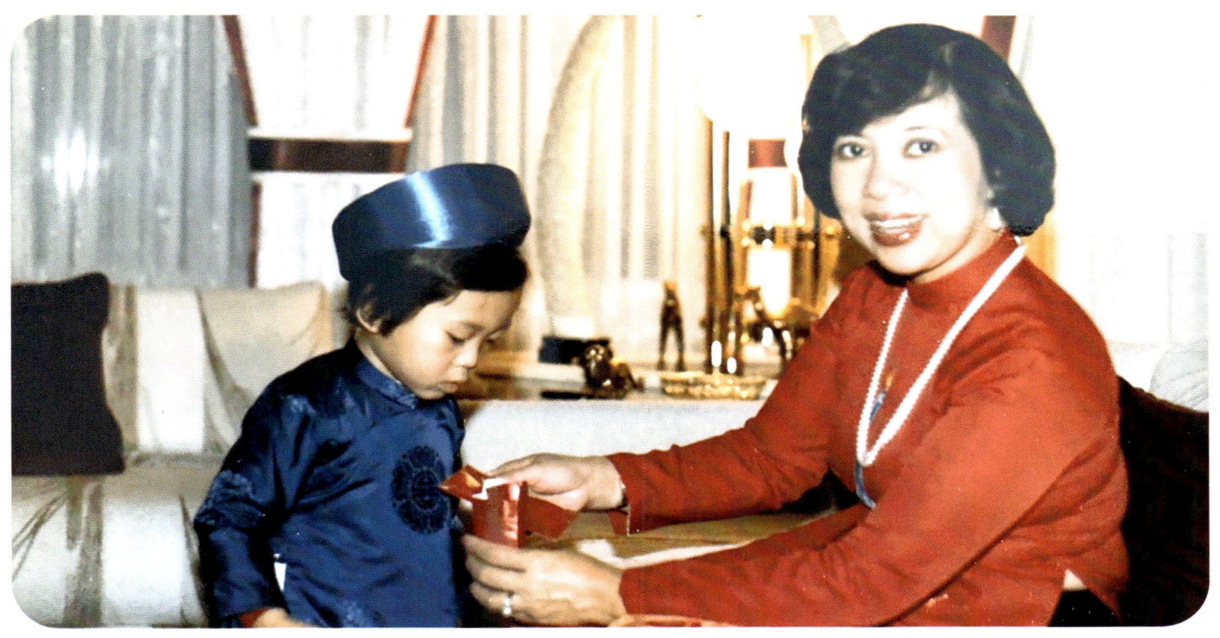

Paul Quốc Trần and his grandmother, circa 1980s.

Paul Quốc Trần

Every day I'm inspired by my parents' journey. Along with the hundreds of thousands of Vietnamese who resettled in the US at such a tumultuous time in the 1970s, forced to forge a new life in unfamiliar places, my mom and dad did what they had to do to survive. My dad (*bố*) always recalls his story with pride. He, a "pioneer" as he calls himself, would co-develop empty lots along stretches of Bolsa Avenue in Westminster into Little Saigon. I'm in awe of the boldness and entrepreneurial spirit he mustered in a place where English wasn't his native language. Mom (*Mẹ*) would be his partner overseeing architectural design and business. I still pass the buildings and shopping plazas today with fond childhood memories of running amuck in parking lots on roller skates with my siblings and cousins, eating banh mi and perusing New Wave tapes from ASIA or Thuy Nga, especially if they had Lynda Trang Đài's image on them.

Fast forward to decades later in New York City. In 2017, post-Trump election, a few of my friends and I, feeling tenuous political strains that threatened our queer community's rights and safety, banded together, which also felt like a natural act of survival. To resist and create a space for our queer Asian community that was not represented in New York nightlife at large was a path we needed to forge.

In the planning of our very first party, we were playfully throwing out ideas of imagery, names, and fun references. We wanted to pay homage to our individual upbringings as a way to reclaim and revisit something from our pasts. Lynda was specific to me as a childhood icon, and she was my first pop diva. From her cassettes of New Wave songs, Thuy Nga variety show videotapes, to singing along to her karaoke laserdiscs in Vietnam on trips in later years, these are the strong memories that defined my youth, but that I had shunned in my adulthood until the creation of the BUBBLE_T parties.

BUBBLE_T is about queer Asian pride and connecting to that aspect of our identity in the diaspora of New York and nightlife. The stills from grainy VHS music videos of the late '80s felt mysterious and nostalgic. I was inspired by the new wave of immigrants carving out an identity for themselves, and creating spaces in which to commune.

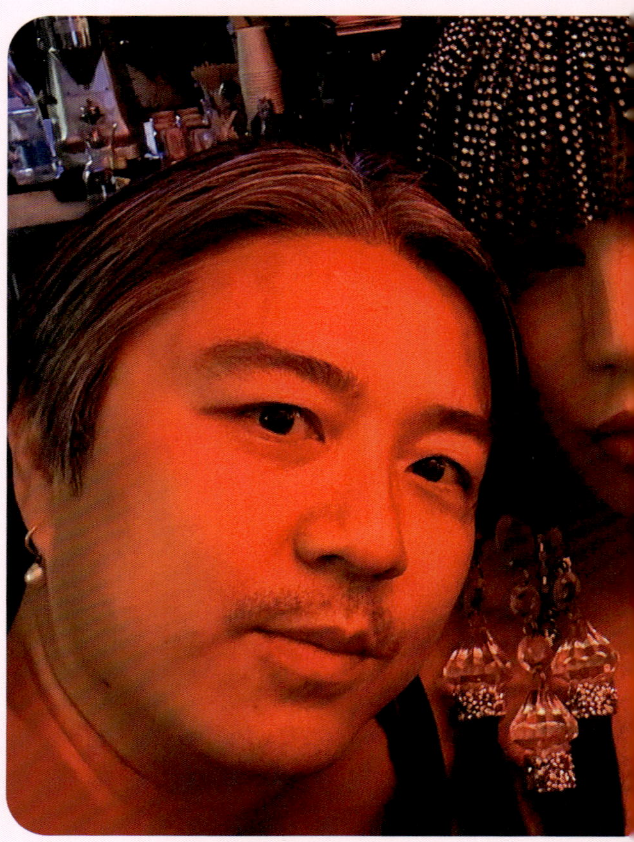

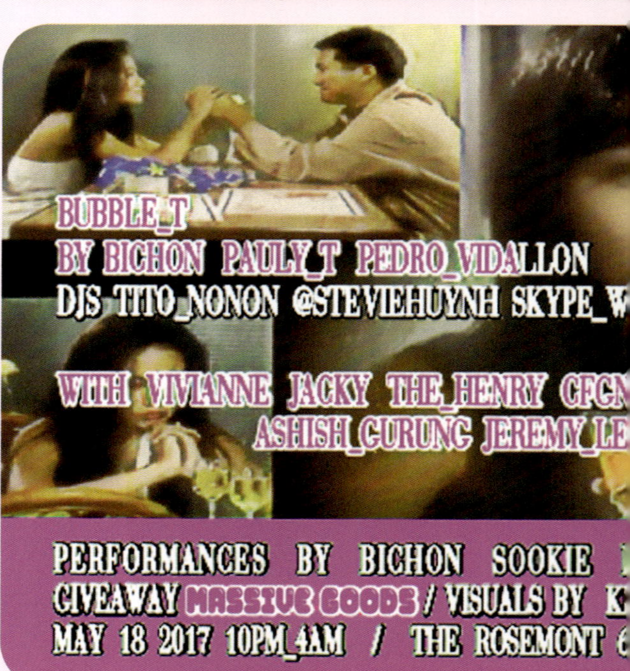

Images from Paul Tran and BUBBLE_T.

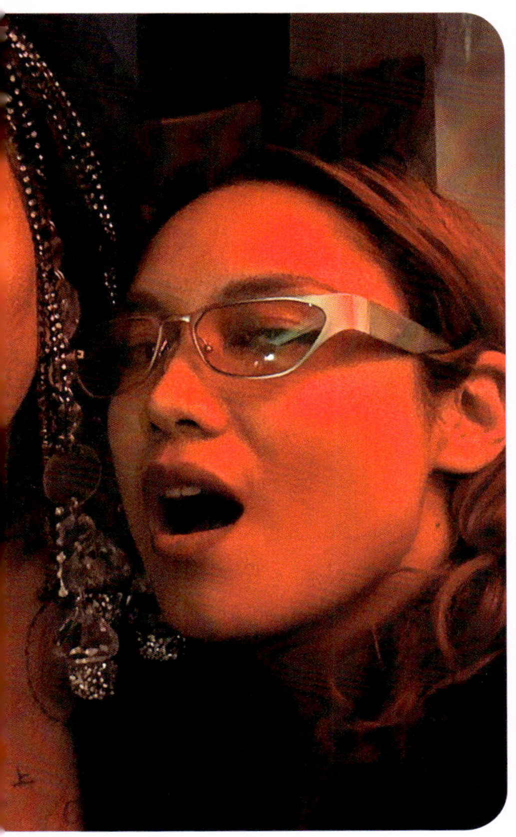

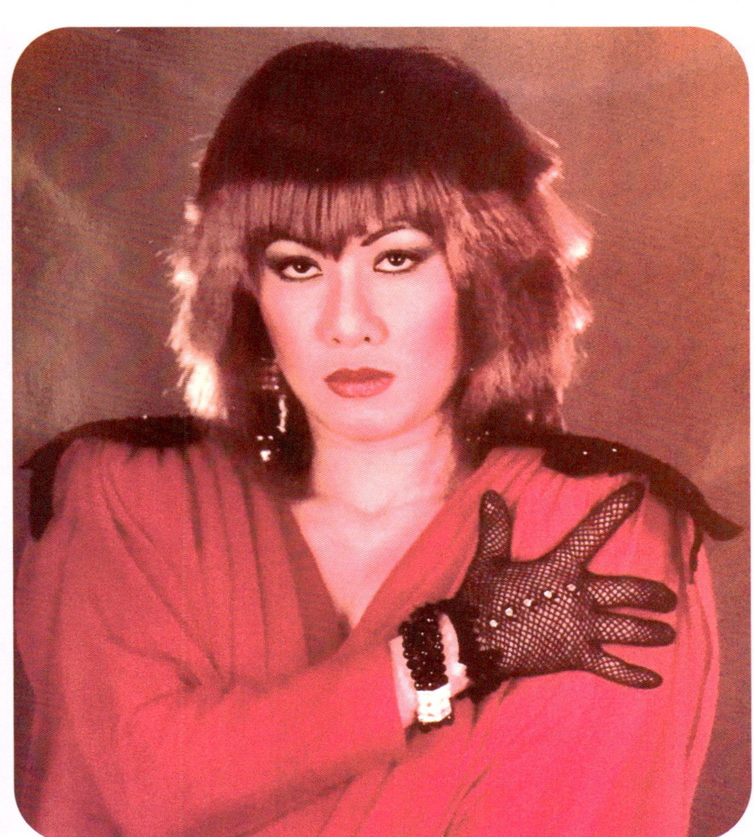

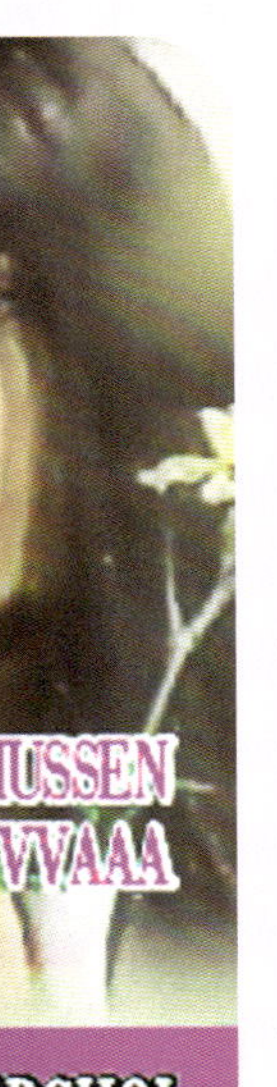

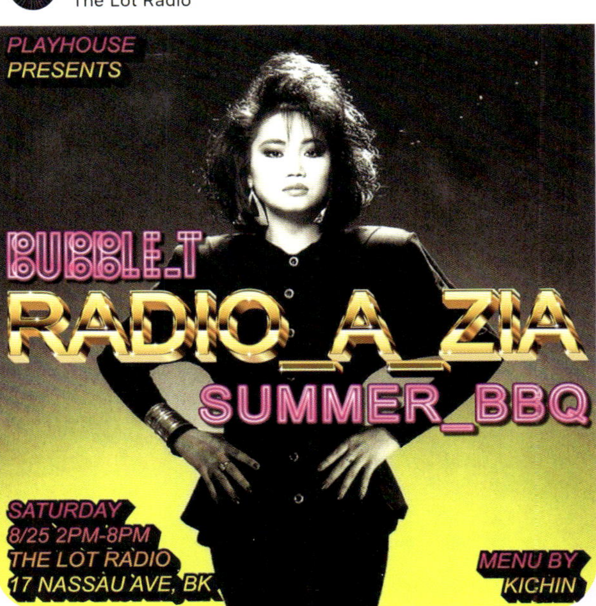
bubble____t
The Lot Radio
PLAYHOUSE
PRESENTS
BUBBLE_T
RADIO_A_ZIA
SUMMER_BBQ
SATURDAY
8/25 2PM-8PM
THE LOT RADIO
17 NASSAU AVE, BK
MENU BY
KICHIN

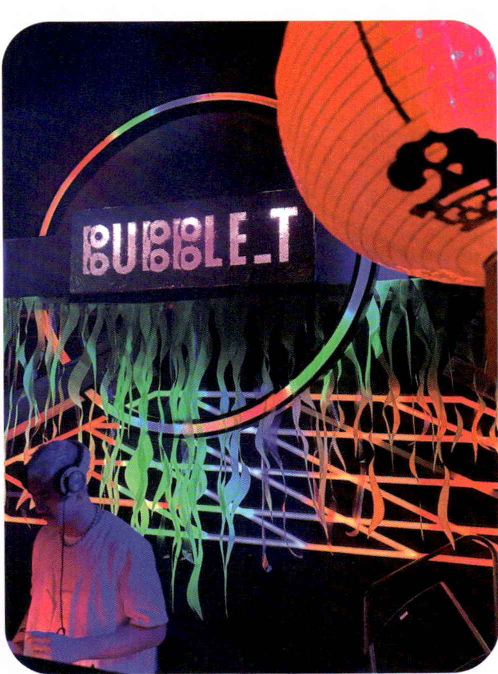
BUBBLE_T

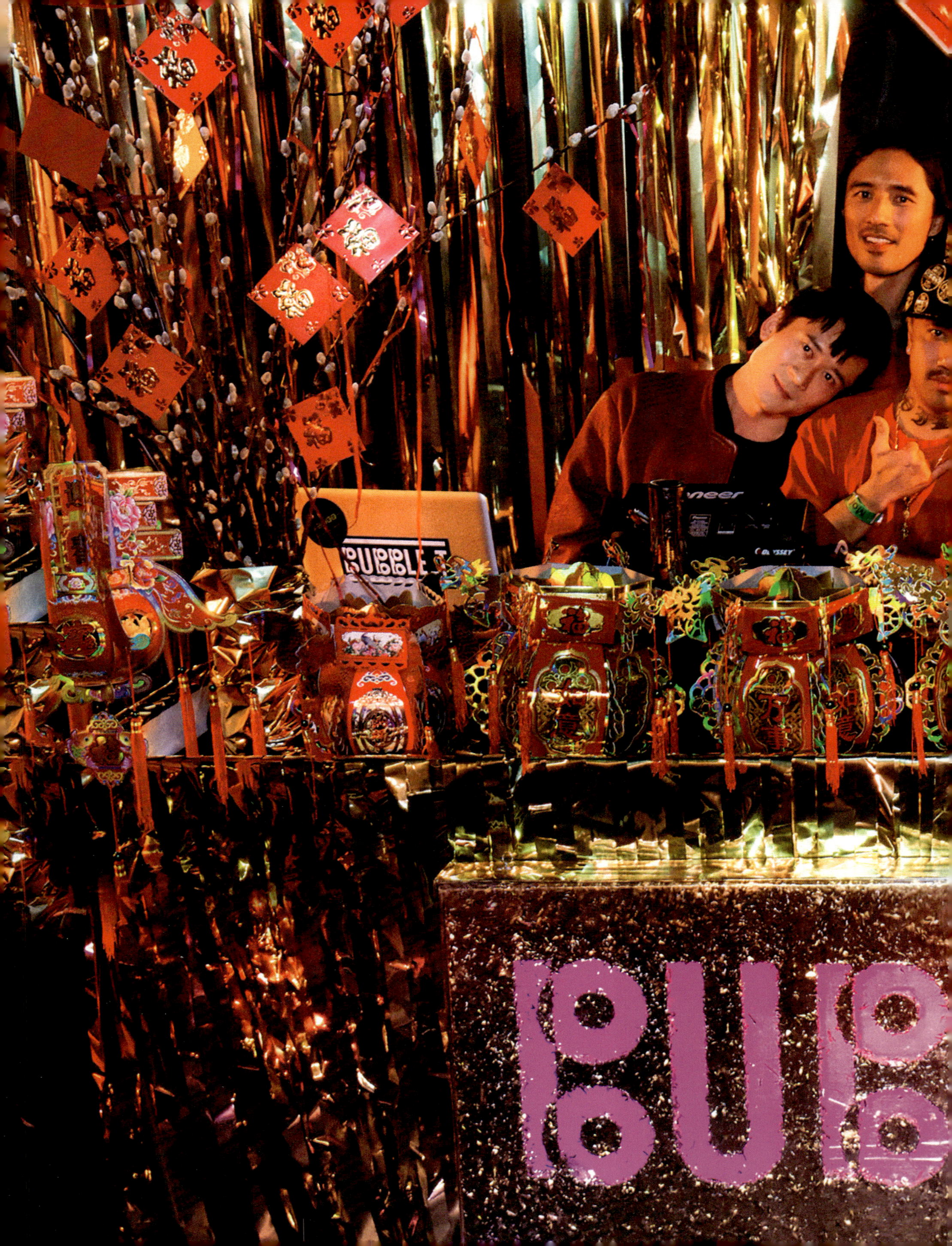

BUBBLE T

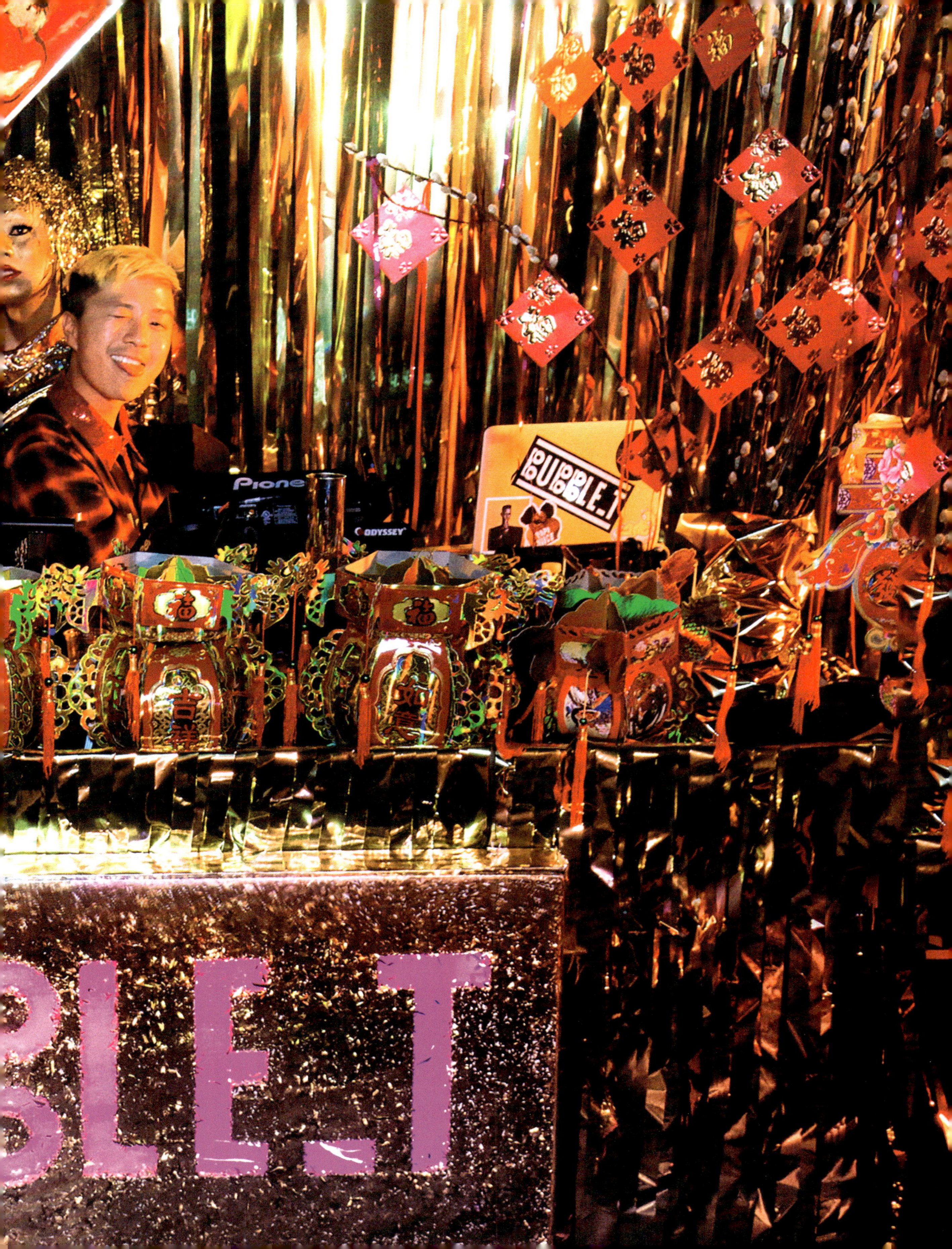
Pione
ODYSSEY
BUBBLE.T
BLE.T

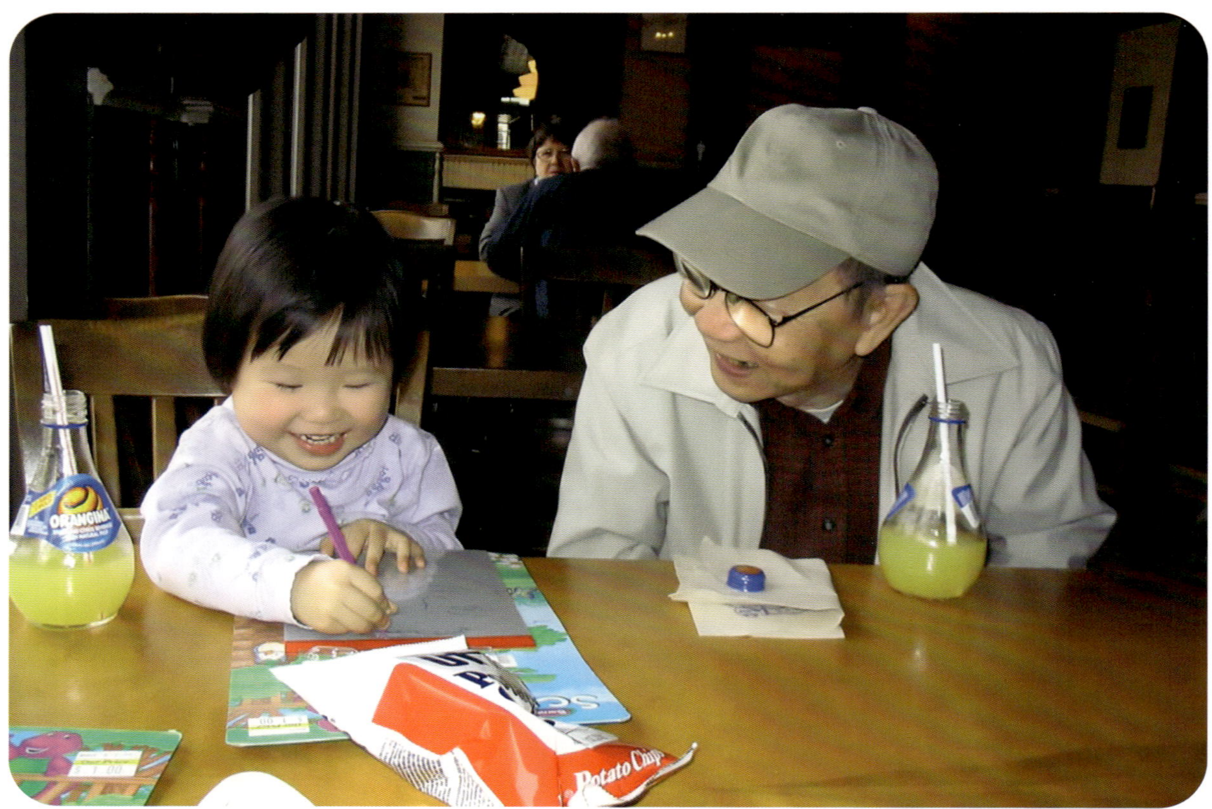

I had just started college when I became fixated on archives. I had so many questions about memory and remembering, about my mother's refugee roots and my father's lack thereof, and how the materiality of our family archives possessed the ability to pierce through time and space, reaching me on one end and their distant childhoods in Vietnam on the other. Working on *NEW WAVE* over the years has only deepened this impulse, sending me down rabbit holes for obscure performance videos, now-defunct Little Saigon clubs, blurry digitizations of more years-old VHS tapes. Let me find you, I'd whisper to myself, wading through the endless pit that is the internet with only a handful of broken Vietnamese search terms to guide me. To be completely honest, I grew up entirely unaware of New Wave music and its ripples in our community. And yet, in the dusty corners of cyberspace— shaped by long abandoned blogs and idle Facebook profiles— I caught glimpses into its life. I've grown quite close to many of the archives included in this project, some of my favorites including a photograph of young men packed together, grinning and throwing their hands up at a party, or the 1987 music video for Hãy Đến Với Em by Giáng Ngọc. The latter opens with the singer vocalizing softly, her gaze floating beyond the viewer, but catching the camera for a split second. The beat kicks in and so does a renewed physicality. What follows is a minute-long synth interlude, her stiff and restrained stance transforming into a self-possessed body swinging across the screen. Yet, there's a certain yearning that radiates as she dances alone on the stage, as if she's the only one left on the dance floor and all the rest have long gone home. Maybe, like me, she's holding out hope for something that's just beyond reach. How lucky of us to have met each other, two girls far removed, right here in the archive.

— Mena Dolinh

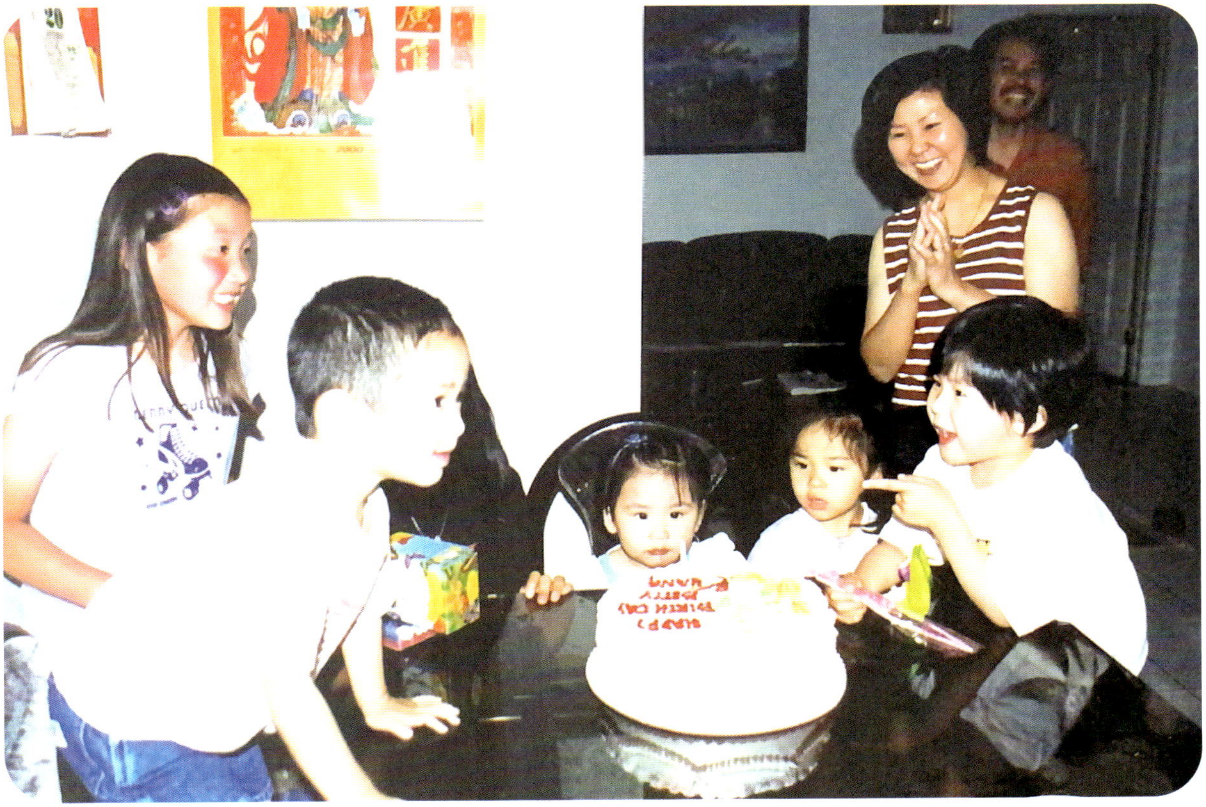

New Wave will be a reminder to me, my team, and hopefully to all readers and viewers, that we can all begin again; we can create a fresh start no matter how scared, how uncertain, how in-between we feel, or how little creativity we may think we have. do carry with you this light and move onwards through electrifying history, unexpected transformation, and new beginnings.

— betty yêń hang

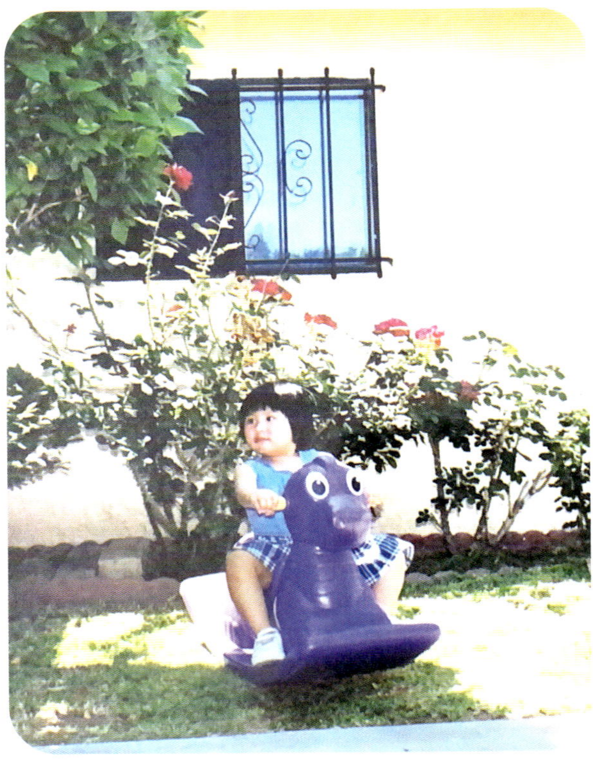

EPILOGUE

WHERE WE'RE GOING

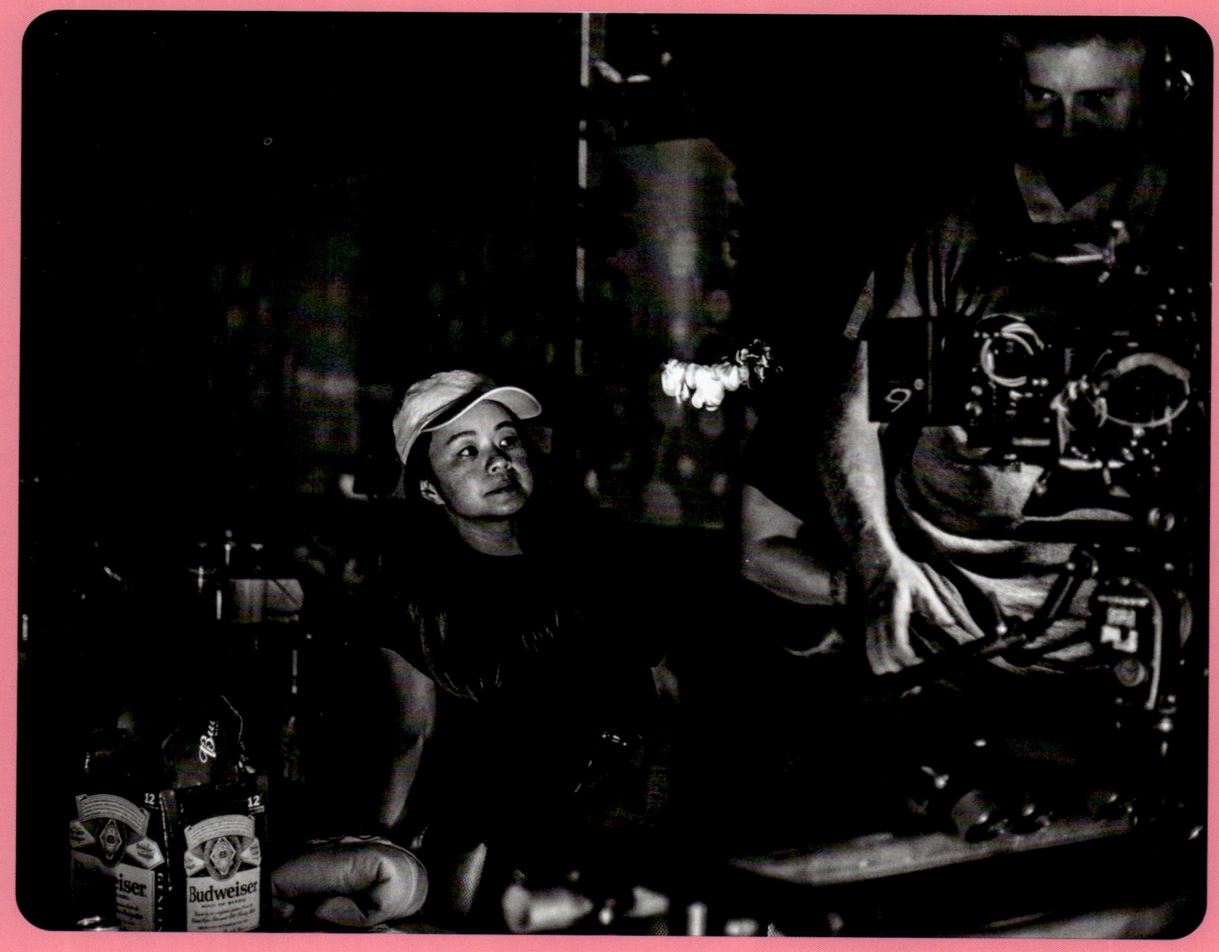

Holding my newborn daughter close in 2018, a flood of memories cascaded, each underscoring moments of vulnerability from my childhood that only fully crystallized after completing my film, *New Wave*, in 2024. Among those memories, one distinctly emerged, a scene of five-year-old me in 1985, in the backseat of a car, probably without a seatbelt, headed to the mall with some wild teenagers. It's not the car nor the trip that remains etched in my brain, but the faces of rebels who happen to be my uncle and aunt. While my mother worked to support our family, her younger teenage siblings were forced into roles of responsibility, caring for my sister and me. This shift in roles not only shaped our family's narrative, but also deepened a rift that led to decades of estrangement from my mother.

The moments I cherished the most were few and far between, when those teenagers could afford a tank of gas to drive us around town, blasting New Wave music through their rattling sound systems. With the volume cranked up and the windows down, it seemed as though the music carried their sorrows away—offering brief reprieves from a life underscored by a tumultuous home, undiagnosed PTSD, and numerous hardships. From the old photos, you'd never know that just a handful of years before that those kids all narrowly escaped death from bombs flying overhead or that in the process of fleeing their homeland, their boat nearly sank at sea. After decades of absorbing violent and tragic American narratives dominated by a toxic male perspective, I realized it was time to tell a different story, centered on joy, celebration, and reinvention.

Each time I looked into my daughter's eyes as the filmmaking process unfolded, my resolve to share our story intensified. Determined to bridge past and present for her, I found the courage to delve deeper into these memories. This journey led me to seek answers from my aunts and uncles, whose stories of survival—intertwined with their love for music, friendship, and escapes—underscored how our family's painful past was crucial for understanding the depth of our bonds.

However, the more I questioned my family, the more they resisted, seemingly unprepared to confront their traumatic memories. Recognizing the fragility of our relationship, I stepped back and sought insights from others in my community. Interestingly enough, the universe seems to provide exactly what you need when you're ready to receive; these strangers became not only participants in my film, but also friends who openly shared their stories with me. Their accounts resonated

Elizabeth Ai on the set of *New Wave* documentary.

with my own experiences and shed light on my estrangement from my mother. These revelations compelled me to establish a narrative foundation that would connect my daughter to her heritage and begin stitching together our family's broken links.

I may never fully recover from a childhood marked by the absence of my mother, a reality many refugees face whose wounds might never fully heal from war and displacement. Yet, the sacrifices of our predecessors who fought to survive have afforded younger generations like mine the privilege to seek healing. Initially, this filmmaking endeavor with New Wave was a means to avoid a painful past, but it evolved into a powerful tool for understanding these realities, unexpectedly guiding me on a path toward healing. Reexploring this past by learning so much from the community who shared a similar lineage has taught me an invaluable lesson—to treasure ordinary moments, like those car rides that can reveal profound truths. By understanding where we come from, we are better equipped to navigate where we are going.

I hope the archives, family photos, personal accounts, and the thoughtful contributions from respected authors will inspire you to narrate your own tales of resistance, rebellion, and reinvention.

Left: Still from the set of *New Wave*. Above, right: Elizabeth Ai and her mother, Lan Tran. Below, right: Elizabeth Ai on the set of *New Wave*.

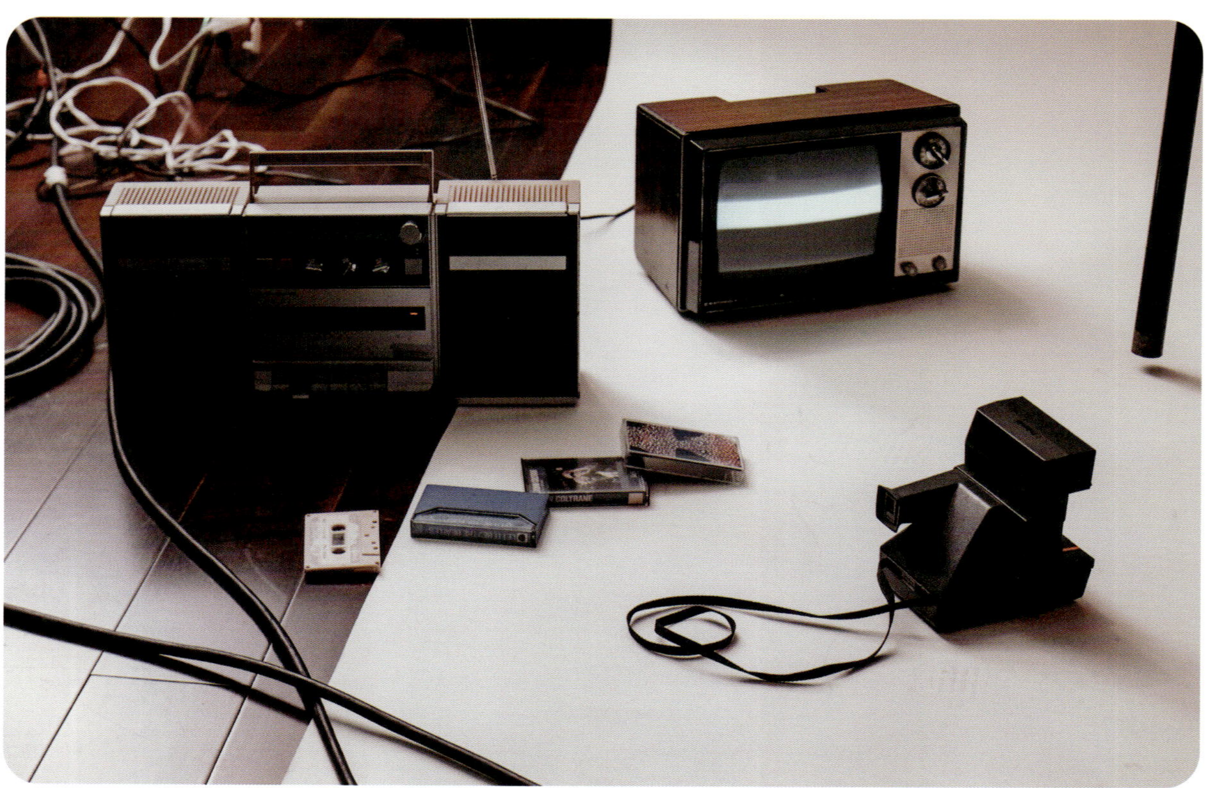

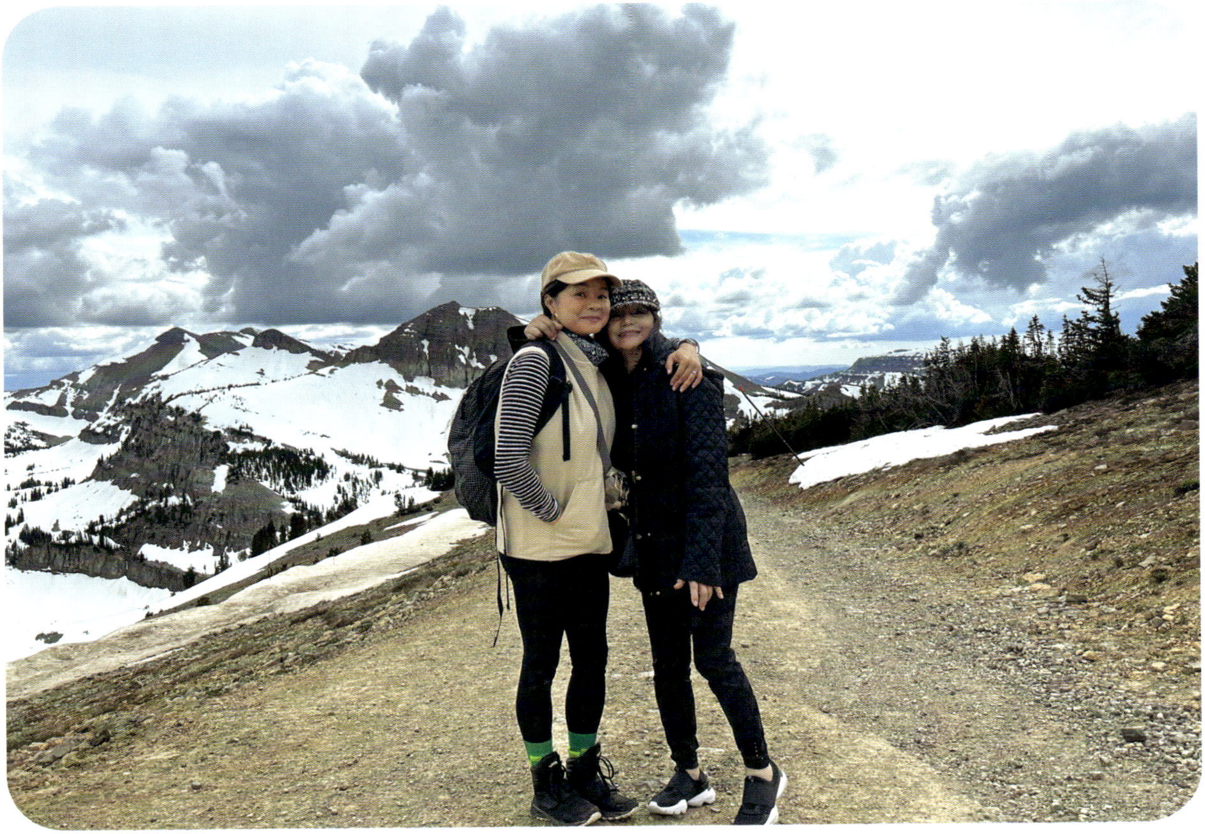

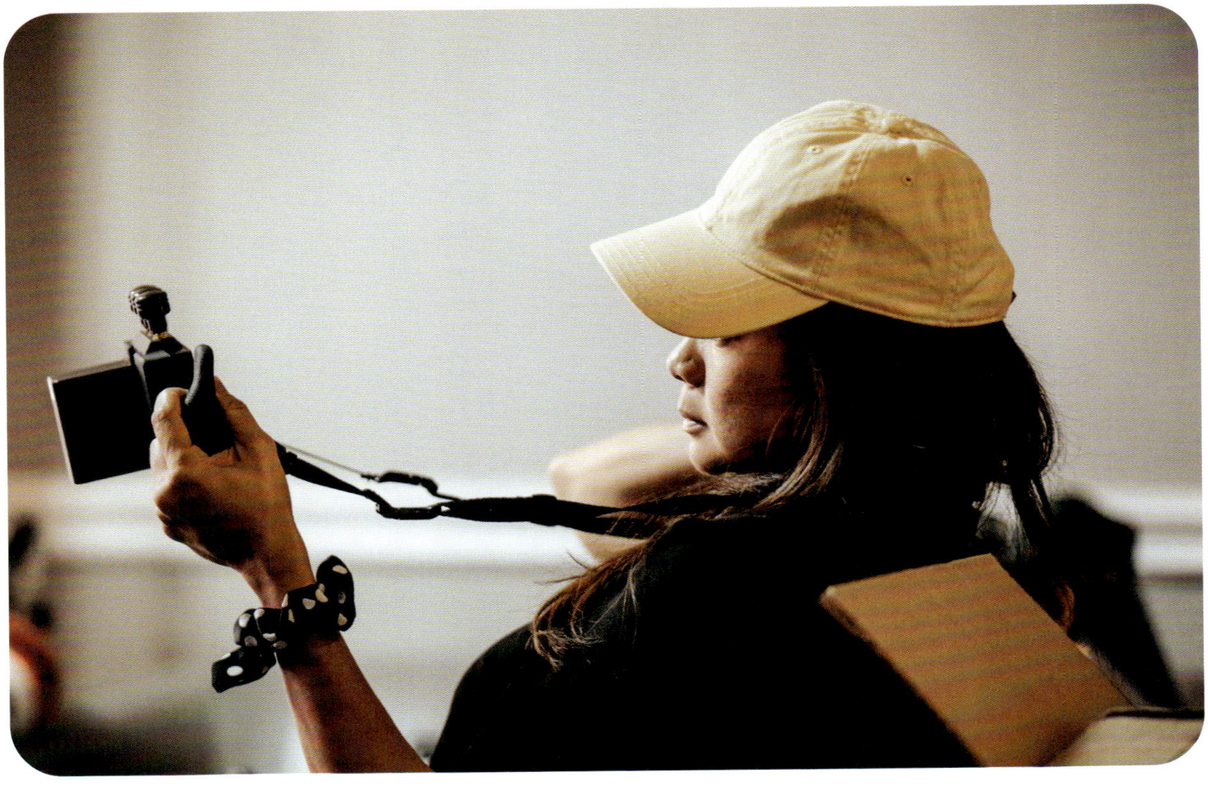

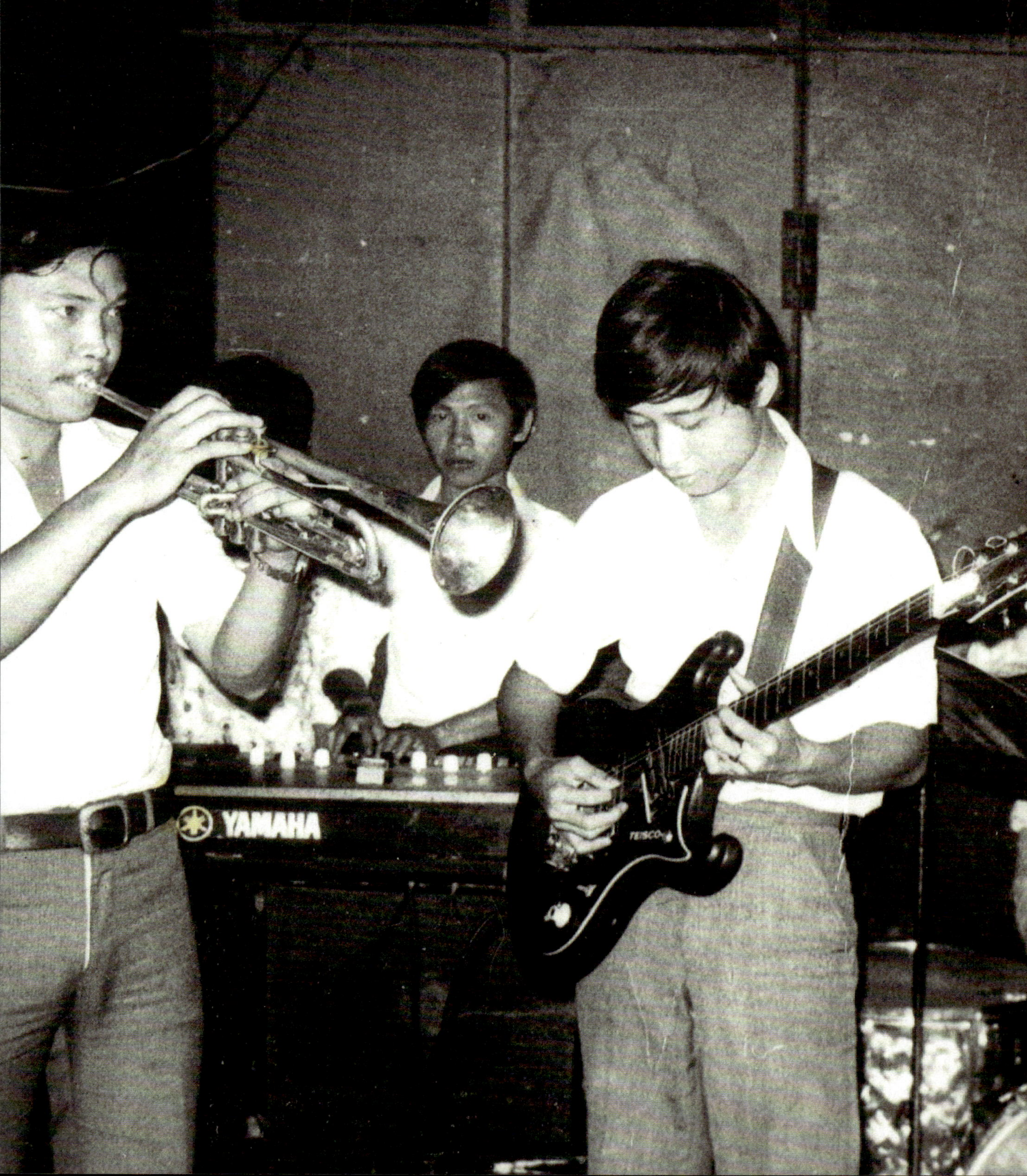
YAMAHA
TEISCO

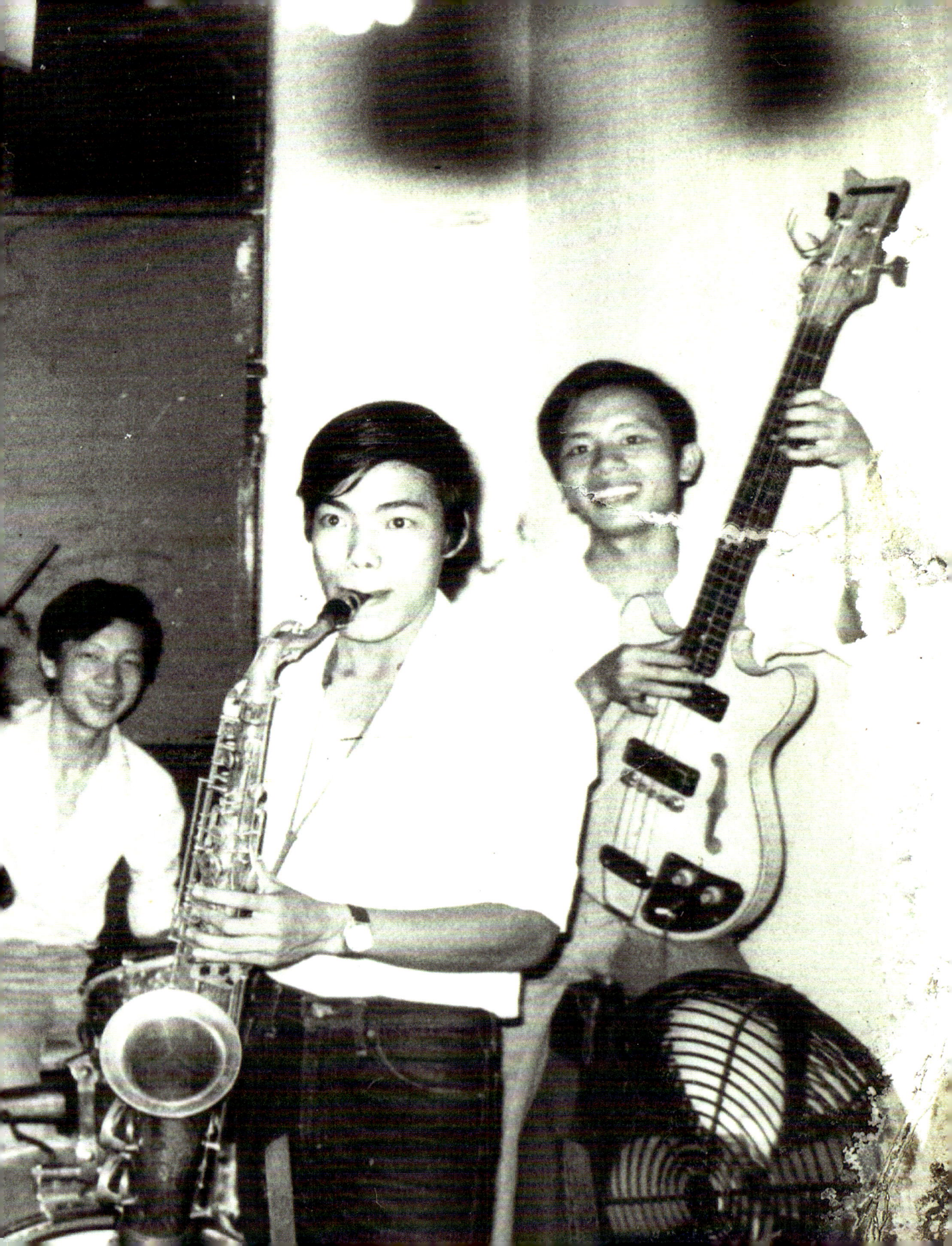

AFTERWORD

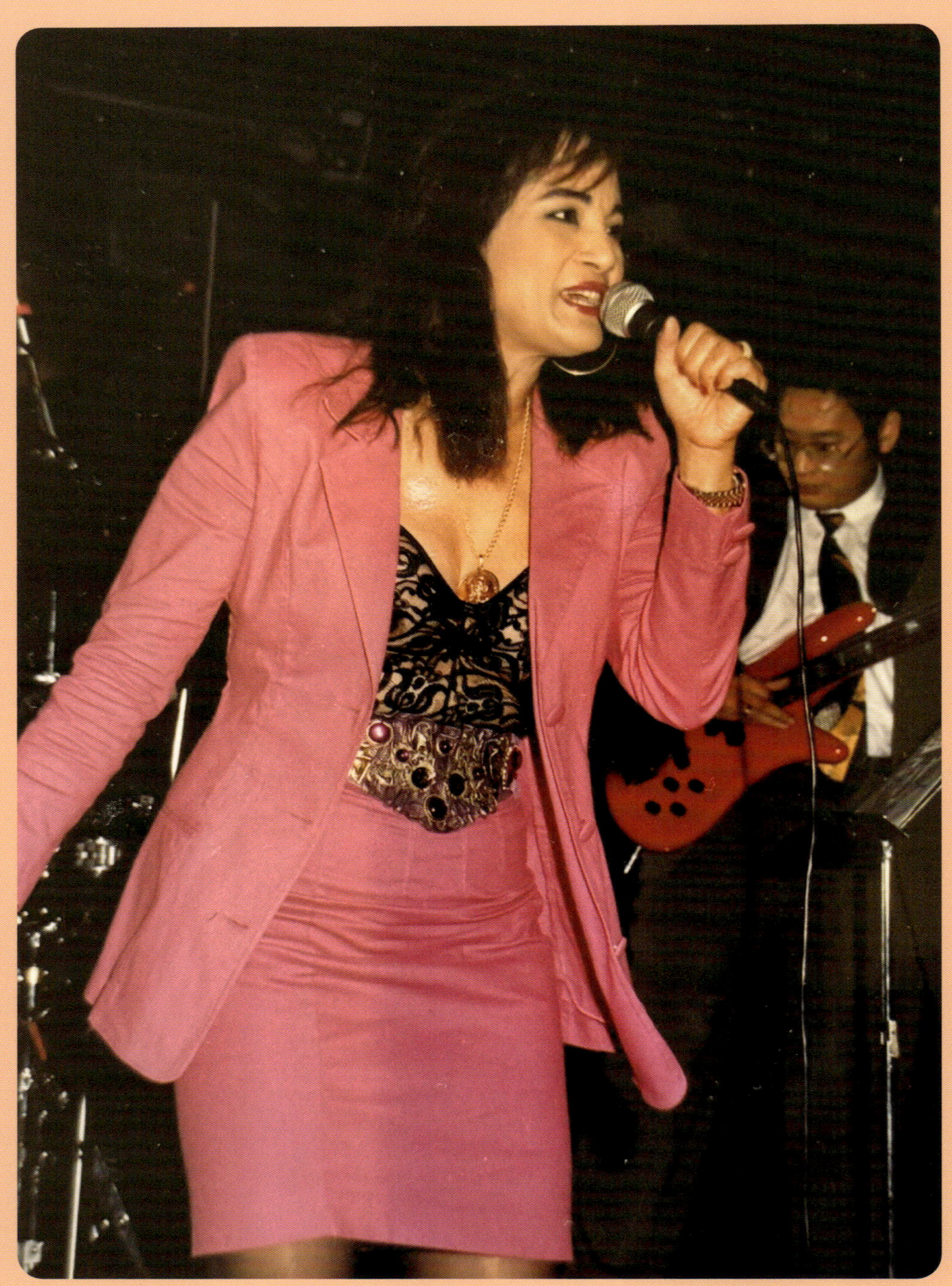

Trace Le

The walls of my childhood were lit by disco balls. The humming sound of the bass was a lullaby intertwined with the faint but powerful sounds of my mother's vocal-runs-turned-melodies. It's past my bedtime, but no one cares, and I wonder if that's a bad thing or a cool thing. But this was my life, and I got to eat all the maraschino cherries I wanted. It was 1995 (ish) and my mom is the "Tina Turner of Vietnam." She's also the woman who raises me (along with my aunt), plays tennis with me, takes me shopping, cooks the best dishes, and tells me I can be whatever I want to be when I grow up, but "just be successful"—all the while establishing for herself a glitzy, gutsy, and very difficult career as an immigrant Vietnamese singer in Orange County, California.

My mom, Carol Kim, first started her singing career in Vietnam, then brought her wave of energy and charisma overseas before the Fall of Saigon in the early 1970s, shaping entertainment for the Vietnamese community who resided in the States. She played an integral part in establishing the transition from traditional folk to modern-day, upbeat, soulful music for Vietnam, and though she wasn't necessarily a centerpiece in the New Wave era, she paved a way for Vietnamese voices. She has been singing for over fifty years and continues to sing her heart out to anyone who'll hear it. It's all she knows. Music gave my mom a life, and so music has been my life as far back I can remember.

Growing up, I naturally wanted to find my own way and interests, and so my great rebellion came in the form of pursuing a bachelor's degree in business and communications. I wanted to be a journalist, or work at an ad agency; at one time, I seriously considered becoming a detective. I worked various jobs and had a couple 9-to-5 careers until music came up and at me in my late twenties—at the age my mom was when she started her singing career. I always wrote song-like things, I guess, but I was always just writing. Poems, essays, confessions, love notes to myself. I never thought I'd be a singer. I was shy as a kid, and though a bit social, I definitely never sang out loud. When I did, it was just to close friends, or at the ceiling in my dorm room.

In 2016, I recorded my first EP in the bathroom of my first LA apartment. Months prior, I did a favor without thinking for a friend by singing on his record, and that experience made me realize: I needed more of this. My mouth, radiating an internal hum on a silver sphere. My voice was heard, and

Carol Kim, Trace Le's mother, performing on stage.

something in me felt lighter. I quit my job as a managing editor, and I told my mom the news. She wasn't surprised. She didn't understand what I did as a living before, but she understood this. She said I always sang and had a good voice, though I have no recollection of when anyone ever heard me; I trusted her. She always knew. And I did, too.

Today, I look at where my life is and see that it was made possible by a woman who left all she knew for what she wanted: freedom. And it's become clearer as I get older that to get to sing, to use your voice, and to just let it out, is one of the most transformational experiences a person can have. My mother and I have always been close, and we have our issues like any mother and daughter, of course. We share a lot of similarities and dreams, but our songs couldn't be more different. While mom's livelihood was anchored in singing mostly covers, the songs she sang were seldom sad. My mom had to sing about joy and hope to help distract herself and her country from what was really going on. A balm of pure entertainment. And though she's unable to understand what I sing about, my privilege to sing and write the sad songs is my own brand of freedom.

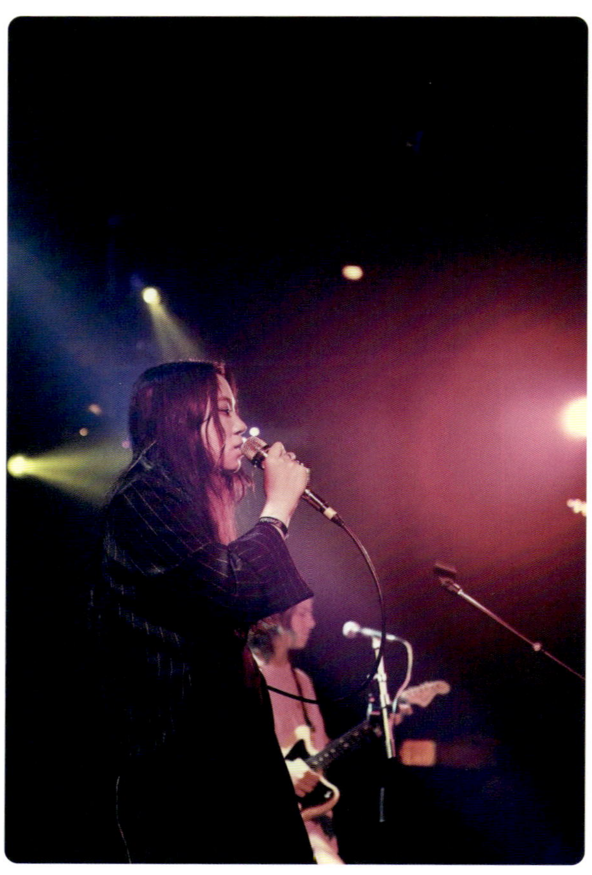

Above: Trace Le performs on stage. Opposite: Trace Le with her mother, Carol Kim.

Through my work, I am grieving what my mom has no time to grieve, or perhaps no capacity to. And I'm becoming more and more comfortable with our individual relationships to music and how it has beautifully alchemized an ongoing healing process that I hope surpasses both our generations. Music is so powerful; it can make you feel it all or help you feel nothing at all, and it's been a gift. And no matter the underlying or obvious tone we use to make it, it will always be the language my mom and I both understand. And through honoring the messages she embodies with her voice, I'm able to sink into the blessing and significance of my own.

LYRICS FROM "TOO MUCH"

Overprotective
Over protective
Of ever being loved I know I'm foolish
My mother made me tough but not enough
I'm losing,
My mind and you're over there doing just fine

I'm hearing things
That tells me we want different things
You stay the same
And I'm the one whose spiraling

So much so much so much
It couldn't work
Too much, too much, too much
I'm finally hurt

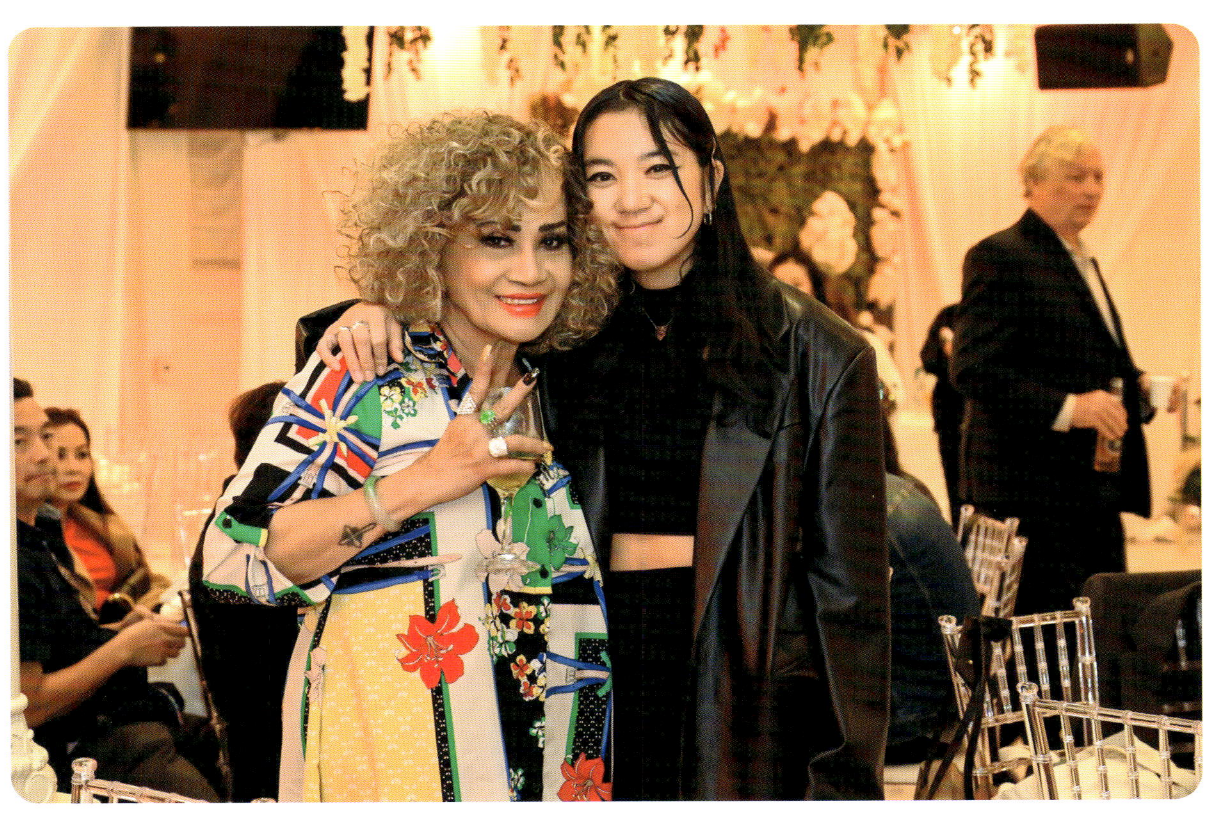

ACKNOWLEDGMENTS

To our Vietnamese diaspora, community, creative collaborators, and contributors: thank you for believing in our stories, and for your unwavering generosity. This project would not have been possible without your support, words, and personal archives.

Asa Ai Hendrickson: motherhood was the unexpected adventure I needed, and your profound questions led me back to our family's history and, ultimately, to myself. I am forever indebted to you for giving me a new lease on life. I hope I make you proud.

Elek Hendrickson: thank you for recognizing the story in New Wave and encouraging me to pursue it. Your steadfast belief in me, your constant challenges to improve, and your unwavering support even in the toughest of times have been my rock. Thank you for the unconditional love, giving me the family I never had but never knew I always wanted.

Rachel Sine: you were there from the first interview through every critical moment throughout the years. In my darkest hour, you helped me find my way back. Your persistence, patience, wit, humor, and relentless belief in me have taught me the true meaning of friendship.

Hannah Bernall: thank you for helping me see when I couldn't and being the first person to help me visualize New Wave. Thank you for shining a light on the darkness and helping me feel less afraid of my scars. I'm so grateful to share this sacred journey of motherhood with you.

Carol Ai: despite our rough upbringing, we always had each other and that meant everything to me. I'm so grateful for the gift that is you. You knew our archives and history needed to become something more tangible, beyond the film. Thank you for introducing me to Mỹ Linh.

Mỹ Linh Triệu Nguyễn: from the moment we met, through the tears and shared experiences, I just knew. Thank you for your unshakable belief in me, our story, and this project from day one. As you wrote, "our hearts are forever bound."

Film Editors: Hee-Jae Park, for your fearless approach, patience, and leadership; Sam Rong, for your openness, vulnerability, and musicality; Nancy Nguyen, for seeing things nobody else could see or understand; Christina Sun Kim, for your deep empathy.

Greg Bernall and Chris Upton: thank you for adding sonic beauty to our film and sticking by the project for years.

Bryant Tse Swanstrom: your cinematic talents have captured our vision more beautifully than I could have ever imagined.

Trace Le and Ariel Loh: for trusting me with your song. Trace for also being faith personified.

To our incredible archival researchers, story believers, and producers of magic: Betty Hang, Julia Huỳnh, Mena Dolinh, So Yun Um. The years have flown by, but you stuck by and kept believing. None of this would be possible without you.

Advisors: Thúy Võ Đặng, Lan Duong, Thao Ha, Ysa Le, Isabelle Pelaud, and Josh Kun. Thank you for showing up, teaching, and believing in a complete rookie.

Diane Quon and Geeta Gandbhir: thank you for blazing trails in our community and taking a chance on me. Your support and leadership over the years has meant everything.

Robina Riccitiello: for being a champion of storytellers and of mothers and daughters. Thank you for working through the narrative with us and helping me investigate my feelings, and putting Heather Box on the case too.

C.Y. Lee: for believing in the music and the memories that follow.

Dug and Linh Song: for your commitment to the arts and deeply understanding.

Simu Liu: for walking the walk and recognizing that we are not a monolith.

Jane Solomon: for sharing your story of music and profound loss, too.

Ian Nguyen: thank you for your vulnerability and sharing your family story with me.

Lynda Trang Đài: thank you for challenging patriarchal norms. You are an inspiration.

Gabrielle Nguyen, and Connie Chweh: thank you for helping make an impact on the world with AZN AMERICANA and extending your friendship to us and so many more in our community.

Myra: for taking care of Carol and me before you could even fully take care of yourself. We are so much better off because of you. Thank you from the bottom of my heart.

Mom: I'm sorry for the things I didn't know and for the decades that slipped away without us understanding one another. Thank you for all the sacrifices you've made for our family. I'm so grateful to be reconnected for the time we have remaining.

Terri Accomazzo: your mentorship and guidance have been crucial. Thank you for believing before we had a film to show and for giving this book more energy and life than it had from its inception.

Thái Tài, thank you for being such a talented superstar and a hero to so many in our community. An extra big thanks for all the amazing photos you took of the stars from the era.

Trizzie Phương Trinh, I'm very grateful to have had the chance to learn more about you and your beautiful journey.

Lê Bá Chư, thank you for bringing our community together way before I was around. It has been such a great privilege to learn about your legacy through Giáng Ngọc Productions.

Trúc Hồ va Anh Tài, thank you both for your major contribution to our diaspora music scene through Anh Tài Band. What an honor to learn about Vietnamese New Wave through you both.

Marie Tô, thank you for our time together and sharing your family's rich musical history as well as your adventures with Lynda Trang Đài.

Thank you to Angel City Press, Los Angeles Public Library, and all the institutions and the incredibly generous people that run them that have provided resources to our team to connect with our community, excavate our history, and share our stories: Sundance (Catalyst, Adobe | Women to Watch, National Endowment for the Humanities Fellowship), Asian American Documentary Network, Better Angels Society, Brown Girls Doc Mafia, California Humanities, Center For Asian American Media, Chicago Media Project, Cinereach, Diasporic Vietnamese Artists Network, Film Independent, Firelight Media, Ford Foundation, International Documentary Association, Los Angeles Institute for the Humanities, Music Nerd, Spark Features, The Gotham, Tribeca Festival, Vietnamese Arts and Letters Association, Wende Museum, Women in Film, and Wyncote Foundation.

Thank you to these generous souls for helping our team cross the finish line: Christine Thanh Huyen Chung, Nicole Jordan-Webber, Katie Lam, Stacy Lam McCarthy, Jenny Le, Tom Nguyen, Brooke Thatawat, Leanne Tran, Alan Tsai, Carl Tydingco, Benjamin Wong, Misherr Wong, and Ty Wu.

To all the New Wavers, those displaced by war, seeking belonging and home, and to the hundreds and hundreds more who have helped, encouraged, and supported but aren't mentioned on this page. Please know, you are loved. Your story is worthy. I'm so grateful to be on this storytelling journey with you and am forever indebted to you all.

Cảm ơn chân thành đến gia đình, bạn bè, và cộng đồng.

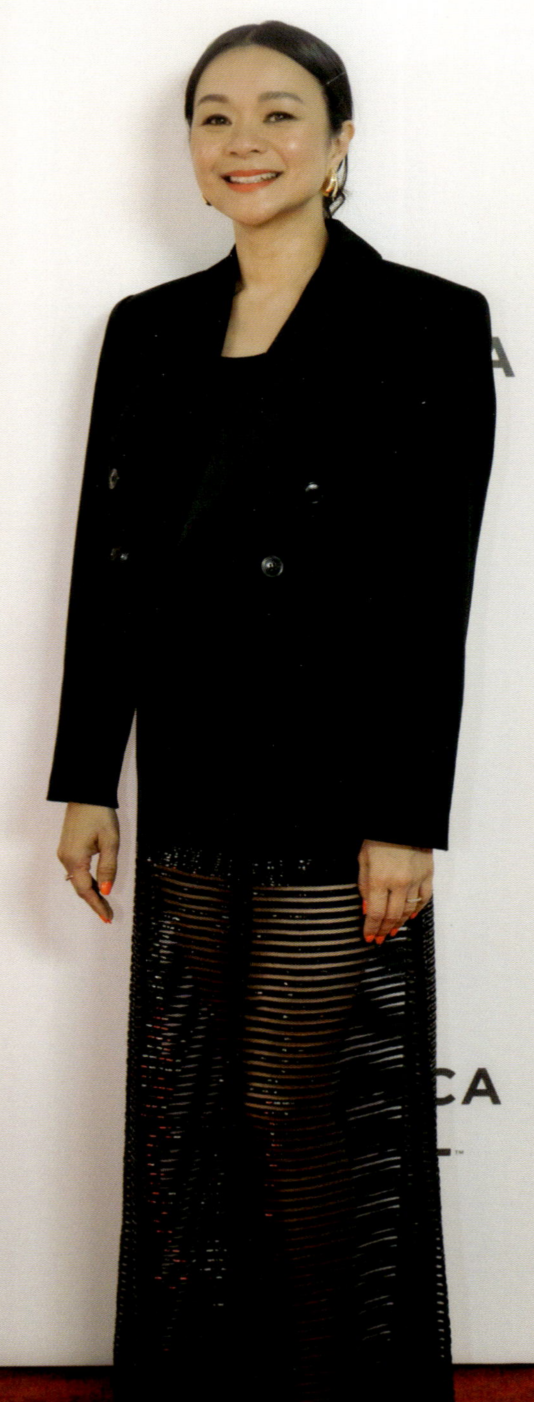
TRIBECA FESTIVAL
TRIBECA FESTIVAL

ABOUT THE AUTHOR

ELIZABETH AI is an award-winning Chinese-Vietnamese American storyteller and filmmaker. Her directorial debut, *New Wave*, premiered at the 2024 Tribeca Festival and was awarded a Special Jury Mention for Best New Documentary Director. Ai writes and produces independent feature films and branded content for companies including ESPN, VICE, and National Geographic, for which she won an Emmy. She produced the documentary features *Dirty Hands: The Art & Crimes of David Choe* (2008), and *A Woman's Work: The NFL'S Cheerleader Problem* (2019). Her narrative features include *Saigon Electric* (2011) and *Ba* (2024). She's an alumnus of Berlinale, Center for Asian American Media, Corporation for Public Broadcasting, Film Independent, Firelight Media, Sundance, and Tribeca. Her work is supported by Adobe, California Humanities, Cinereach, Ford Foundation, Independent Television Service, Knight Foundation, National Endowment for the Humanities, and Sundance.

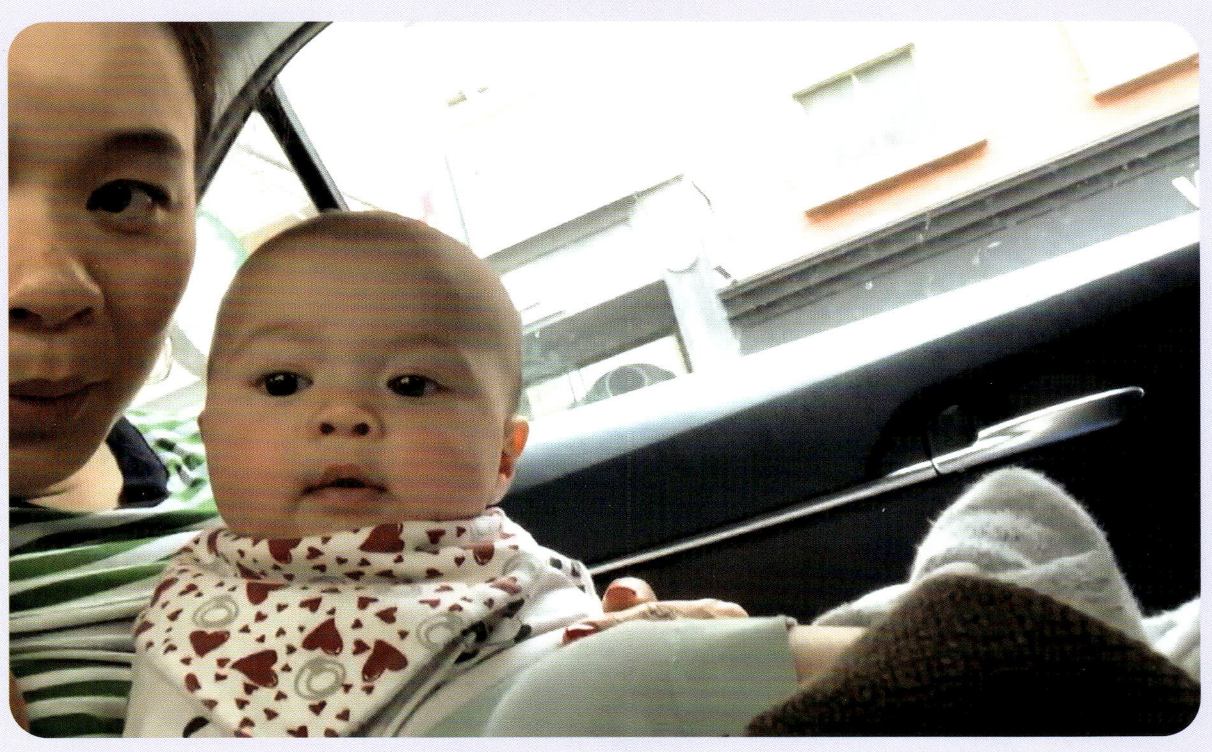

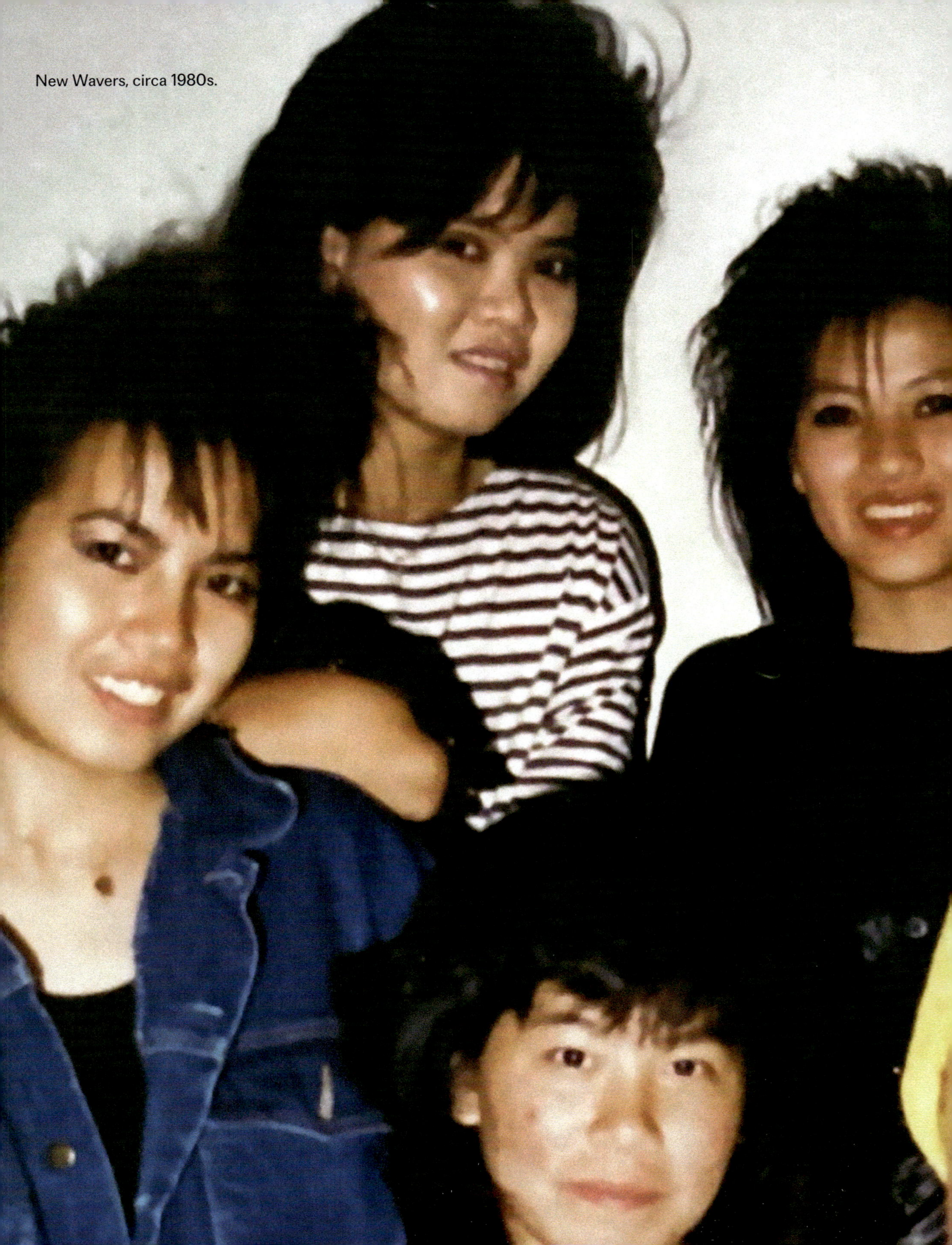

New Wavers, circa 1980s.

ABOUT THE CONTRIBUTORS

THÚY ĐINH is a bilingual critic, literary translator, coeditor of the Vietnamese webzine *Da Màu*, and editor-at-large for the Vietnamese Diaspora at *Asymptote Journal*. Her essays and translations have appeared in *Asymptote*, NPR, NBC Think, Prairie Schooner, *Iron Horse Literary Review*, *dia-CRITICS*, *Manoa*, *Rain Taxi Review of Books*, and *Amerasia*, among others.

LAN DUONG is associate professor in cinema and media studies at the University of Southern California. She is the author of *Treacherous Subjects: Gender, Culture, and Trans-Vietnamese Feminism* and *Transnational Vietnamese Cinemas and the Archives of Memory*. Her book of poems, *Nothing Follows*, was published by Texas Tech University Press in 2023.

THẢO HÀ is a Vietnamese refugee who earned her doctorate in Sociology at the University of Texas at Austin and is a professor at MiraCosta College. She is a published author, content advisor on film and literary projects, and leads multiple non-profits in Southern California.

CAROLYN HUYNH loves writing about messy Asian women who never learn from their mistakes. *The Fortunes of Jaded Women* is her debut novel and was a Good Morning America book club pick and selected as one of the best books of 2022 by NPR. Her next novel, *The Breadwinner*, comes out from Atria in Spring 2025. She resides in Los Angeles with her husband and her chaotic dog.

JULIA HUỲNH is a second-generation Vietnamese Canadian interdisciplinary artist and community archivist. She is a co-creator of Empowered Phụ Nữ and she holds an MA in photography preservation, HBA in art and art history, and a diploma in fine arts.

ERIC NGUYEN earned an MFA in creative writing from McNeese State University. *Things We Lost to the Water* is his debut novel. The book won the 2022 Crook's Corner Book Prize.

TRACE is a Vietnamese American artist from Los Angeles. She tells stories through songwriting, with more than sixty million streams, and her short film, "No More Sad Songs." These hold themes of queerness and the intricacies of emotion. Trace offers language for returning to self with permission to feel it all.

PAUL QUỐC TRẦN is a multidisciplinary designer and a first-generation Vietnamese American born in Los Angeles, California. While living in New York, in 2017, he co-founded BUBBLE_T, a on-going nightlife platform that harnesses community storytelling, music, fashion, and dance to connect the queer Asian diaspora of New York City. BUBBLE_T's core is in shared experience through individual stories and self expression.

MỸ LINH TRIỆU NGUYỄN is an award-winning second-generation Chinese-Vietnamese American designer. She is founder and creative director of STUDIO LHOOQ, a multidisciplinary studio with a holistic approach to branding and design for art and commerce. She holds a masters in graphic design from Yale University.

THÚY VÕ ĐẶNG is a professor and oral historian at UCLA where she co-directs the Community Archives Lab. She is coauthor of *A People's Guide to Orange County* (2022) and Vietnamese in Orange County (2015) and serves as a board member for Arts Orange County and the *Vietnamese American Arts and Letters Association*.

Group photo of the *New Wave* team and Lynda Trang Đài on the red carpet for the world premiere at Tribeca Festival, 2024.

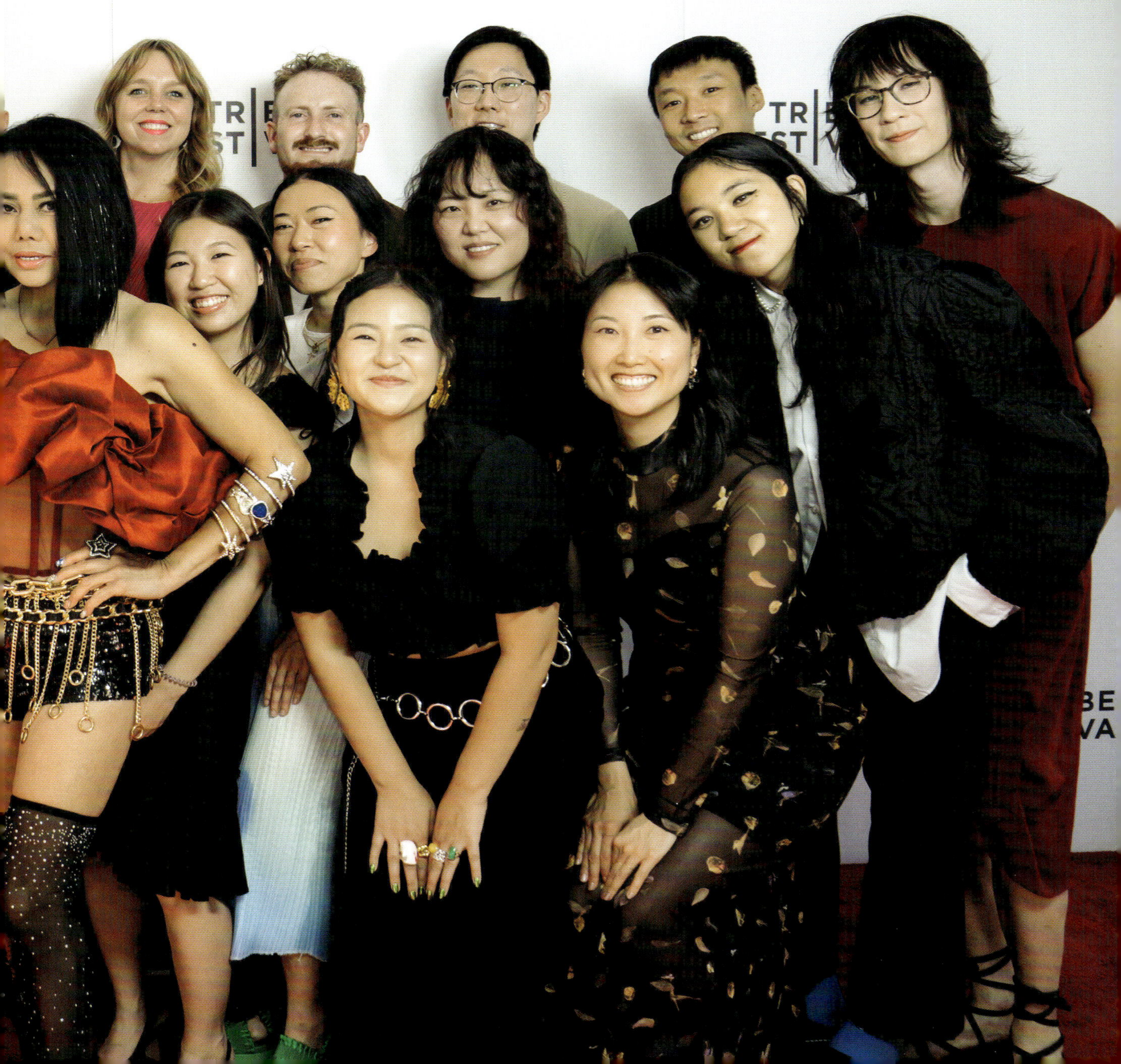
TRIBECA
FESTIVAL

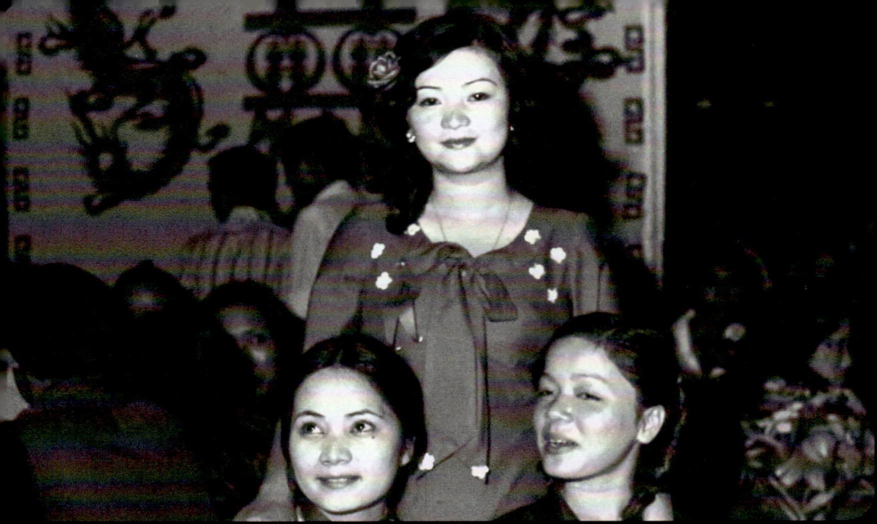

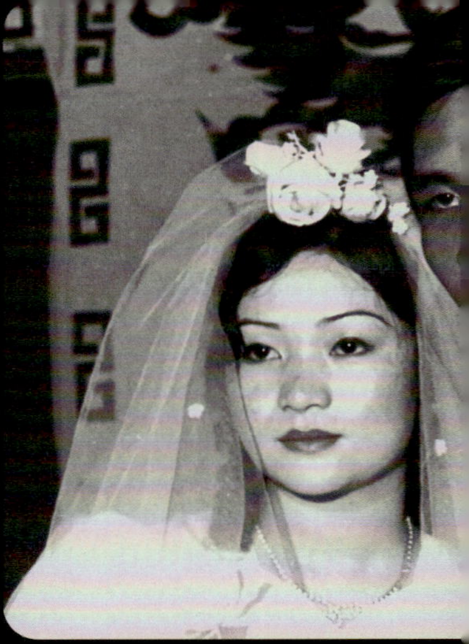

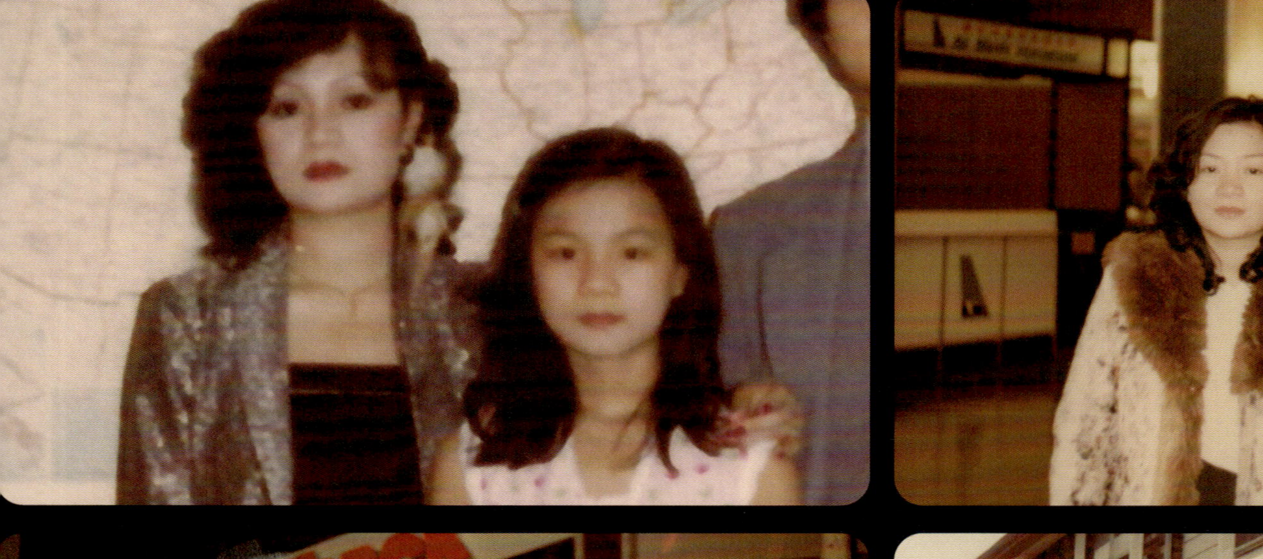

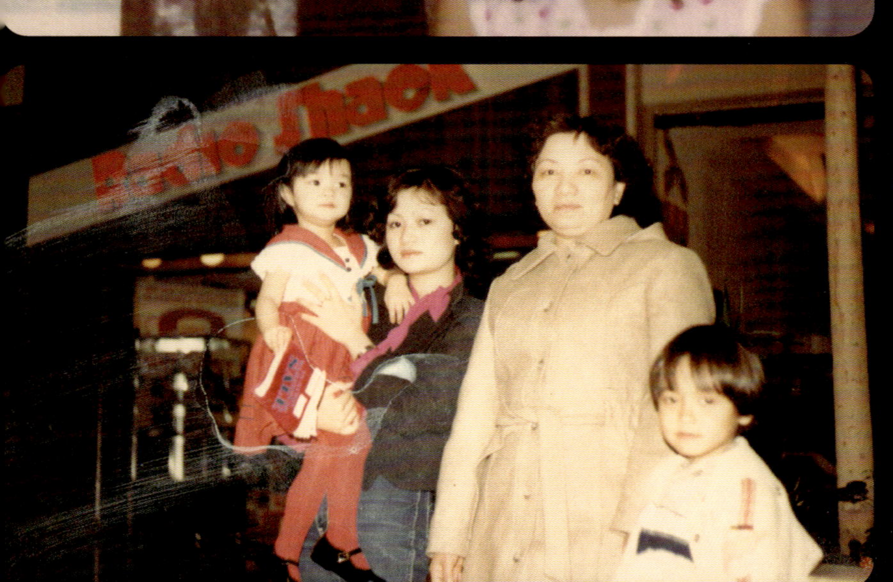
Shack

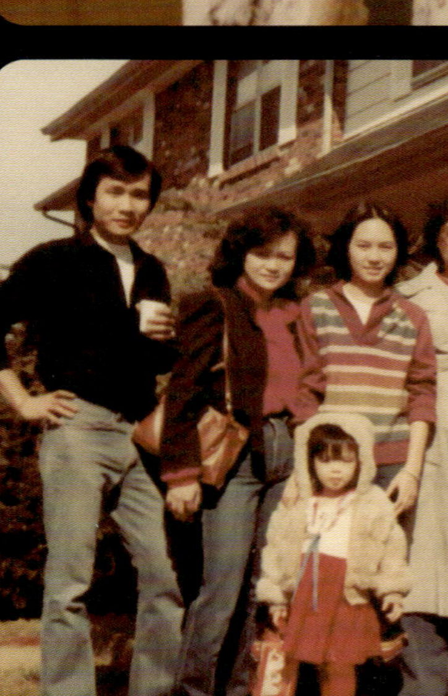

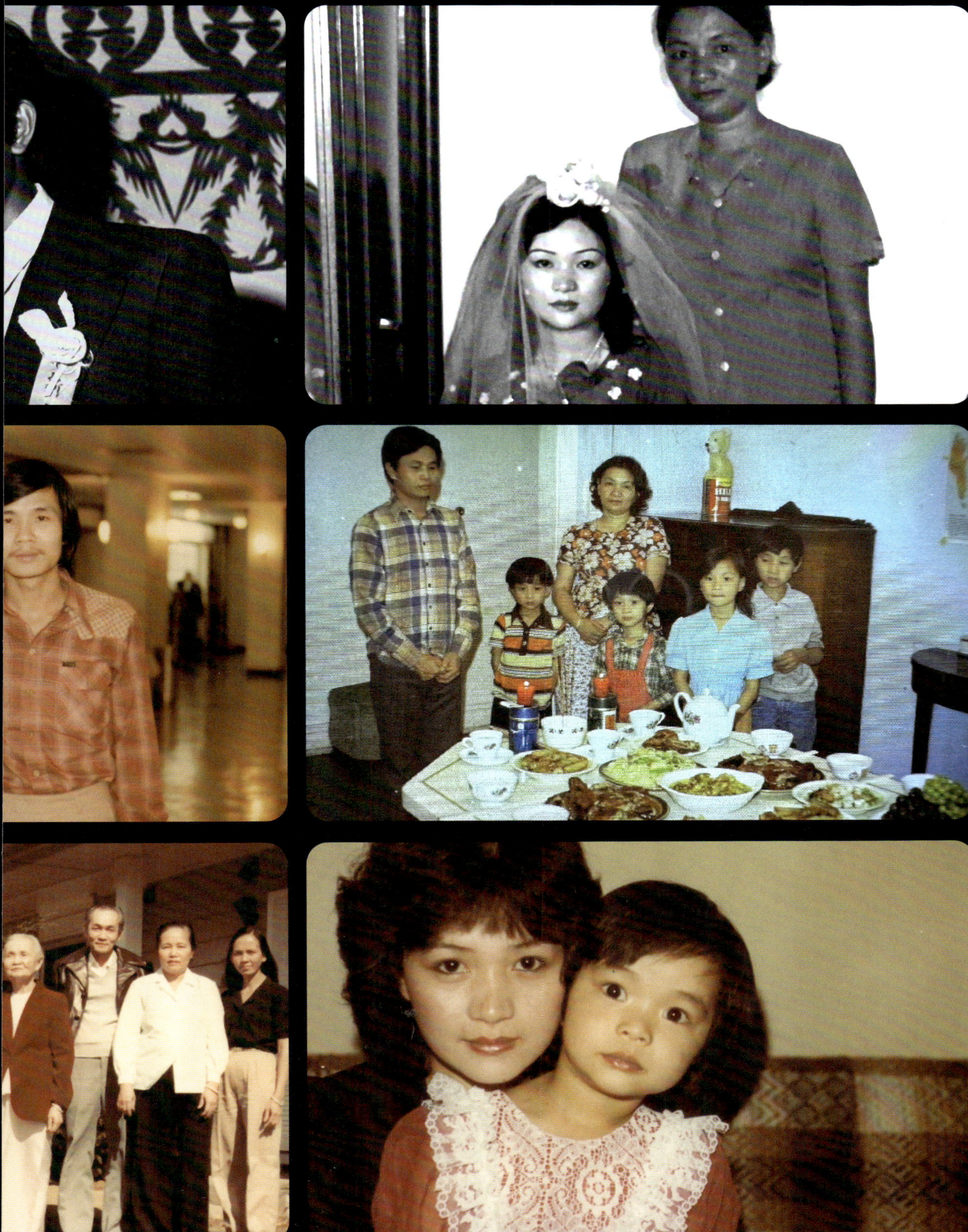

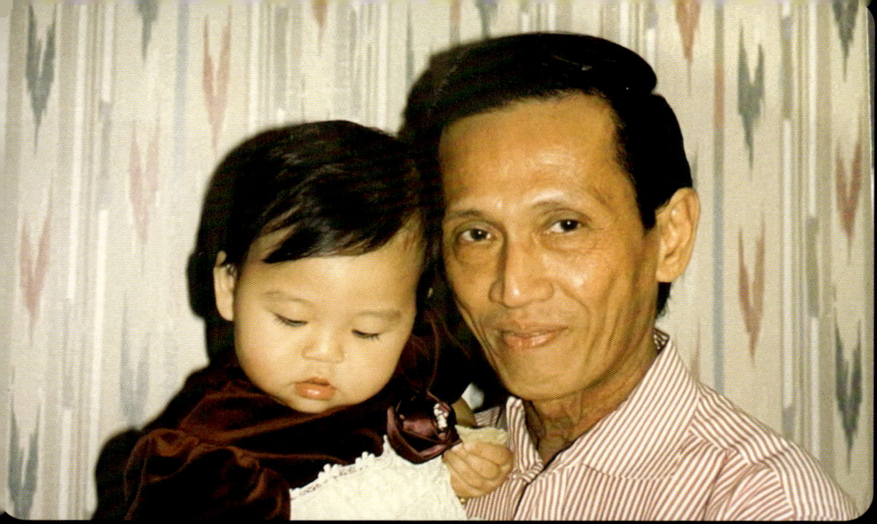

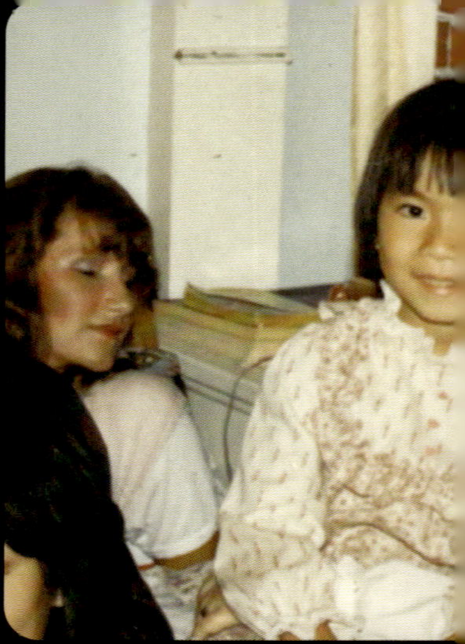

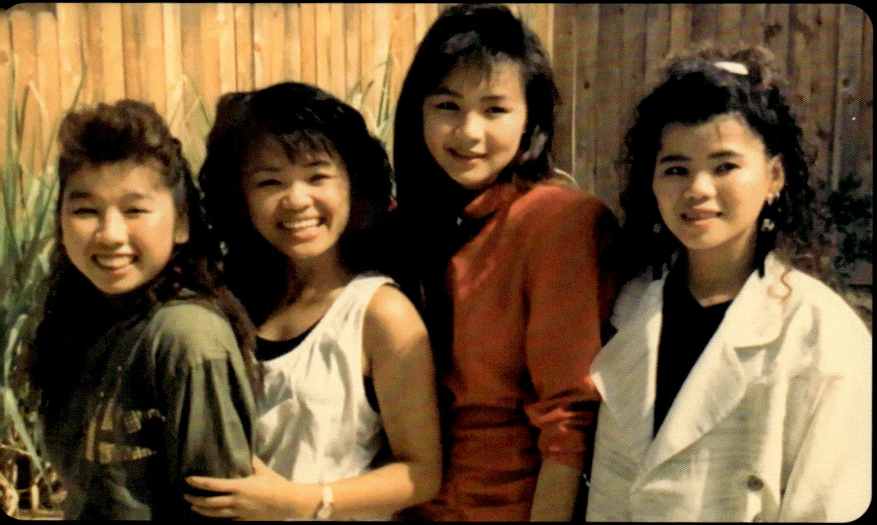

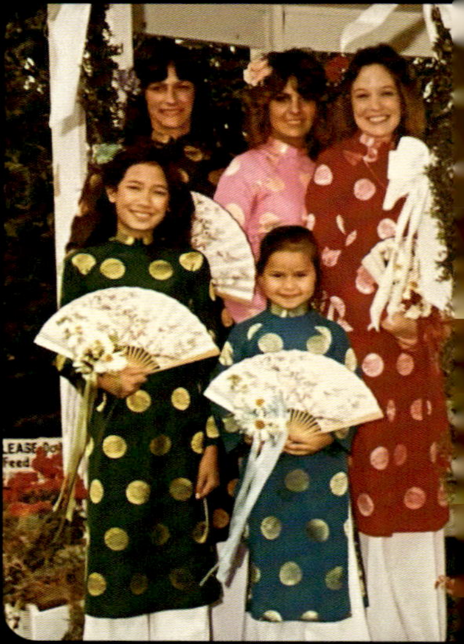

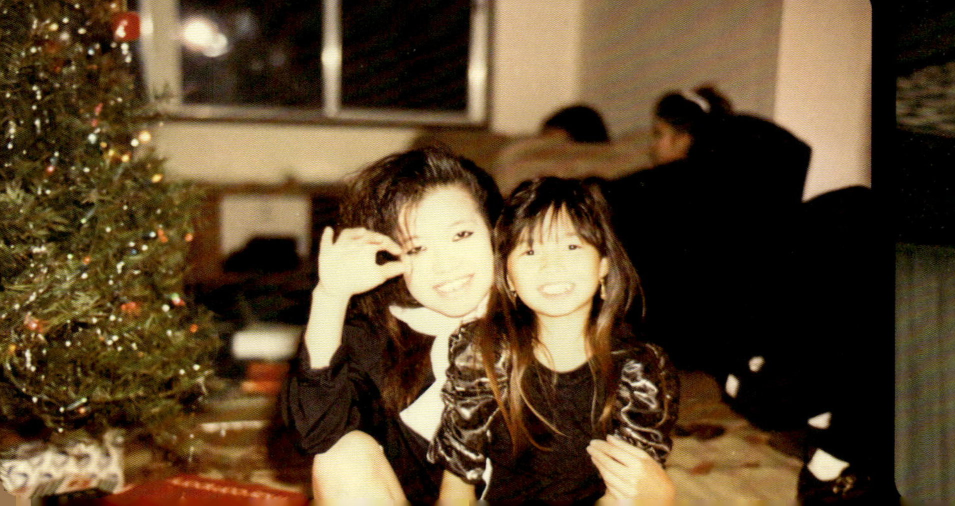

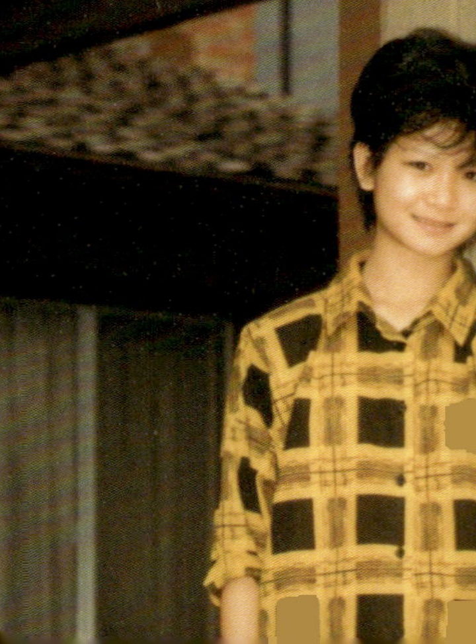

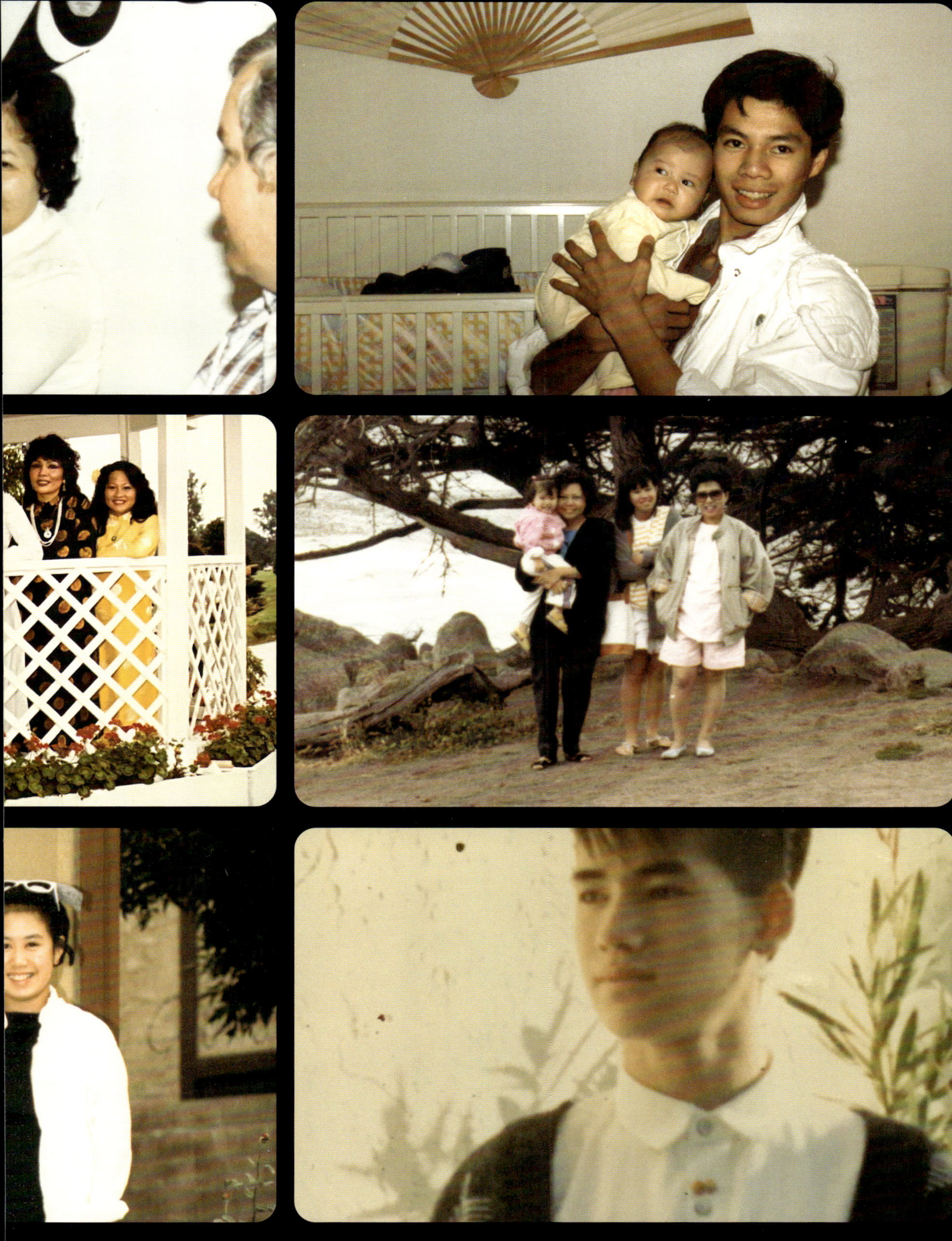

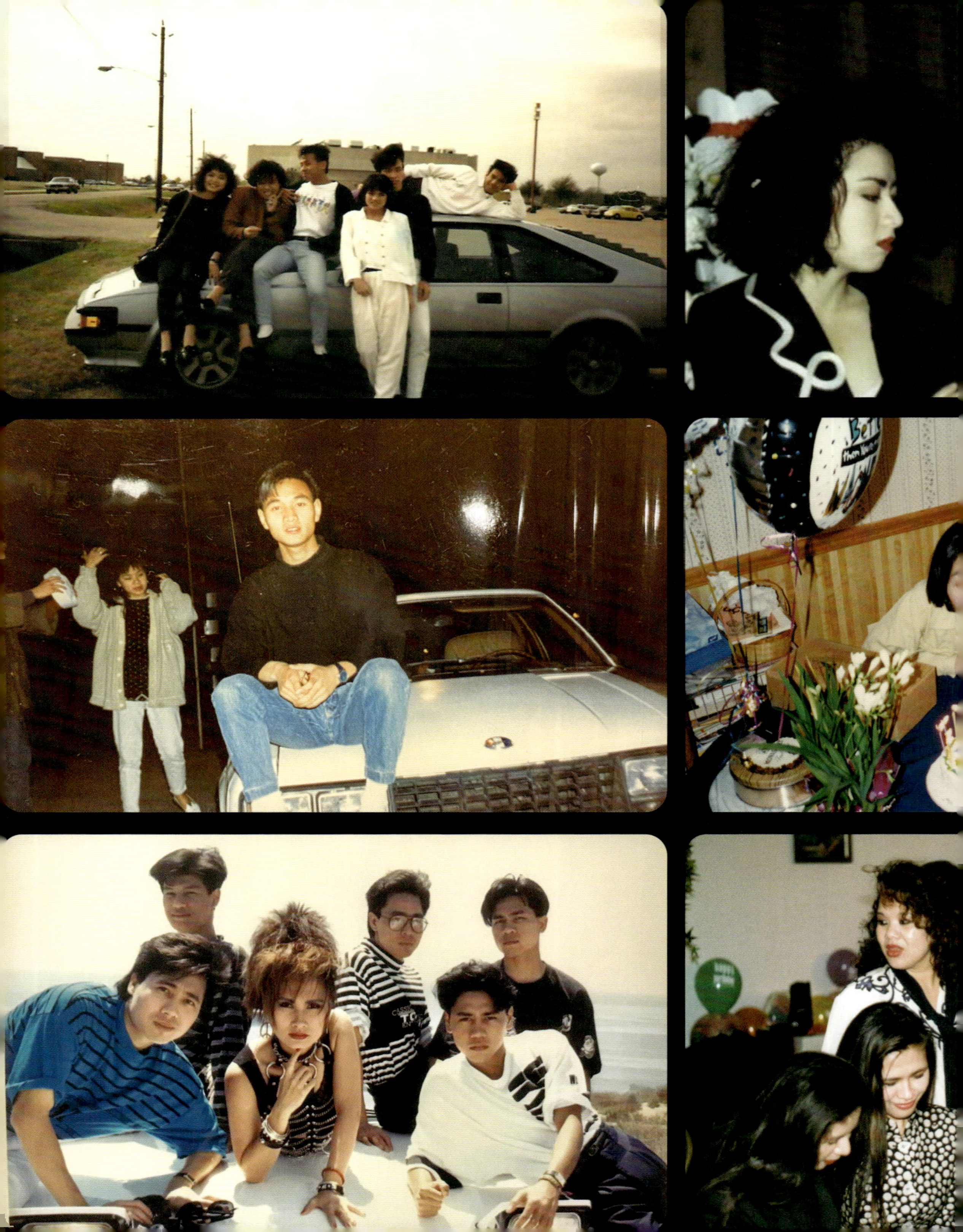

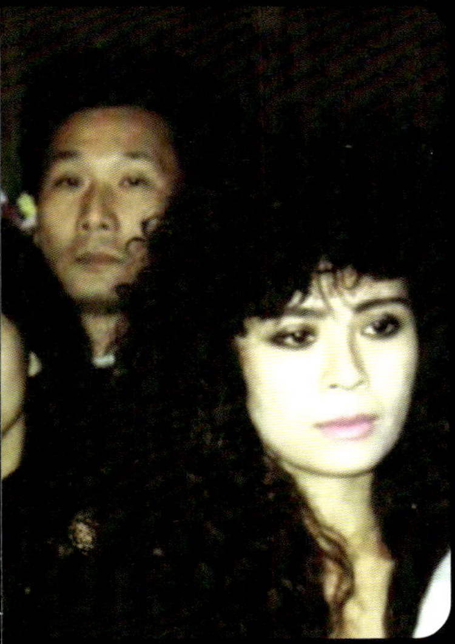

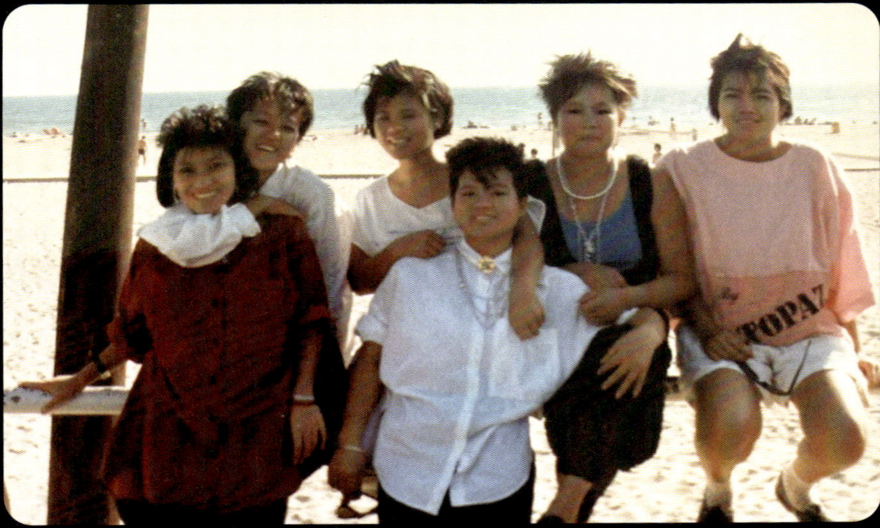

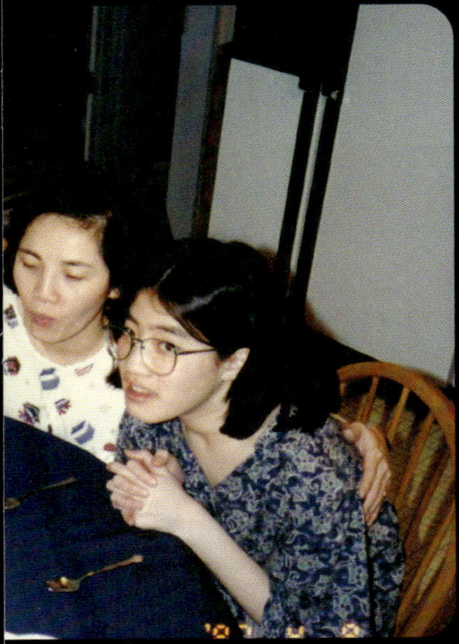

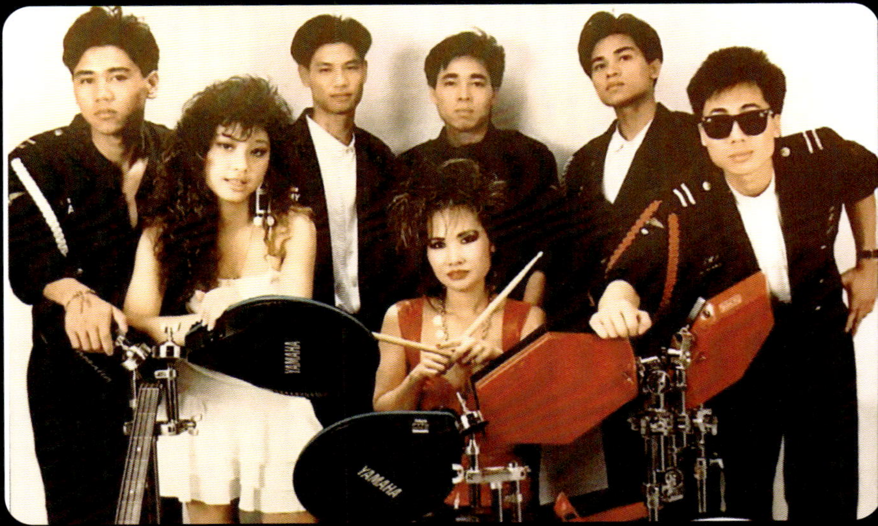

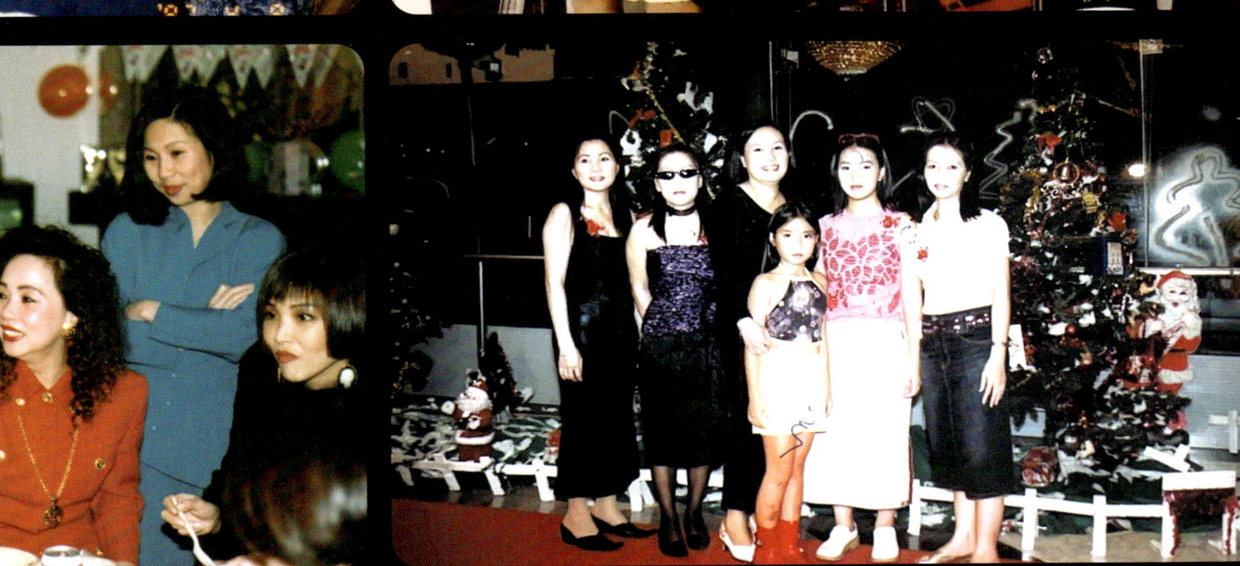

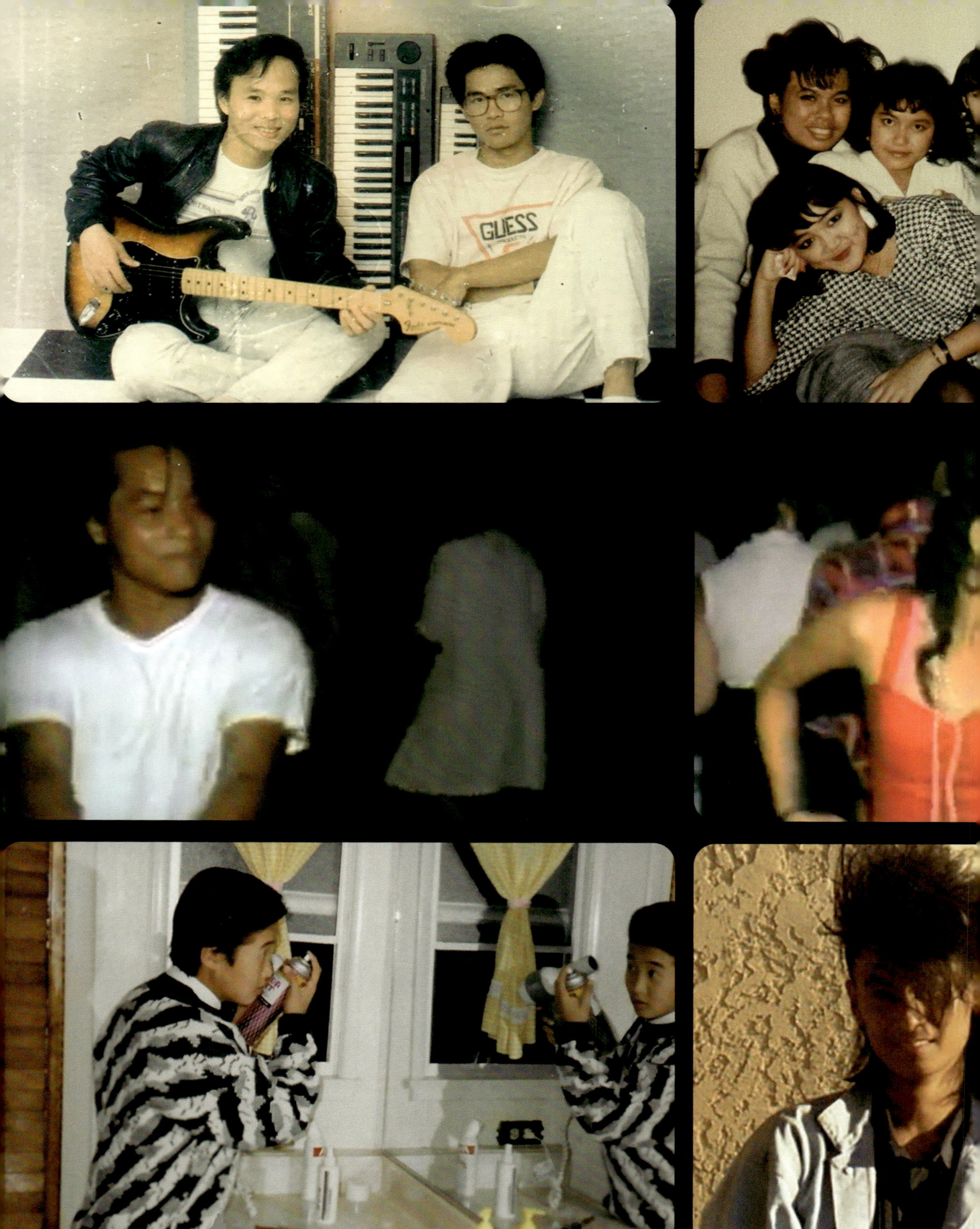
GUESS

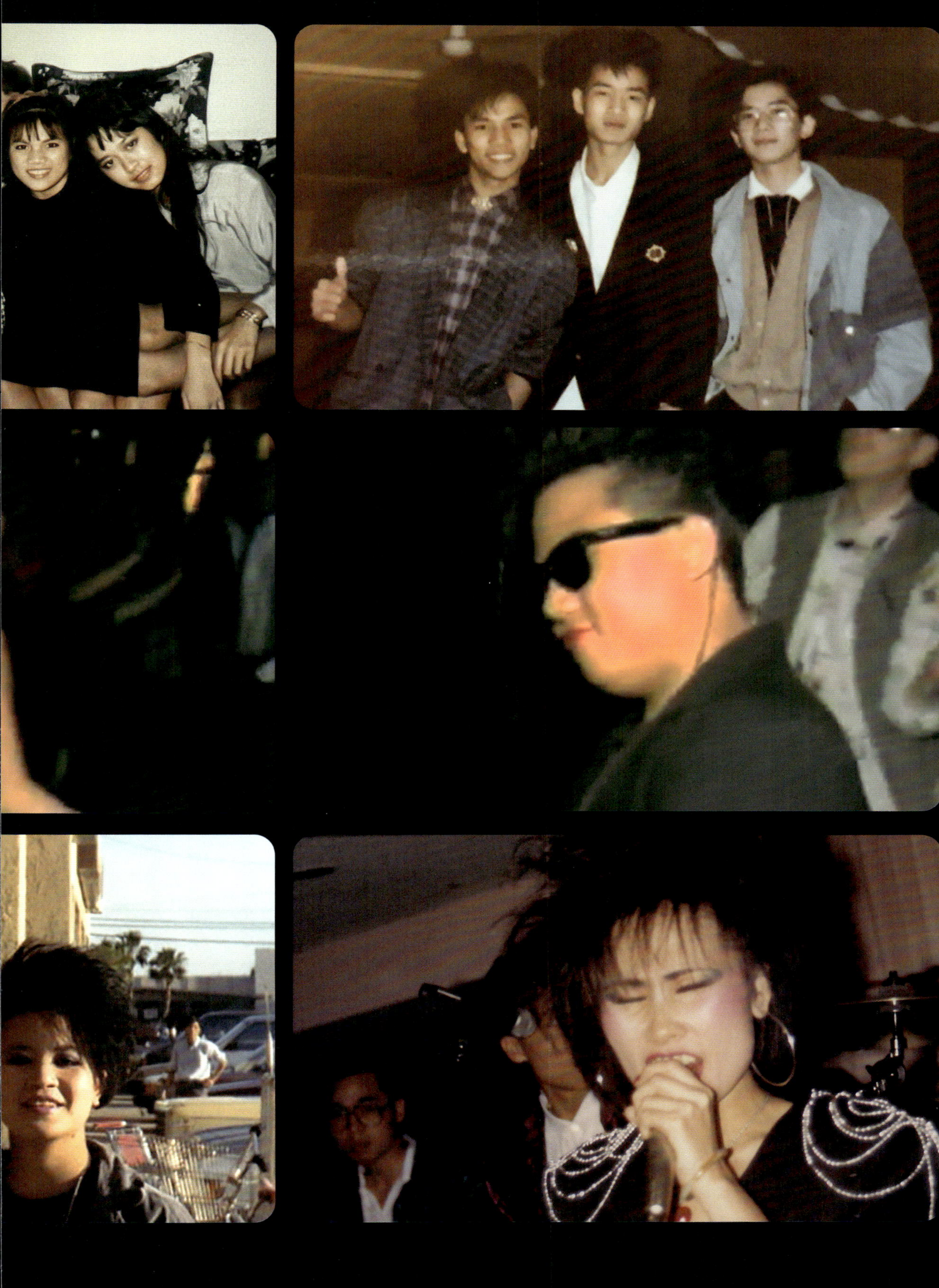

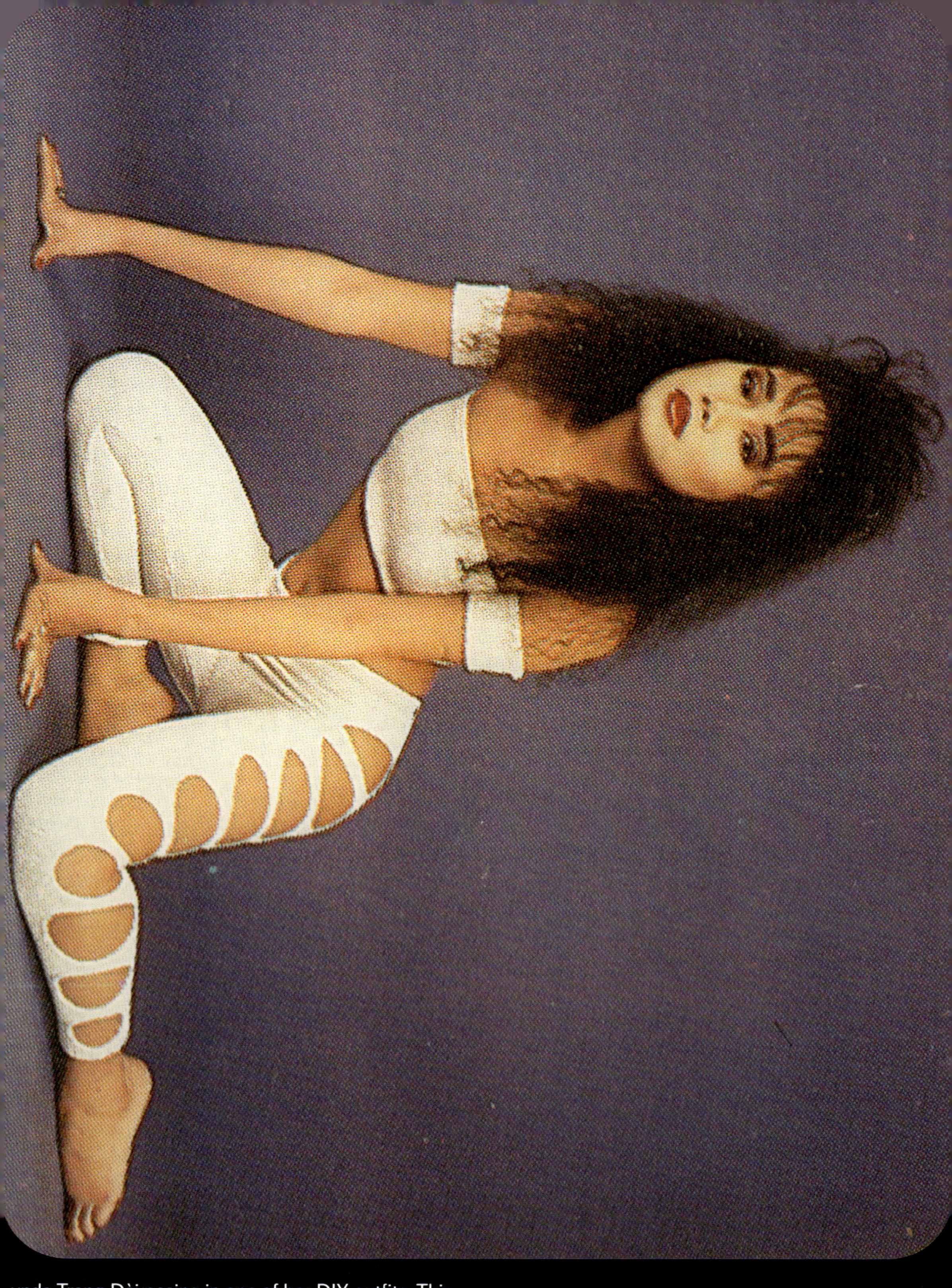

Lynda Trang Đài posing in one of her DIY outfits. This photo was the cover for her original song, "Crazy Love."

PHOTO CREDITS

All of the images in the book are from the author's collection, except as noted below. Many of the images included in this book were submitted from community archives. I tried to represent as broad a view of the New Wave scene as possible; I am deeply grateful for the individuals and record labels who graciously agreed to share their materials. Efforts were made to include as much detail as possible about each photo, but some information was lost to time. Many of these archival materials are rare, and difficult to source; each image was reproduced at the highest possible level with available resources. Efforts were made to ensure proper credit; any necessary corrections will be made in future printings.

Ai Hendrickson, Asa: 167, above
Anh Tài: 163, below; 188 above, left
Ave, Dolly: 151
Bao An Vo, Karyn: front endpaper (reverse); 38; 43, above; 60, above; 60, below
Baris, Sam: 188 center, left; 188 center; 189 center, right
Brightwell, Eric: 76, above; 109, above; 117 (inset); 188 below, center
Bubble_T: 159, below right 158, below
Cao, Diane: 73
Dao, Mitchell: 80, above; 81
Đinh, Thúy: 41, above; 44, above; 44, below; 45; 47; 46; 46, above
Doan Nguyen, Thuc: 186, center
Dolinh, Mena: 162
Family Love, courtesy of Le Toan: 42; 62; 63; back endpapers
Giáng Ngọc Productions, courtesy of Lê Bá Chư: 2, 64-65 (all) 76, below; 84, above; 86-87; 89, below; 98-99 (all); 101, left; 102, above; 103; 134-135 (all); 186 above, center; 186, below; 187, center; 189 below, right; back endpaper (reverse)
Ha, Thao: 75; 108
Han, Minu: 160-161
Han, Samuel: 164; 166; 167, below
Hoang, Kim: 30, below
Huỳnh, Julia: 148
Lambo, Lauren: 155; 156, above
Lam McCarthy, Stacy: 6-7; 178; 187 above, right
lê, mads: 69; 77, below
Le, Tina Snow: 50, above; 153, below
Le, Trace: 170; 172; 173
Le, Ysa: 71, below
Library of Congress: 40; 51
Los Angeles Public Library Photo Collection: Shades of L.A. Collection: 78
Lynda Music, courtesy of Lynda Trang Đài: 8; 146
Newman, Bella: 184 center
Ngo, Danny T.: 189 above, right
Nguyen, Anne: 144-145
Nguyen, Beverly : 43, below
Nguyen, Gabrielle: 184 above, left
Nguyen, Ian: 10-11; 50, below; 54-55; 70; 71, above; 74, below; 82-83; 48, below
Nguyen, Sean: 76, center
Nguyen, Thuy-An J.: 48, above
Nguyen Vaeth, Christine: 79, 186 below, center
Nikko, Sandy: 186 above, left; 188 above, center
Quach, Cindy: 187 below, right
Courtesy of Quốc Sĩ (via Lê Bá Chư): 116-117 (background)
Saigon Kiss, courtesy of Tessa Yến Nguyễn: 152
San Francisco Examiner: 126
Thai, Ha: 185 below, right
Courtesy of Thái Tài: 41, below; 72; 88, above; 88, below; 89, above; 90; 92, below left; 92, above left; 92, above right; 92, below right; 93; 95; 94; 97; 96, above left; 96, below left; 103; 105; 109, below; 110, below; 112, above; 114; 115; 118-119; 120; 121, above; 121, below; 125; 128, above; 128, below; 131; 130; 140; 141; 142-143; 184; 184 center, left; 190; back cover
Tran, Danny: 74, above
Tran, Leanne: 49
Tran, Mary Linh: 58; 66, left; 66, right
Tran, Michael: 52, above; 53; 100, above right; 100, below left; 100, above right; 100, below right; 124, above; 124, below
Tran, Myhuyen: 67; 184 below, left
Tran, Paul and Catherine: 59; 135; 136 above; 136, below; 138
Trần, Paul Quốc: 157; 158, above; 159, above
Tran, Thuy: 156, below
Tranchi, Bao: 184 above, center
Triệu Nguyễn, Mỹ Linh: 185 above, right; 184 below, center; 185 center, right
Trinh, Cindy: 153, above; 176; 180-181
Truong, Hai: 116, above; 188 below, left
Truong, Tammy: 110, above
UC Irvine, Libraries, Southeast Asian Archive: 77, above
Vo Dang, Thuy: 111; 116, below
Vo Huỳnh, Tan: 149
Walker, Quynh-Mi Mimi: 80, below; 80, center
Wu, Hank: 104-105; 112, below
Wu, Myra: 23; 27; 28, below; 28, above; 29; 117, below
yến hang, betty: 163, above; 163, below

New Wave: Rebellion and Reinvention in the Vietnamese Diaspora

By Elizabeth Ai

Design by Mỹ Linh Triệu Nguyễn, STUDIO LHOOQ

Nguyễn Mộng Giác, *Tamarind Road in Summer*, translation by Nhat-Lang Le, Thúy Đinh, May T. Nguyen, courtesy of Nguyễn Diệu Chi.

10 9 8 7 6 5 4 3 2 1

ISBN 978-1-62640-137-2

Library of Congress Cataloging-in-Publication Data is available

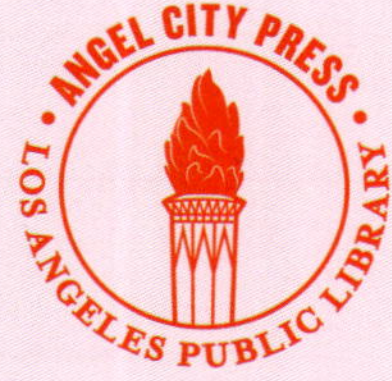

Published by Angel City Press at Los Angeles Public Library
www.angelcitypress.com

Printed in Canada

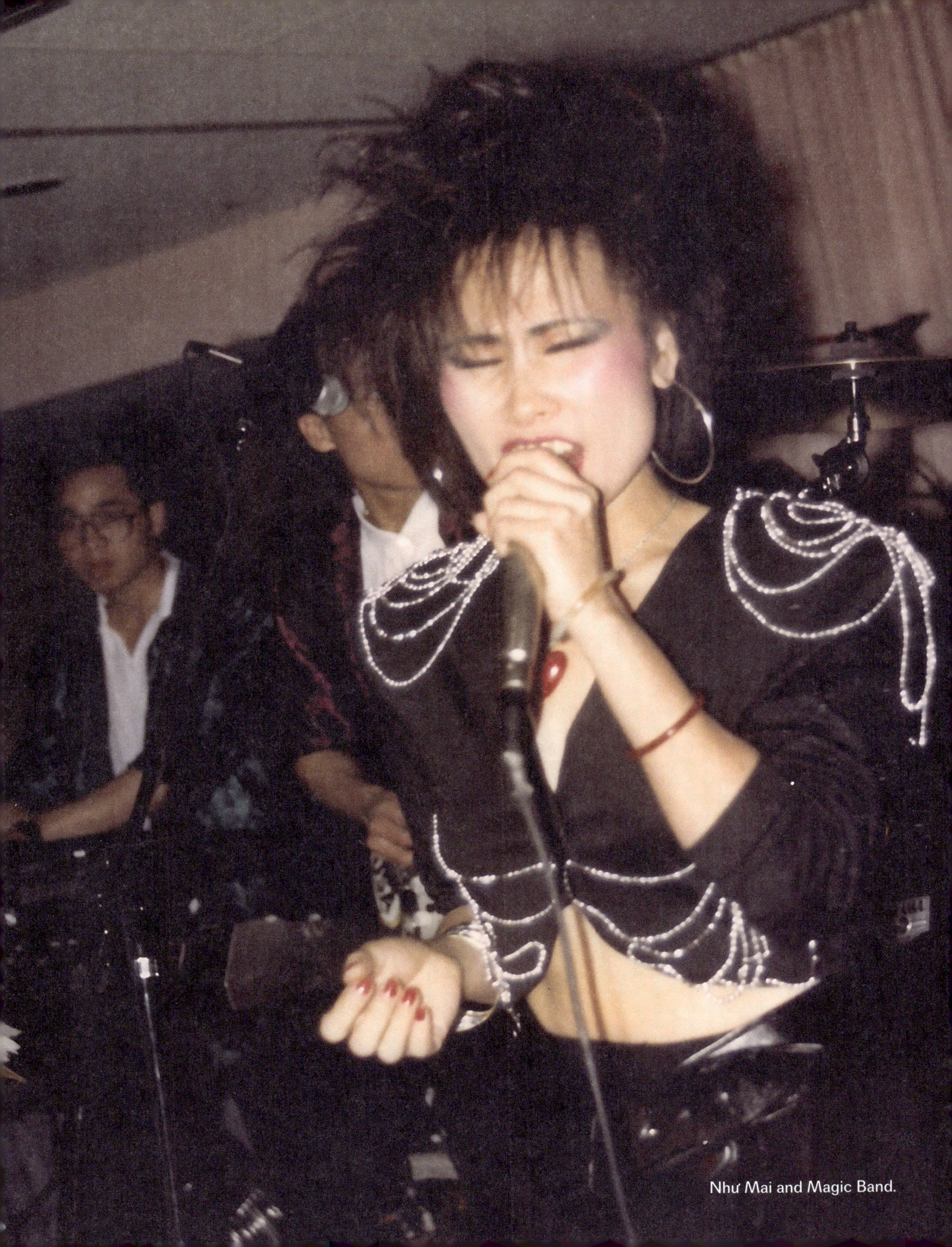

Như Mai and Magic Band.

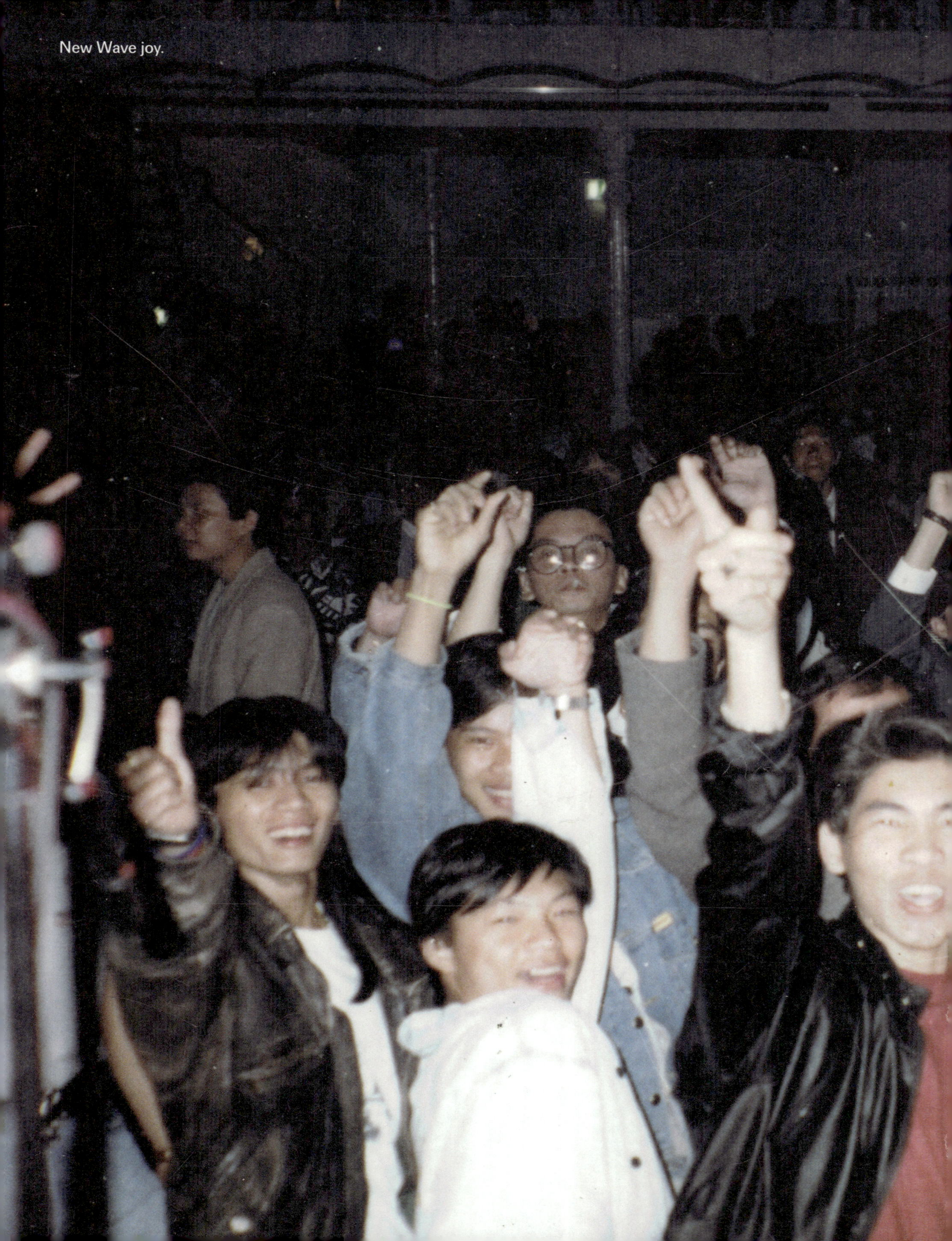

New Wave joy.